Overview

Table of Contents

Foreword

Welcome to *Jesse Liberty's Programming from scratch series*. I created this series because I believe that traditional primers do not meet the needs of every student. A typical introductory computer programming book teaches a series of skills in logical order and then, when you have mastered a topic, the book endeavors to show how the skills might be applied. This approach works very well for many people, but not for everyone.

I've taught programming to over 10,000 students: in small groups, large groups, and through the Internet. Many students have told me that they wish they could just sit down at the computer with an expert and work on a program together. Rather than being taught each skill step by step in a vacuum, they'd like to create a product and learn the necessary skills as they go.

From this idea was born the *Programming from scratch* series. In each of these books, an industry expert will guide you through the design and implementation of a complex program, starting from scratch and teaching you the necessary skills as you go.

You might want to make a *from scratch* book the first book you read on a subject, or you might prefer to read a more traditional primer first and then use one of these books as supplemental reading. Either approach can work; which is better depends on your personal learning style.

All of the *from scratch* series books share a common commitment to showing you the entire development process, from the initial concept through implementation. We do not assume that you know anything about programming: *from scratch* means from the very beginning, with no prior assumptions.

While I didn't write every book in the series, as Series Editor I have a powerful sense of personal responsibility for each one. I provide supporting material and a discussion group on my Web site (www.libertyassociates.com), and I encourage you to write to me at jliberty@libertyassociates.com if you have questions or concerns.

Thank you for considering this book.

Jesse Liberty

Jesse Liberty

from scratch Series Editor

About the Author

Jesse Liberty is the author of the international best seller *Teach Yourself C++ In 21 Days*, as well as *Teach Yourself C++ In 24 Hours* and other books on C++ and object-oriented programming. He writes a regular monthly column for *C++ Report*, the premier magazine on the C++ language. He is president of Liberty Associates, Inc., which provides on-site training in object-oriented software development, as well as mentoring, consulting, and contract programming.

Jesse was a Distinguished Software Engineer at AT&T and Vice President of Electronic Delivery for Citibank. He lives with his wife, Stacey; his daughters, Robin and Rachel; his dog, Milo; and his cat, Fred, in the suburbs of Cambridge, Massachusetts. He can be reached via the Internet at jliberty@libertyassociates.com. Jesse supports his books on his Web site at www.libertyassociates.com (click on Books and Resources).

Dedication

This book is dedicated to the people who made it possible: Stacey, Robin, Rachel, Tracy, Holly, Donald, Hugh, Sara, JoAnna and the incredible team at Que.

Acknowledgments

My name is on the cover, but this book was created by a number of very dedicated people at Que, including Tracy Dunkelberger and Holly Allender. They are among the finest editors and nicest people it has been my pleasure to work with, and they have restored my faith in publishing in general and in Macmillan in particular. Among the many other hard working people at Que are Hugh Vandivier, JoAnna Kremer, and Sara Bosin, all of whom have conspired to make this book far better than it was when I submitted it. The glory is theirs, the mistakes are mine; so send me the email, not them.

I must acknowledge Donald Xie, whom I've never met, but I have worked with him for a few years and my respect and admiration for him continue to grow. He is a *mensch* and he has made me appear to be a better programmer than I am.

Let me add a special word of thanks to Dean Miller and to Richard Swadley. It was Richard who gave the initial push to the *from scratch* series, and Dean who gave it life. My grateful thanks to both.

Thank you also to the approximately 200,000 people who bought my previous books. Finally, I thank you, dear prospective reader, standing there at the bookshelves, leafing through this tome, deciding whether it is the right book for you. It is; so go pay for it, take it home, and read it. We'll both be happy.

Tell Us What You Think!

As the reader of this book, *you* are our most important critic and commentator. We value your opinion and want to know what we're doing right, what we could do better, what areas you'd like to see us publish in, and any other words of wisdom you're willing to pass our way.

As an Associate Publisher for Que Publishing at Macmillan Computer Publishing, I welcome your comments. You can fax, email, or write me directly to let me know what you did or didn't like about this book—as well as what we can do to make our books stronger.

Please note that I cannot help you with technical problems related to the topic of this book, and that due to the high volume of mail I receive, I might not be able to reply to every message.

When you write, please be sure to include this book's title and author as well as your name and phone or fax number. I will carefully review your comments and share them with the author and editors who worked on the book.

Fax: 317.581.4666

Email: programming@mcp.com

Mail: Associate Publisher
          Que Publishing
          201 West 103rd Street
          Indianapolis, IN 46290 USA

Introduction

This book is different from any primer on C++ *ever* written. Here's the difference: All other programming books start by teaching you simple skills that build in difficulty, adding skill upon skill as you go. When you've learned all the skills, the books then demonstrate what you can do: a sample program.

This book does not start with programming technique—it starts with a project. We begin by analyzing and designing the project, and then we implement that design. Programming skills are taught in the context of implementation; first you understand what you are trying to accomplish, and then you learn the skills needed to get the job done.

Learning C++ Doesn't Have to Be Difficult

C++ is perceived to be a very difficult language. I believe that is because most programmers learn with a focus on the *syntax* of the language (what words do you use?) rather than on the *semantics* (what are you trying to say?).

syntax—The proper use of terms and punctuation.

semantics—The meaning and purpose of the code.

There are two ways to learn to speak a foreign language: One way is to memorize dozens of vocabulary words and practice declension of verbs, and the other is to go to the country and interact with native speakers. Different people learn differently, but I can tell you that in my experience, a week in France is worth two years in the classroom.

If I were going to teach you C++ and we worked together, I would not hand you a book at all. I'd sit down with you and we'd write a program together. Along the way, I'd teach you what you need to know, occasionally giving you short pieces to read to flesh out your understanding.

That is exactly how this book works: We'll sit down together and write a program, and along the way I'll teach you what you need to know. From the very first page, we will focus on understanding the problem we are trying to solve and designing a solution, rather than on the syntax of the language.

Compiling the Code

The code in this book should work well with any ANSI/ISO-compliant compiler. I wrote all the sample programs using Microsoft Visual C++ 6.0 on a Pentium II 300Mhz computer with 256MB of RAM. I *highly* recommend that you buy the latest edition of any good 32-bit C++ compiler before attempting to run the code in this book because the language has changed significantly in the past few years.

Unfortunately, I am unable to support your individual compiler, but if it conforms to the language specification, you should have no trouble at all.

Conventions Used in this Book

Some of the unique features in this series include

Geek Speak—An icon in the margin indicates the use of a new term. New terms will appear in the paragraph in *italics*.

> **how too**
> **prō nouns′ it**
>
> **How To Pronounce It**—You'll see an icon set in the margin next to a box that contains a technical term and how it should be pronounced. For example, "cin is pronounced *see-in*, and cout is pronounced *see-out*."

 An icon in the margin indicates code that can be entered, compiled, and run.

EXCURSIONS

Excursions are short diversions from the main topic being discussed, and they offer an opportunity to flesh out your understanding of a topic.

With a book of this type, a topic might be discussed in multiple places as a result of when and where we add functionality during application development. To help make this all clear, we've included a Concept Web that provides a graphical representation of how all the programming concepts relate to one another. You'll find it on the inside front cover of this book.

Notes offer comments and asides about the topic at hand, as well as full explanations of certain concepts.

Tips provide great shortcuts and hints on how to program in C++ more effectively.

Warnings help you avoid the pitfalls of programming, thus preventing you from making mistakes that will make your life miserable.

In addition, you'll find various typographic conventions throughout this book:

- Commands, variables, and other code appear in text in a special `computer font`.
- In this book, I build on existing listings as we examine code further. When I add new sections to existing code, you'll spot it in **`bold computer font`**.
- Commands and such that you type appear in **boldface type**.
- Placeholders in syntax descriptions appear in an *`italic computer font`* typeface. This indicates that you will replace the placeholder with the actual file name, parameter, or other element that it represents.

Breaking the Code

In some instances, when you look at a code listing, you'll notice that some lines of code have been broken in two and that the line numbers have letters. For example, see lines 10 and 10a:

```
10:  if ( ( someCondition || someSecondCondition ) &&
10a:    ( someAlternative || someOtherAlternative ) )
```

What has happened here is that I've broken up a single line of code because it was too long to fit on a single line in this book. The rewrite is still legal C++, and can be typed in just as you find it (without the line numbers, of course).

The letter *a* is a signal to you that normally I'd combine these two lines into one. If this were one long line, it would look like this:

```
10: if ( ( someCondition || someSecondCondition ) && ( someAlternative ||someOtherAlternative ) )
```

In many cases, I must make coding adjustments to break the line and still have legal C++. For example

```
cout << "This is line 10 and you would think this would be one long line of
code" << endl;
```

To break this line of code, I must end the cout statement and add a new one on the subsequent line:

```
10:  cout << "This is line 10 and you would think this would be ";
```

```
10a: cout << "one long line of code" << endl;
```

Again, the resulting code is legal, just not how I might otherwise have written it.

Chapter 1

An Introduction to C++

Computer languages have undergone a dramatic evolution since the first electronic computers were built to assist in artillery trajectory calculations during World War II. Early on, programmers worked with the most primitive computer instructions: machine language. These instructions were represented by long strings of ones and zeros. Soon, assemblers were invented to map machine instructions to human-readable and human-manageable mnemonics such as ADD and MOV.

In time, higher level languages evolved, such as BASIC and COBOL. These languages let people work with something that approximated words and sentences, such as Let I = 100. *Interpreters* and *compilers* translated these instructions back into machine language. An interpreter translates a program as it reads it, turning the program instructions, or *code*, directly into actions. A compiler translates the code into an intermediary form. This step is called *compiling*, and it produces an object file. The compiler then invokes a *linker*, which turns the object file into an executable program.

Because interpreters read the code as it is written and execute the code on the spot, programmers find them easy to work with. Compilers introduce the extra, inconvenient steps of compiling and linking the code. They produce a program that is very fast each time it is run, however, because the time-consuming task of translating the source code into machine language has already been accomplished.

Another advantage of compiled languages such as C++ is that you can distribute the executable program to people who don't have the compiler. With an interpretive language, you must have the interpreter to run the program.

Some languages, such as Visual Basic, call the interpreter the *runtime library*. Java calls its runtime interpreter a *Virtual Machine (VM)*, but in this case, the browser (such as Internet Explorer or Netscape) provides the VM .

For many years, the principle goal of computer programmers was to write short pieces of code that would execute quickly. The program needed to be small because memory was expensive, and it needed to be fast because processing power was also expensive. As computers have become smaller, cheaper, and faster, and as the cost of memory has fallen, these priorities have changed. Today the cost of a programmer's time far outweighs the cost of most of the computers in use by businesses. Well-written, easy-to-maintain code is at a premium. *Easy-to-maintain* means that as business requirements change, the program can be extended and enhanced without great expense.

Programs

The word *program* is used in two ways: to describe individual instructions (or *source code*) that are created by the programmer and to describe an entire piece of executable software. This distinction can cause enormous confusion, so we will try to distinguish between the source code on one hand and the executable file on the other.

Source code can be turned into an executable program in two ways: Interpreters translate the source code into computer instructions, and the computer acts on those instructions immediately. Alternatively, compilers translate source code into a program, which you can run at a later time. Whereas interpreters are easier to work with, most serious programming is done with compilers because compiled code runs much faster. C++ is a compiled language.

Solving Problems

The problems that programmers are asked to solve have been changing. Twenty years ago, programs were created to manage large amounts of raw data. The people writing the code and the people using the program were all computer professionals. Today, many more people use computers , and most know very little about how computers and programs work. Computers are tools that are used by people who are more interested in solving their business problems than struggling with the computer.

Ironically, for programs to become easier for this new audience to use, they have become far more sophisticated. Gone are the days when users typed in cryptic commands at esoteric prompts only to see a stream of raw data. Today's programs use sophisticated "user-friendly interfaces" that involve multiple windows, menus, dialog boxes, and the myriad of metaphors with which we've all become familiar. The programs written to support this new approach are far more complex than those written just ten years ago.

With the development of the Web, computers have entered a new era of market penetration: More people are using computers than ever before, and their expectations are very high. In the few years since the first edition of this book, programs have become larger and even more complex, and the need for object-oriented programming techniques to manage this complexity has become manifest.

As programming requirements have changed, both languages and the techniques used for writing programs have evolved. Although the complete history is fascinating, this book will focus on the transformation from procedural programming to object-oriented programming.

Procedural, Structured, and Object-Oriented Programming

Until recently, programs were thoughta series of procedures that acted upon data. A *procedure*, or *function*, is a set of specific instructions executed one after the other. The data was quite separate from the procedures, and the trick in programming was to keep track of which functions called which other functions and what data was changed. To make sense of this potentially confusing situation, structured programming was created.

The principle idea behind structured programming is as simple as the idea of divide and conquer. Think of a computer program as consisting of a set of tasks. You can break down any task that is too complex to be described simply into a set of smaller component tasks until the tasks are sufficiently small and self-contained enough that you can easily understand them.

For example, computing the average salary of every employee of a company is a rather complex task. You can, however, break it down into the following subtasks:

1. Find out what each person earns.
2. Count how many people you have.
3. Total all the salaries.
4. Divide the total by the number of people you have.

Totaling the salaries can be broken down into the following steps:

1. Get each employee's record.
2. Access the salary.

    3. Add the salary to the running total.

    4. Get the next employee's record.

In turn, obtaining each employee's record can be broken down into the following steps:

    1. Open the file of employees.

    2. Go to the correct record.

    3. Read the data from disk.

Structured programming remains an enormously successful approach for dealing with complex problems. By the late 1980s, however, some of the deficiencies of structured programming had became all too clear.

First, there was a natural desire to think of data (employee records, for example) and what you can do with data (sort, edit, and so on) as a single idea. Procedural programming worked against this, separating data structures from functions that manipulated that data.

Second, programmers found themselves constantly reinventing new solutions to old problems. This is often called "reinventing the wheel," and is the opposite of reusability. The idea behind reusability is to build components that have known properties, and then to be able to plug them into your program as you need them. This is modeled after the hardware world: When an engineer needs a new transistor, she doesn't usually invent one; rather, she goes to the big bin of transistors and finds one that works the way she needs it to, or perhaps modifies it. There was no similar option for a software engineer.

The way we are now using computers—with menus, buttons, and windows—fosters a more interactive, event-driven approach to computer programming. *Event-driven* means that an event happens—the user presses a button or chooses from a menu— and the program must respond. Programs are becoming increasingly interactive, and it has become important to design for that kind of functionality.

The essence of object-oriented programming is to treat data and the procedures that act upon the data as a single "object": a self-contained entity with an identity and certain characteristics of its own.

Why C++?

C++ is the number one language for commercial software development, and C++ programmers are among the best paid in the industry.

Whereas Visual Basic might be easier to learn, it doesn't scale well. That is, it doesn't support large, complex business applications, and it isn't as fast or as efficient as is C++.

For a while, Java seemed to be making inroads, but the tools aren't as mature in Java as they are in C++, the portability is turning out to be more limited than was originally promised, and the programs are not as fast or as efficient as C++ programs. That said, the similarities between programming in C++ and in Java are so great that 90% of what you learn about one applies to the other.

There are many other programming languages and development environments, but when professional programmers need to write large, complex, and efficient programs, the overwhelming majority turns to C++.

C++ is a powerful, efficient, and flexible language, and it is supported by industry-tested tools such as editors for writing programs and debuggers for testing your work. Integrated development environments make programming easier, and application frameworks take the drudgery out of programming for modern operating systems such as Windows NT.

More importantly, C++ was designed to support object-oriented programming.

Why Object-Oriented Programming?

The painful reality is that most commercial software projects fail. They are too late, too unreliable, and too expensive. This is a direct result of the enormous complexity of the programs we are trying to build today, compared with the relative simplicity of programs built just a decade ago.

This crisis has prompted the industry to reevaluate how we do our business, and ultimately to look for new approaches to programming. Many see the advent of object-oriented analysis, design, and programming as the best hope for building products that perform as intended and that are developed on time and on budget.

Managing Complexity

It is estimated that the most complex inventions in history include NASA's Space Shuttle, the Boeing 747, and the Windows Operating System. Simply put, modern programs are among the most complicated things we humans build.

It would be insane for an engineer to set out to build the Space Shuttle without a design. Long before anyone picks up a screwdriver, months—if not years—of work are invested in analyzing the problem the shuttle will solve, and years more are spent perfecting the design.

In fact, no one ever set out to design the shuttle at all; rather, they set out to solve the problem of building reusable spacecraft. Only after the problem was fully understood did they turn their attention to the solution to that problem. The shuttle was a *result* of that analysis and design process, not its cause.

These are the steps for any product: analysis, design, and implementation. *Analysis* is the process of understanding the problem, *design* is the process of imagining a solution, and *implementation* is the process of building to that design.

Object-oriented analysis and design begin by examining the objects in the world and continue by modeling those objects in your program.

Objects

The world is populated by things: cars, dogs, trees, clouds, flowers. That is, things. Each thing has characteristics (fast, friendly, brown, puffy, pretty). Most things have behaviors (move, bark, grow, rain, wilt). We don't think about a dog's data and how we might manipulate it—we think about a dog as a thing in the world, what it is like, and what it does. We are *thing*-oriented beings, and C++ is a *thing*-oriented language.

It is this focus on *objects* (or things), rather than on activities, that sets object-oriented software development apart from other approaches. The overwhelming advantage to this approach is that it corresponds to how we think about the problems we are trying to solve.

The focus on objects is so natural for us that it is hard to see it. We can't imagine a world in which objects have no boundaries and therefore merge into each other. It is inconceivable to think about the oil level in your car without thinking about oil (black, greasy, slick) and car (transportation, fast, red). The entity and the attributes are inextricably tied to our understanding of the world.

Encapsulation

By focusing on *things*, we can *encapsulate* in an object all our understanding of the characteristics and behavior of that object. We treat it as a bounded entity, and its behavior is not spread through our design. That is, we don't keep track of an oil's viscosity in one place and its color in another; rather, we create an oil object and we track both its viscosity and color as attributes of that object.

 encapsulation—Capturing in a single class all the attributes and behavior of an entity.

Encapsulation enables us to think of objects as black boxes—as objects we can use without focusing on how they work.

 black box—An object whose behavior and attributes are known but whose inner workings remain mysterious.

A mechanic must know how the engine and transmission work in your car, but you, as a driver, can use your car without understanding the inner details. The car encapsulates all the details of its constituent parts. All you need to know is its interface: the accelerator, brake, and steering wheel.

Delegation

If you do open the black box of your car and peer through the lid, you won't find an amorphous mass of characteristics, but simply subobjects interacting with one another: engine, transmission, wheels, and so forth. If you open any of these objects you find more objects—for example, the engine consists of spark plugs, manifolds, belts, catalytic converters, and so on. Each in turn comprises smaller and more specialized objects.

 delegation—Assigning responsibility to another object.

When the engine propels the car, it doesn't do all the work in one monolithic object. Instead, it delegates to constituent objects each of the responsibilities. In turn, these objects can delegate to one another. Thus, the engine delegates building up pressure to the pistons, and responsibility for generating the spark is delegated to the spark plug. Responsibility for getting the spark to the built up gas is delegated to the distributor. (Okay, I'm showing my age, but fuel injected engines really *are* a black box to me!)

Perhaps we can see the issue of delegation more clearly in a business analogy. When Bill Gates decides to send you a free copy of Visual C++, he doesn't go down to shipping and stuff it in an envelope. He picks up the phone and tells his administrative assistant to do it. He then forgets about it. He doesn't need to know—nor does he want to know—the details, and by shielding himself from the details he can do other work more efficiently.

The administrative assistant can delegate the responsibility for packing up the latest beta copy to an assistant, and then he can delegate the responsibility for shipping the book to the manager of fulfillment. In fact, the administrative assistant might contribute nothing more than the coordination of the implementation of the plan that was set in motion by Gates.

The director of fulfillment can, in turn, delegate to one or more workers the specialized tasks of stuffing the envelope, getting your address, and taking care of postage. In any case, no one at Microsoft will then fly the software to your house; they will delegate that responsibility either to the U.S. Post Office or to one of the overnight delivery services.

Each individual has a well-understood set of responsibilities, and he delegates these responsibilities to others as appropriate. This division of responsibility enables each individual to focus on doing what he does best, and it creates great flexibility and robustness in the system.

If one package delivery service is more efficient than another, the new delivery service can be "plugged in" to the fulfillment process without breaking any of the other standard steps. In fact, Bill Gates need not even be aware of the change.

Similarly, in object-oriented design, we aim to decouple objects from one another so that the details of how an individual object works are hidden from the other objects with which it interacts. This fosters robust code that is easier to maintain as requirements change.

Specialization

As humans, we have evolved a tremendous capability to categorize and to build hierarchies. This is a natural, inevitable aspect of our humanity; it is hard-wired into who we are. It is how we manage the complexity of the world around us.

Rather than reacting to disparate and inchoate stimuli, our prehistoric ancestors evolved the capability to create and recognize categories and to structure our perception of the world. After we understood that large furry animals with big teeth and claws were dangerous, we categorized lions, tigers, bears, and wolves as animals to avoid, and gazelles, deer, and rabbits as potential food.

We continue to approach the world as populated by things that have characteristics and behavior and that we can organize into groups. In fact, we have formalized some of what we have done into strict taxonomies such as kingdom, phylum, class, order, family, genus, and species.

We see mammals as a specialized form of animals, dogs as a specialized form of mammals, and golden retrievers as a specialized form of dogs. A golden retriever has all the characteristics of a dog, but it specializes certain behavior (such as eagerness to learn, desire to retrieve, and so forth).

specialization—Deriving a new type from an existing type and constraining or altering behavior or characteristics (the *is-a* relationship).

inheritance—Deriving a subclass from a base class to capture specialization.

This is what we mean when we say a golden retriever *is-a* dog and a dog *is-a* mammal. The *is-a* relationship captures specialization.

Generalization and Polymorphism

After we understand the specialization relationship, we can invert it and focus on generalization. Dogs and cats are quite different, but they share certain characteristics: They give birth to live young, they suckle their young, they have hair, and so forth. They share these characteristics with other things: pigs, horses, and so forth. We generalize these characteristics and behaviors into the abstraction *mammal*, which "factors out" the common characteristics of each.

Sometimes we want to focus on the individual *type* (or specialization) of mammal. If we want a pet, we distinguish sharply between dogs and pigs. On the other hand, sometimes we don't care about these specifics—we care only about their shared attributes. Thus, if we are modeling a planet, we might focus on the fact that fish have gills and mammals have lungs. We don't care about the details of dog lungs as opposed to horse lungs; we care only about mammals as a whole.

generalization—Factoring out the common attributes and behavior from a number of classes into a common base class.

polymorphism—The capability to treat many different types of things as one type, or for one thing to take many forms.

In software, we generalize buttons, list boxes, check boxes, and text fields into the more general concept of *widget*. Widgets share the capability to draw themselves on the screen. The mechanics of how each of these widgets draws itself differ from one to the other, but they all know how to do so.

Object-oriented languages enable you to treat the specialized types (or classes) polymorphically. That is, you can tell any window to draw itself, and you don't have to worry about the specifics of how each of the specialized types accomplishes this task. The button draws a circle, the text box draws a rectangle, the check box draws a square—this specialized behavior is hidden (encapsulated) in the individual subtype's implementation of this polymorphic behavior.

We see polymorphism all around us. When we step on the gas, we expect the car to accelerate, even though a carburetor engine does so differently than one with electronic fuel injection or a diesel or rotary engine. These details are hidden; we treat all these specialized types of cars polymorphically.

The Three Pillars

Encapsulation, Specialization, and Polymorphism are the three pillars of object-oriented programming. Together, they enable us to build highly complex programs out of simpler building blocks. This enhances the maintainability, reliability, and robustness of our programs, and it increases the chances of delivering correct code on time and on budget.

How Object-Oriented Analysis and Design Is Done

Object-oriented analysis and design is *iterative*. As we develop software, we go through the entire process of analysis, design, implementation, and testing repeatedly as we strive for enhanced understanding of the requirements. The design directs the implementation, but the details that are uncovered during implementation feed back into the design. Most importantly, we do not try to develop any sizable project in a single, orderly, straight line; rather, we iterate over pieces of the project, constantly improving our design and refining our implementation.

 iterative—A process that repeats and increases its quality with each repetition.

Iterative development can be distinguished from *waterfall development*. In waterfall development, the output from one stage becomes the input to the next, and there is no going back. In a waterfall development process, the requirements are detailed, and the clients sign off ("Yes, this is what I want"). The requirements are then passed on to the designer and set in stone. The designer creates the design (and a wonder to behold it is) and passes it off to the programmer, who implements the design. The programmer in turn hands the code to a quality assurance engineer who tests the code and then releases it to the customer. This is great in theory, but a disaster in practice.

The real-world reality is that we learn things in design that affect our understanding of the requirements, and we learn things in implementation that change our design. The real world is not as compartmentalized as our theory would have it.

Even more problematic is the fact that the software industry is volatile, and requirements change even while we're implementing. Any process that breaks when you change the requirements is doomed to failure. Trying to stop the customer from shifting his priorities is like trying to stop the tide.

In iterative design, the visionary comes up with a concept, and then we begin to work on fleshing out the requirements. As we examine the details, the vision grows and evolves. When we have a good start on the requirements, we begin the design, knowing full well that the questions that arise during design might cause modifications back in the requirements. As we work on design, we begin prototyping and then implementing the product. The issues that arise in development feed back into design and might even influence our understanding of the requirements. Most importantly, we design and implement only pieces of the full product, iterating over the design and implementation phases repeatedly.

Although the steps of the process iterate, it is nearly impossible to describe them in such a cyclical manner. Therefore, I will describe them in sequence: vision (or conceptualization), analysis, design, implementation, testing, and rollout. Don't misunderstand me: In reality, we run through each of these steps many times during the course of the development of a single product. The iterative design process is just hard to present and understand if we cycle through each step, so I'll describe them one after the other.

Following are the steps of the iterative design process:

1. *Conceptualization* is the "vision thing." It is the single sentence that describes the great idea.

2. *Analysis* is the process of understanding the requirements.

3. *Design* is the process of creating the model of your software, from which you generate your code.

4. *Implementation* is writing the code in C++.

5. *Testing* is making sure that you did it right.

6. *Rollout* is getting it to your customers.

Piece of cake. All the rest is details.

conceptualization—The initial vision.

analysis—Understanding the requirements.

design—Creating a model of the solution.

implementation—Writing a program to manifest a design.

testing—Checking your code to make sure it is correct and bug-free.

rollout—Releasing your code to customers.

Object-Oriented Analysis and Design for Small Projects

With large, complex projects, formal analysis and design can save you months of work. Understanding the problem you are trying to solve and designing the solution up front can be a very powerful technique, and I fully document how to do this in my books on object-oriented analysis and design (*Beginning Object-Oriented Analysis and Design*, Wrox Press, ISBN: 1-8610-0133-9; and *Clouds To Code*, Wrox Press, ISBN: 1-8610-0095-2).

For smaller projects, however, the process can be collapsed and simplified. We start by getting the program up and running in its simplest form and then adding features and capabilities as we go. This approach does not scale well. With large complex projects, it is far better to put the time into design before you begin coding—to understand fully what you are going to build before you begin the implementation. For smaller projects, however, there is far less risk. Because the entire project will never overwhelm you with its complexity, you can focus on the code and allow the design to evolve.

That is the approach we'll take in this book, which is perfect for a primer on C++. We will consider what makes for good design, but focus most of our attention where it belongs: on implementation.

The Vision

All great software starts with a vision. One individual has an insight into a product he thinks might be good to build. Rarely do committees create compelling visions.

The very first phase of object-oriented analysis and design is to capture this vision in a single sentence or, at most, a short paragraph. The vision becomes the guiding principle of development, and the team that comes together to implement the vision will refer back to it—and update it if necessary—as it goes forward.

Even if the vision statement comes out of a committee in the marketing department, one person needs to be designated as the visionary. It is the visionary's job to be the keeper of the sacred light. As you progress, the requirements will evolve. Scheduling and time-to-market demands might modify what you try to accomplish in the first iteration of the program, but the visionary must keep an eye on the essential idea to ensure that whatever is produced reflects the core vision with high fidelity. This ruthless dedication, this passionate commitment, sees the project through to completion. If you lose sight of the vision, your product is doomed.

This book will describe the vision, analysis, design, and implementation of Decryptix!, a game designed to help my nine-year-old daughter think logically about problem solving. It is loosely based on the game *Mastermind* by Pressman.

Along the way we will take excursions to explore related aspects of the technology, but the focus will be on our ongoing project. We begin, therefore, with the vision of this project.

1

Decryptix!—The Vision

Decryptix! is a game in which you decode a hidden pattern as quickly as possible, using nothing but successive guesses and the application of logic.

I'll expand on the vision with an example: If I tell you I'm thinking of a five-letter pattern, using five of the letters *a* through *j*, and none of the letters repeats, you might guess *abcde*. If three of these letters are correct and two are in the right position, you might guess *abcfg*. If I then tell you that now only two of these second set of letters are correct and only one is in the right position, you might begin to get an idea of how you can crack this puzzle.

Envisioning

For the purposes of this book, *you* must take on the role of visionary, as well as analyst, designer, implementer, tester, and consumer. To proceed, you need to have a good idea of how Decryptix! might behave after it is working.

As a visionary, you normally know what you have in mind—at least to a first approximation—because it is your vision. Because Decryptix! is not your vision, however, we'll have to cheat. I'll have to share my vision with you a bit more explicitly.

To share my vision of this project, rush right out and buy (or borrow) a copy of the game *Mastermind* by Pressman. This will cost you about $10.00 retail. Be careful, it is quite addictive.

If you can't find the game, you might want to download the working version of Decryptix! from my Web site, `www.libertyassociates.com` (click on Books & Resources). This is truly cheating, but it will give you a good idea of where we are heading.

Before proceeding, spend some time thinking about this game. What does it look like? If you are looking at the toy, consider what it might be like to play the game on a computer. What are the goals of the game? What is good about it, and what are its limitations?

Requirements Analysis

Analysis begins with an understanding of the *problem domain*, the area of business with which we are concerned. In our case, the problem domain is the physical game *Mastermind*. It consists of a game board, colored pegs, and scoring pegs.

problem domain—The area of business or the world with which you will be working and which you will model in your program.

There are two players: the *encoder* and the *decrypter*. The encoder creates a secret pattern of colors (for example, red, blue, white, orange, and purple). It is the decrypter's job to guess the pattern in as few turns as possible.

On his first guess, the decrypter enters a pattern at random (for example, black, white, orange, purple, and green). The encoder then scores the guess, indicating how many colors are correct and how many of them are in the correct position.

Play continues until the decrypter guesses the pattern. Young children tend to guess at random, but older children and adults approach the problem methodically, eliminating choices as being inconsistent with prior results.

Our simulation must use nothing but ANSI/ISO C++. The advantage is that you can write our programs using any compliant compiler, on any platform, and the program will run equally well on a Windows machine, a UNIX box, or a Macintosh. The disadvantage is that we have no icons, windows, buttons, or widgets of any kind. We have only plain, simple text.

Our program won't be pretty, but it will work just fine. Rather than colors, we'll use letters. We can represent ten different colors with the letters *a* through *j*. Rather than using score pegs, we'll just print out a score.

We won't have two players; rather, a single player will interact with the system. The computer will "think" of a pattern, and the player will attempt to guess. The computer will score each attempt until the player gets it right.

If the player becomes confused, he'll want to ask the computer to print out all the guesses to date so that he can look for a pattern. He might also want to quit in the middle of a game, perhaps saving his game so that he can resume it at a later time.

Let's also give the player the option to decide how many letters can be used (for example, five letters means that you can use *a*, *b*, *c*, *d*, and *e*) and how many positions are in the code (for example, three positions means that only three letters are actually used in the code). Finally, the player can choose whether letters are duplicated (if so, the code might be aab).

We'll add one more feature. Young children have a hard time scoring each other's guesses because they tend to be confused when determining how many are correct and how many are in the right position. One way to provide practice is to enable the player to think of a pattern and have the computer attempt to guess it.

Quick and Dirty Design

The initial requirements are fairly simple, but before we begin, let's think about how we might organize this program. We'll need an object to represent the game, which will keep track of how many guesses have been made so far. A guess consists of a string of letters and a score for that string (how many are correct and how many are in the correct position). Because we want to display guesses and keep track of them, this sounds like a pretty good candidate for an object. The Guess object will keep track of the letters and the score, and it will know how to display itself on the screen.

This is sound object-oriented design: a discreet object (the Guess) with a single set of related responsibilities. This allows the game object to not worry about this area of responsibility: When it comes time to display or review a guess, the game can delegate that responsibility to the Guess.

Although things will get more complicated as we add features, we can start with a very simple first iteration. The game will ask how many letters, how many positions, and whether duplicates are allowed. It will then generate a secret code and allow the player to guess, scoring each attempt until the player succeeds or quits.

Future iterations can add the capability for the computer to guess the user's code and to store games and restart them. We'll add features as we go, but we know enough now to get started.

Implementation

In the coming chapters, I'll teach you how to create these classes and how to implement the logic of managing guesses and displaying results. The process of turning your design into code is called implementation, and for many of us it is the most enjoyable part of the development cycle.

Before we can begin, however, we need to discuss the fundamentals. What is a program, how is it created, and what tools do you need?

Programs and Source Code

The word *program* can be used in three ways: as a verb, as a noun that describes individual instructions (or *source code*) that are created by the programmer, or as a noun that describes an entire piece of executable software (as in, "Run this *program* and it spits out the words *Hello world*.")

program—The activity of creating source code ("Did you program that?"), the source code itself ("Can you read my program and see what is wrong?"), or the executable software ("Run this program to fix the problem").

source code—The individual instructions that comprise a C++ program; often simply called *code*.

This distinction can cause enormous confusion, so I will try to distinguish between the source code on one hand and the executable on the other.

A *program* can be defined as either a set of written instructions created by a programmer (source code) or as an executable piece of software.

Following is a bit of source code. I'll explain what all this means later, but here's a little just to give you an idea of what it is like:

```
#include <iostream.h>

int main()
{
    cout << "Decryptix version 0.1\n";
    return 0;
}
```

You can turn source code into an executable program in two ways. Interpreters translate the source code into computer instructions and the computer acts on those instructions immediately. Alternatively, compilers translate source code into a program, which you can run at a later time. Although interpreters are easier to work with, most serious programming is done with compilers because compiled code runs much faster. C++ is a compiled language, so you need a compiler.

Compilers

There are several commercial compilers available, and there are quite a few free compilers on the Internet. Personally, I use Microsoft Visual C++ Enterprise Edition. I started programming in C with the Lightspeed compiler, which became Microsoft C 2.0. I stayed with Microsoft compilers for years, switched to Turbo C and Borland C and then to Turbo C++ and Borland C++, and then switched back when Microsoft brought out Visual C++ 1.5. I've stayed with Microsoft Visual C++ ever since.

Choice of compiler is a personal decision, much like choice of vehicle. Microsoft is, in my opinion, the BMW of compilers, but some people prefer Borland, Watcom, or others.

In any case, the job of the compiler is to turn your source code into a program.

Your Development Environment

This book makes the assumption that your computer has a mode in which you can write directly to the screen without worrying about a graphical environment such as the one in Windows or on a Macintosh.

If you are using Windows, this mode is a DOS box, and Microsoft and the other compilers provide a *console application* or *quick windows mode* that writes directly to a

DOS box, much as the old text-based applications did in the prehistoric days of computing.

Text Editor

Your compiler might have its own built-in text editor, or you might be using a commercial text editor or word processor that can produce text files. The important thing is that whatever you write your program in, it must save simple, plain-text files with no word processing commands embedded in the text. Examples of safe editors include Windows Notepad, the DOS Edit command, Brief, Epsilon, EMACS, and vi. Many commercial word processors, such as WordPerfect, Word, and dozens of others, also offer a method for saving simple text files.

The files you create with your editor are called *source files*, and for C++ they typically are named with the extension .cpp or .CP. In this book, we'll name all the source code files with the .cpp extension, but check your compiler to find out what it needs.

Most C++ compilers don't care what extension you give your source code, but if you don't specify otherwise, many use .cpp by default. Microsoft compilers expect a .cpp extension for C++ code.

If you do not yet have a compiler, and if all this is new to you, I highly recommend that you run out and buy the least expensive Microsoft Visual C++ compiler you can find, so long as it is version 6.0 or later. This will come complete with an Integrated Development Environment that will include a text editor, a compiler, a linker, and a debugger. You don't need to know what these are just yet, but you'll be using all of them extensively as you work your way through this book.

Integrated Development Environment—A programmer's tool that usually includes an editor, a compiler, a linker, a debugger, and possibly additional tools.

Compiling the Source Code

Although the source code in your file is somewhat cryptic and anyone who doesn't know C++ might struggle to understand what it is for, it is still in what we call "human-readable" form. Your source code file is not a program, and it can't be executed, or run, as a program can.

To turn your source code into a program, you use a compiler. How you invoke your compiler and how you tell it where to find your source code varies from compiler to compiler. Check your documentation.

After your source code is compiled, an object file is produced. This file is often named with the extension .OBJ. This is still not an executable program, however. To turn this into an executable program, you must run your linker.

Creating an Executable File with the Linker

C++ programs are typically created by linking together one or more OBJ files with one or more libraries. A *library* is a collection of linkable files that were supplied with your compiler, that you purchased separately, or that you created and compiled. All C++ compilers come with a library of useful functions (or procedures) and classes that you can include in your program. A *function* is a block of code that performs a service, such as adding two numbers or printing to the screen. A *class* is a collection of data and related functions. We'll be talking about classes a lot as we go forward.

Following are the steps to create an executable file:

1. Create a source code file with a .cpp extension.
2. Compile the source code into a file with the .OBJ extension.
3. Link your OBJ file with any needed libraries to produce an executable program.

library—A collection of useful functions.

function—A block of code that performs a service.

class—A collection of data and related functions.

The Development Cycle

If every program worked the first time you tried it, that would be the complete development cycle: Write the program, compile the source code, link the program, and run it. Unfortunately, almost every program, no matter how trivial, can and will have errors, or *bugs*. Some bugs might cause the compile to fail, some might cause the link to fail, and some might only show up when you run the program.

Whatever type of bug you find, you must fix it, and that involves editing your source code, recompiling and relinking, and then rerunning the program. This cycle is represented in Figure 1.1, which diagrams the steps of the development cycle.

Figure 1.1

The steps in the development of a C++ program.

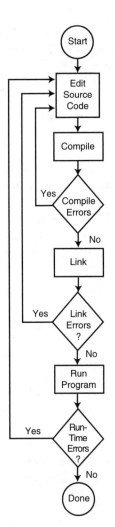

Decryptix.cpp: Your First C++ Program

Type the first program directly into your editor, exactly as shown:

```
#include <iostream.h>

int main()
{
    cout << "Decryptix Version 0.1\n";
       return 0;
}
```

After you are certain it is correct, save the file, compile it, link it, and run it. It will print the words Decryptix version 0.1 to your screen. Don't worry too much about how it works; this is really just to get you comfortable with the development cycle. I will cover every aspect of this program over the next few days.

Make certain you enter this exactly as shown. Pay careful attention to the punctuation.

On the fifth line, the << characters together are the redirection symbol, produced on most keyboards by holding the Shift key and pressing the comma key twice. This line and the next end with a semicolon.

Also check to make sure that you are following your compiler directions properly. Most compilers link automatically, but check your documentation. If you see errors, look over your code carefully and determine how it is different from the code shown here. If you see an error on line 1, for instance `cannot find file iostream.h`, check your compiler documentation for directions on setting up your `include` path or environment variables. If you receive an error that there is no prototype for main, add the line `int main();` just before

```
int main()
```

so that the program becomes

```
#include <iostream.h>

int main();
int main()
{
    cout << "Decryptix Version 0.1\n";
     return 0;
}
```

If you need to add this line here, you need to add it before the beginning of the `main` function in every program in this book. Most compilers don't require this, but a few do.

Compile Errors

Compile-time errors can occur for any number of reasons. Usually they are a result of a typographical or other inadvertent minor error. Good compilers not only tell you what you did wrong, they'll point you to the exact place in your code where you made the mistake. The great ones even suggest a remedy!

You can see this by intentionally putting an error into your program. If Decryptix! ran smoothly, edit it now, and remove the final closing brace.

Listing 1.1   Hello World

```
#include <iostream.h>

int main()
{
    cout << "Hello World!\n";
        return 0;
```

Notice that there is no closing brace this time.

Recompile your program and you see an error that looks similar to the following:

```
Decryptix.cpp, line 5: Compound statement missing
terminating } in function main().
```

This error tells you the file and line number of the problem and what the problem is (although I admit it is somewhat cryptic). Notice that the error message points you to line 5. The compiler wasn't sure whether you intended to put the closing brace before or after the `cout` statement on line 5. Sometimes the errors just point you to the general vicinity of the problem. If a compiler could perfectly identify every problem, it would fix the code itself.

Rollout

When you are writing software, it is imperative that you keep your mind on rolling the software out the door. A full analysis, a great design, and a brilliant implementation are totally worthless if the program never ships. Rollout is the process of getting your code into the hands of end users who will be more than willing to tell you what you did right and wrong. Software development is, in the end, an exercise in the greatest democratic system in the world: free market capitalism.

Next Steps

When your compiler is installed and you've run the Decryptix! program successfully, you are ready to move forward. In the coming chapters, we'll discuss how programs are structured and how to implement Decryptix! as a full featured program. Along the way, we'll examine all the details of C++ and discuss what makes for well-designed programs and how to build software that is reliable and easy to maintain.

Chapter 2

Getting Started

With a fairly simple program such as Decryptix!, my first goal is to get a version up and running—and to keep it running. After it is working, I'll add features, redesigning on-the-fly as I go.

On a large project, this can be a fatally inefficient process. As features are added, the complexity of the overall project grows, and without a good design you end up with code that is hard to maintain.

With a smaller project such as Decryptix!, however, the risk is minimal. If a new feature requires a complete redesign and rewrite of the program, no problem: It only takes a couple of days to write it in the first place.

How Big Is a Small Project?

How small must a program be to design it as you go? I'd argue that any program that takes one person more than a few weeks to program ought to be subject to a more rigorous design process. Here's why: Programs that evolve organically, rather than by design, often have to be rewritten at least once. If doing so is painful, it is worth working out the design up front. If rewriting is trivial, however, nothing was lost by diving right in.

Why Teach a Process that Is Only Good for Smaller Projects?

"Why," I hear you ask, "show an example of organic design if all large projects require formal design?" The answer is fairly straightforward: There's a lot to learn in both programming and design. This book aims to teach programming; you'll find lots of books (including a few I wrote) on object-oriented analysis and design. You can't learn everything at once.

Nothing I teach in this book is inconsistent with good design; we just won't take the time to design everything up front. I don't know about you, but I'm eager to dive into some code.

Bootstrapping Your Knowledge

In a classic C++ primer, I'd start with the structure of the program, introduce statements and expressions, add variables and constants, and then turn to classes. I'd build skill upon skill, and I'd be about 600 pages into the book before you could even begin to write your Decryptix! program.

This book is different. You're going to jump right in and wallow around awhile. Not all of it will make sense at first, and I'll gloss over lots of detail only to return to it later in the book, but the essential flow of the program can be explained pretty quickly. From time to time you'll take an "Excursion" to related—but not strictly relevant—areas of C++.

Creating the Project

This book is designed to be of use regardless of which compiler you are using or what platform (for example, Windows or Mac) you are developing for. From time to time, however, I'll demonstrate how you can accomplish a specific task in Microsoft Visual C++ 6.0. Your compiler might be somewhat different, but the principles are the same. With the knowledge that is provided here you can easily read the documentation for your compiler and make the necessary adjustments.

I begin by creating a project. On the drive on which I installed my compiler I have created a directory called Decryptix Projects. This will house all the versions of the program I will create.

First I start Visual C++ and tell it to create a new Win32 Console Application called Decryptix, as shown in Figure 2.1.

If your compiler offers a *wizard* (a series of dialog boxes that helps you make these decisions), choose whatever provides you with the simplest, text-based, non-windowed, ISO-standard environment. In this case, I choose **empty application**.

After creating the project, Visual C++ drops me in the Integrated Development Environment (IDE). I choose **File**, **New**, and enter a new C++ source file named Decryptix.cpp.

Figure 2.1

Microsoft Visual C++ New Project.

2

In other environments, for example a text editor in UNIX, I'd just open a new file and save it as Decryptix.cpp. Often, in IDEs, saving the file with the .cpp extension signals that this is C++ source code and turns on source code indentation support (and, sometimes, color-coded text!). Source code indentation support means that when you type your source code the editor automatically indents it properly for you. Thus, if you enter

```
if ( someValue > thisValue )
```

and then press **Enter**, the editor automatically indents the next line. (Don't worry about what this code does, it will all be explained in time.)

 Note

To learn what support your editor provides, please check the documentation that comes with your compiler.

Examining the Code

Now take a look at a preliminary version of Decryptix, in Listing 2.1. You can open a file in your project, save it as Decryptix.cpp, and then enter this code, exactly as shown.

 Tip

I strongly advise you to enter all the source code yourself because that is the best way to learn. If you simply can't stand the thought of all that typing, however, you can retrieve this code from the CD that accompanies this book, or you can download this code—and all the code for this book—from my Web site (go to www.libertyassociates.com and click on Books & Resources).

This program is quite advanced, and of course you won't understand much of what you are reading. Don't be intimidated, however; this chapter and Chapter 3, "Program Flow," go over it line by line. You might find, however, that you can get a pretty good idea of what the program is doing just by reading it as prose.

Try running it and examining what it does, and then try matching the code to the output.

Listing 2.1   First Glimpse of Decryptix!

```
0:   #include <iostream>
1:
2:   int main()
3:   {
4:           std::cout << "Decryptix. (c)Copyright 1999 Liberty ";
5:           std::cout << "Associates, Inc. Version 0.2\n " << std::endl;
6:           std::cout << "There are two ways to play Decryptix: ";
7:           std::cout << " either you can guess a pattern I create, ";
8:           std::cout << "or I can guess your pattern.\n\n";
9:
10:          std::cout << "If you are guessing, I will think of a\n ";
11:          std::cout << "pattern of letters (e.g., abcde).\n\n";
12:
13:          std::cout << "On each turn, you guess the pattern and\n";
14:          std::cout << " I will tell you how many letters you \n";
15:          std::cout << "got right, and how many of the correct\n";
16:          std::cout << " letters were in the correct position.\n\n";
17:
18:          std::cout << "The goal is to decode the puzzle as quickly\n";
19:          std::cout << "as possible. You control how many letters \n";
20:          std::cout << "can be used and how many positions\n";
21:          std::cout << " (e.g., 5 possible letters in 4 positions) \n";
22:          std::cout << "as well as whether or not the pattern might\n";
23:          std::cout << " contain duplicate letters (e.g., aabcd).\n\n";
24:
25:          std::cout << "If I'm guessing, you think of a pattern \n";
26:          std::cout << "and score each of my answers.\n\n" << std::endl;
27:
28:          const int minLetters = 2;
29:          const int maxLetters = 10;
30:          const int minPositions = 3;
31:          const int maxPositions = 10;
32:
33:          int howManyLetters = 0, howManyPositions = 0;
34:          bool duplicatesAllowed = false;
35:          int round = 1;
36:
37:          std::cout << "How many letters? (";
38:          std::cout << minLetters << "-" << maxLetters << "): ";
39:          std::cin >> howManyLetters;
40:
```

```
41:        std::cout << "How many positions? (";
42:        std::cout << minPositions << "-" << maxPositions << "): ";
43:        std::cin >> howManyPositions;
44:
45:        char choice;
46:        std::cout << "Allow duplicates (y/n)? ";
47:        std::cin >> choice;
48:
49:        return 0;
50:    }
```

Compile, link, and run this program. In Visual C++ you can do all this at once by pressing **Ctrl+F5**. Here's the output:

Output

```
Decryptix. (c)Copyright 1999 Liberty Associates, Inc. Version 0.2
There are two ways to play Decryptix:
 either you can guess a pattern I create,
or I can guess your pattern.

If you are guessing, I will think of a
 pattern of letters (e.g., abcde).

On each turn, you guess the pattern and
 I will tell you how many letters you
got right, and how many of the correct
 letters were in the correct position.

The goal is to decode the puzzle as quickly
as possible. You control how many letters
can be used and how many positions
 (e.g., 5 possible letters in 4 positions)
as well as whether or not the pattern might
 contain duplicate letters (e.g., aabcd).

If I'm guessing, you think of a pattern
and score each of my answers.

How many letters? (2-10):
```

Analyzing the Code

The very first line of this program (Line 0) is

```
#include <iostream>
```

The goal of this line is to add to your current file the information it needs to support *Input* and *Output streaming*: the capability to read from the keyboard (input) and write to the screen (output).

Input Stream—How data comes into your program; typically from the keyboard.

Output Stream—How data leaves your program; typically to the display.

Here's how it works: C++ now includes a group of supporting code called the standard library, which provides objects to handle input and output. *cin* is an object that handles input from the keyboard, and *cout* is an object that handles output to the screen. The details of how they work are not important at this point, but to use them you must include in your program the file iostream, which provides their definitions. The definition of an object tells the compiler what it needs to know in order for the object to be used.

cin is pronounced *see-in*, and cout is pronounced *see-out*.

You include this file in your program with the #include statement. When your compiler is invoked, the precompiler runs, reading through your program and looking for lines that begin with the # symbol. When it sees #include, it knows it must read in a file. The angle brackets (< and >) say "look in the usual place." When you installed your compiler, it should have set up "the usual place" to look for these files.

Some folks pronounce # as *hash*, others as *cross-hash*. I call it pound, so I pronounce this line of code *pound include eye-oh-stream* .

The net effect is that the file iostream is read into your program at this point, which is just what you want. You can now use the cout object, as you'll see in a few moments.

Note

Using the angle brackets, <iostream> indicates that the precompiler is to "look in the usual place." An alternative is to use double quote marks—for instance "myfile.h"—which say "look in the current project directory and, failing that, look in the usual place."

Namespaces

Unlike the code in Chapter 1, "Introduction," this version uses the new ANSI/ISO standard library header file <iostream> rather than <iostream.h> (note that the new header doesn't use .h).

These headers support the new namespace protocols, which enable you to avoid conflicts in the names of objects and methods when working with code you buy from other vendors. For example, there might be two objects named cout. We solve this by "qualifying" the name with std::, as shown on lines 4–26. This qualification with std:: indicates to the compiler that it is to use the cout object that is defined in the standard (std) library, which comes with your compiler.

Unfortunately, this makes the code look much more complicated and difficult to read.

using namespace std

To simplify this code and to make it easier for us to focus on the issues we care about, I'll rewrite the preceding example by adding the keywords

```
using namespace std;
```

This signals to the compiler that the code I'm writing is within the std (standard) namespace. In effect, it tells the compiler that when it sees cout it is to treat it like std::cout.

Note

All the rest of the code in the book uses this trick, which makes the code much easier to read and follow, at the cost of undermining the protection that namespaces afford.

When you write your commercial applications you might want to eschew the using namespace idiom because you might want to ensure namespace protection.

Listing 2.1a is an exact replica of Listing 2.1, except that it takes advantage of the using namespace idiom.

Listing 2.1a using namespace std

```
0:  #include <iostream>
1: using namespace std;
2:  int main()
3:  {
4:      cout << "Decryptix. (c)Copyright 1999 Liberty ";
5:      cout << "Associates, Inc. Version 0.2\n " << endl;
6:
7:      cout << "There are two ways to play Decryptix: ";
8:      cout << " either you can guess a pattern I create, ";
9:      cout << "or I can guess your pattern.\n\n";
```

continues

Listing 2.1a   continued

```
10:
11:        cout << "If you are guessing, I will think of a\n ";
12:        cout << "pattern of letters (e.g., abcde).\n\n";
13:
14:        cout << "On each turn, you guess the pattern and\n";
15:        cout << " I will tell you how many letters you \n";
16:        cout << "got right, and how many of the correct\n";
17:        cout << " letters were in the correct position.\n\n";
18:
19:        cout << "The goal is to decode the puzzle as quickly\n";
20:        cout << "as possible. You control how many letters \n";
21:        cout << "can be used and how many positions\n";
22:        cout << " (e.g., 5 possible letters in 4 positions) \n";
23:        cout << "as well as whether or not the pattern might\n";
24:        cout << " contain duplicate letters (e.g., aabcd).\n\n";
25:
26:        cout << "If I'm guessing, you think of a pattern \n";
27:        cout << "and score each of my answers.\n\n" << endl;
28:
29:        const int minLetters = 2;
30:        const int maxLetters = 10;
31:        const int minPositions = 3;
32:        const int maxPositions = 10;
33:
34:        int howManyLetters = 0, howManyPositions = 0;
35:        bool duplicatesAllowed = false;
36:        int round = 1;
37:
38:        cout << "How many letters? (";
39:        cout << minLetters << "-" << maxLetters << "): ";
40:        cin >> howManyLetters;
41:
42:        cout << "How many positions? (";
43:        cout << minPositions << "-" << maxPositions << "): ";
44:        cin >> howManyPositions;
45:
46:        char choice;
47:        cout << "Allow duplicates (y/n)? ";
48:        cin >> choice;
49:
50:        return 0;
51:    }
```

Code Spelunking

One of the most powerful ways to learn C++ is to use your debugger. I highly recommend that immediately after entering this code into your project (or downloading it from my site), you compile, link, and run it. You'll need to check your documentation for how to do this, but most modern IDEs offer a menu choice to "Build the entire project."

If you are using Visual C++, you can simply point your cursor at the buttons on the toolbar until you find the ones that compile and link or that build the entire project.

After it is working, set this book aside and pick up the documentation for your debugger, which you'll find with the documentation for your compiler. Set a break point on the first line of code in main() (see line 5 in Listing 2.1). In Visual C++ you just put your cursor on that line and press **F9**, or press the break point toolbar button. Once the break point is set, run to the break point (in Visual C++, press **F5**). Step over each line of code and try to guess what is going on. Again, you'll need to check your documentation for how to step over each line of code (in Visual C++ it is **F10**).

The debugger is one of the last things most primers introduce; I feel that it needs to be one of the very *first* things you learn. If you get stuck, see the exploration of debugging at the end of this chapter.

Every C++ program has a main() function (Listing 2.1, line 2). The general purpose of a function is to run a little code and then return to whomever called you.

 All functions begin and end with parentheses, as you can see on lines 3 and 51. A *function* consists of a series of statements, which are all the lines that are shown between the parentheses.

This is the essence of a structured program. Program flow continues in the order in which the code appears in the file until a function is called. The flow then branches off to the function and follows line by line until another function is called or until the function returns (see Figure 2.2).

In a sense, a function is a subprogram. In some languages, it is called a *subroutine* or a *procedure*. The job of a function is to accomplish some work and then return control to whatever invoked the function.

When main() executes, we execute Statement1. We then branch to line 1 of Func1(). Func1's three lines execute, and then processing returns to main(), where we execute Statement2. Func2 is then called, which in turn calls Func3(). When Func3 completes it returns to Func2(), which continues to run until its own return statement, at which time we return to main() and execute Statement3. We then call Func4(), which executes its own code and then returns to main(), where we execute Statement4.

Figure 2.2

When a program calls a fuction, execution switches to the function and then resumes at the line after the function call.

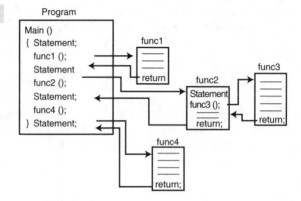

Returning a Value

When a function returns to whoever called it, it can return a value. You'll see later what the calling function can do with that value.

Every function must declare what kind of value it returns: For example, does it return an integer or a character? If a function does not return a value, it declares itself to return void, which means that it returns nothing.

`main()` Is More Equal than Others

`main()` is a special function in C++. All C++ programs begin with `main()`; when `main` ends, the program ends. In a sense, the operating system (Windows, DOS, and so on) calls `main()`.

`main()` always returns an `int` (integer). I'll discuss the various types of values later in the book; for now it is sufficient to know that you must always declare `main` to return an integer.

 **Note**

On some older compilers, you can have `main()` return `void`, but that is not legal under the new ISO standard. It is a good idea to get into the habit of having `main()` return an `int` every time.

You'll notice that `main()` does return an integer (in this case, 0) on line 50. When programs are run from batch files or scripts, you can examine these values. For the programs in this book (and probably for most of the programs you will write), this value is discarded. By convention, you'll return 0 to indicate that the program ran without incident.

Using cout to Print to the Screen

Most of the statements in this very first program are designed to write to the screen. Use the standard output object cout. You send a string of characters to cout by enclosing them in quotation marks and by using the output redirection operator (<<), which you create by holding the Shift key and pressing the comma key twice.

This actually takes advantage of a very advanced feature in C++ called *operator overloading*, which is discussed in detail in Chapter 6, "Using Linked Lists." Fortunately, for now you can use this feature without fully understanding it. The net effect is that the words

```
Decryptix. (c)Copyright 1999 Liberty
```

are sent to the screen.

operator overloading—The capability of user-created types to use the operators that built-in types use, such as +, =, and ==. I explain how to do this in Chapter 6.

Special Printing Characters

Line 5 prints the words

```
Associates, Inc. Version 0.2
```

to the screen. Notice that before the closing quotes, line 5 includes \n. These are two special marks within quoted strings. The slash is called an *escape character*, and when it is found in a quoted string it means "what follows is a special instruction to the compiler." The letter *n*, when it follows the escape character, stands for "new line." Thus, the effect is to print, to the output, a new line.

escape character—A character that serves as a signal to the compiler or precompiler that the letter that follows requires special treatment. For example, the precompiler usually treats the character *n* as a letter, but when it is preceded by the escape character (\n), it indicates a new line.

Notice also that this line ends with

```
<< endl;
```

cout can receive more than just strings. In this case, the redirection operator is being used to send endl.

**how too
pro nouns' it** | endl is pronounced *end-ell* and stands for "end line."

This sends another new line to the output and flushes out the buffers. Buffers will be explained later, when I talk about streams, but the net effect ensures that all the text is written to the screen immediately.

Line 7 begins to print another line, which is continued on line 8 and completed on line 9.

Together, these lines print the following output:

```
Decryptix. (c)Copyright 1999 Liberty Associates, Inc. Version 0.2

There are two ways to play Decryptix: either you can guess a pattern I create,
or I can guess your pattern.
```

Note first that there is no new line after Liberty and before Associates. There was no instruction to cout to print a new line, so none was printed. Two new lines appear after 0.2. The first, created by the \n character, ends the line; the second, created by endl, skips a line.

You can achieve the effect of skipping a line by putting in two \n characters, as shown on line 9.

Table 2.1 illustrates the other special printing characters.

Table 2.1   Special Printing Characters

Character	What it means
\n	new line
\t	tab
\b	rings the bell
\"	prints a double quote
\'	prints a single quote
\?	prints a question mark
\\	prints a backslash

Variables

A *variable* is a place to store a value during the progress of your program.

variable—A place to store a value.

In this case, at line 36, you want to keep track of what round of play you are up to. Store this information in a variable named round:

```
int round = 1;
```

One way to think of your computer's memory is as a series of cubbyholes. Each cubbyhole is one byte, and every byte is numbered sequentially: The number is the address of that memory. Each variable reserves one or more bytes in which you can store a value.

Your variable's name (round) is a label on one of these cubbyholes, which enables you to find it easily without knowing its actual memory address.

Think of it like this: When you jump in a cab in Washington, D.C., you can ask for 1600 Pennsylvania Avenue, or you can ask for The White House. The identifier "The White House" is the name of that address.

Figure 2.3 is a schematic representation of this idea. As you can see from the figure, round starts at memory address 103. Depending on the size of round, it can take up one or more memory addresses.

Figure 2.3

A schematic representation of memory.

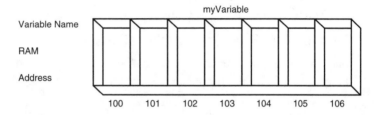

RAM

Variable Name

Address

myVariable

100   101   102   103   104   105   106

RAM—Random access memory. When you run your program, it is loaded into RAM from the disk file. All variables are also created in RAM. When programmers talk about memory, they are usually referring to RAM.

Setting Aside Memory

When you define a variable in C++, you must tell the compiler what kind of variable you are declaring: an int, char, and so forth. The type tells the compiler the size of the variable. For example, a char is 1 byte, and on modern computers an int is 4 bytes; thus, the variable round consumes four bytes (cubbyholes) of memory.

Defining a Variable

You define a variable by stating its type, followed by one or more spaces, the variable name, and a semicolon:

```
int round;
```

The variable name can be virtually any combination of letters, but it cannot contain spaces. Legal variable names include x, J23qrsnf, and myAge. It is good programming practice to use variable names that tell you what the variables are for. This makes them easier to understand, which makes it easier for you to maintain your program.

Case Sensitivity

C++ is case sensitive; therefore, a variable named round is different from Round, which is different from ROUND. Avoid using multiple variables whose names differ only by capitalization—it can be terribly confusing.

Some compilers enable you to turn case sensitivity off. Don't be tempted to do this. Your programs won't work with other compilers, and other C++ programmers will be very confused by your code.

Keywords

C++ reserves some words, and you cannot use them as variable names. These are keywords that are used by the compiler to control your program. Keywords include if, while, for, and main. Your compiler manual probably provides a complete list, but generally, any reasonable name for a variable is almost certainly not a keyword.

Creating More Than One Variable at a Time

You can create more than one variable of the same type in one statement by writing the type and then the variable names, separated by commas. For example

```
int howManyLetters, howManyPositions;
bool valid, duplicatesAllowed;
```

Assigning Values to Your Variables

Back in listing 2.1, at line 36, a local variable is defined by stating the type (int) and the variable name (round).

This actually allocates memory for the variable. Because an int is four bytes, this allocates four bytes of memory. When the compiler allocates memory, it reserves the memory for the use of your variable and assigns the name that you provide (in this case, round).

Scope

Scope refers to the region of a program in which an identifier—something that is named, such as an object, variable, function, or constant—is valid. When I say a variable has *local scope*, I mean that it is valid within a particular function.

scope—The region of a program in which an identifier (that is, the name of something) is valid.

local scope—When an identifier has local scope, it is valid within a particular function.

There are other levels of scope (global, static member, and so on) that I will discuss as I progress through the program.

The Value of Variables

Local variables, such as round, have a value when they are created regardless of whether you initialize them. If you don't initialize them (as shown here), whatever happened to already be in the bit of memory is assigned to them—that is, a random *garbage* value.

It is good programming practice to *initialize* your variables. When you initialize a variable, you create it and give it a specific value, all in one step:

```
int round = 1;
```

This creates the variable round and initializes it with the value 1.

Just as you can define more than one variable at a time, you can initialize more than one variable. For example,

```
    int howManyLetters = 0, howManyPositions = 0;
```

initializes the two variables howManyLetters, each to the value 0. You can even mix definitions and initializations:

```
int howManyLetters = 0, round, howManyPositions = 2;
```

This example defines three variables of type int, and it initializes the first and third.

EXCURSION

Characters

On line 46 of Listing 2.1, you created a character variable (type char) named choice. On most computers, character variables are 1 byte, enough to hold 256 values. A char can be interpreted as a small number (0–255) or as a member of the ASCII set. ASCII stands for the American Standard Code for Information Interchange. The ASCII character set and its ISO (International Standards Organization) equivalent are a way to encode all the letters, numerals, and punctuation marks.

ASCII—The American Standard Code for Information Interchange.

ISO—The International Standards Organization.

You create a character by placing the letter in single quotes. Therefore, 'a' creates the character *a*.

In the ASCII code, the lowercase letter *a* is assigned the value **97**. All the lower- and uppercase letters, all the numerals, and all the punctuation marks are assigned values between **1** and **128**. Another 128 marks and symbols are reserved for use by the computer maker.

Characters and Numbers

When you insert a character—'a', for example—into a char variable, what is really there is just a number between 0 and 255. The compiler knows, however, how to translate back and forth between characters and one of the ASCII values.

The value/letter relationship is arbitrary; there is no particular reason that the lowercase *a* is assigned the value **97**. As long as everyone (your keyboard, compiler, and screen) agrees, there is no problem. It is important to realize, however, that there is a big difference between the value **5** and the character '5'. The latter is actually valued at **53**, much as the letter 'a' is valued at **97**.

Listing 2.2 is a simple program that prints the character values for the integers 32–127. Pay no attention to the details of this program—we will walk through how this works later in the book.

Listing 2.2   **Printing out the Characters**

```
    #include <iostream >
using namespace std;
int main()
    {
    for (int i = 32; i<128; i++)
      cout << (char) i;
    return 0;
    }
```

Output

```
!"#$%G'()*+,./0123456789:;<>?@ABCDEFGHIJKLMNOP
_QRSTUVWXYZ[\]^'abcdefghijklmnopqrstuvwxyz<¦>~s
```

 Note   Your computer might print a slightly different list.

Built-In Types

C++ comes right out of the box with knowledge of a number of primitive built-in types. The type of a variable or object defines its size, its attributes, and its capabilities.

For example, an int is, on modern compilers, 4 bytes in size. It holds a value from -2,147,483,648 to 2,147,483,647. For more on bytes and why 2,147,483,648 is a round number, see Appendix A, "Binary and Hexadecimal."

You might think that an integer is an integer, but it isn't quite. The keyword `integer` refers to a four-byte value, but only if you are using a modern compiler on a modern 32-bit computer. If your software or computer is 16-bit, however, an integer might be only two bytes. The keyword `short` usually refers to a two-byte integer, and the keyword `long` most often refers to a four-byte integer, but neither of these is certain. The language requires only that a `short` is shorter than or equal to an integer, and an integer is shorter than or equal to a `long`. On my computer, a `short` is 2 bytes and an integer is 4, as is a `long`.

ISO C++ provides the types that are listed in Table 2.2.

Table 2.2   Variable Types

Type	Size	Values
unsigned short `int`	2 bytes	0 to 65,535
short `int`	2 bytes	-32,768 to 32,767
unsigned long `int`	4 bytes	0 to 4,294,967,295
long `int`	4 bytes	-2,147,483,648 to 2,147,483,647
`int` (16-bit)	2 bytes	-32,768 to 32,767
`int` (32-bit)	4 bytes	-2,147,483,648 to 2,147,483,647
unsigned `int` (16-bit)	2 bytes	0 to 65,535
unsigned `int` (32-bit)	4 bytes	0 to 4,294,967,295
`char`	1 byte	256 character values
`float`	4 bytes	1.2e-38 to 3.4e38
`double`	8 bytes	2.2e-308 to 1.8e308
`bool`	1 byte	`true` or `false`

Note ISO C++ recently added a new type, `bool`, which is a `true` or `false` value. `bool` is named after the British mathematician George Bool (1815-1864), who invented Boolean algebra, a system of symbolic logic.

Size of Integers

This book assumes that you are using a 32-bit computer (for example, a Pentium) and that you are programming with a 32-bit compiler. With that development environment, an integer is always 4 bytes. Listing 2.3 can help you determine the size of the built-in types on your computer, using your compiler.

Listing 2.3   Finding the Size of Built-In Types

```
1:    #include <iostream>
2:    using namespace std;
3:    int main()
4:    {
5:      cout << "The size of an int is:\t\t";
5a:     cout << sizeof(int)     << " bytes.\n";
6:      cout << "The size of a short int is:\t";
6a:     cout << sizeof(short)   << " bytes.\n";
7:      cout << "The size of a long int is:\t";
7a:     cout << sizeof(long)    << " bytes.\n";
8:      cout << "The size of a char is:\t\t";
8a:     cout << sizeof(char)    << " bytes.\n";
9:      cout << "The size of a float is:\t\t";
9a:     cout << sizeof(float)   << " bytes.\n";
10:     cout << "The size of a double is:\t";
10a:    cout << sizeof(double) << " bytes.\n";
11:     cout << "The size of a bool is:\t";
11a:    cout << sizeof(bool) << " bytes.\n";
12:         return 0;
13:   }
```

Output

```
The size of an int is:          4 bytes.
The size of a short int is:     2 bytes.
The size of a long int is:      4 bytes.
The size of a char is:          1 bytes.
The size of a float is:         4 bytes.
The size of a double is:        8 bytes.
The size of a bool is:          1 bytes.
```

Note   On your computer, the number of bytes presented might be different. If the number of bytes reported for an int (the first line of output) is 2 bytes, you are using an older (and probably obsolete) 16-bit compiler.

Tip   If you are using Visual C++, you can run your program with **Ctrl+F5**. Your ouput displays, followed by

```
Press any key to continue
```

This gives you time to look at the output; then, when you press a key, the window closes.

If your compiler does not provide this service, you might find that the text scrolls by very quickly, and then you are returned to your IDE.

2

In this case, add the following line to the top of the file:

```
#include <conio.h>
```

Add the following line just before `return 0;`:

```
    _getch();
```

This causes your program to pause after all the output is completed; it waits for you to press the spacebar or other character key. Add these lines to every sample program.

Analysis

Most of Listing 2.3 is probably pretty familiar to you. The one new feature is the use of the `sizeof()` operator, which is provided by your compiler and tells you the size of the object you pass as a parameter. For example, on line 5, the keyword `int` is passed into `sizeof()`. Using `sizeof()`, I determined that on my computer an `int` is equal to a long `int`, which is 4 bytes.

Using an Integer Variable

In Decryptix!, we want to keep track of how many different letters the code can contain. Because this is a number (between **1** and **26**), you can keep track of this value with an `int`. In fact, because this number is very small, it can be a short `int`, and because it must be a positive number, in can be an unsigned short `int`.

Using a short `int` might save me two bytes. There was a time when such a savings was significant; today, however, I rarely bother. Short `int`s can be written just as short, so it is the height of profligacy to waste bytes because I'm too lazy to write short rather than `int`.

When I was a boy, bytes were worth something, and I watched every one. Today, for most applications, bytes are cheap. They are the pennies of programming, and these days most programmers just keep a small cup of bytes out on the counter and let customers take them when they need a few, occasionally tossing extra bytes into the cup for the next person to use.

In the 1960s, many programmers worked in primitive languages, which represented dates as characters. Each number in the date consumed one byte (so 1999 consumed 4 bytes). Obsessive concern about saving a byte here and a byte there led many programmers to shorten dates from four digits (1999) to two (99), thus saving two bytes and creating the Y2K problem.

For the vast majority of programs, the only built-in types to be concerned with are `int`, `char`, and `bool`. Now and again you'll use unsigned `int`s, `float`s, and `double`s. Of course, most of the time you'll use your own programmer-created types.

Signed and Unsigned

After you determine the size of an integer, you're not quite done. An integer (and a short and a long) can be *signed* or *unsigned*. If it is signed, it can store negative and positive numbers. If it is unsigned, it can store only positive numbers.

Because signed numbers can store negative as well as positive numbers, the absolute value they can store is only half as large.

Wrapping Around an Unsigned Integer

The fact that unsigned long integers have a limit to the values they can hold is only rarely a problem—but what happens if you *do* run out of room?

When an unsigned integer reaches its maximum value, it wraps around and starts over, much like a car odometer. Listing 2.4 shows what happens if you try to put too large a value into a short integer.

Listing 2.4 Wrapping Around an Unsigned Integer

```
1: #include <iostream>
2: using namespace std;
3:  int main()
4:  {
5:      unsigned short int smallNumber;
6:      smallNumber = 65535;
7:      cout << "small number:" << smallNumber << endl;
8:      smallNumber++;
9:      cout << "small number:" << smallNumber << endl;
10:     smallNumber++;
11:     cout << "small number:" << smallNumber << endl;
12:      return 0;
13:  }
```

```
small number:65535
small number:0
small number:1
```

On line 4, `smallNumber` is declared to be an unsigned short `int`, which on my computer is a two-byte variable that can hold a value between `0` and `65,535`. On line 5, the maximum value is assigned to `smallNumber`, and it is printed on line 6 using the standard output library function. Note that because we did not add the line `using namespace std;` we must explicitly identify `cout`. The keyword endl is also part of the standard library and must be explicitly identified.

On line 7, `smallNumber` is *incremented*; that is, one is added to it. The symbol for incrementing is `++` (as in the name *C++*, an incremental increase from C). Thus, the value in `smallNumber` is `65,536`. However, unsigned short integers can't hold a number larger than `65,535`, so the value is wrapped around to `0`, which is printed on line 8.

incremented—When a value is incremented, it is increased by one.

On line 9, `smallNumber` is incremented again, and then its new value, 1, is printed.

Wrapping Around a Signed Integer

A signed integer is different from an unsigned integer in that half of the values you can represent are negative. Instead of picturing a traditional car odometer, you might picture one that rotates up for positive numbers and down for negative numbers. One mile from 0 is either 1 or -1. When you run out of positive numbers, you run right into the largest negative numbers and then count back down to 0. Listing 2.5 shows what happens when you add 1 to the maximum positive number in short integer.

Listing 2.5   Wrapping Around a Signed Integer

```
1:  #include <iostream>
2: using namespace std;
3:  int main()
4:  {
5:      short int smallNumber;
6:      smallNumber = 32767;
7:      cout << "small number:" << smallNumber << endl;
8:      smallNumber++;
9:      cout << "small number:" << smallNumber << endl;
10:     smallNumber++;
11:     cout << "small number:" << smallNumber << endl;
12:     return 0;
13: }

small number:32767
small number:-32768
small number:-32767
```

On line 4, `smallNumber` is declared to be a signed short integer. (If you don't explicitly say that it is unsigned, it is assumed that it is signed.) The program proceeds much as the preceding program does, but the output is quite different.

The bottom line is that just like an unsigned integer, the signed integer wraps around from its highest positive value to its highest negative value.

Constants

The point of a variable is to store a value. I call it a variable because it might vary: That is, the value might change over the course of the program. `howManyLetters` starts out as 0, but is assigned a new value based on the user's input.

At times, however, you need a fixed value—one that won't change over the course of the program. The minimum number of letters a user is allowed to choose is an example of a fixed value; the programmer determines it long before the program runs.

A fixed value is called a *constant*. There are two flavors of constants: literal and symbolic.

Literal Constants

A *literal constant* is a value that is typed directly into your program wherever it is needed. For example

```
int howManyLetters = 7;
```

howManyLetters is a variable of type int; 7 is a literal constant. You can't assign a value to 7, and its value can't be changed.

Symbolic Constants

Like variables, *symbolic constants* are storage locations, but their contents never change during the course of your program. When you declare a constant, what you are really doing is saying to the compiler, "Treat this like a variable, but if I ever change the value stored here, let me know." The compiler then tells you with a compiler error.

You'll define minLetters to be a symbolic constant—specifically, a constant integer whose value is 2. Note that the constant minLetters is used on a number of different lines of code. If you decide later to change the value to 3, you need to change it only in one place—the change affects many lines of code. This helps you avoid bugs in your code. Changes are localized, so there is little chance of one line assuming that the minimum number of letters is two, whereas another line assumes that it is three.

There are actually two ways to declare a symbolic constant in C++. The old, traditional, and now obsolete way is with a preprocessor directive: #define.

Defining Constants with `#define`

To define a constant in the traditional way, enter the following code:

```
#define minLetters 2
```

Note that when it is declared this way, `minLetters` is of no particular type (`int`, `char`, and so on). `#define` does a simple text substitution. Every time the preprocessor sees the word `minLetters`, it puts in the text 2.

Because the preprocessor runs before the compiler, your compiler never sees your constant; it sees the number 2. Later, when I discuss debugging, you'll find that `#defined` constants do not appear as symbolic constants in the debugger; you see only the literal value (2).

Defining Constants with `const`

Although `#define` works, there is a newer, much better way to define constants in C++:

```
const int minLetters = 2;
```

This creates the symbolic constant `minLetters` but ensures that it has a particular type—`integer`. If you try to write

```
const int minLetters = 3.2;
```

the compiler complains that you have declared it to be an `int` but that you are trying to initialize it with a `float`.

EXCURSION

The purpose of a debugger is to enable you to peek inside the machine and watch your variables change as the program runs. You can accomplish a lot with a debugger, and aside from your text editor, it is your most important tool.

Unfortunately, most novices don't become comfortable with their debugger until very late in their experience of C++. This is a shame because the debugger is a terrific learning tool.

Although every debugger is different and you definitely want to consult your documentation, this excursion illustrates how you might debug Listing 2.1 using the Microsoft Visual C++ 6.0 Enterprise Edition debugger. Your exact experience might vary, but the principles are the same.

Follow these steps:

1. Create a project called Decryptix.

2. Open a new file called decryptix.cpp.

3. Enter the program as it is written or download it from my Web site.

4. Place the cursor on the first line after the opening brace and press **F9**. You see a red dot in the margin next to that line, indicating a break point (see Figure 2.4).

Figure 2.4

Figure 2.4

A break point showing in Visual C++.

5. Press **Go** (**F5**). The debugger starts, and your code runs.

6. Choose **View/Debug Windows** and make sure that the Watch and Variables windows are open (see Figure 2.5).

Figure 2.5

Checking that the Watch and Variables windows are open.

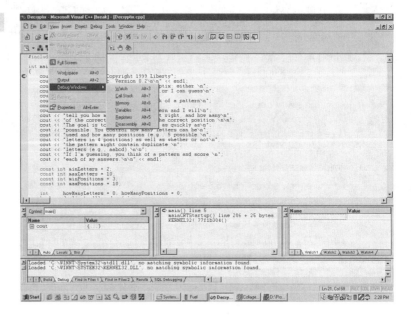

7. Press **Step Over** (**F10**) to walk through the code line by line.

8. Scroll down to the line on which `duplicatesAllowed` is defined, and place a break point there. Press **Go** (**F5**) to run until this second break point.

9. Note in the variables window that `howManyLetters` and `howManyPositions` are zero, but that `duplicatesAllowed` has a random value (see Figure 2.6).

Figure 2.6

Looking at values in the debugger.

10. Press **Step Over** (**F10**) to step over this one line of code. This causes `duplicatesAllowed` to be created and initialized. Note that the value that is shown in the variables window is now correct (`false` is indicated as **0**, and `true` is indicated as **1**). Note also that `round` has a random value. Press **F10** again; `round` is initialized to **1**.

11. Explore the debugger and read through the documentation and help files. The more time you spend in the debugger, the more you will come to appreciate its tremendous value, both for finding bugs and for helping you understand how programs work.

Chapter 3

Program Flow

This chapter takes a look at how programs progress, how loops are created, and how programs branch based on user input and other conditions.

Building Robustness

Listing 2.1 in Chapter 2, "Getting Started," is vulnerable to incorrect user input. For example, what happens if the user asks for 35 letters or says, "Use five letters in six positions without duplicates." This, of course, is impossible: You can't put five letters into six positions without duplicating at least one letter. How do you prevent the user from giving you bogus data?

A *robust program* is one that can handle any user input without crashing. Writing highly robust code is difficult and complex. Therefore, we won't set a goal of handling absolutely any bogus data, but we will attempt to deal with a few highly predictable errors.

 robust—A program is robust when it can handle incorrect user input or other unanticipated events without crashing.

Listing 3.1 illustrates a more complex version of the code you just considered. Before it is discussed, take a look at it and see if you can make some guesses about what it is doing.

Listing 3.1   A More Complex Version of Decryptix!

```
0:   #include <iostream>
1:   using namespace std;
2:   int main()
3:   {
4:     cout << "Decryptix. (c)Copyright 1999 Liberty";
5:     cout << "Associates, Inc. Version 0.2\n\n" << endl;
6:     cout << "There are two ways to play Decryptix: either";
7:     cout << "you can guess a pattern I create,\n";
8:     cout << "or I can guess your pattern.\n\n";
9:     cout << "If you are guessing, I will think of a pattern\n";
10:    cout << "of letters (e.g., abcde).\n\n";
11:    cout << "On each turn, you guess the pattern and I will\n";
12:    cout << "tell you how many letters you got right, and how many\n";
13:    cout << "of the correct letters were in the correct position.\n\n";
14:    cout << "The goal is to decode the puzzle as quickly as\n";
15:    cout << "possible. You control how many letters can be\n";
16:    cout << "used and how many positions (e.g., 5 possible \n";
17:    cout << "letters in 4 positions) as well as whether or not\n";
18:    cout << "the pattern might contain duplicate \n";
19:    cout << "letters (e.g., aabcd).\n\n";
20:    cout << "If I'm guessing, you think of a pattern and score \n";
21:    cout << "each of my answers.\n\n" << endl;
22:
23:
24:    int round = 1;
25:    int howManyLetters = 0, howManyPositions = 0;
26:    bool duplicatesAllowed = false;
27:    bool valid = false;
28:
29:    const int minLetters = 2;
30:    const int maxLetters = 10;
31:    const int minPositions = 3;
32:    const int maxPositions = 10;
33:
34:
35:    while ( ! valid )
36:    {
37:       while ( howManyLetters < minLetters
38:          ¦¦ howManyLetters > maxLetters )
39:       {
40:          cout << "How many letters? (";
41:          cout << minLetters << "-" << maxLetters << "): ";
42:          cin >> howManyLetters;
43:          if ( howManyLetters < minLetters
44:             ¦¦ howManyLetters > maxLetters )
45:          {
46:             cout << "please enter a number between ";
47:             cout << minLetters << " and " << maxLetters << endl;
48:          }
```

```
49:        }
50:
51:        while ( howManyPositions < minPositions
52:            || howManyPositions > maxPositions )
53:        {
54:          cout << "How many positions? (";
55:          cout << minPositions << "-" << maxPositions << "): ";
56:          cin >> howManyPositions;
57:          if ( howManyPositions < minPositions
58:              || howManyPositions > maxPositions )
59:          {
60:             cout << "please enter a number between ";
61:             cout << minPositions <<" and " << maxPositions << endl;
62:          }
63:        }
64:
65:        char choice = ' ';
66:        while ( choice != 'y' && choice != 'n' )
67:        {
68:           cout << "Allow duplicates (y/n)? ";
69:           cin >> choice;
70:        }
71:
72:        duplicatesAllowed = choice == 'y' ? true : false;
73:
74:        if ( ! duplicatesAllowed
75:           && howManyPositions > howManyLetters )
76:        {
77:          cout << "I can't put " << howManyLetters;
78:          cout << " letters in " << howManyPositions;
79:          cout << " positions without duplicates! Please try again.\n";
80:           howManyLetters = 0;
81:           howManyPositions = 0;
82:        }
83:        else
84:        valid = true;
85:     }
86:
87:   return 0;
88: }
```

What Are You Trying to Accomplish?

Line 35 brings us to the first line of code after the initialization of the local variables and constants.

The goal with this piece of code is to prompt the user for a series of pieces of information. Specifically, you want to know how many letters he or she will use (for example, five letters means *a*, *b*, *c*, *d*, and *e*), how many positions (for example, three positions means there are three letters that are actually used in the code), and whether you'll allow duplicates (can one letter repeat?)

The problem is that the user might not give you valid information. For example, the user might tell you to use four letters in five positions with no duplicates. This, unfortunately, is not physically possible. You want to make sure that you have reasonable choices before moving forward with the program.

> **Note** Let me pause and point out that in a real commercial program, it is not unusual for literally dozens—or even hundreds—of lines of code to be devoted to catching and responding appropriately to bogus user input. You will not endeavor to be quite that robust here, but you do want to trap the obvious mistakes and ask the user to try again.

Solving the Problem with Loops

The essential approach to solving this problem is to do some work (ask the user for input), test a condition (determine whether the data makes sense), and, if the condition fails, start over.

This is called a *loop*; C++ supports a number of different looping mechanisms.

loop—A section of code that repeats.

Remember that you've created two constant integers for the values you need: minLetters and maxLetters. Because you initialized howManyLetters to zero, when you start out, howManyLetters is of course less than minLetters, assuming that minLetters is greater than zero.

You want to continue to prompt and then reprompt the user while howManyLetters is either less than the minimum or more than the maximum. To do this, you'll create a while loop.

The syntax for the while statement is as follows:

```
while ( condition )
statement;
```

condition is any C++ expression, and statement is any valid C++ statement or block statements. When condition evaluates to true, statement executes, and then condition is tested again. This continues until condition tests false, at which time the while loop terminates and execution continues on the first line following statement.

Your `while` statement might be

```
while ( howManyLetters < minLetters )
{
    //...
}
```

> **Note**
>
> The symbol
>
> `//...`
>
> indicates that I've left out code that you're not considering at the moment.

Relational Operators

Relational operators determine whether two numbers are equal, or whether one is greater or less than the other. Every relational statement evaluates to either `true` or `false`.

relational operator—A symbol (for example, > or <) that is used to determine the relative size of two objects. Relational operators evaluate to `true` or `false`.

If the integer variable `howManyLetters` has the value 1 and the constant `minLetters` has the value 2, the expression

```
howManyLetters < minLetters
```

returns `true`.

A `while` loop continues while the expression is true, so if `howManyLetters` is 1 and `minLetters` is 2, the expression is true and the `while` loop will in fact execute.

Note that I talk about a single statement executing. It is also possible to execute a *block* (that is, a group) of statements.

Blocks and Compound Statements

A statement can be a single line or it can be a block of code that is surrounded by braces, which is treated as a single statement. Although every statement in the block must end with a semicolon, the block itself does not end with a semicolon.

The block of code itself can consist of any number of statements, but it is treated as a single statement.

This enables you to run several statements as the execution of a single `while` loop.

Not only can you test whether one variable is less than another, you can test whether one is larger, or even whether they are the same.

There are six relational operators listed in Table 3.1, which also shows each operator's use and some sample code.

Table 3.1   Relational Operators

Name	Operator	Sample	Evaluates
Equals	==	100 == 50;	false
		50 == 50;	true
Not Equals	!=	100 != 50;	true
		50 != 50;	false
Greater Than	>	100 > 50;	true
		50 > 50;	false
Greater Than or Equals	>=	100 >= 50;	true
		50 >= 50;	true
Less Than	<	100 < 50;	false
		50 < 50;	false
Less Than or Equals	<=	100 <= 50;	false
		50 <= 50;	true

Warning   Many novice C++ programmers confuse the assignment operator (=) with the equals operator (==). This can create a nasty bug in your program.

Logical Operators

The problem with this `while` loop is that it tests only whether `howManyLetters` is less than the constant `minLetters`; you also need to test to find out whether `howManyLetters` is greater than `maxLetters`.

You *can* test them separately:

```
while ( howManyLetters < minLetters )
{
     //...
}

while ( howManyLetters > maxLetters )
{
     //...
}
```

This will work, but the code within both `while` loops will be identical. In fact, what you are really trying to say is that you want to repeat this work while `howManyLetters` is less than `minLetters` or while `howManyLetters` is greater than `maxLetters`. C++ enables you to make exactly that test using the *logical OR operator* (¦¦). You create the logical OR operator by pressing **Shift+** twice.

The Logical OR Operator

In this case, you are asking for the `while` loop to continue as long as either condition is true, so you use logical OR:

```
while ( howManyLetters < minLetters ¦¦ howManyLetters > maxLetters )
{
    //...
}
```

This code says that the statement (between the braces) is executed if it is true that `howManyLetters` is less than `minLetters` or if it is true that `howManyLetters` is greater than `maxLetters` (or if both conditions are true).

The Logical AND Operator

At other times, you might want to continue only if both conditions are true, in which case you want to use `while (condition 1 and condition 2)`. The *logical AND operator* (&&) handles this condition. A logical AND statement evaluates two expressions, and if both expressions are true, the logical AND statement is true as well.

For example, you can test the following:

```
while ( howManyLetters > minLetters && howManyLetters < maxLetters )
{
    //...
}
```

this statement executes only if it is true that `howManyLetters` is greater than `minLetters` and if it is also true that `howManyLetters` is less than `maxLetters`.

logical operator OR—¦¦ created by two vertical lines, by pressing **Shift+backslash** (\) twice.

logical operator AND—&& created by two ampersands, by pressing **Shift+7** twice.

The `if` Statement

An `if` statement allows you to take action only if a condition is true (and to skip the action or do something else if the condition is false). You use `if` statements every day:

> If it is raining, I'll take my umbrella.
>
> If I have time, I'll walk the dog.
>
> If I don't walk the dog, I'll be sorry.

The simplest form of an `if` statement is this:

```
if (expression)
    statement;
```

The *expression* in the parentheses can be any expression at all, but it usually contains one of the relational expressions. If the expression has the value `false`, the statement is skipped. If it evaluates to `true`, the statement executes. Once again, the statement can certainly be a compound statement between braces, as you see here.

The Logical NOT Operator

A *logical NOT statement* (`!`) evaluates `true` if the expression that is being tested is false. This is confusing at first, but an example will help. I might start by saying, "If it is raining, I'll bring my umbrella":

```
if ( raining )
  BringUmbrella();
```

How do I express that I'll only go for a walk if it is *not* raining?

```
if ( ! raining )
   GoForWalk();
```

I can also reverse these:

```
if ( ! raining )
  LeaveUmbrella;

if ( raining )
  GoForWalk;
```

You get the idea.

Thus

```
if ( ! valid )
```

is true only if `valid` is false.

logical NOT—Evalutes `true` when something is not true, and `false` when it *is* true.

You can use this nifty construct to turn your logical OR statement into a logical AND statement without changing its meaning. For example

```
while ( howManyLetters < minLetters ¦¦ howManyLetters > maxLetters )
```

is exactly the same thing as

```
while ( (! (howManyLetters > minLetters) ) &&
(! (howManyLetters > maxLetters ) _) )
```

The logic of this is easy to understand if you use values. Assume that `minLetters` is 2, `maxLetters` is 10, and `howManyLetters` is 0.

In that case, the `while` loop executes because the left part of the statement is true (0 is less than 2). In an OR statement, only one side must be true for the entire statement to return `true`.

Thus,

```
while ( howManyLetters < minLetters ¦¦ howManyLetters > maxLetters )
```

becomes

```
while ( 0 < 2 ¦¦ 0 > 10 ) // substitute the values
```

becomes

```
while ( true ¦¦ false ) // evaluate the truth of each side
```

becomes

```
while ( true ) // if either is true, the statement is true
```

The second statement,

```
while ( (! (howManyLetters > minLetters) ) &&
(! (howManyLetters > maxLetters ) ) )
```

becomes

```
while ( (! (0 > 2) ) && (! (0 > 10 ) _) )
```

Now each side must be evaluated. The NOT symbol reverses the truth of what follows. It is as if this said, "While it is *not* true that zero is greater than 2 *and* it is *not* true that zero is greater than 10."

Thus you get

```
while ( (! (false) ) && (! (false ) _) )
```

When you apply NOT to `false`, you get `true`:

```
while ( (true) ) && (true) )
```

With an AND statement, both sides must be true; in this case they are, so the statement will execute.

Short Circuit Evaluation

When the compiler is evaluating an AND statement such as

```
while ( (x == 5) && (y == 5) )
```

the compiler evaluates the truth of the first statement (x==5); if this fails (that is, if x is not equal to five), the compiler does not go on to evaluate the truth or falsity of the second statement (y == 5) because AND requires that both be true.

Similarly, if the compiler is evaluating an OR statement such as

```
while ( (x == 5) ¦¦ (y == 5) )
```

if the first statement is `true` (x == 5), the compiler never evaluates the second statement (y == 5) because the truth of either is sufficient in an OR statement.

Relational Precedence

Relational operators and logical operators, because they are C++ expressions, each return a value of `true` or `false`. Like all expressions, they have a precedence order (see Appendix B, "Operator Precedence") that determines which relations are evaluated first. This fact is important when determining the value of the statement

```
if ( x > 5 &&  y > 5  ¦¦ z > 5)
```

It might be that the programmer wanted this expression to evaluate `true` if both x and y are greater than 5 or if z is greater than 5. On the other hand, the programmer might have wanted this expression to evaluate `true` only if x is greater than 5, and if it is also true that either y is greater than 5 or z is greater than 5.

If x is 3 and y and z are both 10, the first interpretation is true (z is greater than 5, so ignore x and y), but the second is false (it isn't true that x is greater than 5, and it therefore doesn't matter what is on the right side of the && symbol because both sides must be true.)

Although precedence determines which relation is evaluated first, parentheses can both change the order and make the statement clearer:

```
if (  (x > 5)  && (y > 5 ¦¦  z > 5) )
```

Using the values that were mentioned earlier, this statement is false. Because it is not true that x is greater than 5, the left side of the AND statement fails, so the entire statement is false. Remember that an AND statement requires that both sides be true: Something isn't both "good tasting" AND "good for you" if it isn't good tasting.

> **Note**
>
> It is often a good idea to use extra parentheses to clarify what you want to group. Remember, the goal is to write programs that work and that are easy to read and understand. It is easier to understand
>
> ```
> (8 * 5) + 3
> ```
>
> than
>
> ```
> 8 * 5 + 3
> ```
>
> even though the result is the same.

Putting It All Together

Following is the while statement you'll use to see whether you have a reasonable number of letters:

```
while ( howManyLetters < minLetters || howManyLetters > maxLetters )
{
    //...
}
```

This reads "As long as the condition is true, do the work between the braces." The condition that is tested is that either howManyLetters is less than minLetters OR howManyLetters is greater than maxLetters.

Thus, if the user enters 0 or 1, howManyLetters is less than minLetters, the condition is true, and the body of the while loop executes.

do while

Because howManyLetters is initialized to zero, you know that this while loop will run at least once. If you do not want to rely on the initial value of howManyLetters but you want to ensure that the loop runs at least once in any case, you can use a slight variant on the while loop—the do while loop:

```
do statement
    while ( condition )
```

This says that you will do the body of the loop while the condition is true. The loop must run at least once because the condition is not tested until after the statement executes the first time. So you can rewrite your loop as follows:

```
do
{
    //...
} while ( howManyLetters < minLetters || howManyLetters > maxLetters )
```

You know you need a `do while` loop when you are staring at a `while` loop and find your self saying, "Dang, I want this to run at least once!"

do while—A `while` loop that executes at least once and continues to exit while the condition that is tested is true.

Enumerated Constants

When I have constants that belong together, I can create *enumerated* constants. An enumerated constant is not quite a *type*; it is more of a collection of related constants.

The syntax for enumerated constants is to write the keyword enum, followed by the enumeration name, an open brace, each of the legal values (separated by commas), and a closing brace and a semicolon. Here's an example:

```
enum COLOR { RED, BLUE, GREEN, WHITE, BLACK };
```

This statement performs two tasks:

1. It makes COLOR the name of an enumeration.
2. It makes RED a symbolic constant with the value 0, BLUE a symbolic constant with the value 1, GREEN a symbolic constant with the value 2, and so on.

Every enumerated constant has an integer value. If you don't specify otherwise, the first constant has the value 0 and the rest count up from there. Any one of the constants can be initialized with a particular value, however, and those that are not initialized count upward from the ones before them. Thus, if you write

```
enum Color { RED=100, BLUE, GREEN=500, WHITE, BLACK=700 };
```

RED has the value 100; BLUE, the value 101; GREEN, the value 500; WHITE, the value 501; and BLACK, the value 700.

In this case you'll create an enum called BoundedValues and establish the values you need:

```
enum BoundedValues
{
minPos = 2,
maxPos = 10,
```

```
minLetters = 2,
maxLetters = 26
};
```

This replaces the four constant integers described previously. Frankly, there often is little advantage to enumerated constants, except that they keep these values together in one place. If, on the other hand, you are creating a number of constants and you don't particularly care what their value is so long as they all have unique values, enumerated constants can be quite useful.

Enumerated constants are most often used for comparison or testing, which is how you use them here. You'll test whether minLetters is greater or less than these enumerated values.

Returning to the Code

Let's look at the code beginning on line 37 and ending on line 49:

```
37:        while ( howManyLetters < minLetters
38:              || howManyLetters > maxLetters )
39:        {
40:            cout << "How many letters? (";
41:            cout << minLetters << "-" << maxLetters << "): ";
42:            cin >> howManyLetters;
43:            if ( howManyLetters < minLetters
44:                || howManyLetters > maxLetters )
45:            {
46:                cout << "please enter a number between ";
47:                cout << minLetters << " and " << maxLetters << endl;
48:            }
49:        }
```

The goal of this statement is to continue to prompt the user for an entry that is greater than minLetters and smaller than maxLetters.

The purpose of the if statement is to issue a reminder message if the number that is entered is out of bounds. Here's how the code reads in words:

```
37:        while ( howManyLetters < minLetters
38:              || howManyLetters > maxLetters )
```

While it is either true that the value howManyLetters is smaller than minLetters or it is true that howManyLetters is greater than maxLetters,

```
cout << "How many letters? (";
cout << minLetters << "-" << maxLetters << "): ";
cin >> howManyLetters;
```

prompts the user and captures the user's response in the variable howManyLetters:

```
if ( howManyLetters < minLetters
|| howManyLetters > maxLetters )
```

Test the response; if it is either smaller than `minLetters` or greater than `maxLetters`,

```
{
    cout << "please enter a number between ";
    cout << minLetters << " and " << maxLetters << endl;
}
```

prints out the reminder message.

The logic of this next `while` loop, shown on line 51, is identical to the preceding one.

Getting a Boolean Answer from the User

It is now time to ask the user whether he or she wants to allow duplicates (on line 72). You have a problem, however. The local variable `duplicatesAllowed` is of type `bool`, which, you'll remember, is a type that evaluates either to `true` or `false`.

You cannot capture a Boolean value from the user. The user can enter a number (using `cin` to save it in an `int` variable) or a character (using `cin` to save it in a character variable). There are some other choices as well, but Boolean is not one of them.

Here's how you'll do it: You'll prompt the user to enter a letter, *y* or *n*, and you'll then set the Boolean value based on what is entered.

The first task is to capture the response, and here you need something very much like the `while` logic that was shown previously for the letters. That is, you create a variable, as shown on line 65, initialize it to an invalid answer (in this case, space), and then continue to prompt until the user gives you an acceptable answer (`'y'` or `'n'`):

```
char choice = ' ';
while ( choice != 'y' && choice != 'n' )
{
    cout << "Allow duplicates (y/n)? ";
    cin >> choice;
}
```

Begin by defining and initializing a character variable, `choice`. You can initialize it to a space by enclosing a space in single quotes, as described in Chapter 2.

Once again, you use a `while` loop to test whether you have valid data. This time, you will test to see whether `choice` is not equal to `'y'` or `'n'`.

If it is true that `choice` is not equal to (`!=`) `'y'`, and it is also true that `choice` is not equal to `'n'`, the expression returns `true` and the `while` statement executes.

Your next task is to test the value in `choice` (which must now be `'y'` or `'n'`) and set `duplicatesAllowed` accordingly. You can certainly use an `if` statement:

```
if ( choice == 'y')
    duplicatesAllowed = true;
else
    duplicatesAllowed = false;
```

Equality Operator ==

The equality operator (`==`) tests whether two objects are the same. With integers, two variables are equal if they have the same value (for example, if x is assigned the value 4 and y is assigned the value 2*2, they are equal). With character variables, they are equal if they have the same character value. No surprises here. We test for equality on line 72 to see if `choice` is equal to the letter `'y'`.

equality operator (==)—Determines whether two objects have the same value. Be careful with this; you need two equal signs. A single equal sign (=) indicates *assignment* in C++. Thus, if you write

a = b

in C++ you assign the value currently in b to the variable a. If you want to test if they are equal, you must write

a == b

else

Often your program wants to take one branch if your condition is true, another if it is false. The keyword `else` indicates what the compiler is to execute if the tested expression evaluates `false`:

```
if (expression)
    statement;
else
    statement;
```

else—An `else` statement is executed only when an `if` statement evaluates to `false`.

Thus, the code shown says, "If `choice` is equal to y, set `duplicatesAllowed` to `true`; otherwise (`else`), set it to `false`."

The Conditional (or ternary) Operator

You're trying to assign the value `duplicatesAllowed` depending on the value of `choice`. In English you might want to say, "Is `choice` equal to y? If so, set `duplicatesAllowed` equal to `true`; otherwise, set it to `false`."

C++ has an operator that does exactly what you want.

The conditional operator (?:) is C++'s only ternary operator: It is the only operator to take three terms.

> **Note**
>
> The *arity* of an operator describes how many terms are used. For example, a *binary* operator, such as the addition operator (+), uses two terms: a+b. In this case, a and b are the two terms.
>
> C++ has a few *unary* operators, but you've not seen them yet. The conditional operator is C++'s only ternary operator, and thus the terms *conditional* operator and *ternary* operator are often used interchangeably.

arity—How many terms an operator uses.

unary—An operator that uses only one term.

binary—An operator that uses two terms.

ternary—An operator that uses three terms.

The conditional operator takes three terms and returns a value. In fact, all three terms are expressions; that is, they can be statements that return a value:

```
(expression1) ? (expression2) : (expression3)
```

This line is read as follows: "If expression1 is true, return the value of expression2; otherwise, return the value of expression3." Typically, this value is assigned to a variable.

Thus, line 72 shows

```
duplicatesAllowed = (choice == y) ? true : false;
```

Figure 3.1 illustrates each of the operators and terms.

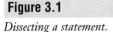

Figure 3.1

Dissecting a statement.

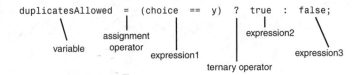

This line is read as follows: "Is it true that `choice` equals the character `'y'`? If so, assign `true` to `duplicatesAllowed`; otherwise, assign `false`."

After you are comfortable with the conditional operator, it is clean, quick, and easy to use.

Putting It All Together

You are now ready to analyze the `while` loop, beginning at line 35. You start at line 27 by establishing `valid` as a Boolean operator that is initialized to `false`.

```
while ( ! valid )
```

The `while` loop executes while `valid` is false. Because `valid` was initialized to `false`, the `while` loop will certainly execute the first time through. This `while` loop begins with the opening brace on line 36 and ends at the closing brace on line 86.

This entire loop continues to execute until and unless `valid` is set to `true`.

Within this `while` loop are a series of interior `while` loops that solicit and test the values for `howManyLetters`, `howManyPositions`, and, ultimately (if indirectly), `duplicatesAllowed`:

```
( ! duplicatesAllowed && howManyPositions > howManyLetters )
```

Finally, after the values are gathered, on line 74 you test the logic of the choices. If it is true that duplicates are not allowed, and it is also true that `howManyPositions` (provided by the user) is greater than the number the user chose for `howManyLetters`, you have a problem: You need to put five letters in six positions without duplicating any letters—it can't be done.

In this case, you execute the `if` statement and write to the screen, "I can't put five letters in six positions without duplicates! Please try again." You then reinitialize `howManyLetters` and `howManyPositions` to zero. Make sure that you understand why. Hint: check the `while` loops in which these variables are assigned the user's choice.

If, on the other hand, the `if` statement fails (if duplicates are allowed or if `howManyPositions` is not greater than `howManyLetters`), the `else` statement executes, `valid` is set to `true`, and the `while` loop terminates.

Chapter 4

Creating Classes

In Chapter 3, "Program Flow," you began to put logic into main() to gather the user's preference. In this chapter you'll look at creating classes to do this work.

Why Classes?

Although it is possible—and perhaps tempting—to just flesh out main() with the additional functionality you want to add to this program, it is a very bad idea.

The point of object-oriented programming is to create objects and assign them responsibility for specific aspects of the game. This fosters encapsulation, and with it maintainability and extensibility.

Maintainability means that the programs can be maintained at less expense. *Extensibility* means that you can add features without breaking the existing code.

As we design and implement classes, I'll discuss *design heuristics*: guidelines for designing excellent software.

design heuristics—Guidelines for quality in design.

The very first—and perhaps most important—object-oriented design heuristic is that each class needs to have a single area of responsibility, and each object needs to collaborate with other objects to accomplish more complicated tasks.

As a rule, C++ programmers tend to keep main() very simple. Its job is only to create the first object and set off the chain of events that lead to these objects accomplishing their assigned tasks.

You'll begin by creating a Game class that is responsible for keeping track of the user's preferences and getting the game underway.

Creating New Types: Class

Although the built-in types are fine for storing values, they are limited in the complexity of the information they can manage.

Built-in types can be combined, however, into user-defined types that can be far more complex.

For example, suppose you want to store the number of letters from which you'll allow the player to choose and the number of positions (for example, choosing among three numbers in two positions, without duplicates, makes the following codes possible: ab, ba, ac, ca, bc, and cb). You can store these two values in variables, or you can store both of them along with the decision as to whether to allow duplicates—all within a Game class.

A class not only has values—it also has capabilities. Just as you know that an int can be added, subtracted, multiplied, and divided, a Game can be set up, played, restarted, quit, and saved.

Interface Versus Implementation

We draw a sharp distinction between the declaration of a class and its implementation. The declaration of a class tells the compiler about the attributes of the class and what its capabilities are. We often refer to this declaration as the class's *interface*.

Every method that is declared in the interface must be implemented: You must write the code that shows how it works.

interface—The declaration of the methods of a class.

implementation—The code showing how the class methods work.

Clients

Classes provide services to clients of the class. The client of your class is any programmer (even you!) who creates instances of your class in his code.

Note It is regrettable that the generic pronoun in Standard English is masculine, and this is especially exacerbated by the fact that the programming profession is disproportionately male. Please understand that the masculine pronoun is intended to be generic.

Programmers use the term *client* in many ways. For example, if class A calls a method in class B, we say that A is a client of B. If I write class A and I call code you wrote in class B, I am a client of your code. If my computer calls code running on your computer, my computer is a client of your (server) computer. And so on.

All these share the same essential characteristic: The client receives a service from the server.

The client of your class needs to know what your class does, but not how it works. If you create an `employee` class, your client needs to know that the employee can tell him his hire date, but your client does not need to know how your `employee` class keeps track of that date. You can store it in memory, on disk, or in a central database, but that is not important to your client. He cares about the interface (*can supply date*), not the implementation (*retrieve date from file*). Thus, the client treats your code as a *black box*.

client—Any code that makes use of a class.

Looking at the Code

Before we discuss classes, let's take a quick look at the new code that is declaring the `Game` class. Once again, there is much here that will be new, but by reading through the code you can get a good idea of how it works—even before we go through it in detail.

Listing 4.1   Game.h

```
0:  class Game
1:  {
2:  public:
3:      Game();
4:      ~Game();
```

continues

Listing 4.1   continued

```
5:      void Play();
6:
7:      bool duplicatesAllowed;
8:      int howManyLetters;
9:      int howManyPositions;
10:      int round;
11:  };
```

Declaring the Class

A class is declared by writing the keyword `class`, followed by the class name and an opening brace (as shown at line 0). The declaration is ended by a closing brace and a semicolon.

> **Note**
>
> The keyword `public` is needed as it is shown in line 2. We'll cover what this word does in a later chapter. For now, please be sure to place the keyword `public`, followed by a colon, at the start of every class declaration.

Classes and Objects

A *class* is a type. When you make instances of that type, they are called *objects*. In fact, the action of creating an object is called *instantiation*.

class—Defines a new type.

object—An instance of the type defined by a class.

instantiation—Creating an instance of a class: an object.

Novice programmers often confuse classes with objects. The type of something (the class) tells you what it is (cat), what it can do (purr, eat, jump), and what attributes it has (weight and age). Individual objects of that type have specific objects (nine pounds, two years old.)

Member Variables

When this code was in `main()`, you had a number of local variables: `duplicatesAllowed`, `howManyLetters`, `howManyPositions`, and `round`.

These variables are now moved into the class, and they become members of the class itself starting at line 7.

Member variables represent attributes of the objects of that class type. In other words, we are now saying that every Game object will keep track of whether duplicates are allowed in that game, how many letters and how many positions are to be used in the game, what the current round is, and that these are the attributes of the class Game.

 member variable—Data that is owned by a particular object of a class, and which represents attributes of that class.

Member variables are different from normal variables only in that they are scoped to a specific class. This is actually a very powerful aspect of object-oriented programming. The details of these values and their management are now delegated to the Game class and can be made invisible to the clients of that class.

Member Methods or Functions

The Game class has two principal activities:

- **Setup**—Get the user's preferences and choose a secret code.
- **Play**—Ask the user for guesses and score the guesses based on how many are correct and how many are in the correct position.

You provide these capabilities to a class by giving the class member methods, which are also called *member functions*. A member method is a function that is owned by a class—a method that is *scoped* to a particular class.

 When we say that a member method is *scoped* to a class, we mean that the identifier that is the member method is visible only within the context of the class or an object of that class.

It is through these member methods that an object of a class achieves its behavior.

The Size of Objects

The size of an object is the sum of the sizes of the member variables that are declared for its class. Thus, if an int is 4 bytes and your class declares three integer member variables, each object is 12 bytes. Functions have no size.

Files

You create a class in two steps: First, the interface to the class is declared in a *header file*; second, the member methods are created in a *source code file*.

header file—A text file that contains the class declaration. Traditionally named with the .h extension.

source file—A text file that contains the source code for the member methods of a class. Traiditionally named with the .cpp extension.

The header file typically has an extension of .h or .hpp, and the source code file has the extension .cpp. So for your Game class, you can expect to find the declaration in the file Game.h and the implementation of the class methods in Game.cpp.

Constructors

It is not uncommon for a class to require a bit of setting up before it can be used. In fact, an object of that class might not be considered valid if it hasn't been set up properly. C++ provides a special method to set up and initialize each object, called a *constructor*, as shown at line 3.

In this case, you want the constructor to initialize each of the member variables. For some member variables, you'll *hard wire* a reasonable value; for example, you'll keep track of what round of play you are on, and of course, you'll start with round 1.

hard wire—A programming term that means that the value is written into the code and doesn't change each time you run the program.

For other member variables, you must ask the user to choose an appropriate starting value. For example, you'll ask the user to tell you whether duplicates are allowed, how many letters are to be used, and how many positions are to appear in the secret code.

A constructor (line 3) has the same name as the class itself, and never has a return value.

The absence of a return value does not, in this case, mean that it returns void. Constructors are special: They have no return value. There are only two types of methods for which this is true—constructors and destructors.

Destructors

The job of the destructor (line 4) is to tear down the object. This idea will make more sense after we talk about allocating memory or other resources. For now, the destructor won't do much, but as a matter of form, if I create a constructor, I always create a destructor.

Implementing the Methods

The header file provides the interface. Each of the methods is named, but the actual implementation is not in this file—it is in the implementation file (See Listing 4.2).

Listing 4.2 Game.cpp

```
0:  #include "Game.h"
1:  #include <iostream.h>
2:
3:
4:  Game::Game():
5:  round(1),
6:  howManyPositions(0),
7:  howManyLetters(0),
8:  duplicatesAllowed(false)
9:  {
10:     enum BoundedValues
11:     {
12:        minPos = 2,
13:        maxPos = 10,
14:        minLetters = 2,
15:        maxLetters = 26
16:     };
17:     bool valid = false;
18:     while ( ! valid )
19:     {
20:        while ( howManyLetters < minLetters
21:           || howManyLetters > maxLetters )
22:        {
23:           cout << "How many letters? (";
24:           cout << minLetters << "-" << maxLetters << "): ";
25:           cin >> howManyLetters;
26:           if ( howManyLetters < minLetters
27:              || howManyLetters > maxLetters )
28:           {
29:              cout << "please enter a number between ";
30:              cout << minLetters << " and " << maxLetters << endl;
31:           }
32:        }
33:
34:        while ( howManyPositions < minPos
35:           || howManyPositions > maxPos )
36:        {
37:           cout << "How many positions? (";
38:           cout << minPos << "-" << maxPos << "): ";
39:           cin >> howManyPositions;
```

continues

Listing 4.2   continued

```
40:            if ( howManyPositions < minPos
41:                || howManyPositions > maxPos )
42:            {
43:                cout << "please enter a number between ";
44:                cout << minPos <<" and " << maxPos << endl;
45:            }
46:        }
47:
48:        char choice = ' ';
49:        while ( choice != 'y' && choice != 'n' )
50:        {
51:            cout << "Allow duplicates (y/n)? ";
52:            cin >> choice;
53:        }
54:
55:        duplicatesAllowed = choice == 'y' ? true : false;
56:
57:        if ( ! duplicatesAllowed &&
58:            howManyPositions > howManyLetters )
59:        {
60:          cout << "I can't put " << howManyLetters;
61:          cout << " letters in " << howManyPositions;
62:          cout << " positions without duplicates! Please try again.\n";
63:          howManyLetters = 0;
64:          howManyPositions = 0;
65:        }
66:        else
67:            valid = true;
68:    }
69:
70:
71:  }
72:
73:  Game::~Game()
74:  {
75:
76:  }
77:
78:  void Game::Play()
79:  {
80:
81:  }
```

Listing 4.3 provides a short driver program that does nothing but instantiate an object of type Game.

Listing 4.3   Decryptix.cpp

```
0: #include <iostream >
1: #include "Game.h"
2:
3: int main()
4: {
5:     Game theGame;
6:     return 0;
8: }
```

Including the Header

The compiler can't know what a Game is without the definition, which is in the header file. To tell the compiler what a Game object is, the first thing you do in the implementation file is to #include the file with the definition of the Game class, in this case Game.h (as shown on line 1 of Listing 4.2).

It is desirable to minimize the number of header files that are included in other header files. Having many include statements within a header file can risk the creation of circular references (a includes b, which includes c, which includes a) that won't compile. This can also introduce *order dependence*, which means that the proper execution of your code depends on files being added in the "correct order." This makes for code that is difficult to maintain.

There is no limit to the number of header files you might want to include in implementation files, but keep the includes in your header file to a minimum.

Implementing the Constructor

A member function definition begins with the name of the class, followed by two colons (the scoping operator), the name of the function, and its parameters. On line 4 in Listing 4.2, you can see the implementation of the constructor.

scope operator—The pair of colons between the class name and the method.

identifier—Any named thing: object, method, class, variable, and so on.

Like all methods, the constructor begins with an open brace ({) and ends with a closing brace (}). The body of the constructor lies between the braces.

Initialization

In the exploration of variables, I talked about the difference between assignment and initialization. Member variables can be initialized as well. In fact, the constructor actually executes in two steps:

- Initialization
- Construction

Construction is accomplished in the body of the constructor. Initialization is accomplished through the syntax that is shown: After the closing parentheses on the constructor, add a colon. For each member variable you want to initialize, write the variable name, followed by the value to which you want to initialize it (enclosed in parentheses). Note also that you can initialize multiple members by separating them with commas. There must be no comma after the last initialized value.

Thus, on line 5 in Listing 4.3, you see round initialized to the value 1, howManyPositions to the value 0, howManyLetters to the value 0, and duplicatesAllowed to the value false.

 Note

> The new line I've placed between each initialized value is only for the convenience of the programmer. I can just as easily put them all on one line, separated by spaces:
>
> ```
> Game::Game():
> round(1),
> howManyPositions(0),
> howManyLetters(0),
> duplicatesAllowed(false)
> {
> ```

All this initialization occurs before the body of the constructor runs, beginning on line 10 of Listing 4.2.

 We talk of methods or functions running, being executed, or being called, depending on context. These all mean the same thing: Program execution branches to the function, beginning at the first line and proceeding from there until it reaches a return statement.

Within the body of the constructor, you see that an enumerated constant, BoundedValues, is created, and a *local* variable, valid, is created and initialized on line 17.

This local variable, valid, will exist only for the duration of the constructor. Because this value is needed only temporarily and is not part of the permanent state of the object (it is not an attribute of the class Game), do not make it a member variable.

Just as valid is a variable that is local to the constructor, the instance of Game that is created in main() is local to main() (Listing 4.3, line 5). Declare it like you declare any other variable—by declaring its type (Game), and then the name of the object itself (theGame). You can name the object anything you want, but it is best to name it something meaningful so that the code can be easily understood.

By defining this object, you bring it into existence, and that causes the constructor to be invoked automatically.

Normally, methods are called *explicitly*. The constructor, however, is called *implicitly* when the object is created, and the destructor is called implicitly when the object is destroyed. When a method is called implicitly, the call doesn't appear in your code: It is understood to be the result of another action. Thus, when you create an object, you implicitly call the constructor; when you delete an object, you implicitly call the destructor. Not only do you not have to call these methods explicitly, you are prohibited from doing so.

There are two ways to see this explicitly. One way is to add a temporary output line to the constructor and destructor (as shown in Listing 4.4), and to main() (as shown in Listing 4.5).

Listing 4.4   Implicit Call to Constructor and Destructor

```
 0:  #include "Game.h"
 1:  #include <iostream>
 2:
 3:  Game::Game():
 4:       round(1),
 5:       howManyPositions(0),
 6:       howManyLetters(0),
 7:       duplicatesAllowed(false)
 8:  {
 9:      cout << "In the Game constructor\n"" << endl;
10:  }
11:
12:  Game::~Game()
13:  {
14:      cout << "In the Game destructor\n" << endl;
15:  }
16:
17:  void Game::Play()
18:  {
19:
20:  }
```

Listing 4.5   Driver Program for Listing 4.4

```
0:   #include <iostream>
1:   #include "Game.h"
2:
3:   using namespace std;
4:
5:   int main()
6:   {
7:       cout << "Creating the game\n" << endl;
8:       Game theGame;
9:       cout << "Exiting main\n" << endl;
10:       return 0;
11:   }
```

Output

```
Creating the game

In the Game constructor

Exiting main

In the Game destructor
```

Here we've stripped the constructor down to do nothing except print an informative message. As you can see, creating the Game object causes the constructor to be invoked. Returning from main() ends the function and implicitly destroys any local objects. This causes the destructor to be invoked, which prints an equally informative message.

Using the Debugger

Although this works, it is tedious to add these printout messages; in any case, you can only infer the effect because you don't actually see the constructor being invoked. The debugger is a far more powerful tool.

Load Listings 4.1, 4.2, and 4.3 into a project and compile, link, and run it. Now, put a break point on line 5 in Listing 4.3—the creation of the Game object. You are ready to see what this does, so step into the function call. You find yourself at the opening brace to the constructor.

The debugger is a powerful tool for learning C++. It can show you explicitly what is happening in your program as it runs. Because you'll be using the debugger throughout this book, you might want to take a few minutes and read the documentation that came with your programming environment to learn more about how to use your debugger.

Examining the Constructor

Careful examination of the constructor reveals that you have, essentially, duplicated the logic you had in `main()` in the preceding chapter. The one exception is that you are now capturing and storing the user's preferences in member variables as shown on lines 25, 39, and 52. These member variables are part of the object and will, therefore, persist and contain these values after the constructor returns.

The Other Methods

The `Game` object has two other methods: a destructor and the `Play()` method. At this time neither of these methods has any action, and you'll note that `Play()` is not yet called. This *stubbed out* function exists only to remind the programmer of his intent—that eventually this class will include a meaningful `Play()` method.

 When a programmer wants to show a method or function but does not want to do the work of implementing that function, he *stubs it out*. He creates a stub function that does nothing more than return, or at most prints, a message "in myTestMethod" and then returns.

Storing the Pattern

The computer creates a pattern that the human player guesses. How is this pattern to be stored? Clearly, you need the capability to store between `minLetters` and `maxLetters` characters as a pattern against which you can compare the human's guesses.

 Let me explain the preceding sentence because this is exactly how programmers talk about a problem like this: "The capability to store between `minLetters` and `maxLetters` characters." This sentence is easier to understand if we use sample values: If `minLetters` is 2 and `maxLetters` is 10, this sentence means that you need the capability to store between 2 and 10 letters in a pattern.

Programmers become comfortable using variables rather than absolute values in their formulations of a problem. The astute reader might also note that in fact we store these values (`minLetter` and `maxLetter`) as constants, not variables. That is true, but the values can vary from one compiled version to another, so they are variable in the more general sense.

So how *do* you store the computer's secret code? Let's assume that the player chooses seven possible letters with five positions, and the computer generates a secret code of `acbed`. How do you store this string of letters?

You have several options. You can use the built-in array class or the standard library string, you can create your own data structure to hold the letters, or you can use one of the standard library collection classes.

The rest of this chapter examines arrays in some detail; in coming chapters you'll turn to other alternatives.

What Is an Array?

An *array* is a fixed-size collection of data storage locations, each of which holds the same type of data. Each storage location is called an *element* of the array.

 array—A fixed size collection of data.

You declare an array by writing the type, followed by the array name and the subscript. The *subscript* is the number of elements in the array, surrounded by square brackets. For example

```
long LongArray[25];
```

declares an array of 25 long integers, named LongArray. When the compiler sees this declaration, it sets aside enough memory to hold all 25 elements. Because each long integer requires 4 bytes, this declaration sets aside 100 contiguous bytes of memory, as illustrated in Figure 4.1.

 subscript—The number of elements in an array.

Figure 4.1

Declaring an array.

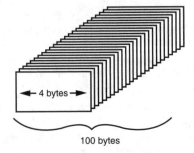

4 bytes

100 bytes

Initializing Arrays

You can initialize a simple array of built-in types, such as integers and characters, when you first declare the array. After the array name, put an equal sign (=) and a list of comma-separated values enclosed in braces. For example

```
int IntegerArray[5] = { 10, 20, 30, 40, 50 };
```

declares `IntegerArray` to be an array of five integers. It assigns `IntegerArray[0]` the value `10`, `IntegerArray[1]` the value `20`, and so on.

If you omit the size of the array, an array that is just big enough to hold the initialization is created. Therefore, if you write

```
int IntegerArray[] = { 10, 20, 30, 40, 50 };
```

you create exactly the same array as you did in the preceding example.

If you need to know the size of the array, you can ask the compiler to compute it for you. For example

```
int IntegerArrayLength = sizeof(IntegerArray)/sizeof(IntegerArray[0]);
```

sets the `int` variable `IntegerArrayLength` to the result that is obtained by dividing the size of the entire array by the size of each individual entry in the array. That quotient is the number of members in the array.

You cannot initialize more elements than you've declared for the array. Therefore,

```
int IntegerArray[5] = { 10, 20, 30, 40, 50, 60};
```

generates a compiler error because you've declared a five-member array and initialized six values. You can, however, write

```
int IntegerArray[5] = { 10, 20};
```

Uninitialized array members have no guaranteed values; therefore, any value might be in an array member if you don't initialize it.

Initializing Character Arrays

You can use a special syntax for initializing character arrays. Rather than writing

```
char alpha[] = { 'a', 'b', 'c' };
```

you can write

```
char alpha[] = "abc";
```

This creates an array of four characters and initializes with the three letters shown, followed by a NULL character. It is exactly as if you had written

```
char alpha[4] = {'a','b','c',0}
```

It adds the NULL because NULL-terminated strings have special meaning in C and C++.

C-Style Strings

C++ inherits from C the capability to create *strings*, which are meaningful groups of characters used to store words, phrases, and other strings of characters. These strings are represented in C and C++ as NULL-terminated arrays of characters. The old C library string.h, still a part of C++, provides methods for manipulating these strings: copying them, printing them, and so on.

The new Standard Library now includes a far better alternative: the string class. Objects of type string offer all the functionality of old C-style NULL-terminated arrays of characters, but with all the benefits of being well-defined types. That is, the new libraries are object-oriented, type safe, and well encapsulated.

You'll look at string objects in some detail as we go forward, and along the way I'll review some of the details of how C-style strings are used. For now, you're actually using this array of characters as a simple array, and it is not NULL-terminated. You are using the array as a collection. The objects that are being collected happen to be characters, but they can just as easily be integers or anything else you can store in an array.

Array Elements

You access each of the array elements by referring to an offset from the array name. Array elements are counted from zero. Therefore, the first array element is arrayName[0].

In the version of the program we'll examine for the rest of this chapter, you'll add a member variable solution, which will hold an array of characters that represent the solution to the code generated by the compiler.

The declaration for that array is

```
char solution[maxPos+1];
```

This creates an array of characters that can hold exactly one more than maxPos characters. maxPos is a symbolic constant defined to 10, so this defines an array of 11 characters. The 11th character is the NULL character.

Because arrays count from offset 0, the elements in this array are solution[0], solution[1], solution[2]...solution[9].

Writing Past the End of an Array

When you write a value to an element in an array, the compiler computes where to store the value, based on the size of each element and the subscript. Suppose that you ask to write over the value at solution[5], which is the sixth element. The compiler multiplies the offset (5) by the size of each element. Since this is a char array, each element is 1 byte, so the math is fairly simple. The compiler then moves that many bytes (5) from the beginning of the array and writes the new value at that location.

If you ask to write at solution[12], the compiler ignores the fact that there is no such element. It computes how far past the first element it is to look, and then writes over whatever is at that location. This can be virtually any data, and writing your new value there might have unpredictable results. If you're lucky, your program will crash immediately. If you're unlucky, you'll get strange results elsewhere in your program, and you'll spend weeks trying to find the bug.

Fence Post Errors

It is so common to write to one past the end of an array that this bug has its own name. It is called a *fence post error*. This refers to the problem in counting how many fence posts you need for a 10-foot fence if you need one post for every foot: Most people answer ten, but of course you need 11. Figure 4.2 makes this clear.

4

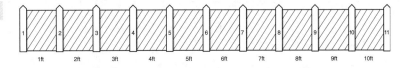

This sort of "off by one" counting can be the bane of any programmer's life. Over time, however, you'll get used to the idea that a 25-element array counts only to element 24, and that everything counts from zero.

Fence post errors are responsible for one of the great misunderstandings of our time: when the new millennium begins. A millennium is 1,000 years. We are ending the second millennium of the Common Era, and we are about to start the third—but when, exactly?

The first Millennium began with the year 1 and ended with the year 1000. The second Millennium runs from 1001 to 2000. The third will begin on January 1, 2001. (Don't tell the newspapers.)

Of course, to a C++ programmer this is all wrong. We begin counting with 0, and 1K is 1,024, thus the third C++ Millennium begins on January 1, 2048. Call it the $Y2K_2$ problem.

Some programmers refer to ArrayName[0] as the *zeroth* element. Getting into this habit is a big mistake. If ArrayName[0] is the zeroth element, what is ArrayName[1], the *oneth*? If so, when you see ArrayName[24], will you realize that it is not the 24th element, but rather the 25th? It is far better to say that ArrayName[0] is at offset zero and is the first element.

Generating the Solution

Now that you have an array to hold the solution, how do you add letters to it? You want to generate letters at random, and you don't want the user to be able to guess the solution. The C++ library provides a method, rand(), which generates a pseudo-random number. It is pseudo-random in that it always generates numbers in the same predictable order, depending on where it starts—but they appear to be random.

You can increase the apparent randomness of the numbers that are generated if you start the random number generator with a different *starting* number (which we call a seed number) each time you run the program.

You provide rand() with a seed number by first calling srand() and passing in a value. srand (*seed random*) gives the random number generate a starting point to work from. The seed determines the first random number that will be generated.

If you don't call srand() first, rand() behaves as if you have called srand() with the seed value 1.

You want to change the seed value each time you run the program so that you'll invoke one more library function: time(). The function time returns the system time, expressed as a large integer.

> Interestingly, it actually provides you with the number of seconds that have elapsed since midnight, January 1, 1970, according to the system clock. This date, 1/1/1970, is known as the *epoch*, the moment in time from which all other computer dates are calculated.

The time() function takes a parameter of type time_t, but we don't care about this because it is happy taking the NULL value instead:

```
srand( (unsigned)time( NULL ) );
```

The sequence, then, is to call time(), pass in NULL, cast the returned value to unsigned int, and pass that result to srand(). This provides a reasonably random value to srand(), causing it to initialize rand() to a nearly-random starting point.

> Let's talk about casting a value. When you cast a value to unsigned you say to the compiler, "I know you don't think this is an unsigned integer, but I know better, so just treat it like one." In this case, time() returns the value of type time_t,

> but you know from the documentation that this can be treated as an unsigned integer—and an unsigned integer is what `srand()` expects. Casting is also called "hitting it with the big hammer." It works great, but you've disconnected the sprinklers and disabled the alarms, so be sure you know what you're doing.

Now that you have a random number, you need to convert it into a letter in the range you need. To do this, you'll use an array of 26 characters, the letters *a–z*. By creating such an array, you can convert the value 0 to a, the value 1 to b, and so on.

Quick! What is the value of *z*? If you said 25, pat yourself on the back for not making the fence post error of thinking it would be 26.

We'll call the character array `alpha`. You want this array to be available from just about anywhere in your program. Earlier we talked about local variables, variables whose scope is limited to a particular method. We also talked about class member variables, which are variables that are scoped to a particular object of a class. A third alternative is a *global variable*.

global variable—A variable with no limitation in its scope—visible from anywhere in your program.

The advantage of global variables is that they are visible and accessible from anywhere in your program. That is also the bad news—and C++ programmers avoid global variables like the plague. The problem is that they can be changed from any part of the program, and it is not uncommon for global variables to create tricky bugs that are terribly difficult to find.

Here's the problem: You're going along in your program and everything is behaving as expected. Suddenly, a global variable has a new and unexpected value. How'd that happen? With global variables, it is difficult to tell because they can be changed from just about anywhere.

In this particular case, although you want `alpha` to be visible throughout the program, you don't want it changed at all. You want to create it once and then leave it around. That is just what constants are for. Instead of creating a global variable, which can be problematic, you'll create a *global constant*. Global constants are just fine:

```
const char alpha[] = "abcdefghijklmnopqrstuvwxyz";
```

global constant—A constant with no limitation in its scope—visible from anywhere in your program.

This creates a constant named `alpha` that holds 27 characters (the characters *a–z* and the terminating `NULL`). With this in place,

`alpha[0]`

evaluates to *a*, and

`alpha[25]`

evaluates to *z*.

 Note   We'll include the declaration of `alpha` in a new file called definedValues.h, and we'll #include that file in any file that needs to access `alpha`. This way, we create one place for all our global constants (all our defined values), and we can change any or all of them by going to that one file.

Listing 4.5   Adding Characters to the Array

```
0:  for ( i = 0; i < howManyPositions; )
1:  {
2:      int nextValue = rand() % (howManyLetters);
3:      char c = alpha[nextValue];
4:      if ( ! duplicatesAllowed && i > 0 )
5:      {
6:          int count = howMany(solution, c);
7:          if ( count > 0 )
8:              continue;
9:      }
10:     // add to the array
11:     solution[i] = c;
12:     i++;
13: }
14: solution[i] = '\0';
15:
16: }
```

On line 0 you create a `for` loop to run once for each position. Thus, if the user has asked for a code with five positions, you'll create five letters.

On line 2 you call `rand()`, which generates a random value. You use the modulus operator (%) to turn that value into one in the range 0 to `howManyLetters-1`. Thus, if `howManyLetters` is 7, this forces the value to be 0, 1, 2, 3, 4, 5, or 6.

Let's assume for the purpose of this discussion that `rand()` first generates the value 12, and that `howManyLetters` is 7. How is the value 12 turned into a value in the range 0 through 6? To understand this, you must start by examining *integer division*.

Integer division is somewhat different from everyday division. In fact, it is exactly like the division you originally learned in fourth grade. "Class, how much is 12 divided by seven?" The answer, to a fourth grader, is "One, remainder five." That is, seven goes into 12 exactly once, with five "left over."

integer division—When the compiler divides two integers, it returns the whole number value and loses the remainder.

When an adult divides 12 by 7, the result is a real number (1.714285714286). Integers, however, don't have fractions or decimal parts, so when you ask a programming language to divide two integers, it responds like a fourth grader, giving you the whole number value without the remainder. Thus, in integer math, 12/7 returns the value 1.

Just as you can ask the fourth grader to tell you the remainder, you can use the modulus operator (%) to ask your programming language for the remainder in integer division. To get the remainder, you take 12 modulus 7 (12 % 7), and the result is 5. The modulus operator tells you the remainder after an integer division.

This result of a modulus operator is always in the range zero through the operand minus one. In this case, zero through seven minus one (or zero through six). If an array contains seven letters, the offsets are 0–6, so the modulus operator does exactly what you want: It returns a valid offset into the array of letters.

On line 3 you can use the value that is returned from the modulus operator as an offset into alpha, thus returning the appropriate letter. If you set howManyLetters to 7, the result will be that you'll always get a number between zero and six, and, therefore, a letter in the range *a* through *g*—exactly what you want!

Next, on line 4 you check to see whether you're allowing duplicates in this game. If not, enter the body of the if statement.

Remember, the bang symbol (!) indicates *not*, so

```
if ( ! duplicatesAllowed )
```

evaluates true if duplicatesAllowed evaluates false. Thus, if not, duplicatesAllowed means "if we're not allowing duplicates." The second half of the and statement is that *i* is greater than zero. There is no point in worrying about duplicates if this is the first letter you're adding to the array.

On line 6 you assign to the integer variable count the result of the member method howMany(). This method takes two parameters—a character array and a character— and returns the number of times the character appears in the array. If that value is greater than zero, this character is already in the array and the continue statement causes processing to jump immediately to the top of the for loop, on line 0. This tests *i*, which is unchanged, so proceed with the body of the for loop on line 2, where you'll generate a new value to try out.

If howMany() returns zero, processing continues on line 11, where the character is added to solution at offset i. The net result of this is that only unique values are added to the solution if you're not allowing duplicates. Next, i is incremented (i++) and processing returns to line 0, where i is tested against howManyPositions. When i is equal to howManyPositions, the for loop is completed.

Finally, on line 14 you add a NULL to the end of the array to indicate the end of the character array. This enables you to pass this array to cout, which prints every character up to the NULL.

Note To designate a NULL in a character array, use the special character '\0'. To designate NULL otherwise, use the value 0 or the constant NULL.

Examining the Defined Values File

Take a look at Listing 4.6, in which we declare our constant array of characters alpha.

Listing 4.6 definedValues.h

```
0:   #ifndef DEFINED_VALUES
1:   #define DEFINED_VALUES
2:
3:   #include <iostream>
4:   using namespace std;
5:
6:   const char alpha[] = "abcdefghijklmnopqrstuvwxyz";
7:
8:   const int minPos = 2;
9:   const int maxPos = 10;
10:  const int minLetters = 2;
11:  const int maxLetters = 26;
12:
13:  #endif
```

This listing introduces several new elements. On line 0 you see the precompiler directive #ifndef. This is read "if not defined," and it checks to see whether you've already defined whatever follows (in this case, the string DEFINED_VALUES).

If this test fails (if the value DEFINED_VALUES is already defined), nothing is processed until the next #endif statement, on line 13. Thus, the entire body of this file is skipped if DEFINED_VALUES is already defined.

If this is the first time the precompiler reads this file, that value will not yet be defined; processing will continue on line 2, at which point it will be defined. Thus, the net effect is that this file is processed exactly once.

The #ifndef/#define combination is called an *inclusion guard*, and it guards against multiple inclusions of the same header file throughout your program. Every header file needs to be guarded in this way.

inclusion guards—Inclusion guards are added to header files to ensure that they are included in the program only once.

4

We intend to include the definedValues.h header file into all our other files so that it constitutes a global set of definitions and declarations. By including, for example, iostream.h here, we don't need to include it elsewhere in the program.

On line 6 you declare the constant character array that was discussed earlier. On lines 8–11 you declare a number of other constant values that will be available throughout the program.

In this chapter

- *Inline Implementation*
- *Constant Member Methods*
- *The Signature*
- *Passing by Reference and by Value*
- *Pointers*
- *Arrays*
- *Using ASSERT*
- *String Manipulation*

Chapter 5

Playing The Game

The declaration of the Game object builds on the material we've covered so far, and it adds a few new elements you'll need to build a robust class. Let's start by taking a look at the code (see Listing 5.1) and then discussing it in detail.

Listing 5.1 Game.h

```
1:    #ifndef GAME_H
2:    #define GAME_H
3:
4:    #include "def0514.h"
5:
6:    class Game
7:    {
8:    public:
9:        Game();
10:       ~Game()          {}
11:       void Display(const char * charArray) const
12:       {
13:           cout << charArray << endl;
14:       }
15:       void Play();
16:       const char * GetSolution() const
17:       {
18:           return solution;
19:       }
20:    void Score(const char * thisGuess, int & correct, int & position);
21:
22:    private:
```

continues

Listing 5.1   continued

```
23:        int howMany(const char *, char);
24:        char solution[maxPos];
25:        int howManyLetters;
26:        int howManyPositions;
27:        int round;
28:        bool duplicates;
29:    };
```

Once again, you see inclusion guards on line 1, and you now see the naming pattern that I'll use throughout this book. The inclusion guard will typically have the name of the class or file, in all uppercase, followed by the underscore (_) and the uppercase letter *H*. By having a standard for the creation of inclusion guards, you can reduce the likelihood of using the same guard name on two different header files.

On line 4, we include definedValues.h. As promised, this file will be included throughout the program.

On line 6, we begin the declaration of the Game class. In the public section we see the public interface for this class. Note that the public interface contains only methods, not data; in fact, it contains only those methods that we want to expose to clients of this class.

On line 9, we see the default constructor, as described in Chapter 4, "Creating Classes," and on line 10, we see the destructor. The destructor, as it is shown here, has an *inline* implementation, as do Display() (lines 11 to 14) and GetSolution (lines 16 to 19).

Inline Implementation

Normally, when a function is called, processing literally jumps from the calling function to the called function.

The processor must stash away information about the current state of the program. It stores this information in an area of memory known as the *stack*, which is also where local variables are created.

stack—An area of memory in which local variables and other information about the state of the program are stored.

The processor must also put the parameters to the new function on the stack and adjust the instruction pointer (which keeps track of which instruction will execute next), as illustrated in Figure 5.1. When the function returns, the return value must be popped off the stack, the local variables and other local state from the function must be cleaned up, and the registers must be readjusted to return you to the state you were in before the function call.

Figure 5.1

The instruction pointer.

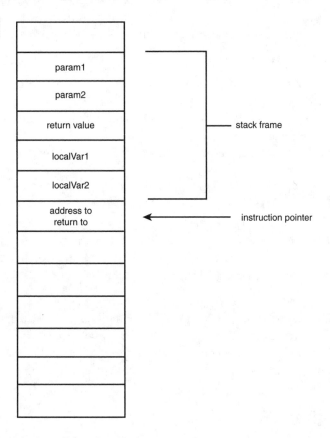

param1

param2

return value — stack frame

localVar1

localVar2

address to return to ← instruction pointer

5

An alternative to a normal function call is to define the function with the keyword `inline`. In this case, the compiler does not create a real function: It copies the code from the inline function directly into the calling function. No jump is made. It is just as if you had written the statements of the called function right into the calling function.

Note that inline functions can bring a heavy cost. If the function is called 10 times, the inline code is copied into the calling functions each of those 10 times. The tiny improvement in speed you might achieve is more than swamped by the increase in size of the executable program. Even the speed increase might be illusory. First, today's optimizing compilers do a terrific job on their own, and there is almost never a big gain from declaring a function inline. More importantly, though, the increased size brings its own performance cost.

If the function you are calling is very small, it might still make sense to designate that function as inline. There are two ways to do so. One is to put the keyword inline into the definition of the function, before the return value:

```
inline int Game::howMany()
```

An alternative syntax for class member methods is just to define the method right in the declaration of the class itself. Thus, on line 19 you might note that the destructor's implementation is defined right in the declaration. It turns out that this destructor does nothing, so the braces are empty. This is a perfect use of inlining: There is no need to branch out to the destructor, just to take no action.

Constant Member Methods

Take a look at Display on lines 11–14. After the argument list is the keyword const. This use of const means, "I promise that this method does not change the object on which you invoke this method," or, in this case, "I promise that Display() won't change the Game object on which you call Display()."

const methods attempt to enlist the compiler in helping you to enforce your design decisions. If you believe that a member method ought not change the object (that is, you want the object treated as if it were read-only), declare the method constant. If you then change the object as a result of calling the method, the compiler flags the error, which can save you from having a difficult-to-find bug.

The Signature

On line 20, we see the *signature* for the member method Score(). The signature of a method is the name (Score) and the parameter list. The declaration of a method consists of its signature and its return value (in this case, void).

signature—The name and parameter list of a method.

Before we examine this signature in detail, let's talk about what this method does and what parameters it needs. The responsibility of this method is to examine the player's guess (an array of characters) and to score it on how many letters he correctly found, and of those letters, how many were in the right place.

Let's take a look at how this will be used. Listing 5.2 shows the Play() method, which calls Score().

Listing 5.2   The `Play` Method

```
0:    void Game::Play()
1:    {
2:        char guess[80];
3:        int correct = 0;
4:        int position = 0;
5:
6:        //…
7:            cout << "\nYour guess: ";
8:        Display(guess);
9:
10:       Score(guess,correct,position);
11:       cout << "\t\t" << correct << " correct, " << position
12:         << " in position." << endl;
13:    }
```

I've elided much of this method (indicated by the //... marks), but the code with which we are concerned is shown. We ask the user for his guess and store it in the character array guess on line 2. We display guess by calling Display() on line 8 and passing guess in as a parameter. We then score it by calling Score() on line 10 and passing in guess and two integer variables: correct (declared on line 3) and position (declared on line 4). Finally, we print the values for correct and position on lines 11 and 12.

Score() adjusts the values of correct and position. To accomplish this, we must pass in these two variables *by reference*.

Passing by Reference and by Value

When you pass an object into a method as a parameter to that method, you can pass it either by reference or by value. If you pass it by reference, you are providing that function with access to the object itself. If you pass it by value, you are actually passing in a copy of the object.

passing by reference—Passing an object into a function.

passing by value—Passing a copy of an object into a function.

This distinction is critical. If we pass correct and position by value, Score() cannot make changes to these variables back in Play(). Listing 5.3 illustrates a very simple program that shows this problem.

Listing 5.3   Illustrating Pass by Value

```
0:   #include <iostream>
1:   using namespace std;
2:
3:   class Game
4:   {
5:   public:
6:       Game(){};
7:       ~Game(){}
8:       void Play();
9:       void Score(int correct, int position);
10:
11:  private:
12:       int howManyLetters;
13:       int howManyPositions;
14:  };
15:
16:  void Game::Score(int  correct, int  position)
17:  {
18:      cout << "\nBeginning score. Correct: ";
19:      cout << correct << " Position: " << position << endl;
20:      correct = 5;
21:      position = 7;
22:      cout << "Departing score. Correct: ";
23:      cout << correct << " Position: " << position << endl;
24:  }
25:
26:   void Game::Play()
27:  {
28:      int correct = 0;
29:      int position = 0;
30:
31:      cout << "Beginning Play. Correct: ";
32:      cout << correct << " Position: " << position << endl;
33:      correct = 2;
34:      position = 4;
35:      cout << "Play updated values. Correct: " ;
36:      cout << correct << " Position: " << position << endl;
37:      cout << "\nCalling score..." << endl;
38:      Score(correct, position);
39:      cout << "\nBack from Score() in Play. Correct: ";
40:      cout << correct << " Position: " << position << endl;
41:  }
42:
43:  int main()
44:  {
45:
46:      Game theGame;
47:      theGame.Play();
48:      return 0;
49:  }
```

Output

```
50: Beginning Play. Correct: 0 Position: 0
51: Play updated values. Correct: 2 Position: 4
52:
53: Calling score...
54:
55: Beginning score. Correct: 2 Position: 4
56: Departing score. Correct: 5 Position: 7
57:
58: Back from Score() in Play. Correct: 2 Position: 4
```

Analysis

The very first thing to note is that I've moved everything into one file: Decryptix.cpp. This is for convenience only. In a real program, the declaration of Game would be in Game.h, the implementation of Game would be in Game.cpp, and so forth.

Let's examine the code. On line 6, you see that we've simplified the constructor to take no action, and we've implemented it inline. For the purpose of this illustration, we don't need to focus on anything except the invocation of Score() from Play(). On line 9, you might notice that I've simplified the signature of Score():, eliminating the array of characters. We'll come back to how to pass an array into a function later, but for now I want to focus on the two integer variables, correct and position. Note that in this illustration the ampersand (&) is gone: We're now passing by value, not by reference.

Program flow begins in main(), toward the bottom of the file on line 43. On line 46 we create an instance of a Game object, and at (16) we invoke (or call) the method Play() on that method.

This call to Play() causes program flow to jump to the beginning of Play() on line 26. We start by initializing both correct and position to 0, on line 28. We then print these values on line 32, which is reflected in the output on line 50.

Next, on lines 33 and 34 we change the values of correct and position to 2 and 4, respectively, and then on line 36 we print them again, which is shown in the output on line 51.

On line 38 we invoke Score(), passing in correct and position. This causes the program flow to jump to the implementation of Score(), which is shown on lines 16–24.

The signature of Score() at its implementation matches that of Score() in the class declaration, as it must. Thus, correct and position are passed in by value. This is exactly as if you had declared local variables in this function and initialized them to the values they had in Play().

On line 19 we print correct and position and, as the output shows on line 55, they match the values they had in Play().

On lines 20 and 21, we change these values to 5 and 7, and then on line 23 we print them again to prove that the change occurred; this appears in the output at line 56.

Score() now returns, and program flow resumes on 39; the values are printed again, as shown in the output on line 58.

Until this moment, everything has proceeded according to plan; however, the values back in Play() are not changed, even though you know they were in Score(). Step through this in your debugger, and you'll find that the values *are* changed in Score(), but when you are back in Play(), they are unchanged.

As you have probably already guessed, this is the result of passing the parameters by value. If you make one tiny change to this program and declare the values to be passed by reference, this program works as expected (see Listing 5.4).

Listing 5.4   Passing by Reference

```
0:   #include <iostream>
1:   using namespace std;
2:
3:   class Game
4:   {
5:   public:
6:       Game(){}
7:       ~Game(){}
8:       void Play();
9:       void Score(int & correct, int & position);
10:
11:  private:
12:       int howManyLetters;
13:       int howManyPositions;
14:  };
15:
16:  void Game::Score(int & rCorrect, int & rPosition)
17:  {
18:       cout << "\nBeginning score. Correct: " << rCorrect
18a:      << " Position: " << rPosition << endl;
19:       rCorrect = 5;
20:       rPosition = 7;
21:  cout << "Departing score. Correct: "; << rCorrect;
21a: cout << " Position: " << rPosition << endl;
22:  }
23:
24:  void Game::Play()
```

```
25:  {
26:      int correct = 0;
27:      int position = 0;
28:
29:      cout << "Beginning Play. Correct: " << correct;
29a:     cout << " Position: " << position << endl;
30:      correct = 2;
31:      position = 4;
32:      cout << "Play updated values. Correct: " << correct;
32a:     cout << " Position: " << position << endl;
33:      cout << "\nCalling score..." << endl;
34:      Score(correct, position);
35:      cout << "\nBack from Score() in Play. Correct: " << correct;
35a:     cout << " Position: " << position << endl;
36:  }
37:
38:  int main()
39:  {
40:
41:      Game theGame;
42:      theGame.Play();
43:      return 0;
44:  }
```

Output

```
45: Beginning Play. Correct: 0 Position: 0
46: Play updated values. Correct: 2 Position: 4
47:
48: Calling score...
49:
50: Beginning score. Correct: 2 Position: 4
51: Departing score. Correct: 5 Position: 7
52:
53: Back from Score() in Play. Correct: 5 Position: 7
```

Analysis

The only change in this version is to the signature of Score() (on line 9), which is matched in the implementation (on line 16). The parameter names (for example, rCorrect) need not match between the declaration and the implementation.

Note The parameter names are actually optional at the declaration. If you leave them off, the program compiles without error. As a general programming practice, however, be sure to include good parameter names even though they are not required. They serve as documentation and make your source code easier to understand.

The invocation of `Score()` on line 34 does not change at all. The client of `Score()` doesn't have to manage the fact that you are now passing `correct` and `position` by reference.

The output illustrates on line 53 that the change to the values in `Score()` did change the values back in `Play()`. This happens because this time no copy was made—you were changing the actual values.

References and Passing by Reference

The change in the signature is a change in type. You have changed `correct` from the integer

```
int correct
```

into a reference to an integer:

```
int & rCorrect
```

A *reference* is a special type that acts as an alias.

reference—A type that acts as an alias to an existing object.

The references `rCorrect` and `rPosition` are used within `Score()` exactly as if they were normal integer variables, but the values assigned to them are actually assigned to the original variables—`correct` and `position`—back in `Play()`.

The name I've given it, `rCorrect`, is a clue to me that this is a reference. I tend to prepend reference variables with the letter *r* and pointers (discussed later) with the letter *p*, but the language does certainly not require this. You can name the variables in `Score()` and the variables in `Play()` using exactly the same names, but it makes the source code a bit more difficult to understand.

prepend—Programmers use the term *prepend* to indicate that you add something to the beginning of a term or variable. Thus, we prepend the letter *p* to variable names for pointers. The Free Online Dictionary of Computing
(`http://www.instantweb.com/foldoc/foldoc.cgi?query=prepend`) defines *prepend* as follows: /pree *pend*/ (by analogy with *append*) To prefix or add to the beginning.

It is important to distinguish between passing *by* reference and passing *a* reference. There are two ways to pass by reference. So far we've examined one way: using a reference. Let's take a look at the alternative—pointers.

Pointers

Your throat tightens, your pulse quickens, and a cold, sickening dread grows in the pit of your stomach. Nothing unnerves new C++ programmers as does working with pointers. Well, relax. When you understand that a pointer is nothing more than a variable that holds the *address in memory* of another variable, pointers are a piece of cake.

What is a pointer?

When you create objects in your program, you create them in memory.

When you create the local variable `correct` in the method `Play()`, `correct` is kept in memory. Later you'll examine where in memory variables live, but for now it doesn't matter. What does matter is that `correct` is in memory, and every location in memory has an address. Normally, you don't care about the specific address of an object because you have a label (or name), for example, `correct`. If you need to get to `correct`, you can do so with its label.

You can get the address of `correct` by using the address-of operator (`&`):

```
&correct;
```

 **Note**   The address-of operator (&) uses the same ampersand that we used to identify references. The compiler can tell which you want by context.

When you have the address of `correct`, you can stash that address in a pointer. A pointer is a variable that holds the address of some object in memory.

 pointer—A variable that holds the address of an object.

Memory Addresses

You can imagine that each memory location is ordered sequentially, as an offset from some arbitrary starting point. Picture, if you will, a series of cubbyholes, all aligned and numbered, perhaps as shown in Figure 5.2.

Every integer, character, or object you create is stored in these addresses. Because each cubby holds one byte, a 4-byte integer such as `correct` takes up four such locations.

Figure 5.2

Memory as cubbyholes.

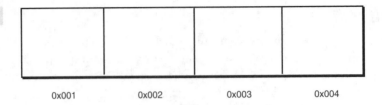

0x001   0x002   0x003   0x004

correct's address is just the first byte of that storage location. Because the compiler knows that an integer is 4 bytes, if its address is 0x001, the compiler knows it occupies 0x001, 0x002, 0x003, and 0x004, and therefore puts the next integer at 0x005–0x008.

 **Note** These addresses are in hexadecimal, which is a base-16 numbering system. If you are curious about this, please see Appendix A, "Binary and Hexadecimal."

There are two perspectives on what is stored in these locations. One is the bit perspective, which is pretty close to how the compiler "thinks" about memory (see Figure 5.3).

Figure 5.3

How the compiler thinks about data in memory.

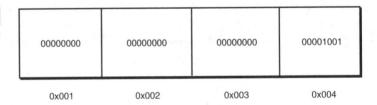

| 00000000 | 00000000 | 00000000 | 00001001 |

0x001   0x002   0x003   0x004

From this perspective, the four bytes are filled with binary digits. How these values are interpreted is irrelevant to the compiler. The bits might represent an integer, a character, or an address somewhere else in memory. We'll return to that idea in a moment.

The point is that the compiler doesn't know or care how to interpret the bits—it just knows what is stored at a given location. To the programmer, however, this memory is conceived somewhat differently (as shown in Figure 5.4).

To the programmer, the value 5 is stored at this location like a letter in a mailbox. The programmer doesn't much care how the bits are configured, he just knows that the value is stashed away at a particular location.

Figure 5.4

How programmers think about data in memory.

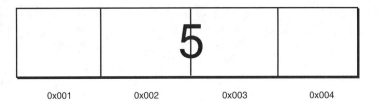

0x001   0x002   0x003   0x004

Let's return to the idea that you can store a memory address. This is a powerful idea. We show here that the value 5 is stored at memory location 0x001. What if you take that address, 0x001 (which in binary is 00000000 00000000 00000000 00000001), and you stash that pattern at another address in memory: 0x1101 (see Figure 5.5).

Figure 5.5

Storing the address.

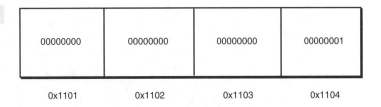

0x1101   0x1102   0x1103   0x1104

 Note

There are some simplifying assumptions here that do not distort the point of this discussion. For example, these are not real memory locations, and values are often stored in memory in a slightly different order than is shown. In addition, compilers often store values at even boundaries in memory.

Here you see that at location 1101, you have stored the value 0x001: the memory location at which you stored the value 5.

At that *pointed to* address, you hold the value 5 as illustrated in Figure 5.4. You can now assign this address to a variable that holds an address—a pointer. You declare a pointer by indicating the type of object it points to (in this case, int), followed by the pointer operator (*), followed by the name of the variable:

```
int * pCorrect;
```

This declares pCorrect to be a pointer to an integer. You can then assign the address of any integer, in this case correct, to that pointer:

```
pCorrect = &correct;
```

Thus, pCorrect now contains the address of the score, as shown in Figure 5.6.

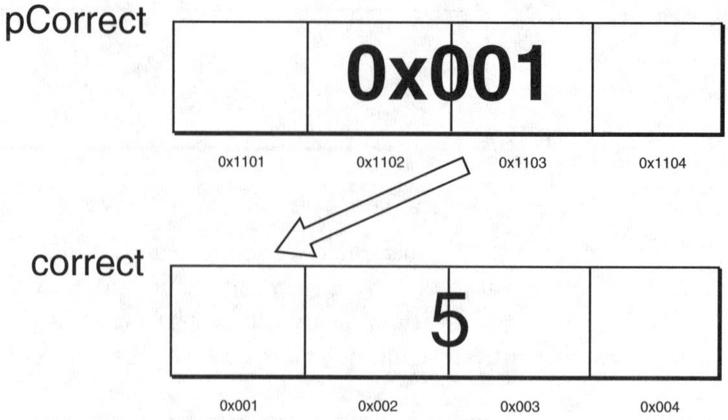

Figure 5.6

pCorrect points to correct.

pCorrect is a pointer to an integer. The integer itself, correct, is stored at 0x001, and pCorrect stores the address of that integer.

The pointer does not have to be in the same method as the variable. In fact, by passing the address into a method and manipulating it with a pointer, you can achieve the same pass by reference effect you achieved using references. Listing 5.5 illustrates this point by rewriting Listing 5.4 using pointers.

Listing 5.5   Using Pointers

```
0:   #include <iostream>
1:   using namespace std;
2:
3:   class Game
4:   {
5:   public:
6:       Game(){}
7:       ~Game(){}
8:       void Play();
9:       void Score(int * correct, int * position);
10:
11:  private:
12:       int howManyLetters;
13:       int howManyPositions;
14:  };
15:
16:  void Game::Score(int * pCorrect, int * pPosition)
17:  {
18:       cout << "\nBeginning score. Correct: " << * pCorrect
18a:        << " Position: " << * pPosition << endl;
19:       * pCorrect = 5;
20:       * pPosition = 7;
21:       cout << "Departing score. Correct: " << * pCorrect
21a:        << " Position: " << * pPosition << endl;
```

```
22:  }
23:
24:  void Game::Play()
25:  {
26:      int correct = 0;
27:      int position = 0;
28:
29:      cout << "Beginning Play. Correct: " << correct
29a:       << " Position: " << position << endl;
30:      correct = 2;
31:      position = 4;
32:      cout << "Play updated values. Correct: " << correct
32a:       << " Position: " << position << endl;
33:      cout << "\nCalling score..." << endl;
34:      Score(&correct, &position);
35:      cout << "\nBack from Score() in Play. Correct: " << correct
35a:       << " Position: " << position << endl;
36:  }
37:
38:  int main()
39:  {
40:
41:      Game theGame;
42:      theGame.Play();
43:      return 0;
44:  }
```

Output

```
45: Beginning Play. Correct: 0 Position: 0
46: Play updated values. Correct: 2 Position: 4
47:
48: Calling score...
49:
50: Beginning score. Correct: 2 Position: 4
51: Departing score. Correct: 5 Position: 7
52:
53: Back from Score() in Play. Correct: 5 Position: 7
```

Analysis

The signature to Score() has changed again, as shown on lines 9 and 16. This time, pCorrect and pPosition are declared to be *pointers to* int: They hold the address of an integer.

On line 34, Play() calls Score() and passes in the addresses of correct and position using the address-of operator (&). There is no reason to declare a pointer here. All you need is the address, and you can get that using the address-of operator.

The compiler puts this address into the pointers that are declared to be the parameters to Score(). Thus, on line 34, the variables pCorrect and pPosition are filled with the addresses of correct and position, respectively.

Dereferencing

On line 18 you want to print the values of correct and position. You don't want the values of pCorrect and pPosition because these are addresses. Rather, you want to print the values at the variables whose addresses these pointers hold.

Similarly, on line 19 and 20 you want to set a new value into the variable whose address is stored in pCorrect. You do *not* want to write

```
pCorrect = 5;
```

because that assigns 5 to pCorrect, and pCorrect needs an address, not a simple integer value.

Note   This will compile, but it stores the address 5 to this pointer, which is a disaster waiting to happen.

The *dereference operator* (*) is used. Again, this is the pointer operator, but its meaning is understood in context.

dereference operator—The dereference operator is used to access the object to which the pointer points.

The dereference operator returns the object whose address is stored in the pointer. Thus

```
*pCorrect
```

returns the variable correct. By writing

```
*pCorrect = 5;
```

we store the value 5 in correct.

how too pro nouns' it

I read the statement

```
*pCorrect = 5
```

as "set the value at pCorrect to 5." That is, assign 5 to the variable whose address is stored in pCorrect.

Getting the Operators Straight

There are two hurdles for a novice programmer—syntax and semantics—and pointers challenge you on both. The syntax is different because the same symbols (& and *) are used for many different purposes. The asterisk is used for multiplication, for the declaration of a pointer, and for dereferencing:

```
z = x * y; // z equals x multiplied by y
int * ptr; // declare a pointer
```

*ptr = 7; // assign 7 to the dereferenced pointerSimilarly, the ampersand is used for references, for the address-of operator, and for logical AND:

```
if ( x && y ) // if x and also y
ptr = &x; // address-of operator
```

int & x = y; // initialize a referenceMore important than the confusing syntax is the difficulty with semantics. When I assign the value 5 on line 19, realize that I'm assigning 5 to correct in Play() indirectly through the pointer that is passed into Score().

5

Arrays

Listing 5.6 reproduces the excerpt of Play() that we were examining in Listing 5.2 when we went off on the discussion of pointers. Remember that on line 10 we call Score() with three parameters, the first of which is our array of characters—guess. We've considered the two other parameters, correct and position, which are passed by reference using references. How is guess passed?

Listing 5.6 `Play`

```
          0:  void Game::Play()
1:  {
2:      char guess[80];
3:      int correct = 0;
4:      int position = 0;
5:
6:      //…
7:          cout << "\nYour guess: ";
8:          Display(guess);
9:
10:         Score(guess,correct,position);
11:         cout << "\t\t" << correct << " correct, " << position
11a:            << " in position." << endl;
12:  }
```

You must always pass arrays by reference; this is fairly easy to accomplish because C++ supports a close symmetry between arrays and pointers.

Every nonstatic member method has, as a hidden parameter, a pointer called the **this** pointer. The **this** pointer has the address of the object itself. When you write

```
const char * Game::GetSolution()
{
     return solution;
}
```

the compiler invisibly turns it into

```
const char * Game::GetSolution(Game * this)
{
     return this->solution;
}
```

You are free to use the **this** pointer explicitly: you can write your code as follows

```
const char * Game::GetSolution()
{
     return this->solution;
}
```

but there is little point in doing so. That said, there are times when you will use the **this** pointer explicitly to obtain the address of the object itself. We'll discuss this later in the book.

When you declare the member method **const**, the compiler changes the **this** pointer from a pointer to an object into a pointer to a *constant* object. Thus, the compiler turns the following code

```
const char * Game::GetSolution() const
{
     return solution;
}
```

into

```
const char * Game::GetSolution(const Game * this) const
{
     return this->solution;
}
```

The constant **this** pointer enforces the constancy of class **method**.

Arrays as Pointers

The name of an array (in our case, guess) is thought of as a pointer to the first element in the array. You can access elements of an array using the offset operator ([ ]), or by using the name of the array and what is called *pointer arithmetic*. Listing 5.7 illustrates this relationship between pointers and arrays.

pointer arithmetic—You can determine how many objects are in a range by subtracting the address of one pointer from another.

Listing 5.7   Relationship Between Pointers and Arrays

```
0:   #include <iostream>
1:   using namespace std;
2:
3:   int main()
4:   {
5:       char myString[80];
6:       strcpy(myString,"Hello there");
7:       cout << "myString is " << strlen(myString)
7a:         << " characters long!" << endl;
8:       cout << "myString: " << myString << endl;
9:       char c1 = myString[1];
10:      char c2 = *(myString + 1);
11:      cout << "c1: " << c1 << " c2: " << c2 << endl;
12:      char * p1 = myString;
13:      char * p2 = myString + 1;
14:      cout << "p1: " << p1 << endl;
15:      cout << "p2: " << p2 << endl;
16:      cout << "myString+1: " << myString+1 << endl;
17:      myString[4] = 'a';
18:      cout << "myString: " << myString << endl;
19:      *(myString+4) = 'b';
20:      cout << "myString: " << myString << endl;
21:      p1[4] = 'c';
22:      cout << "myString: " << myString << endl;
23:      *(p1+4) = 'd';
24:      cout << "myString: " << myString << endl;
25:      myString[4] = 'o';
26:      myString[5] = '\0';
27:      cout << "myString: " << myString << endl;
28:      return 0;
29:  }
```

Output

```
30: myString is 11 characters long!
31: myString: Hello there
32: c1: e c2: e
33: p1: Hello there
```

5

```
34: p2: ello there
35: myString+1: ello there
36: myString: Hella there
37: myString: Hellb there
38: myString: Hellc there
39: myString: Helld there
40: myString: Hello
```

Analysis

On line 5, we create a character array that is large enough to hold the string. On line 6 we use the old-fashioned C-style string library routine strcpy to copy into our array a null-terminated string with the words *Hello there*.

On line 7 we use the C-style library routine strlen to obtain the length of the string. This measures the number of characters until the first NULL and returns that value as an integer, which is printed by cout and shown on line 30.

On line 8 we pass the array to cout, which treats the name of the array (myString) as a pointer to the first byte of the string. cout knows that when it is given an array name it is to print every character until the first NULL. This is shown on line 30.

On line 9 we create a character variable, c1, which is initialized with the character at offset 1—that is, the second character in the array, e.

On line 13 we treat myString as a pointer and add one to it. When you add one to a pointer, the compiler looks at the type of the object that is pointed to, which in this case is char. It uses the type to determine the size of the object, which in this case is one byte. It then returns the address of the next object of that size. If this were a pointer to int, it would return the address of the next int, four bytes later in memory.

Take the address that is returned (myString+1) and dereference it; this returns the character at that address. Then initialize a new character variable, c2, with that character. Note that c2 is not a pointer; by dereferencing, you're actually getting a character, and that is what is assigned to c2.

We print these two characters on line 11, and the printout is on line 32.

On line 12 we create a pointer to a character and assign it to myString. Because the name of the array acts as a pointer to the first byte of the array, p1 now also points to the first byte. On line 13 we create a second pointer and point it to the second character in the array. These are printed on lines 14 and 15 and shown at lines 33 and 34). This illustrates that in each case cout acts as expected, printing the string beginning at the byte that is pointed to and continuing until the first NULL. These have the same printout as on line 18, which uses the string offset directly and which is shown on line 35.

On line 21 we use the offset operator to change the character that is stored at offset 4 (the fifth character). This is printed, and the output appears on line 36.

You can accomplish the same thing on line 16 by using pointer arithmetic and dereferencing the address that is returned; see the output on line 37. Because p1 is pointing to myString, you can use the offset operator on the pointer on line 21. Remember that the name of the array is a pointer to the first element—and that is exactly what p1 is. The effect on line 38 is identical.

Similarly, on line 23 we can use pointer arithmetic on p1 and then dereference the resulting address, just as we did with the array name. The resulting printout is shown on line 39.

On line 25 we change the value back to 'o' using the offset operator, and then we insert a null at offset 5. You can do the same thing with pointer arithmetic, but you get the point. As you probably remember, cout prints only to the first null, so the string hello is printed; nothing further in the array is printed, however, even though the word *there* still remains. This is shown on line 40.

Passing the Array as a Pointer

We said earlier that guess is passed by reference, as a pointer. What you see passed in Listing 5.6 is the name of the array, which is a pointer to the first element in the array:

```
Score(guess,correct,position);
```

In Score() this first parameter must be declared as a pointer to character, which it is. Listing 5.8 reproduces Listing 5.1, the declaration of the Game class.

Listing 5.8   Reproducing Listing 5.1

```
0:  #ifndef GAME_H
1:  #define GAME_H
2:
3:  #include "de0514.h"
4:
5:  class Game
6:  {
7:  public:
8:      Game();
9:      ~Game(){}
10:     void Display(const char * charArray)const{ cout << charArray <<
```

continues

Listing 5.8   continued

```
10a:                                                    endl;}
11:    void Play();
12:    const char * GetSolution() const { return solution; }
13:    void Score(const char * thisGuess, int & correct, int & position);
14:
15:  private:
16:      int howMany(const char *, char);
17:      char solution[maxPos];
18:      int howManyLetters;
19:      int howManyPositions;
20:      int round;
21:      bool duplicates;
22:  };
23:
24:  #endif
```

You can see on line 13 that the first parameter to Score() is declared as a pointer to char, just as we require. Listing 5.9 shows the implementation of the Score() method.

Listing 5.9   Implementing score()

```
0:void Game::Score(const char * thisGuess, int & correct, int & position)
1:  {
2:      correct = 0;
3:      position = 0;
4:
5:      for ( int i = 0; i < howManyLetters; i++)
6:      {
7:          int howManyInGuess = howMany (thisGuess, alpha[i]);
8:          int howManyInAnswer = howMany (solution, alpha[i]);
9:          correct += howManyInGuess < howManyInAnswer ?
10:                        howManyInGuess : howManyInAnswer;
11:
12:      }
13:
14:      for ( int j = 0; j < howManyPositions; j++)
15:      {
16:          if ( thisGuess[j] == solution[j] )
17:              position++;
18:      }
19:
20:  }
```

The signature on the implementation agrees, as it must, with the declaration. thisGuess is a pointer to char and is the same array as guess in Play(). Because guess was passed by reference (as arrays must be), this is the same array, and changes to this array are reflected back in Play.

Because you must pass by reference but you do not want to allow `Score()` to change this array (and there is no reason for it to do so), declare the parameter to be a pointer to a constant `char` rather than a pointer to `char`. This keyword `const` says to the compiler, "I don't intend to change the object that is pointed to, so tell me if I do." This way, the compiler taps you on the shoulder if you attempt to make such a change and says, "Excuse me, sir, but you've changed an object when you promised you wouldn't. Not cricket, sir." (Your compiler's error message might vary).

Let's walk through this implementation of `Score()` line by line. On lines 2 and 3, we initialize both integers, `correct` and `position`, to `0`. If we take no other action, the score is zero correct and zero in position.

On line 5 we begin a `for` loop that will run once for each letter in `thisGuess`. The body of the `for` loop consists of three statements.

On line 7 a local variable—`howManyInGuess`—is initialized to store the result of calling the private member method `howMany()`. When we call `howMany`, we pass in the pointer to the array as the first parameter and the letter at `alpha[i]` as the second parameter.

This is a classic C++ statement, which does at least three things at once. Let's take the statement apart.

The first thing that happens is that `alpha[i]` is returned. The first time through this loop, `alpha[0]` is returned, which is `'a'`. The second time through, `'b'` is returned, and so forth.

This letter becomes the second parameter to the call to `howMany()`. If you look back at the declaration of `Game`, you'll find that `howMany()` is a private method that takes two parameters: a pointer to a constant `char` (the guess from `Play()`) and a character. Listing 5.10 shows the implementation of `howMany()`.

Listing 5.10   Implementing `Game::HowMany()`

```
0:   inline int Game::howMany(const char * theString, char c)
1:   {
2:       int count = 0;
3:       for ( int i = 0; i < strlen(theString); i++)
4:     {
5:           if ( theString[i] == c )
6:               count ++;
7:     }
8:       return count;
9:   }
```

The purpose of this method is to return the number of times an individual letter occurs in an array of characters. On line 2 the counter is initialized to zero. On line 3 we begin a `for` loop that iterates through every `position` in the array.

On line 5 we test each character to see whether it matches the character that was sent in to be tested; if so, we increment the counter. Note that the braces at lines 4 and 7 are not technically necessary, but as Donald Xie pointed out when editing this book, they do make the code much easier to read.

Finally, on line 8 we return that value.

In Listing 5.9, on line 7, we now have a value on the right side of the assignment that represents how many times `alpha[i]` occurs in `thisGuess`: that is, in the array that is passed in from `Play()`.

On line 8, we compute the same value for the solution. The value of `correct` is the lesser of these two, which we accomplish on lines 9 and 10 by using the ternary operator to find the smaller value.

An example makes this clearer: If the solution has *aabba* and the guess has *ababc*, we examine the first letter *a*. `howMany()` returns 2 for the guess and 3 for the solution, so the player has the lesser, 2, correct.

On lines 14–18, we iterate again through the loops, this time testing on line 16 to see whether the character at a specific offset in `thisGuess` is the same as the character at the same offset in the solution. If so, another letter is in the right position.

Because `correct` and `position` were passed in as references, the changes that are made in `Score()` are reflected back in `Play()`.

Using ASSERT

Before moving on, I want to demonstrate how this code can be made both more reliable and more understandable through the use of `ASSERT`.

The purpose of `ASSERT` is to test your assumptions when you are debugging your code, but to have no effect at all when you release your final production version.

When you are debugging your code, you signal your compiler to enter *debug mode*. When you are ready to release your program to the paying public, you rebuild in *release mode*. Debug mode brings along a lot of debugging information that you don't want in release mode.

Thus, in debug mode, you can write

```
ASSERT ( position <= correct )
```

Here you are simultaneously documenting your belief that `position` must never be larger than `correct`. (You can never have five in the correct position if you only have four correct letters!) You are also testing that assertion each time the code runs to prove that you are right. In debug mode, if `position` ever is larger than `correct`, this `ASSERT` statement fails and an error message is written.

When your program is ready to be released, the `ASSERT` macro magically disappears and has no effect on the efficiency of your code.

How ASSERT Works

`ASSERT` is typically implemented as a *macro*. Macros are left over from C; they are type-unsafe routines that are processed not by the compiler but by the precompiler, the same beast that handles your `#include` and `#define` statements. In fact, a macro *is* a `#define` statement.

macro—A text substitution by the precompiler. Macros can act as small subprograms.

EXCURSION

Macros

A macro function is a symbol that is created using **#define**, which takes an argument much like a function does, and which replaces the macro and its argument with a *substitution string*. For example, you can define the macro **TWICE** as follows:

```
#define TWICE(x) ( (x) * 2 )
```

Then in your code you write

```
TWICE(4)
```

The entire string **TWICE(4)** is removed and the value **4*2** is substituted. When the precompiler sees **TWICE(4)**, it substitutes ((4) * 2). That is just what you want because 4*2 evaluates to 8, so **TWICE** will have done just the work you expected.

A macro can have more than one parameter, and each parameter can be used repeatedly in the replacement text. Two common macros are **MAX** and **MIN**:

```
#define MAX(x,y) ( (x) > (y) ? (x) : (y) )
#define MIN(x,y) ( (x) < (y) ? (x) : (y) )
```

MAX returns the larger of two values (x and y), and MIN returns the lesser. Thus,

```
MAX(7,5) is 7, and MIN(7,5) is 5.
```

In a macro function definition, the opening parenthesis for the parameter list must

Note

immediately follow the macro name, with no spaces. The preprocessor is not as forgiving of white space as is the compiler.

Why All the Parentheses?

You might be wondering why there are so many parentheses in these macros. The preprocessor does not demand that parentheses be placed around the arguments in the substitution string, but the parentheses help you avoid unwanted side effects when you pass complicated values to a macro. For example, if you define MAX as

```
#define MAX(x,y) x > y ? x : y
```

and pass in the values **5** and **7**, the macro works as intended. If you pass in a more complicated expression, however, you'll get unintended results, as shown in Listing 5.11.

Listing 5.11   Unintended Macro Results

```
0:
1:   #include <iostream.h>
2:
3:   #define CUBE(a) ( (a) * (a) * (a) )
4:   #define THREE(a) a * a * a
5:
6:   int main()
7:   {
8:       long x = 5;
9:       long y = CUBE(x);
10:      long z = THREE(x);
11:
12:      cout << "y: " << y << endl;
13:      cout << "z: " << z << endl;
14:
15:      long a = 5, b = 7;
16:      y = CUBE(a+b);
17:      z = THREE(a+b);
18:
19:      cout << "y: " << y << endl;
20:      cout << "z: " << z << endl;
21:      return 0;
22:  }
```

```
***Please Insert Output icon herey: 125
z: 125
y: 1728
z: 82
```

Analysis

On line 1, we use the old-fashioned iostream.h so that we can avoid using namespaces. This is perfectly legal in C++, and it is common in writing very short demonstration programs.

On line 3, the macro **CUBE** is defined, with the argument **x** put into parentheses each time it is used. On line 4, the macro **THREE** is defined, without the parentheses. It is intended for these macros to do exactly the same thing: to multiply their arguments times themselves, three times.

In the first use of these macros, on line 16, the value **5** is given as the parameter and both macros work fine. CUBE(5) expands to ((5) * (5) * (5)), which evaluates to 125, and THREE(5) expands to 5 * 5 * 5, which also evaluates to 125.

In the second use, on line 17, the parameter is 5 + 7. In this case, CUBE(5+7) evaluates to

```
( (5+7) * (5+7) * (5+7) )
```

which evaluates to

```
( (12) * (12) * (12) )
```

which in turn evaluates to 1,728. THREE(5+7), however, evaluates to

```
5 + 7 * 5 + 7 * 5 + 7
```

Because multiplication has a higher precedence than addition, this becomes

```
5 + (7 * 5) + (7 * 5) + 7
```

which evaluates to

```
5 + (35) + (35) + 7
```

which finally evaluates to 82.

Macros Versus Functions

Macros suffer from four problems in the eyes of a C++ programmer. First, because all macros must be defined on one line, they can be confusing if they become large. You can extend that line by using the backslash character (\), but large macros quickly become difficult to manage.

Second, macros are expanded inline each time they are used. This means that if a macro is used a dozen times, the substitution appears 12 times in your program, rather than appearing once as a function call does. On the other hand, they are usually quicker than a function call because the overhead of a function call is avoided.

The fact that they are expanded inline leads to the third problem, which is that the macro does not appear in the intermediate source code that is used by the compiler, and therefore it is not visible in most debuggers. By the time you see it in the debugger, the substitution is already accomplished. This makes debugging macros tricky.

The final problem, however, is the largest: Macros are not type-safe. Although it is convenient that absolutely any argument can be used with a macro, this completely undermines the strong typing of C++ and so is anathema to C++ programmers.

That said, the ASSERT macro is a good example of a time when this is not a bug, but a feature: One ASSERT macro can test any condition, mathematical or otherwise.

String Manipulation

The preprocessor provides two special operators for manipulating strings in macros. The *stringizing operator* (#) substitutes a quoted string for whatever follows the stringizing operator. The *concatenation operator* (##) bonds two strings together into one.

stringizing operator (#)—Substitutes a quoted string for whatever follows the stringizing operator.

concatenation operator (##)—Bonds two strings together into one.

Stringizing

The stringizing operator(#) puts quotes around any characters that follow the operator, up to the next white space. Thus, if you write

```
#define WRITESTRING(x) cout << #x
```

and then call

```
WRITESTRING(This is a string);
```

the precompiler turns it into

```
cout << "This is a string";
```

Note that the string This is a string is put into quotes, as is required by cout.

Concatenation

The concatenation operator (##) enables you to bond together more than one term into a new word. The new word is actually a token that can be used as a class name, a variable name, or an offset into an array—or anywhere else a series of letters might appear.

Assume for a moment that you have five functions named fOnePrint, fTwoPrint, fThreePrint, fFourPrint, and fFivePrint. You can then declare

```
#define fPRINT(x) f ## x ## Print
```

and then use it with fPRINT(Two) to generate fTwoPrint, and with fPRINT(Three) to generate fThreePrint.

Predefined Macros

Many compilers predefine a number of useful macros, including __DATE__, __TIME__, __LINE__, and __FILE__. Each of these names is surrounded by two underscore characters to reduce the likelihood that the names will conflict with names you've used in your program.

When the precompiler sees one of these macros, it makes the appropriate substitutes. For __DATE__, the current Date is substituted; for __TIME__, the current time is substituted. __LINE__ and __FILE__ are replaced with the source code line number and filename, respectively. Note that this substitution is made when the source is precompiled, not when the program is run. If you ask the program to print __DATE__, you do not get the current date; instead, you get the date the program was compiled. These defined macros are very useful in debugging.

Although many compilers do provide an ASSERT macro, it will be instructive to create our own, shown in Listing 5.12.

Listing 5.12 An ASSERT Macro

```
0:  #define DEBUG
1:
2:  #ifndef DEBUG
3:      #define ASSERT(x)
4:  #else
5:      #define ASSERT(x) \
6:              if (! (x)) \
7:              { \
8:                  cout << "ERROR!! Assert " << #x << " failed\n"; \
9:                  cout << " on line " << __LINE__  << "\n"; \
10:                 cout << " in file " << __FILE__ << "\n";  \
11:             }
12: #endif
```

On line 0, we define the value DEBUG, which we test on line 2. In the production version we'll remove the definition of DEBUG, and the test on line 2 will fail. When the test fails, this macro defines ASSERT(x) to do nothing, as shown on line 3. If the test succeeds, as it will while we are debugging, this macro defines ASSERT as shown on line 5.

In a macro, any line ending with \ continues on the next line as if both were on the same line. The entire set of lines from line 5 to line 11 is thus considered a single line of the macro. On line 6, whatever is passed to the macro (x) is tested; if it fails, the body of the if statement executes, writing an error message to the screen.

On line 8, we see the stringizing macro at work, and the following lines take advantage of the __FILE__ and __LINE__ macros that are supplied by the compiler vendor.

I don't show ASSERT macros everywhere they might appear in this book because they can detract from the point that is being made; at other times, however, they can greatly clarify the program. For example, I'd rewrite Score() as shown in Listing 5.13.

Listing 5.13   Rewriting Score with ASSERT

```
0:void Game::Score(const char * thisGuess, int & correct, int & position)
1:  {
2:      correct = 0;
3:      position = 0;
4:
5:      ASSERT ( strlen(thisGuess) == howManyPositions )
6:      ASSERT ( strlen(solution) == howManyPositions )
7:
8:      for ( int i = 0; i < howManyLetters; i++)
9:      {
10:         int howManyInGuess = howMany (thisGuess, alpha[i]);
11:         int howManyInAnswer = howMany (solution, alpha[i]);
12:         correct += howManyInGuess < howManyInAnswer ?
12a:                 howManyInGuess : howManyInAnswer;
13:      }
14:
15:     for (  i = 0; i < howManyPositions; i++)
16:     {
17:         if ( thisGuess[i] == solution[i] )
18:             position++;
19:     }
20:
21:     ASSERT ( position <= correct )
22:
23:  }
```

The ASSERT on line 5 documents and tests my assumption that the string passed in as thisGuess is exactly howManyPositions long. The ASSERT on line 6 does the same for the solution. Finally, the ASSERT on line 21 documents and tests my assumption that the number in the correct position can never be greater than the number of correct letters.

Through the Program Once, by the Numbers

Listing 5.14 provides the complete listing of this program. Let's walk through one round, line by line.

Listing 5.14   Using ASSERT (def0514.h)

```
1:      #ifndef DEFINED
2:      #define DEFINED
3:
4:      #include <iostream>
5:      using namespace std;
6:
7:      const char alpha[] = "abcdefghijklmnopqrstuvwxyz";
```

```
8:     const int minPos = 2;
9:     const int maxPos = 10;
10:    const int minLetters = 2;
11:    const int maxLetters = 26;
12:
13:    #define DEBUG
14:
15:    #ifndef DEBUG
16:       #define ASSERT(x)
17:    #else
18:       #define ASSERT(x) \
19:                if (! (x)) \
20:                { \
21:                    cout << "ERROR!! Assert " << #x << " failed\n"; \
22:                    cout << " on line " << __LINE__ << "\n"; \
23:                    cout << " in file " << __FILE__ << "\n";  \
24:                }
25:    #endif
26:
27:    #endif
```

game0514.h

```
28:    #ifndef GAME_H
29:    #define GAME_H
30:
31:    #include "def0514.h"
32:
33:    class Game
34:    {
35:    public:
36:        Game();
37:        ~Game(){}
38:        void Display(const char * charArray) const
39:        {
40:            cout << charArray << endl;
41:        }
42:    void Play();
43:    const char * GetSolution() const { return solution; }
44:    void Score(const char * thisGuess, int & correct, int & position);
45:
46:    private:
47:        int HowMany(const char *, char);
48:        char solution[maxPos+1];
49:        int howManyLetters;
50:        int howManyPositions;
51:        int round;
52:        bool duplicates;
53:    };
54:
55:    #endif
```

continues

Listing 5.14 continued

game0514.cpp

```
56:    #include <time.h>
57:    #include "game0514.h"
58:
59:    void Game::Score(const char * thisGuess, int & > rCorrect, int &
>       rPosition)
60:    {
61:        rCorrect = 0;
62:        rPosition = 0;
63:
64:        ASSERT ( strlen(thisGuess) == howManyPositions)
65:        ASSERT ( strlen(solution) == howManyPositions)
66:        int i;
67:        for ( i = 0; i < howManyLetters; i++)
68:        {
69:            int howManyInGuess = HowMany (thisGuess, alpha[i]);
70:            int howManyInAnswer = HowMany (solution, alpha[i]);
71:            rCorrect += howManyInGuess < howManyInAnswer ?
72:                            howManyInGuess : howManyInAnswer;
73:        }
74:
75:        for (  i = 0; i < howManyPositions; i++)
76:        {
77:            if ( thisGuess[i] == solution[i] )
78:                rPosition ++;
79:        }
80:
81:        ASSERT ( rPosition <= rCorrect)
82:
83:    }
84:
85:    Game::Game():
86:        round(1),
87:        howManyPositions(0),
88:        howManyLetters(0),
89:        duplicates(false)
90:    {
91:
92:        bool valid = false;
93:        while ( ! valid )
94:        {
95:            while ( howManyLetters < minLetters ¦¦
96:                    howManyLetters > maxLetters )
97:            {
98:                cout << "How many letters? (";
99:                cout << minLetters << "-" << maxLetters << "): ";
100:               cin >> howManyLetters;
101:               if ( howManyLetters < minLetters ¦¦
102:                    howManyLetters > maxLetters )
```

```
103:                  cout << "please enter a number between ";
104:                  cout << minLetters << " and " << maxLetters << endl;
105:            }
106:
107:        while ( howManyPositions < minPos ||
107a:           howManyPositions > maxPos )
108:        {
109:            cout << "How many positions? (";
110:            cout << minPos << "-" << maxPos << "): ";
111:            cin >> howManyPositions;
112:            if ( howManyPositions < minPos ||
112a:                     howManyPositions > maxPos )
113:            cout << "please enter a number between ";
114:            cout << minPos <<" and " << maxPos << endl;
115:        }
116:
117:        char choice = ' ';
118:        while ( choice != 'y' && choice != 'n' )
119:        {
120:            cout << "Allow duplicates (y/n)? ";
121:            cin >> choice;
122:        }
123:
124:        duplicates = choice == 'y' ? true : false;
125:
126:        if ( ! duplicates && howManyPositions > howManyLetters )
127:        {
128:            cout << "I can't put " << howManyLetters;
128a:           cout << " letters in ";
129:            cout << howManyPositions;
130:            cout << " positions without duplicates! ";
131:            cout << Please try again.\n";
132:            howManyLetters = 0;
133:            howManyPositions = 0;
134:        }
135:        else
136:            valid = true;
137:    }
138:
139:    int i;
140:    for (i = 0; i < maxPos; i++ )
141:        solution[i] = 0;
142:
143:    srand( (unsigned)time( NULL ) );
144:
145:    for ( i = 0; i < howManyPositions; )
146:    {
147:        int nextValue = rand() % (howManyLetters);
148:        char c = alpha[nextValue];
149:        if ( ! duplicates && i > 0 )
150:        {
```

continues

Listing 5.14　continued

```
151:                    int count = HowMany(solution, c);
152:                    if ( count > 0 )
153:                        continue;
154:                }
155:                // add to the array
156:                solution[i] = c;
157:                i++;
158:            }
159:            solution[i] = '\0';
160:
161:    }
162:
163:    void Game::Play()
164:    {
165:        char guess[80];
166:        int correct = 0;
167:        int position = 0;
168:        bool quit = false;
169:
170:        while ( position < howManyPositions )
171:        {
172:
173:            cout << "\nRound " << round << ". Enter ";
174:            cout << howManyPositions << " letters between ";
175:            cout << alpha[0] << " and ";
175a:           cout << alpha[howManyLetters-1] << ": ";
176:
177:            cin >> guess;
178:
179:            if ( strlen(guess) != howManyPositions )
180:            {
181:                cout << "\n ** Please enter exactly ";
182:                cout << howManyPositions << " letters. **\n";
183:                continue;
184:            }
185:
186:
187:            round++;
188:
189:            cout << "\nYour guess: ";
190:            Display(guess);
191:
192:            Score(guess,correct,position);
193:            cout << "\t\t" << correct << " correct, ";
194:            cout << position << " in position." << endl;
195:        }
196:
197:        cout << "\n\nCongratulations! It took you ";
198:
199:        if ( round <= 6 )
```

```
200:            cout << "only ";
201:
202:        if ( round-1 == 1 )
203:            cout << "one round!" << endl;
204:        else
205:            cout << round-1 << " rounds." << endl;
206:    }
207:
208:
209:    inline int Game::HowMany(const char * theString, char c)
210:    {
211:        int count = 0;
212:        for ( int i = 0; i < strlen(theString); i++)
213:        if ( theString[i] == c )
214:            count ++;
215:        return count;
216:    }
```

decr0514.cpp

5

```
217:    #include "def0514.h"
218:    #include "game0514.h"
219:
220:    int main()
221:    {
222:        cout << "Decryptix. (c)Copyright 1999 Liberty ";
223:        cout << "Associates, Inc. Version 0.3\n\n" << endl;
224:        bool playAgain = true;
225:
226:        while ( playAgain )
227:        {
228:            char choice = ' ';
229:            Game theGame;
230:            theGame.Play();
231:
232:            cout << "\nThe answer: ";
233:            theGame.Display(theGame.GetSolution());
234:            cout << "\n\n" << endl;
235:
236:            while ( choice != 'y' && choice != 'n' )
237:            {
238:                cout << "\nPlay again (y/n): ";
239:                cin >> choice;
240:            }
241:
242:            playAgain = choice == 'y' ? true : false;
243:        }
244:
245:        return 0;
246:    }
```

We begin by loading this program in the debugger and placing a break point on line 222, as illustrated in Figure 5.7. Your particular debugger might look somewhat different, but the essentials are probably the same. Choose Run to break point (in Microsoft Visual Studio, this is **F5**).

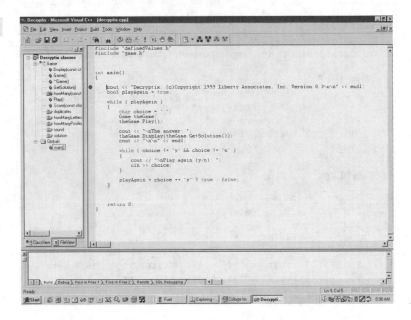

By the time the program has stopped at this break point, it has loaded the two header files, definedValues.h and Game.h.

Loading definedValues brings us to line 1, where the inclusion guards are checked and we find that DEFINED has not yet been defined. Thus, the body of definedValues is read, which brings in iostream (line 4) and which declares (line 5) that we are using the standard namespace.

The global constants are defined on line 7, and ASSERT is defined on line 18.

Including Game.h brings us to line 31, where we attempt to include definedValues. This brings us back to line 1, where the inclusion guards protect us by determining that DEFINED has already been defined, so the rest of definedValues.h is ignored. Returning to line 33, we find the declaration of the Game class.

The constructor and destructor are declared lines 36 and 37. Lines 38–41 are the Display routine, which prints to the screen any character array that is passed in. On line 42 is the heart of the class: the Play() method. On line 43 I've added a new method, GetSolution(), which simply returns the solution as a pointer to a constant character—exactly what is needed by Display(). Finally, on line 44 we see the Score() method, which takes an array of characters (passed in by reference as a pointer to a constant character), and two references to integers.

 Note

> Part of the private interface—not exposed to the public but used by the class's methods to aid in implementation—are several state variables (such as howManyLetters on line 49 and howManyPositions on line 50) that indicate which round we're playing (on line 51) and whether we're allowing duplicates (on line 52).

In addition, line 48 shows the array that holds the solution to the game; line 47 shows a helper function, which is used by other methods of this class to determine how many instances of a particular character are found within any array of characters. You'll see how all the methods work as we step through the code.

Our break point on line 222 causes the program to stop before it prints to the screen. See your debugger's documentation for how to *step over* a function call; in Microsoft's debugger it is **F10**. Pressing step-over causes the copyright notice to print, and then the Boolean value. playAgain is initialized to true. This is used in the test on line 226, and of course this test passes because the value was just initialized one line earlier.

This brings us into the body of the while statement, where we create an instance of a Game object on line 229. This causes program flow to jump to the constructor of the Game object on line 85. We see that the member variables are initialized, and we enter the while loop on line 93. On lines 95 and 96 we test whether howManyLetters (initialized to 0) is less than minLetters (set in definedValues.h to 2). Because this proves true, the second half of the OR statement (howManyLetters > maxLetters) is not even evaluated; instead, we enter the while loop on line 98.

The user is prompted to enter how many letters he'll be guessing in this instance of the game. We'll choose 4; that value is stored in the member variable howManyLetters on line 100.

On line 101 we test to ensure that we have a legal value; if not, we print a reminder to the player. Program flow loops back up to line 95, where the value is checked; if we have a valid value we proceed on line 107, where the same logic is applied to the number of positions. We'll choose 3.

On line 121 we prompt the user to tell us whether he wants to allow duplicates. Note that this is not robust code: If the user enters *Y* rather than *y* (that is, uppercase rather than lowercase), the `while` statement continues to prompt him until he gets it right. We'll fix that up in the next version. For now, we'll enter `n`.

On line 124 we test the value that is received; if it is `'y'`, we set `duplicates` to `true`; otherwise, we set it to `false`. In this case, we set it to `false` because we've entered `'n'`.

Take a look at the member variables, as shown in Figure 5.8.

Figure 5.8

Examining member variables.

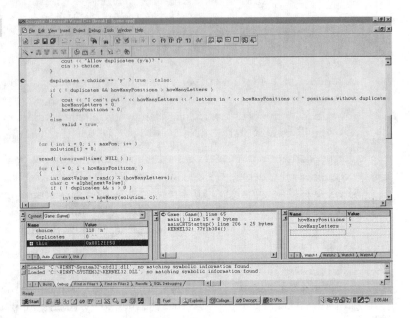

Notice, in the variables window in the lower-left corner, that `choice` has the value `'n'`, and in the watch window in the lower-right, that you have `howManyLetters` 4, and `howManyLetters` 3. Also note, in the variables window, that `duplicates` is shown as `0`. My debugger cannot handle bools, so it shows `true` as 1 and `false` as 0. This is legal in C++ (`0` does evaluate `false` and all other integers evaluate `true`), but it might be better if the debugger showed the actual Boolean value.

 Note

These images are from the Visual C++ debugger. In other environments you may find a different display, but you should be able to see the same values and information.

On line 126 we test the logic of the user's choices. If he asks for three letters in four positions without duplicates, we point out that this is impossible.

On line 140 we iterate through the entire array, setting every member to zero. It is interesting to put solution into a watch window in the debugger and step through this loop watching as each offset member of the array is changed to zero. Note that this is zero the numeric value, not *0* the character. In C++, 0 is the value of NULL, so this loop sets our character array to contain nothing but NULLs.

At line 143 we use srand to seed the random number generator. You might find it interesting to step into the call to time, but this is not relevant to our discussion here.

On line 145 we begin the work of populating the solution array. First, the local counter variable i is initialized to zero.

> **Note**
>
> You might find that many C++ programmers use the variables i, j, k, l, and m as counter variables in for loops, and many can't even tell you why. Why not a? Why not counter?
>
> This is a perfect example of historical anachronisms living on past the time they make any sense. Back in the ancient days of mainframe computing, early versions of FORTRAN (FORmula TRANslator) used only the variables i, j, k, l, and m as legal counting variables. My second computing language was FORTRAN IV, which I learned in high school in 1971. ("You had zeros? We had to use *o*s!") Old habits die hard.
>
> Just as an aside, my first programming language was Monrobot machine language (*1*s and *0*s), which we programmed using paper tape. The computer on which we ran this also had an assembler called QuickComp, which was used by the programming students. To use QuickComp, you had to load a machine language "loader" by running the appropriate tape before running your program. A few of us hacked the QuickComp tape so that on loading it printed go away, I'm sleeping and then shut down the system. In those days, programming, and my sense of humor, were a lot simpler.

On line 147 we examine the result of applying the modulus operator to the result of calling rand() and howManyLetters. If you want to see this at work, rewrite this line as follows:

```
// int nextValue = rand() % (howManyLetters);
int randResult = rand();
int nextValue = randResult % (howManyLetters);
```

This way you can see the result from rand() (stored in randResult), and then the effect of the modulus operator.

The first time I ran this on my machine, randResult was 17,516. I note that howManyLetters is 4. 17,516 divided by 4 is equal to exactly 4,379. Thus, there is no remainder, so the value that is returned by the modulus operator is 0.

On line 148 the character variable c is set to the letter at offset 0 in alpha ('a').

On line 149 we test the value of duplicates (in this case, false) and whether i is greater than zero. In this case, i is zero, so the if statement is skipped. On line 156 solution[0] is set to a. Then i is incremented to 1 and is compared with howManyPositions at 41. (Notice that we do not do the increment in the body of the for loop.) This is because we only want to increment i if we get to line 156. We'll see the alternative in just a moment.

On line 147 we generate nextValue again. On my computer this generates a randResult of 14846 and a nextValue of 2. Does this make sense? howManyLetters is 4. It turns out that 14,846 divided by 4 is 3,711, with a remainder of 2. (3,711 times 4 is 14,844). Thus the modulus operator returns 2, and the character c is assigned alpha[2] or c.

This time the if statement at line 149 returns true, and we enter the body of the if statement. On line 151 we assign the result of calling HowMany to the variable count, passing in the solution array and the letter c.

Program flow branches to line 209. The array is now represented as a pointer. On line 211 the local variable count is initialized to zero. On line 212 we iterate through the string that is passed in (the solution), and each time through the loop we test whether the value at the current offset is equal to the character that is passed in (c).

This time, strlen(theString) is 1. You can test this by inserting a line between, rewriting line 212 as follows:

```
int stringLength = strlen(theString);
for ( int i = 0; i < stringLength; i++ )
```

C++ programmers snicker at this kind of code, with lots of temporary variables, but I've come to believe strongly that this is the right way to do things. By introducing the temporary variable stringLength, you can examine this value in the debugger in a way that is not possible with the more compact version of this code (in which strlen is used in the for loop test).

We see that this first time stringLength is 1, so the for loop runs only once. Because theString[0] is 'a' and our character c is 'c', the if statement fails and count is not incremented. The for loop then ends, and the value 0 is returned. Program flow now resumes at the line immediately following line 151, where the returned value (count) is tested. Because it is not greater than zero, the continue statement does not execute, and program flow continues on line 156 where the character 'c' is added to the array and, once again, i is incremented.

The third time through the for loop at on line 145, my computer generates the value 5,092, which is also exactly divisible by four, returning a nextValue of 0 and a character of 'a'. This time, when we enter howMany, the character matches, so the counter is incremented and the value 1 is returned from howMany. In this case, when the flow resumes at the line just after the call to howMany on line 151, the if statement returns true (1 is greater than 0), so the continue statement executes. This causes the program flow to immediately return to line 145, where we will generate and test a new value.

This is why you don't want to increment i: After all, you have not yet put a value into solution[2]. Thus, i remains at 2, but the call on line 147 generates a different value; this time, the value is 1,369, which sets nextValue to 1 and the character value c to 'b'. Because 'b' does not yet appear in our array, it is added, and i is incremented. i is now 3, the test on line 145 fails (3 is not less than 3), and we fall through to line 159 where solution[3] is set to null.

The result of all this is that solution looks like this:

```
solution[0]: 'a'
solution[1]: 'c'
solution[2]: 'b'
solution[3]: 0
```

The constructor now ends, and we resume on line 230 back in main(). This immediately calls Play(), so processing branches to the implementation of Play() on line 163. The local variables correct and position are initialized to 0 (check your local variables window in your debugger), and the user is prompted to enter a guess on line 173. That guess is stored on line 177 in the array you created on line 165.

We'll guess abc. This fails the test on line 179 because the string length of guess is 3, which is equal to howManyPositions and thus fails the test of not being equal. Processing skips the body of the if statement and continues on line 187, where the member variable round is incremented from zero to 1. On line 190 this guess is passed to Display(), where it is shown to the user; then, on line 192, it is passed into Score().

You can step over Display (in Visual C++, press **F10**) and then into Score (in Visual C++, press **F11**) to follow those parts of the program that are of immediate interest. Stepping into Score() causes program flow to branch to line 59.

We immediately set the values that are referenced by rCorrect and rPosition to 0. We then assert that our assumptions about the sizes of these arrays are correct. On line 67, we enter a for loop in which we'll iterate through each array, testing every possible letter and creating a count of how many are correct.

The first time in this loop, i is 0 and therefore passes the test of being less than howManyLetters (which is 3). The first call to HowMany() passes in the current guess (abc), and the letter *a* (alpha[0]) and returns the value 1. The second call passes in the solution (acb) and the character 'a' and also returns 1.

The next line tests whether howManyInGuess (which is 1) is less than howManyInAnswer (also 1). This is false, so it returns the third part of this ternary operator: howManyInAnswer (which, again, is 1). This value of 1 is added to rCorrect, incrementing it from 0 to 1.

We repeat this for all three letters in the two arrays. Next, on line 75, we reset i to 0 and test whether thisGuess[0] is equal to solution[0]. thisGuess[0] is 'a', and solution[0] is also 'a', so rPosition is incremented from 0 to 1. On the second time through the loop, thisGuess[1] is 'b', but solution[1] is 'c', so rPosition is not incremented. On the third time through, thisGuess[2] is 'c' and solution [1] is 'b', so again, rPosition is not incremented.

There is no need to return a value from this method (which is why it is marked void) because the variables rPosition and rCounter are references to the local variables back in Play(). When we return from Score(), these values are printed and we see that correct is 3 and position is 1.

This returns us to the top of the while loop on line 170; position (now 1) is compared with howManyPositions (currently 3). Because it is still smaller, we're not yet done, and we repeat the loop, offering the user a second guess.

This time let's guess acb. The score we receive is three correct and three in position, and this while loop ends. Program flow resumes on line 197, where we print a congratulatory message. Play() then returns, dropping us on line 232 in main(), where the answer is displayed and you are offered (on line 236) the opportunity to play again.

If you decide *not* to play again, the value 0 is returned to the operating system on line 245 and the program ends.

On line 230 we invoke the Play() method.

This causes program flow to jump to line 163. To see this, step into this method from line 230. Your debugger brings you to line 163. A few local variables are created and initialized, and then on line 170 we check the value of position (which is zero) to see if it is less than howManyPositions.

Chapter 6

Using Linked Lists

The problem with using arrays is that you must declare their size at compile time rather than at runtime.

compile time   When you compile the program.

runtime   When you run the program.

This means that you must guess, in advance, how much memory you need to allocate. If you guess wrong and you allocate too little, you run out of room and your program breaks. If, on the other hand, you allocate more than you need, you waste memory.

In Decryptix! this isn't a very big problem because we create only two arrays: one to hold the solution and one to hold the guess. We can just create a pair of arrays large enough to hold the biggest legal solutions and the largest possible guess, and let it go at that.

In other programs, however, fixed size arrays are so wasteful of memory as to be unusable. Software designers are often asked to consider how their program will *scale:* How will they perform as they become larger and handle more data? Programs that use fixed size arrays rarely scale well.

Scaling a program refers to the capability to do more: to handle larger and more complex data sets, more users, or more frequent access. When a program scales, it becomes bigger and typically more complex, and all the weaknesses in performance and maintainability surface.

To solve the problem of fixed size arrays, we need the capability to store data in some form of data structure or collection that grows *dynamically*, which means that it grows as it needs to while the program runs.

Dynamic Data Structures

Over the years, computer scientists have struggled with this issue. In the past, procedural programmers created complex data structures to hold data efficiently. Object-oriented programmers talk about *collection classes*, classes that are designed to hold collections of other objects.

collection class   A class designed to hold a collection of other objects.

Collection classes are built on top of traditional data structures as higher-level abstractions, but the problem they are solving is the same: How do we efficiently deal with large sets of data or objects?

We need a variety of collection classes because our needs and priorities differ from program to program. Sometimes we care about adding objects to the collection quickly. Other times, we don't mind if there is a slight delay adding objects, but we want the capability to find objects quickly. In other programs, the emphasis is on using little memory or little disk space.

The Standard Template Library

The C++ Standard Library now offers a suite of *collection classes* called the Standard Template Library (STL), which is described in coming chapters. The STL classes are designed to hold collections of objects, including built-in objects such as characters and more complex (and dramatically larger) user-defined objects. Most importantly, the STL code has been optimized, debugged, and tested so that you don't have to do this work yourself.

Before considering the STL in detail, however, it is helpful to create our own rather simple collection class, at least once, to see what is involved.

We'll rewrite Decryptix! to use a *linked list* rather than an array. A linked list is a very simple data structure that consists of small containers that can be linked together as needed, and each of which is designed to hold one object.

linked list   A simple data structure in which each element in the list points to data and to the next element in the list.

Each individual container is called a *node*. The first node in the list is called the *head*, and the last node in the list is called the *tail*.

node   An element in a data structure.

head   The first node in a linked list.

tail   The last node in a linked list.

Lists come in three fundamental forms. From simplest to most complex, they are

- Singly linked
- Doubly linked
- Trees

In a singly linked list, each node points forward to the next one, but not backward. To find a particular node, start at the top and go from node to node, as in a treasure hunt ("The next node is under the sofa"). A doubly linked list enables you to move backward and forward in the chain. A tree is a complex structure built from nodes, each of which can point in two or three directions. Figure 6.1 shows these three fundamental structures.

Figure 6.1

Singly linked, doubly linked, and tree structures.

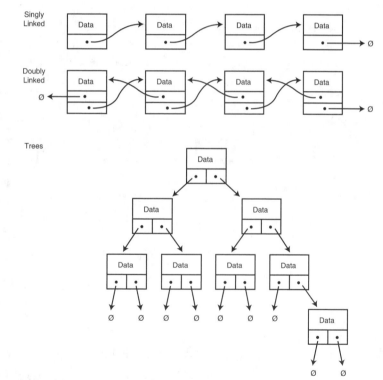

Linked Lists

We'll build the simplest form of linked list, a singly linked list that is not sorted. Characters are added in the order in which they are received (just as they are in an array).

We'll actually create the linked list three times. The first time we'll take a rather simplistic, traditional approach just to get a good sense of how a linked list works. The second time we'll design a somewhat more object-oriented linked list and see whether we can add some solid object-oriented design heuristics to our solution. Finally, we'll use the linked list to illustrate the concept of abstract data types.

Understanding Linked Lists

Our simplest linked list consists of nothing but nodes. A node is a tiny object with two members. The first member is a pointer to the thing we're storing, in our case a single character. The second member is a pointer to another node. By stringing nodes together, we create a linked list.

When there are no more nodes in the list, the last node points to NULL. Figure 6.2 shows what our linked list looks like. The first node in the list (the head node) points to its data (A) and also to the second node in the list. This second node in turn points to its data and also to the third node. The third node is the tail node, and it points to its data and to null, signifying that there are no more nodes in the list.

Figure 6.2

Simple linked list.

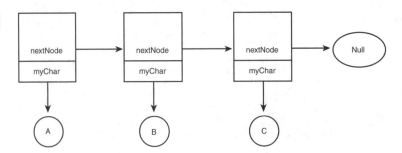

Let's implement this linked list and then see how we might use it, instead of an array, to hold our solution. To get started, however, we need only create the Node class and fill it with a list of characters. Listing 6.1 has the declaration for our Node class.

Note   During the development of a program, I'm often confronted with a new technology, in this case the linked list. Rather than trying to figure out how to use it in my program while also figuring out how to implement it, I usually first implement the technology with a simple *driver program*. That is, I'll take it out of context and create a very simple program that does nothing but exercise the new technology. After it is working, I'll go back and integrate it into the real program.

Listing 6.1 The Node Class Declaration

```
0:  class Node
1:  {
2:  public:
3:      Node(char c);
4:      ~Node();
5:      void Display () const;
6:      int HowMany (char c) const;
7:      void Insert (char c);
8:
9:  private:
10:      char GetChar ();
11:      Node * GetNext ();
12:      char myChar;
13:      Node * nextNode;
14:  };
```

Let's start by looking at the constructor on line 3. A node is created by passing in a character by value. Rather than keeping a pointer to the character, our Node class keeps a copy of the character on line 12. With a tiny 1-byte object, this is sensible. With larger objects, you'll want to keep a pointer to avoid making a copy.

Note In C++, pointers are typically 4 bytes. With a 1-byte object, it is cheaper to keep a copy (one byte of memory used) than to keep a pointer (4 bytes of memory used). With large user-defined types, it can be far more expensive to make the copy, in which case a pointer or reference is used.

Node provides three methods in addition to its constructor and destructor. On line 5 we see Display(), whose job it is to print the characters that are stored in the list. The method HowMany() also takes a character and returns the number of times that character appears in the list. Finally, Insert() takes a character and inserts it into the list. Listing 6.2 shows the implementation of these simple methods.

Listing 6.2 Implementing Node

```
0:  #include <iostream>
1:  using namespace std;
2:
3:  #include "node0601.h"
4:
5:  Node::Node(char c):
```

continues

Listing 6.2   continued

```
 6:    myChar(c),nextNode(0)
 7:    {
 8:    }
 9:
10:    Node::~Node()
11:    {
12:        if ( nextNode )
13:            delete nextNode;
14:    }
15:
16:
17:    void Node::Display() const
18:    {
19:        cout << myChar;
20:        if ( nextNode )
21:            nextNode->Display();
22:    }
23:
24:
25:    int Node::HowMany(char theChar) const
26:    {
27:        int myCount = 0;
28:        if ( myChar == theChar )
29:            myCount++;
30:        if ( nextNode )
31:            return myCount + nextNode->HowMany(theChar);
32:        else
33:            return myCount;
34:    }
35:
36:    void Node::Insert(char theChar)
37:    {
38:        if ( ! nextNode )
39:            nextNode = new Node(theChar);
40:        else
41:            nextNode->Insert(theChar);
42:    }
```

The constructor on line 5 receives a character and initializes its myChar member variable on line 6. The constructor also initializes its nextNode pointer to zero   that is, to null. When the Node is created, it points to nothing further along in the list.

The destructor on line 10 tests the pointer on line 12, and if the pointer is not NULL, the destructor deletes it.

`Display()`, on line 17, prints the character that is held by the current node on line 19, and then calls `Display()` on the `nextNode` in the list, if any (on line 20). In this way, by telling the first node to display itself, you cause every node in the list to display itself.

A Simple Driver Program

On line 25, `HowMany()` takes a character and returns the number of times that character exists in the list. The implementation of this is tricky and instructive because this type of implementation is common in C++. Explaining how this works in words is much less effective than tracing it in the debugger. To do that, we need a driver program, shown in Listing 6.3.

Listing 6.3   Driver Program

```
0:  #include "def0514.h"
1:  #include "node0601.h"
2:
3:  int main()
4:  {
5:      Node head('a');
6:      head.Insert('b');
7:      int count = head.HowMany('a');
8:      cout << "There are " << count << " instances of a\n";
9:      count = head.HowMany('b');
10:     cout << "There are " << count << " instances of b\n";
11:     cout << "\n\nHere's the entire list: ";
12:     head.Display();
13:     cout << endl;
14:
15:     return 0;
16: }
```

Output

```
There are 1 instances of a
There are 1 instances of b

Here's the entire list: ab
```

Before we examine HowMany, let's look at the driver. Its job is to generate two letters and add them to the list. To do this, it creates a first node, called the *head node*, on line 5, and initializes it with the value 'a'. It then tells the head node to insert one more letter ('b'), starting on line 6.

Our linked list now looks like Figure 6.3.

Figure 6.3

With two nodes.

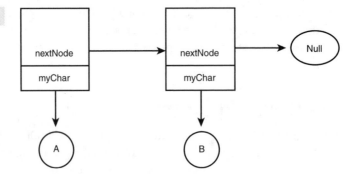

On line 0 we #include DefinedValues.h, shown in Listing 6.4.

Listing 6.4 def0514.h

```
1:    #ifndef DEFINED
2:    #define DEFINED
3:
4:    #include <iostream>
5:    using namespace std;
6:
7:    const char alpha[] = "abcdefghijklmnopqrstuvwxyz";
8:    const int minPos = 2;
9:    const int maxPos = 10;
10:    const int minLetters = 2;
11:    const int maxLetters = 26;
12:
13:    #define DEBUG
14:
15:    #ifndef DEBUG
16:        #define ASSERT(x)
17:    #else
18:        #define ASSERT(x) \
19:                if (! (x)) \
20:                { \
21:                    cout << "ERROR!! Assert " << #x << " failed\n"; \
22:                    cout << " on line " << __LINE__ << "\n"; \
23:                    cout << " in file " << __FILE__ << "\n";   \
```

```
24:                    }
25:     #endif
26:
27:     #endif
```

Analysis

This file serves to define constants we'll need in this program.

Let's not examine how `Insert()` works just yet, but rather assume that the letter *b* is in fact inserted into the list. We'll return to how this works in just a moment, but let's first focus on `HowMany()` works.

The `HowMany()` Method

On line 7 we ask how many instances of `'a'` there are, and on line 9 we ask the same about how many instances of `'b'` there are. Let's walk through the call to `howMany` on line 9. Put a break point on this line, and run the program to the break point.

The program runs as expected and stops at the following line:

```
count = head.HowMany('b');
```

Stepping into this line of code brings you to the top of `HowMany()`:

```
int Node::HowMany(char theChar) const
{
```

Let's step line by line. The first step initializes `myCount` to `0`, which you can probably see in the local variables window of your debugger.

Which node are we looking at? We'll be entering the `HowMany()` method once for each node. How can we tell where we are? Remember that every nonstatic member method has a pointer called the `this` pointer, which holds the address of the object itself.

You can examine the value of the `this` pointer in your debugger. Take note of the address of the `this` pointer while you are here in `HowMany()`. On my machine, it is `0x0012ff6c`, but yours might be different. The particular value doesn't matter   just write down whatever you have. This is the address of the node we're examining.

Step to the next line, where `myChar` is compared with `theChar`. Examine the `myChar` member variable (`'a'`) and the local variable `theChar` (`'b'`), again in your local variables window.

Note You might need to expand your `this` pointer to see the member variables, or you might need to click on a different debugger window to find them.

Clearly, these values are not the same, so the `if` statement fails. `myCount` remains at `0`.

Step again to the next `if` statement. The `nextNode` pointer should be nonzero. On my machine, it is `0x004800a0`. Your value will differ; again, although the absolute value doesn't matter, write down whatever you get.

Because `nextNode` is nonzero, the `if` statement evaluates `true`, and you step to the following line:

```
return myCount + nextNode->HowMany(theChar);
```

What do you expect to happen if you step *into* this line? The first thing to be evaluated is

```
nextNode->HowMany(theChar);
```

This calls the `howMany()` method through the `nextNode` pointer. This, in fact, calls `howMany()` on the object to which `nextNode` points. Remember that `nextNode` had a value, the address of the next node in the list. Let's step in.

The debugger appears to go to the top of the same method. Where are we? Examine the `this` pointer in your debugging window (you might first have to step to the first line of the method). On my machine, the `this` pointer has changed to `0x004800a0`, which was exactly the value previously held in the `nextNode` pointer. Aha! We're now in the second node in the list. We can imagine that our list looks like Figure 6.4.

Figure 6.4

Nodes with addresses.

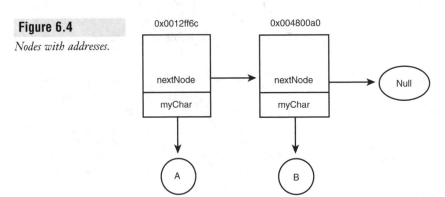

We are running `HowMany` in the *second* node. Once again, `HowMany()` begins by initializing the local variable `myCount`, on line 27, to `0`. Be careful here, the `myCount` we're

looking at now is local to this iteration of HowMany(). The myCount back in the first node has its own local value.

HowMany() then tests the character that is passed in against the character it is storing on line 28; if they match, it increments the counter. In this case, they do match, so we compare myChar ('b') with theChar (also 'b'). They match, so myCount is incremented.

Stepping again brings us to the next if statement:

```
30:    if ( nextNode )
```

This time nextNode is NULL (you should see all zeros in its value in your local variables window). As expected, the second node's nextNode points to NULL. The if statement fails and the else statement executes, returning myCount, which has the value 1.

We step into this line and appear to be right back at the return statement. Examine the this pointer, however, and you'll find that we're back in the first node. The value that is returned (1) is added to the value in myCounter (now 0), and it is this combined value that is returned to the calling function, main().

As an exercise, try revising main() to insert the values a, b, c, b, and b. This produces the linked list that is shown in Figure 6.5. Make sure you understand why HowMany() returns the value 3 when passed in 'b'.

Figure 6.5

Linked list with abcbb.

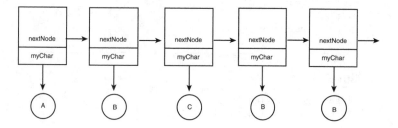

Insert() in Detail

Now is the time to examine the implementation of Insert(), as shown on line 36 in Listing 6.2 and reproduced here for your convenience:

```
36:  void Node::Insert(char theChar)
37:  {
38:      if ( ! nextNode )
39:          nextNode = new Node(theChar);
40:      else
41:          nextNode->Insert(theChar);
42:  }
```

The goal of this method is to insert a new character (theChar) into the list.

Note that on line 39 we use the keyword new to create a new Node object. This is explained in full in just a few pages; for now, all you need to know is that this creates a new object of type Node.

Let's start over, creating the linked list from Figure 6.5, using the code shown in Listing 6.5.

Listing 6.5   Decryptix **Driver Program**

```
0:   #include "def0514.h"
1:   #include "node0601.h"
2:
3:   int main()
4:   {
5:       Node head('a');
6:       head.Insert('b');
7:       head.Insert('c');
8:       head.Insert('b');
9:       head.Insert('b');
10:      int count = head.HowMany('a');
11:      cout << "There are " << count << " instances of a\n";
12:      count = head.HowMany('b');
13:      cout << "There are " << count << " instances of b\n";
14:      cout << "\n\nHere's the entire list: ";
15:      head.Display();
16:      cout << endl;
17:
18:      return 0;
19:   }
```

Output

```
There are 1 instances of a
There are 3 instances of b

Here's the entire list: abcbb
```

On line 5 we create the first Node object, which we call head. Set a break point on that line and run to the break point. Stepping in takes you to the constructor of the Node object:

```
 Node::Node(char c):
myChar(c),nextNode(0)
{
}
```

This does nothing but initialize the member variables. We now have a node whose myChar character variable contains 'a' and whose nextNode pointer is NULL.

Returning to `main()`, we step into the call to

```
head.Insert('b');
```

Step into this code from Listing 6.2, which is once again reproduced for your convenience:

```
36:   void Node::Insert(char theChar)
37:   {
38:       if ( ! nextNode )
39:           nextNode = new Node(theChar);
40:       else
41:           nextNode->Insert(theChar);
42:   }
```

On line 38 we test to see whether `nextNode` is NULL. In this case it is, so we must create a new node. The last time we created a node, we simply declared it and passed in the value to store ('a'). This time we do something different, calling the new operator. Why?

Until now, all the objects you've created were created on the stack. The stack, you'll remember, is where all local variables are stored, along with the parameters to function calls. To understand why creating your new node object on the stack won't work, we need to talk a bit more about what the stack is and how it works.

6

EXCURSION

Understanding the Stack

The stack is a special area of memory that is allocated for your program to hold the data required by each of the functions in your program. It is called a stack because it is a *last-in, first-out* (LIFO) queue, much like a stack of dishes at a cafeteria (see Figure 6.6).

Figure 6.6

A LIFO stack.

LIFO means that whatever is added to the stack last will be the first thing that is taken off. Other queues are more like a line at a theater, which is called *first in, first out* (FIFO): The first one on line is the first one off.

LIFO Last in, first out, like plates on a stack.

FIFO First in, first out, like people on line to buy tickets at a theater.

Interestingly, most airplanes board and unboard coach like a FIFO stack. The people at the rear of the plane are the first to board and the last to get off. Of course, first class is a FIFO structure first class passengers are the first ones in and the first ones out.

When data is pushed onto the stack, the stack grows; as data is popped off the stack, the stack shrinks. It isn't possible to pop a dish off the stack without first popping off all the dishes placed on after that dish, and it isn't possible to pop data off a stack without first popping all the data added above your data.

A stack of dishes is a fine analogy as far as it goes, but it is fundamentally wrong. A more accurate mental picture is of a series of cubbyholes, aligned top to bottom. The top of the stack is whatever cubby the stack pointer happens to be pointing to. The *stack pointer* is just a pointer whose job is to keep track of the top of the stack.

stack pointer A pointer that keeps track of the top of the stack.

Each of the cubbies has a sequential address, and one of those addresses is kept in the stack pointer register. Everything below that magic address, known as the top of the stack, is considered to be on the stack. Everything above the top of the stack is considered to be off the stack, and therefore invalid. Figure 6.7 illustrates this idea.

Figure 6.7

The instruction pointer.

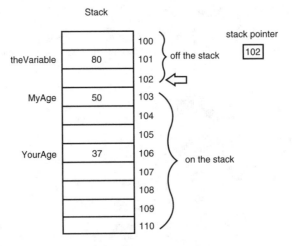

When data is put on the stack, it is placed into a cubby above the stack pointer, and then the stack pointer is moved up to indicate that the new data is now on the stack.

When data is popped off the stack, all that really happens is that the address of the stack pointer is changed because it moves down the stack. Figure 6.8 makes this rule clear.

*Moving the stack
pointer.*

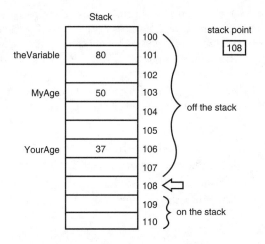

The Stack and Functions

Here's what happens when a program that is running on a PC under DOS branches to a function:

1. The address in the instruction pointer is incremented to the next instruction past the function call. That address is then placed on the stack, and it will be the return address when the function returns.

2. Room is made on the stack for the return type you've declared. On a system with two-byte integers, if the return type is declared to be `int`, another two bytes are added to the stack, but no value is placed in these bytes.

3. The address of the called function, which is kept in a special area of memory that is set aside for that purpose, is loaded into the instruction pointer, so the next instruction executed will be in the called function.

4. The current top of the stack is noted and is held in a special pointer called the *stack frame*. Everything that is added to the stack from now until the function returns is considered local to the function.

5. All the arguments to the function are placed on the stack.

6. The instruction that is now in the instruction pointer executes, thus executing the first instruction in the function.

7. Local variables are pushed onto the stack as they are defined.

8. When the function is ready to return, the return value is placed in the area of the stack that is reserved at step 2.

9. The stack is then popped all the way up to the stack frame pointer, which effectively throws away all the local variables and the arguments to the function.

10. The return value is popped off the stack and assigned as the value of the function call itself.

11. The address that is stashed away in step 1 is retrieved and put into the instruction pointer.

12. The program resumes immediately after the function call, with the value of the function retrieved.

Some of the details of this process change from compiler to compiler, or between computers, but the essential ideas are consistent across environments. In general, when you call a function, the return address and parameters are put on the stack. During the life of the function, local variables are added to the stack. When the function returns, these are all removed by popping the stack.

For our purposes, the most important thing to note about this process is that when a function returns, all the local variables are popped off the stack and destroyed.

As was described previously, if we create the new node in `InsertNode` on the stack, when the function returns, that node is destroyed. Let's try it. We'll just change `Insert` to create a local node, and we'll stash away the address of that local `Node` in `nextNode`. Listing 6.6 illustrates the change.

 Warning   These changes compile and link, but will crash when you run the program.

Listing 6.6   Local Nodes

```
0:   void Node::Insert(char theChar)
1:   {
2:       if ( ! nextNode )
3:       {
4:           Node localNode(theChar);
5:           nextNode = &localNode;
6:       }
7:       else
8:           nextNode->Insert(theChar);
9:
```

When I run this program, it quickly crashes. Here's what happens: When we create the head `Node`, its `nextNode` pointer is null. When we call `Insert()` on the head node, the `if` statement returns `true`, and we enter the body of the `if` statement on line 4. We create a `localNode` object and assign its address to `nextNode`. We then return from `Insert`. At that moment, the stack unwinds, and the local node we created is destroyed.

Now, all that happens when that local node is destroyed is that its destructor runs and the memory is marked as reusable. Sometime later, we might assign that memory to a different object. Still later, we might use the `nextNode` pointer and *bang!* the program crashes.

Using new

This is a classic example of when you need to create an object on the heap. Objects that are created on the heap are *not* destroyed when the function returns. They live on until you delete them explicitly, which is just what we need.

Unlike objects on the stack, objects on the heap are unnamed. You create an object on the heap using the new operator, and what you get back from new is an address, which you must assign to a pointer so that you can manipulate (and later delete) that object.

Let's look again at Insert() from Listing 6.2:

```
36:    void Node::Insert(char theChar)
37:    {
38:        if ( ! nextNode )
39:            nextNode = new Node(theChar);
40:        else
41:            nextNode->Insert(theChar);
42:    }
```

The logic of this code is that we test to see whether the nextNode pointer is pointing to an object on line 38; if it is not, we create a new object on the heap and assign its address to nextNode.

When we create the new object, we call new, followed by the type of the object we are creating (Node) and any parameters we need to send to the constructor (in this case, theChar).

If this object does point to another node, we invoke Insert on that object, passing along the character we're trying to solve. Eventually we reach the end of the list   a node that does not point to any other node   and we can create a new node and tag it to the end of the list.

new and delete

Many details are involved in using new effectively, which we'll discuss as we come to them. There is one, however, that I want to discuss immediately. When you create an object on the heap using new, you own that object, and you must clean it up when you are done with it. If you create an object on the heap and then lose the pointer, that object continues to use up memory until your program ends, but you can't access that memory.

When you have an object that you can't access anymore but that continues to consume memory, we say it has *leaked out* of the program. Memory leaks are of significant concern to C++ programmers. You solve memory leaks by the judicious application of delete(). We see this in the destructor in Listing 6.2, copied here:

```
10:   Node::~Node()
11:   {
12:       if ( nextNode )
13:           delete nextNode;
14:   }
```

When we are ready to destroy the linked list, we call delete on the head node (implicitly by returning from the function in which the head node was created on the stack, or explicitly if the head node was created on the heap). The destructor examines its own nextNode, and if the nextNode pointer is not null, the destructor deletes the node to which it points. This mechanism knocks down all the dominoes, each object deleting the next object as part of its own sequence of destruction.

Let's modify main() to create the head node on the heap, and we'll delete it explicitly when we're done with the list. To make all this clear, we'll add printouts to the constructors and destructors to see our progress. Listing 6.7 is the entire program, which we'll walk through in some detail.

Listing 6.7a   Node.h

```
1:    class Node
2:    {
3:    public:
4:        Node(char c);
5:        ~Node();
6:
7:        void Display () const;
8:        int HowMany (char c) const;
9:        void Insert (char c);
10:
11:   private:
12:        char myChar;
13:        Node * nextNode;
14:   };
```

Listing 6.7b   Node.cpp

```
15:   #include <iostream.h>
16:   #include "L0607.h"
17:
18:   Node::Node(char theChar):
19:   myChar(theChar),nextNode(0)
20:   {
21:       cout << "In constructor of Node(" << this << ")\n";
```

```
22:        }
23:
24:        Node::~Node()
25:        {
26:            cout << "In destructor of Node(" << this << ")\n";;
27:            if ( nextNode )
28:                delete nextNode;
29:        }
30:
31:
32:        void Node::Display() const
33:        {
34:            cout << this << ": " << myChar << endl;
35:            if ( nextNode )
36:                nextNode->Display();
37:        }
38:
39:
40:        int Node::HowMany(char theChar) const
41:        {
42:            int myCount = 0;
43:            if ( myChar == theChar)
44:                myCount++;
45:            if ( nextNode )
46:                return myCount + nextNode->HowMany(theChar);
47:            else
48:                return myCount;
49:        }
50:
51:        void Node::Insert(char theChar)
52:        {
53:            if ( ! nextNode )
54:                nextNode = new Node(theChar);
55:            else
56:                nextNode->Insert(theChar);
57:        }
```

Listing 6.7c   Driver.cpp

```
58:        #include <iostream.h>
59:        #include "L0607a.h"
60:
61:        int main()
62:        {
63:            Node * pHead = new Node('a');
64:            pHead->Insert('b');
65:            pHead->Insert('c');
66:            pHead->Insert('b');
67:            pHead->Insert('b');
68:            int count = pHead->HowMany('a');
```

continues

Listing 6.7c   continued

```
69:           cout << "There are " << count << " instances of a\n";
70:           count = pHead->HowMany('b');
71:           cout << "There are " << count << " instances of b\n";
72:           count = pHead->HowMany('c');
73:           cout << "There are " << count << " instances of c\n";
74:           cout << "\n\nHere's the entire list:\n";
75:           pHead->Display();
76:           cout << "Deleting pHead..." << endl;
77:           delete pHead;
78:           cout << "Exiting main()..." << endl;
79:           return 0;
80:       }
```

Output

```
81:    In constructor of Node(0x00430060)
82:    In constructor of Node(0x00431DB0)
83:    In constructor of Node(0x00431D70)
84:    In constructor of Node(0x00431D30)
85:    In constructor of Node(0x00431CF0)
86:    There are 1 instances of a
87:    There are 3 instances of b
88:    There are 1 instances of c
89:
90:
91:    Here's the entire list:
92:    0x00430060: a
93:    0x00431DB0: b
94:    0x00431D70: c
95:    0x00431D30: b
96:    0x00431CF0: b
97:    Deleting pHead...
98:    In destructor of Node(0x00430060)
99:    In destructor of Node(0x00431DB0)
100:    In destructor of Node(0x00431D70)
101:    In destructor of Node(0x00431D30)
102:    In destructor of Node(0x00431CF0)
103:    Exiting main()...
```

The best way to follow the progress of this code is to put the code in the debugger and set a break point in main() at line 63. Run the program to the break point and note that we are going to create a new node and initialize it to hold the letter 'a'. The address of this new node is stashed away in the Node pointer pHead. Now, step in at line 63. You might step into the new operator. If so, just step back out and step in again, which brings you to the constructor for Node on line 18.

Sure enough, the character 'a' was passed in (now designated theChar), and this character is used to initialize the member variable myChar. The node's second member variable, nextNode, which is a pointer to a Node object, is also initialized with the value 0 or NULL. Finally, as you step through the constructor, a message is printed on line 21, the effect of which is shown on line 81.

Notice that the this pointer is not dereferenced, so its actual value is printed: That is, the address of the Node object on the heap whose constructor we are now discussing.

If you continue stepping, you'll return from the constructor back to main() on line 64, where we intend to call the Insert() method on that Node. We do so indirectly, using the pointer that holds its address, and we pass 'b' to the Insert method in the hope that a new Node will be created and appended to the list to hold this new value.

Step in at on line 30 and you enter the Insert() method of Node on line 51, where the parameter theChar holds the value 'b'. On line 53 you test the Node's nextNode pointer, which is NULL (or 0), the value to which you initialized it just a moment ago. The if statement returns true. Take a moment and reflect on why.

If a pointer has a nonzero value, it evaluates true. With a 0 value, it evaluates false. Thus, asking if a pointer is false is the same as asking if it is null.

The not operator turns false to true. Thus, (! nextNode) will evaluate true if nextNode is zero (false). Thus

```
if ( ! nextNode )
```

will evaluate true and the if statement will execute as long as nextNode points only to NULL (zero).

To most programmers, this is so idiomatic that

```
if ( ! nextNode )
```

really means "if nextNode doesn't yet point to anything…" and we don't much think through all the convoluted logic that makes that work.

In any case, the if statement executes by calling newNode, passing in theChar, and assigning the address that results to nextNode. Calling new immediately invokes the constructor, so stepping into this line brings us to the Node constructor on line 18. Once again, a message is printed on line 82), and we return from the constructor, assigning the address that is returned from new to the nextNode pointer of the first node.

Before leaving Insert, let's examine the this and the nextNode pointers. You should find that this has an address that is equal to the first address printed because we are now back in that first node. You should find that the nextNode pointer has the address of the object we just created. Sure enough, we now have a linked list with two objects in it.

Continuing causes us to return from Insert() back to main(), where the same logic is repeated to insert 'c', 'b', and once again 'b'.

If you don't want to work your way through the logic repeatedly, continue to step over these lines until you reach line 70. We are now ready to determine how many instances of 'b' exist in the program.

Step into this line of code. This takes you into Node::HowMany() on line 40, in which the parameter theChar has the value 'b'. On line 42 we'll initialize myCount to 0. On line 43 we test myChar, which has the value 'a', against theChar, which has the value 'b'. This test fails, so we fall through to line 45, where we test to see whether nextNode is nonzero; it is. This causes us to execute the body of the if statement:

```
return myCount + nextNode->HowMany(theChar);
```

Step into this line. You find yourself in HowMany() for the second node. Continue stepping. myChar is 'b' this time, and it thus matches theChar. We increment myCount and test nextNode. Again it is nonzero, so again we step in, this time to the third node in the list.

In the third node, myChar is 'c', so it does not match myChar; but nextNode is nonzero, so we step into the fourth node.

In the fourth node, mychar is 'b', and we increment myCount to 1. Why is it set to 1 and not to 2, given that this is the second node with 'b'? The answer is that myCount is local to this invocation of HowMany() and therefore can't know about the previous values. Again, nextNode is nonzero, so we now step into the fifth node.

Take a look at the this pointer and expand it in your local variables window. You are now looking at the local member variables for the fifth node object. myChar is 'b', and nextPointer is 0. Thus, we increment myCount; then the test for nextPointer fails, so we return myCount.

We thus return the value 1 to the call from the fourth node. This value is added to the myCount variable (also 1), summing to 2, and this value is now returned to the third node. The third node's myCount is 0, so the value 2 is now returned to the second node. Its myCount variable is 1, so 3 is returned to the first node. The first node's myCount is 0, so 3 is returned to main().

It is very important that you understand how this was accomplished. You might find that using pencil and paper and drawing a picture (see Figure 6.9) makes this easier to understand.

Figure 6.9

Walking the list to get the answer.

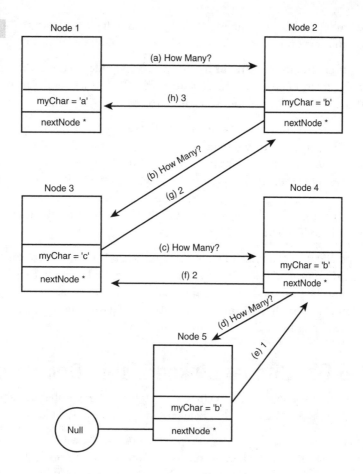

As you continue to step out of the function calls, you'll find yourself popping up through the calls to HowMany(), unwinding your way from Node 5 to 4, 3, 2, and back to Node 1. Step into and out of this set of calls repeatedly until you can match what is happening in your debugger to the diagram in Figure 6.9.

When this is comfortable, continue stepping over code lines until you get to the call to Display on line 74. Here you are calling Display() on pHead. Step into this method call and you'll be in Display() for your first node on line 32. Step into the method and note the address of the this pointer, which confirms that you are in the first Node in the list. myChar is printed on line 34 (printing 'a'), and the nextNode pointer is checked on line 45. It returns true, so Display() is called on the second node in the list.

Step into this call, and you are back at line 32. Step in and notice that the this pointer now reflects the address of the second node, as you'd expect. On line 34, the member variable myChar is printed ('b'), and once again we call Display(), this time on the third node.

This continues until the fifth node prints its value. Because the fifth node does not point to another node, the if statement fails, and we return through the various Display() method invocations, back to main().

On line 77 we call delete on pHead. To see what this does, place a break point on line 24 and go until the break point. You find yourself in the destructor of the head node. On line 26 we print the address of the first (head) node, and then on line 27 we test nextNode, which points to the second node. We delete that object, causing us to come to the destructor for the second node, where the logic is repeated. The second node deletes the third node, the third node deletes the fourth node, and the fourth node deletes the fifth.

The client of the linked list, in this case main(), never had to call HowMany() or Display() on any node except the head node, and it doesn't have to delete any node except the head node. The maintenance of the list is managed by the list itself. Commands such as Display() or delete are passed along the list as required, each node falling like a domino into the next in the list.

Using Our Simple Linked List in Decryptix!

We are just about ready to change the type of the member variable solution in the Game class. Until now, it has been an array; we want it to be a linked list.

Let's examine all the places we use Solution to see what our linked list must be able to accomplish, and whether our list of Nodes is up to the task.

Following are the lines in Game in which we refer to the solution:

```
theGame.Display(theGame.GetSolution());
int howManyInAnswer = howMany (solution, alpha[i]);
if ( thisGuess[i] == solution[i] )
```

That is, we must have the capability to retrieve the solution and display it, count the instances of a particular character in the solution, and retrieve the character at a given offset.

Rather than expose the workings of the Node object to the Game, I've chosen to create a small class that will serve as an interface to the nodes, which I'll call LinkedList. Listing 6.8 shows the declaration of the LinkedList class.

Listing 6.8   `LinkedList` Declared

```
0: include "nod0603.h"
1:
2:  class LinkedList
3:  {
4:  public:
5:      LinkedList();
6:      ~LinkedList();
7:      bool Add (char c, bool dupes = true);
8:      void Display () const { headNode->Display() }
9:      int HowMany (char c) const;
10:      char operator[] (int offset);
11: private:
12:      Node * headNode;
13:  };
```

To the client (in this case, Game), LinkedList *is* the linked list structure. The client is oblivious to the existence of nodes (note that headNode is private).

The best way to understand the implementation of these methods is to see them in action. Let's change Game to use a LinkedList as its solution, as shown in Listing 6.9.

6

Listing 6.9   The `Game` Class Declaration

```
0:  #include "List0606_LL.h"
1:
2:  class Game
3:  {
4:  public:
5:      Game ();
6:      ~Game () {}
7:      void Display (const LinkedList * pList) const
7a:      { pList->Display(); }
8:      const LinkedList &  GetSolution    () const { return solution; }
9:      void Play ();
10:      void Score (const char * thisGuess, int &
10a:          correct, int & position);
11:
12: private:
13:      int HowMany (const char * theString, char theChar);
14:
15:      bool duplicates;
16:      int howManyLetters;
17:      int howManyPositions;
18:      int round;
19:      LinkedList solution;
20:  };
```

`Game` is unchanged except for the last line, where the `solution` member variable is changed to type `LinkedList`.

When one class contains another, as `Game` contains `LinkedList`, it can do so by value or by reference. `LinkedList` contains `Node` by reference (see Figure 6.10).

Figure 6.10

Containing the node by reference.

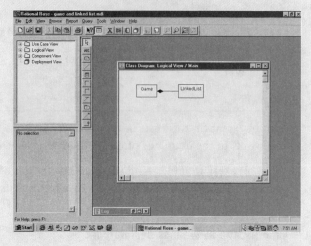

`Game`, on the other hand, contains `LinkedList` by value and is diagrammed in the UML as shown in Figure 6.11. The filled in diamond indicates *by value*.

Figure 6.11

Containing linked list by value.

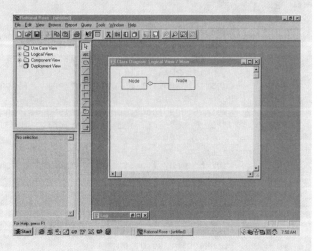

Run it!

Let's run through one play of Decryptix! and see how the `LinkedList` is used. Our driver program is unchanged, as shown in Listing 6.10. We begin by instantiating a `Game` object, which brings us into `Game`'s constructor as shown in Listing 6.11.

When you make an instance of an object, you are said to *instantiate* it.

 Note

To save room, I've left out the beginning of `Game`'s constructor, in which the member variables `howManyLetters`, `howManyPositions`, and `duplicates` are set because this logic is unchanged.

Listing 6.10 Decryptix!.cpp

```
0:   #include "def0514.h"
1:   #include "game0607.h"
2:
3:   int main()
4:   {
5:       cout << "Decryptix. (c)Copyright 1999 Liberty";
5a:          cout << Associates, Inc. Version 0.4\n\n" << endl;
6:       bool playAgain = true;
7:
8:       while ( playAgain )
9:       {
10:          char choice = ' ';
11:          Game theGame;
12:          theGame.Play();
13:
14:          cout << "\nThe answer: ";
15:          theGame.GetSolution().Display();
16:          cout << "\n\n" << endl;
17:
18:          while ( choice != 'y' && choice != 'n' )
19:          {
20:              cout << "\nPlay again (y/n): ";
21:              cin >> choice;
22:          }
```

continues

Listing 6.10   **continued**

```
23:
24:            playAgain = choice == 'y' ? true : false;
25:        }
26:
27:        return 0;
28:    }
```

Listing 6.11   **Implementing** Game

```
1:    Game::Game():
2:        round(1),
3:        howManyPositions(0),
4:        howManyLetters(0),
5:        duplicates(false)
6:    {
7:
8:    //...
9:
10:       srand( (unsigned)time( NULL ) );
11:
12:       for ( int i = 0; i < howManyPositions; )
13:       {
14:           int nextValue = rand() % (howManyLetters);
15:           char c = alpha[nextValue];
16:           if ( solution.Add(c, duplicates) )
17:               i++;
18:       }
19:
20:       cout << "Exiting constructor. List: ";
21:       solution.Display();
22:
23:    }
```

We pick up the logic on line 14, within the for loop in which we create our random numbers, turn them into characters on line 20, and then add them to solution on line 21. It is here, when we call solution.add(), that the logic of the LinkedList comes into play. This invokes LinkedList::Add(), as shown in Listing 6.12.

Listing 6.12   **Implementing** LinkedList

```
1:
2:    bool LinkedList::Add(char theChar, bool dupes)
3:    {
4:        bool inserted = false;
5:
6:        if ( ! headNode )
7:        {
```

```
 8:            headNode = new Node(theChar);
 9:            inserted = true;
10:         }
11:         else if ( dupes || HowMany(theChar) == 0 )
12:         {
13:             headNode->Insert(theChar);
14:             inserted = true;
15:         }
16:
17:         return inserted;
18:    }
19:
20:    int LinkedList::HowMany(char theChar) const
21:    {
22:         return headNode->HowMany(theChar);
23:    }
24:
25:    char LinkedList::offset(int offSetValue)
26:    {
27:        Node * pNode = headNode;
28:        for ( int i = 0; i < offSetValue && pNode; i++ )
29:            pNode = pNode->GetNext();
30:
31:        ASSERT ( pNode );
32:        char c =  pNode->GetChar();
33:        return c;
34:    }
35:
36:    char LinkedList::operator[](int offSetValue)
37:    {
38:        Node * pNode = headNode;
39:        for ( int i = 0; i < offSetValue && pNode; i++ )
40:            pNode = pNode->GetNext();
41:
42:        ASSERT ( pNode );
43:        char c =  pNode->GetChar();
44:        return c;
45:    }
```

On line 6, LinkedList checksto see whether it already has a headNode. To do this, it checks its headNode pointer, which was initialized to NULL in LinkedList's constructor. If that is pointer is still NULL, no headNode exists, so one is now created, passing in the character to be stored.

The constructor to Node was considered earlier (refer to Listing 6.3). Remember that the Node's member variable myChar is initialized with the character passed in (theChar), and its member variable nextNode is initialized with NULL as shown in Listing 6.13.

Listing 6.13 Node Constructor

```
0:  Node::Node(char theChar):
1:  myChar(theChar),nextNode(0)
2:  {
3:  }
```

This effectively adds the character to the linked list, storing it in the head node.

If there already is a HeadNode, (that is, the pointer is not NULL), we have a list already and must decide whether we want to add the character. If we are accepting duplicates or if the character does not appear in the list already (line 11), we add it by calling Insert on the headNode (line 13). I already described HeadNode()::Insert in Listing 6.3.

We determine whether the character is in the list on line 11 by calling LinkedList::HowMany(), as shown in Listing 6.14.

Listing 6.14 LinkedList's HowMany Method

```
0:  int LinkedList::HowMany(char theChar) const
1:  {
2:      return headNode->HowMany(theChar);
3:  }
```

As you can see, LinkedList does nothing but pass along the character to the headNode, calling the logic that was considered earlier (in Listing 6.3). The LinkedList method HowMany() is considered a *wrapper* method: It wraps around the Node::HowMany() method, encapsulating its interface, but delegating all the work to the encapsulated method.

wrapper   A class is a wrapper for another when it provides a public interface but delegates all the work to the contained class.

method   A method is a wrapper for another method when it provides an encapsulating interface to that method but delegates all the work to the wrapped method.

Playing the Game

After the solution member linked list is populated, the Game object is fully constructed and the next line in main() is a call to the Game's Play() method. This was considered earlier, and you probably remember that Play() solicits a guess from the player and then calls Game::Score().

Game::Score() was also considered earlier, but because solution is now a linked list, this is worth another look. I've reproduced Game::Score() in Listing 6.15 for your convenience.

Listing 6.15 **The `score` Method**

```
0:void Game::Score(const char * thisGuess, int & correct, int & position)
1: {
2:      correct = 0;
3:      position = 0;
4:
5:
6:      for ( int i = 0; i < howManyLetters; i++)
7:      {
8:          int howManyInGuess = HowMany(thisGuess, alpha[i]);
9:          int howManyInAnswer = solution.HowMany(alpha[i]);
10:     correct += howManyInGuess < howManyInAnswer ?
10a:            howManyInGuess : howManyInAnswer;
11:      }
12:
13:     for (  i = 0; i < howManyPositions; i++)
14:     {
15:         if ( thisGuess[i] == solution[i] )
16:             position++;
17:     }
18:
19:     ASSERT ( position <= correct )
20:
21: }
```

On line 9, we must determine how many times each character appears in `solution`. We do this by calling `HowMany()` on `solution`, passing in each character in turn. This calls `LinkedList::HowMany()`, which, as we just saw, calls `Node::HowMany()`.

On line 15, we compare the letter at each offset into `thisGuess` with the letter at the same offset in `solution`. The `Node` class does not provide an offset operator, but the `LinkedList` class must if we are to make this comparison.

Solving the Problem with a Member Method

You can solve this problem by implementing an `offset` method and calling that method by changing line 15 to read

```
15:         if ( thisGuess[i] == solution.offset(i) )
```

The implementation of the `offset` method is shown in Listing 6.16.

Listing 6.16 **The `offset` Operator**

```
0:  char LinkedList::offset(int offSetValue)
1:  {
2:      Node * pNode = headNode;
```

continues

Listing 6.16 continued

```
3:        for ( int i = 0; i < offSetValue && pNode; i++ )
4:            pNode = pNode->GetNext();
5:
6:        ASSERT ( pNode );
7:        char c =  pNode->GetChar();
8:        return c;
9:    }
```

The offset is passed into this method as a parameter. We make a new, local pointer, pNode, and we assign to that pointer the address that is currently held in headNode. Thus, both pointers now point to the same object on the heap, as shown in Figure 6.12.

The goal of the for loop on line 3 in Listing 6.16 is to tick through the linked list, starting at the head node, and find the node that corresponds to offSetValue.

As we tick through each node, we must also check that pNode continues to point to a valid node (that is, we have not reached the end of the list). This protects us from trying to get an offset that is too large for the list.

We put the test for whether the offset continues to point to a valid Node right into the for loop by adding it to the test condition:

```
i < offSetValue && pNode;
```

This tests that the counter i is not greater than the offset value that was passed in (that is, we're still ticking through the list) and that pNode has a nonzero (that is, non-NULL) value.

On line 4 we assign to pNode the address returned by GetNext(). The call to Node::GetNext() simply returns the address that is stored in that node's nextNode pointer. The net effect of this is that pNode now points to the next node in the list.

This for loop continues until i is no longer less than offSetValue. Thus, if offSetValue is 5, this for loop causes pNode to point to the sixth node in the list, just as you want it to.

On line 6, we assert that we are still pointing to a valid object (belt and suspenders!), on line 7 we extract from that node the character it holds, and on line 8 we return that character.

The net effect of all this is that if you call offset(5), you get back the character at the fifth offset: that is, the sixth character in the list.

This works great, but it isn't how arrays work. You never write

```
myArray.offset(5);
```

You write

```
myArray[5];
```

It would be nice if our linked list supported the same syntax.

Operator Overloading

C++ provides the capability for the designer of a class to give that class the same operators that are available in the built-in class, such as +, -, ==, <, >, and so forth. This is called *operator overloading*. The goal of operator overloading is to allow your class to behave as if it were a built-in type.

operator overloading   The ability to program operators such as plus (+) or assignment (=) for classes.

How You Accomplish Operator Overloading

C++ has a specific syntax dedicated to creating operators for your classes. We'll examine how the offset operator ([ ]) is overloaded because that is what we need right now in the code; we'll return to operator overloading throughout the book, however, because it is a powerful technique with many subtleties.

To create the offset operator, you use the following syntax:

```
char operator[](int offSetValue);
```

When you write solution[5], the compiler automatically converts this to solution.operator[].

The implementation for this overloaded operator is identical to the offset method shown in Listing 6.14, as illustrated in Listing 6.17. The only difference is in the signature of the method.

Listing 6.17   LinkedList's offset Operator

```
0:  char LinkedList::operator[](int offSetValue)
1:  {
2:      Node * pNode = headNode;
3:      for ( int i = 0; i < offSetValue && pNode; i++ )
4:          pNode = pNode->GetNext();
5:
6:      ASSERT ( pNode );
7:      char c =  pNode->GetChar();
8:      return c;
9:  }
```

As you can see, the body is identical; it is just the signature on line 0 that is different:

```
0:   char LinkedList::operator[](int offSetValue)
```

Once again, the return value is a `char`, but this time we see the keyword `operator`, followed by the operator we're overloading, and then the parameter that is needed by that operator.

You invoke this method by writing

```
solution[5];
```

which the compiler translates into

```
solution.operator[](5);
```

setting the parameter `offset` to the value passed in (5).

With this implementation in place, the `Play()` method can test the value of `solution[i]`, and thus the `Play()` method remains unchanged from when we were using arrays.

Passing Objects by Value

After the `Game` is fully constructed, we return to `main()`, where the `Play()` method is invoked. When we return from `Play()`, we see this line:

```
theGame.GetSolution().Display();
```

This causes the `Game`'s `GetSolution()` method to be called, returning a reference to a `LinkedList`; then the method `Display()` is called on that reference to a `LinkedList` object.

It is clearer to write

```
const LinkedList & linkedListConstantReference =
    theGame.GetSolution();
linkedListConstantReference.Display();
```

This compiles equally well and makes a bit more explicit what we're up to.

We declare `linkedListConstantReference` to be a reference to a constant `LinkedList` object because that is what `GetSolution()` is declared to return in Game.h:

```
class Game
{
//...

    const LinkedList &  GetSolution () const { return solution; }
//...
}
```

Let's pick this apart:

- `const`, `LinkedList`, and `&` together represent the return value: a reference to a constant `LinkedList` object.
- `GetSolution` is the name of the method, `GetSolution`.
- `()` is the parameter list, which in this case is empty.
- `const` declares this member method to be constant.
- `return solution` is the inline implementation, in which we return the member variable `solution`.

Because the return value is declared to be a constant reference to a `LinkedList`, we actually don't return `solution` itself. Instead, we return a constant reference to `solution`.

Note

The fact that we return a reference to a constant object limits what you can do with that object. For example, you can only call constant member methods using that reference. If the reference is to a constant object, you can't change that object, and calling a method that is not constant risks changing the object. The compiler enforces this constraint. We're fine here because the only method we call with this reference is `Display()`, which is a constant member method of `LinkedList`.

Why Is It a Reference?

Why bother returning the `LinkedList` object by reference at all? Why not just return it by value?

```
LinkedList GetSolution () const { return solution; }
```

This has the advantage of not being constant: You can do anything you want with this object. Because it is a copy of the original, you won't affect `solution` at all. The net effect in this case is the same: You can still call `Display`, only this time you'll call it on the copy.

The answer is that it is more expensive to make a copy, but to understand why, we must examine what happens when you pass an object by value, this is the subject of the next chapter, "The Canonical Methods."

The Canonical Methods

Method Overloading

In C++ it is legal to have more than one method with the same name, as long as the *signature* is different. Remember that the signature is the combination of the name and the list of parameters. Thus, methods can differ in their names, they can differ in their list of parameters, or they can differ in both.

The best way to illustrate this is with a few simple demonstration classes. After we've covered the concepts, we'll circle back and see how all this works with linked lists and nodes.

The Shape Classes

Let's start by imagining a Shape class. The following methods can all exist in our class:

```
class Shape
{
public:
    void CreateSquare(int side);
    void CreateRectangle(int side);
    void CreateRectangle(int width, int height);
    void CreateRectangle(Point upperLeft, Point lowerRight);
}
```

We can assume that CreateSquare(int side) makes a square whose sides are the size that is passed in as a parameter. CreateRectangle(int side), I've decided, will create a rectangle whose height is the size that is passed in and whose width will be twice its height. Notice that these two methods differ in name, but not in parameter list.

`CreateRectangle(int width, int height)` will create a rectangle based on two values, a width and height. Its signature differs from `CreateRectangle(int side)` by the number of parameters passed.

`CreateRectangle(Point upperLeft, Point lowerRight)` also creates a rectangle, but this time we pass in two `Point` objects—presumably, user-defined types that hold a specific location. This differs from `CreateRectangle(int width, int height)` not in the number of parameters, but rather in the type of the parameters.

All these methods can coexist in the same class declaration. This is a common practice among C++ programmers and can be very powerful.

Overloading Constructors

In fact, you can overload constructors as well as member methods. For example, we can imagine a `Rectangle` class rather than a `Shape` class. When we are ready to create a rectangle, we might want to pass in a single integer, a pair of integers, or a pair of points, just as we did previously. This is perfectly legal, and we can write

```
class Rectangle
{
    Rectangle(int side);
    Rectangle(int width, int height);
    Rectangle(Point upperLeft, Point lowerRight);
//...
}
```

This class now has three constructors. When we're ready to instantiate rectangles, we can use any of the three:

```
int main()
{
    //...
    Rectangle rect1(25);
    Rectangle rect2(30,50);
    Rectangle rect3(PointOne, PointTwo);
}
```

Presumably, in the early part of `main()` we created two point objects, `PointOne` and `PointTwo`, which are passed into the third constructor.

What if we want to create a rectangle without passing a value? We might decide that, by default, rectangles are 5×7 unless we indicate otherwise. For this, we use the default constructor. A *default constructor* is any constructor that takes no parameters.

The Miranda Methods

The default constructor is one of four methods that the compiler provides for you if you don't create them yourself:

- The default constructor
- The default destructor
- The copy constructor
- The assignment operator

I call these the *Miranda methods*: "You have the right to a constructor. If you can't afford a constructor, one will be supplied for you by the compiler, free of charge." Of course, like Miranda lawyers, the methods you get might or might not be good enough to meet your needs. If you want more control over the method, you'll have to supply your own. Let's look at what the Miranda methods are and what they do.

The Default Constructor

If you do not create a constructor for your class, the compiler will give you one implicitly. When objects of your class are created, it will call this implicit constructor. It turns out that the one that is provided by the compiler takes no parameters and does nothing at all.

Because the constructor that is provided for you by the compiler takes no parameters, many people think that the term *default constructor* refers to the constructor that is provided by the compiler. In fact, *any* constructor that takes no parameters— whether the compiler provides it or you write your own—is called a default constructor.

 default constructor—A constructor that takes no parameters.

Because your compiler provides a default constructor if you don't write a constructor, you might say that you get the default constructor *by default*.

For any nontrivial class, you *always* want to write your own constructor, even if it has no work to do. This is good programming practice, and it documents that you didn't just forget to create one, you intentionally created one that does nothing.

We'll add the default constructor to our class, as illustrated in Listing 7.1.

Listing 7.1   Illustrating the Default Constructor

```
0:  #include <iostream>
1:  using namespace std;
2:
3:  class Point
4:  {
5:  public:
6:      Point (int x, int y): itsX(x), itsY(y) {}
7:      ~Point(){}
8:      int GetX()const { return itsX;}
9:      int GetY()const { return itsY;}
10: private:
11:     int itsX;
12:     int itsY;
13: };
14:
15: class Rectangle
16: {
17: public:
18: Rectangle(): itsWidth(5), itsHeight(7){}
19: Rectangle(int side): itsWidth(side), itsHeight(side*2){}
20: Rectangle(int width, int height):itsWidth(width), itsHeight(height){}
21: Rectangle(Point upperLeft, Point lowerRight);
22: ~Rectangle(){}
23:     int GetWidth() const { return itsWidth; }
24:     int GetHeight() const { return itsHeight; }
25: private:
26:     int itsWidth;
27:     int itsHeight;
28: };
29:
30: Rectangle::Rectangle(Point upperLeft, Point lowerRight):
31: itsWidth(lowerRight.GetX() - upperLeft.GetX()),
32: itsHeight(lowerRight.GetY() - upperLeft.GetY())
33: {}
34:
35: int main()
36: {
37:     Point ul(5,5);
38:     Point lr(20,15);
39:
40:     Rectangle r1;
41:     Rectangle r2(3);
42:     Rectangle r3(7,12);
43:     Rectangle r4(ul,lr);
44:
45:     cout << "r1: " << r1.GetWidth() << "x" << r1.GetHeight() << endl;
46:     cout << "r2: " << r2.GetWidth() << "x" << r2.GetHeight() << endl;
```

```
47:      cout << "r3: " << r3.GetWidth() << "x" << r3.GetHeight() << endl;
48:      cout << "r4: " << r4.GetWidth() << "x" << r4.GetHeight() << endl;
49:
50:      return 0;
51:  }
```

Output

r1: 5x7
r2: 3x6
r3: 7x12
r4: 15x10

Analysis

We begin at line 3 by creating a `Point` class. This class manages an x and y offset on the screen, where the lower-left corner is `0,0` and we count up pixel by pixel as we head up and to the right. Figure 7.1 illustrates a rectangle and its `Point` coordinates.

Figure 7.1

Illustrating point coordinates.

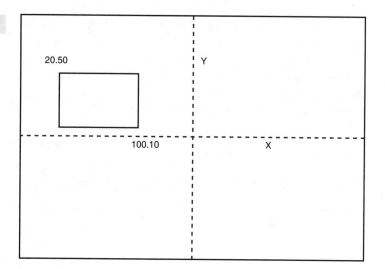

The `Point` constructor on line 2 takes as its argument an x and y offset and initializes its member variables. The `Accessor` functions that are shown on lines 8 and 9 simply return these values.

The `Rectangle` class, shown on lines 15–28, is as we described previously, complete with four overloaded constructors. The default constructor on line 18 initializes the member variables `itsWidth` to 5 and `itsHeight` to 7.

The second constructor, on line 19, accepts a single value and creates a rectangle twice as wide as it is tall. The third `Rectangle` takes two values, one for the height and one for the width. Note that all these methods are shown inline to save space. The fourth constructor, on line 21, is a bit more complex and is shown out of line, just below the class definition on lines 30–33. This initializes `itsWidth` with the difference between the x values of the upper-left point and the lower-right.

The destructor on line 22 does nothing, but it is included for the reasons stated: When I create constructors I always create the destructor.

In `main()` I create two points (line 37), initializing them with the values 5,5 and 20,15. These are used as arguments to the `Rectangle` constructor on line 43. The other constructors are shown on lines 40–42. Note that the call to the default constructor on line 40 does not require the use of parentheses at all. When you invoke the default constructor, you can leave off the parentheses. This is unusual, but it was implemented to make the creation of objects of user-defined classes more like the creation of simple variables such as integers.

The output reflects that each of these constructors operated as expected.

When Do You Get a Compiler-Supplied Constructor?

I said earlier that the compiler creates a default constructor for you if you don't create your own. This is true, but if you create *any* constructor, the compiler does *not* provide a constructor for you. Because we have created a `Rectangle` constructor that takes arguments (one integer, two integers, or two points), the compiler does not give us a default constructor; if we want one, we must create it explicitly, as shown at line 18.

The Default Destructor

Just to confuse you further, the compiler creates a destructor for you if you don't create one yourself—the *default destructor*. No destructors take any parameters, so it turns out that the one that is provided by the compiler doesn't either; but in this case the term *default* refers to what the compiler provides for you.

default destructor—The destructor provided by the compiler. The default destructor does nothing.

I've explicitly created my own default constructor, and having written a destructor, I won't get the default destructor.

This is unnecessarily confusing because we use the term *default* in two different ways, but that is how C++ programmers talk about it, so you might want to get it straight.

default—Something you get when you don't specify otherwise. Thus, a destructor that is provided if you don't specify one is the default destructor.

When you create an object of a call, you call the constructor and specify the parameters. If you call a constructor that takes no arguments, it is the default constructor.

To recap: The default constructor is one that takes no parameters, regardless of whether you write your own or the compiler provides one for you by default. If you *do* write any constructors, the compiler does not create a default constructor for you, so you must create your own.

The default destructor, on the other hand, is the one that is provided by the compiler. If you write your own, it is not called the default destructor.

The default destructor does nothing, as was the case with the one we wrote ourselves:

```
~Rectangle(){}
```

As a rule, if I write any constructors, I also always write my own destructors—even if they do nothing. I do so to remind myself that I intended for the destructor to do nothing, and that I've explicitly created one that does nothing. In fact, doing nothing is something I do quite well.

Of course, if I allocate memory, I can use my nifty destructor to clean up after that memory and thus avoid memory leaks.

The Copy Constructor

All this leads us to the copy constructor, which is called when we copy an object by value (as we propose to do with LinkedList). Remember the LinkedList? This is a chapter about the LinkedList (with thanks to Arlo Guthrie).

Because the linked list copy constructor is a bit tricky, let's stay with our Rectangle class a bit longer. To make the next point clear, Listing 7.2 modifies the Rectangle class to store a pair of Point objects as member variables. Let's give this class a copy constructor and see what it does.

Listing 7.2   The Point Class Declaration

```
1:    #include <iostream>
2:    using namespace std;
3:
4:    class Point      // holds x,y coordinates
5:    {
6:    public:
7:        Point (int x, int y);
8:        Point (const Point & rhs);
9:        ~Point()
10:       {
11:           cout << "In Point destructor(";
12:           cout << this << ")" << endl;
13:       }
14:       void SetX(int x) { itsX = x; }
15:       void SetY(int y) { itsY = y; }
16:       int GetX()const { return itsX;}
17:       int GetY()const { return itsY;}
18:   private:
19:       int itsX;
20:       int itsY;
21:   };    // end of Point class declaration
22:
23:   class  Rectangle
24:   {
25:   public:
26:
27:       Rectangle (int top, int left, int bottom, int right);
28:       Rectangle(const Rectangle& rhs);
29:       ~Rectangle()
30:       {
31:           cout << "In Rectangle destructor (";
32:           cout << this << ")" << endl;
33:       }
34:
35:
36:       Point GetUpperLeft() const { return itsUpperLeft; }
37:       Point GetLowerRight() const { return itsLowerRight; }
38:       int GetDepth() const { return itsDepth;  }
39:
40:
41:       int GetWidth() const;
42:       int GetHeight() const;
43:       int GetArea() const;
44:
45:   private:
46:       Point itsUpperLeft;
47:       Point itsLowerRight;
48:
49:       int itsDepth;
50:
```

```
51:    };
52:
53:    int GetArea(Rectangle r)
54:    {
55:        cout << "\nIn GetArea()..." << endl;
56:        return r.GetArea();
57:    }
58:
59:    int GetAreaByRef(const Rectangle& rectRef)
60:    {
61:        cout << "In GetAreaByRef(const Rectangle&)..." << endl;
62:        return rectRef.GetArea();
63:    }
64:
65:    int GetAreaByRef(const Rectangle * const pRect)
66:    {
67:        cout << "In GetAreaByRef(const Rectangle * const)...";
68:        cout << endl;
69:        return pRect->GetArea();
70:    }
71:
72:    Rectangle::Rectangle(int top, int left, int bottom, int right):
73:    itsUpperLeft(left,top),
74:    itsLowerRight(right,bottom)
75:    {
76:        cout << "In rectangle constructor(";
77:        cout << this << ")\n" << endl;
78:    }
79:
80:    Rectangle::Rectangle(const Rectangle & rhs):
81:    itsLowerRight(rhs.GetLowerRight()),
82:    itsUpperLeft(rhs.GetUpperLeft()),
83:    itsDepth(rhs.GetDepth())
84:    {
85:        cout << "In Rectangle copy constructor(";
86:        cout << this << ")\n" << endl;
87:    }
88:
89:    int Rectangle::GetWidth() const
90:    {
91:        int rightX = itsLowerRight.GetX();
92:        int leftX = itsUpperLeft.GetX();
93:        int width = rightX - leftX;
94:        cout << "GetWidth. rightX: " << rightX;
95:        cout << " leftX:   " << leftX << ".  Width:   ";
96:        cout << width << endl;
97:        return width;
98:    }
99:
100:   int Rectangle::GetHeight() const
101:   {
```

continues

Listing 7.2   continued

```
102:            int topY = itsUpperLeft.GetY();
103:            int bottomY = itsLowerRight.GetY();
104:            int height = topY - bottomY;
105:            cout << "GetHeight. topY: " << topY << " bottomY: ";
106:            cout << bottomY << ".  Height: " << height << endl;
107:            return height;
108:    }
109:
110:    // compute area of the rectangle by finding corners,
111:    // establish width and height and then multiply
112:    int Rectangle::GetArea() const
113:    {
114:        int Width = GetWidth();
115:        int Height = GetHeight();
116:        return (Width * Height);
117:    }
118:
119:    Point::Point (int x, int y):
120:    itsX(x),
121:    itsY(y)
122:    {
123:        cout << "In Point constructor(";
124:        cout << this << ")" << endl;
125:    }
126:
127:    Point::Point(const Point & rhs):
128:    itsX(rhs.GetX()),
129:    itsY(rhs.GetY())
130:    {
131:        cout << "In Point copy constructor(";
132:        cout << this << ")" << endl;
133:    }
134:
135:    int main()
136:    {
137:        cout << "Constructing the rectangle..." << endl;
138:        Rectangle r1 (100, 20, 50, 80 );
139:
140:        cout << "\nCalling GetArea()..." << endl;
141:        cout << "r1 area: " << GetArea(r1);
142:        cout << "\n" << endl;
143:
144:
145:        cout << "Calling GetAreaByRef(const Rectangle&)...";
146:        cout << endl;
147:        cout << "r1 area: " << GetAreaByRef(r1);
148:        cout << "\n" << endl;
149:
150:
151:        cout << "Calling GetAreaByRef(const Rectangle * const)...";
```

```
152:         cout << endl;
153:         cout << "r1 area: " << GetAreaByRef(&r1) << "\n" << endl;
154:
155:         return 0;
156:     }
```

Output

Constructing the rectangle...
In Point constructor(0012FF60)
In Point constructor(0012FF68)
In rectangle constructor(0012FF60)

Calling GetArea()...
In Point copy constructor(0012FEE8)
In Point copy constructor(0012FEF0)
In Rectangle copy constructor(0012FEE8)

In GetArea()...
GetWidth. rightX: 80 leftX: 20. Width: 60
GetHeight. topY: 100 bottomY: 50. Height: 50
In Rectangle destructor (0012FEE8)
In Point destructor(0012FEF0)
In Point destructor(0012FEE8)
r1 area: 3000

Calling GetAreaByRef(const Rectangle&)...
In GetAreaByRef(const Rectangle&)...
GetWidth. rightX: 80 leftX: 20. Width: 60
GetHeight. topY: 100 bottomY: 50. Height: 50
r1 area: 3000

Calling GetAreaByRef(const Rectangle * const)...
In GetAreaByRef(const Rectangle * const)...
GetWidth. rightX: 80 leftX: 20. Width: 60
GetHeight. topY: 100 bottomY: 50. Height: 50
r1 area: 3000

In Rectangle destructor (0012FF60)
In Point destructor(0012FF68)
In Point destructor(0012FF60)

Analysis

The purpose of this code is to explore what happens when you pass an object by value or by reference into a method. The object we're passing is a Rectangle that consists of an integer and a pair of Point objects. The Point objects, in turn, consist of two integers.

Let's cut to the chase: When you pass an object by value, the compiler makes a temporary copy of it by calling the copy constructor.

When we walk through this code, you'll find that when you pass Rectangle by value, its copy constructor is called to make the copy. In that copy, the Point member variables must be copied, so their copy constructors are called. Later, the copy must be destroyed, so the Rectangle's destructor and the Point's destructor must be called.

You can see the effect of this by examining the output. The first line shows the construction of the rectangle instantiated in main(). We see two points constructed along with the rectangle. The Point constructor's this pointer has the same address as the rectangle's constructor because the point is part of the rectangle. You can imagine that in memory the rectangle looks like Figure 7.2.

Figure 7.2

The rectangle in memory.

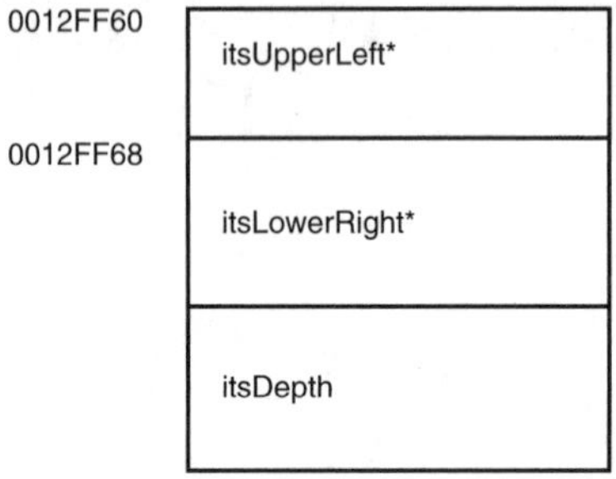

The next part of the output shows the call to GetArea, which is immediately followed by a call to the Point copy constructor. This creates a new point at memory location 0012FEE8, a second Point constructor (making a copy of itsLowerRight), and then a call to the Rectangle copy constructor.

The output continues from within GetArea(), printing the value of the area. Then, when we leave GetArea(), we see the destructor run for the temporary copies that are made. Checking the address, we confirm that it is the copies that are being destroyed.

The output goes on to show calls into GetAreaByRef, first passing in a reference to the Rectangle, and then a pointer to the Rectangle; in neither case is a copy made.

This is very expensive: It consumes memory and time. When you pass by reference, you avoid all these copies and save that time and memory.

Let's briefly walk through the example and see how all this works. We begin in main() at line 135. On line 138, we instantiate an instance of a Rectangle class, passing in the coordinates 100,20,50,80, representing the top-left and bottom-right corners of the rectangle.

Put a break point on this line and run to the break point. Stepping into the constructor (line 80), we see the member variables `itsUpperLeft` and `itsLowerRight` being initialized. If we step in once more, we go to the `Point` constructor (line 119), where `itsUpperLeft` is constructed. We will step into the `Point` constructor twice before returning to the body of the `Rectangle` constructor.

After `r1` is constructed, program flow returns to `main` (line 140), where we invoke `GetArea`, passing in `r1` (line 141). Stepping in brings us to the copy constructor. We don't call the copy constructor explicitly, but the compiler calls it. Why? Because we've said that we want to pass `Rectangle` by value, and that is a signal to the compiler that a copy must be made. Implicit copies are made by calls to the copy constructor.

Try this experiment: Comment out the copy constructor, both in the declaration of the `Rectangle` class and in the implementation. Run the program again and examine the output. You won't see a call to the `Rectangle` copy constructor (you deleted it), but you will see a call to the `Point` copy constructor. Who's calling `Point`'s copy constructor? Clearly, a copy of the `Rectangle` is being created; but where?

This is the Miranda copy constructor at work: The compiler has written a hidden copy constructor for you.

The hidden copy constructor does nothing but make a bitwise copy of each member variable in the class. In this case, it works just as well as the one we've written. To understand why this is not good enough for all purposes, we'll need to modify `Rectangle`. Before we do, though, let's finish stepping through this program.

We want to uncomment out the `Rectangle` copy constructor so that we are back to having our own explicit copy constructor.

 Note   To uncomment out the code, just remove the comments.

When we invoke `GetArea` and pass in `r1`, program flow jumps to the `Rectangle` copy constructor (line 80). The member variable `itsLowerRight` is constructed, passing in the value that is returned from the original's value, returned by `GetLowerRight()`. You'll step into `Rectangle::GetLowerRight` (line 37), which returns a `Point` by value. Hey! Presto! a `Point` copy constructor is called, as is reflected in the output.

After the copy of the `Rectangle` is complete, program flow continues in `GetArea()` (line 53). When this method returns (line 56), the copy must be destroyed. Program flow jumps to the `Rectangle` destructor (line 29), and from there to the `Point` destructor (line 9).

After all the temporaries are destroyed, we pick up back in main() (line 143). We now call GetAreaByRef, passing in a reference to a Rectangle object.

We actually pass in a *constant* reference—a reference to a constant object. This means that we can only call const methods on that object, which is fine because that is what we intend to do. Step into the call to GetAreaByRef. Zoom! You're in the method without a stop over in the copy constructor. Because we're passing by reference, no copy is made, so there is no call to the copy constructor.

When this concludes, we return to main() (line 151) and are ready to call GetAreaByRef() again, this time passing in a pointer.

There are two interesting things to note about this second call (line 153). First, GetAreaByRef is a global method: It is not part of any class. This was true for GetArea() and, of course, for main() as well. However, GetAreaByRef() is over-loaded. You can overload any global method, just as you can a member method, as long as the signature is different. Because the first instance uses a constant reference and the second uses a constant pointer to a constant object, the compiler can tell which you mean to invoke by the type of argument you provide. That is, in the first case main sends in the rectangle (line 147), and in the second instance main() sends in the *address* of the rectangle (line 153).

The second thing to note is that we see the keyword const used twice in this declaration. The first const says that the Rectangle to which you are pointing is constant. This means that you can't use this pointer to modify that Rectangle. In other words, you can only call constant methods. This is exactly like the use of const in the reference.

The second const modifies the pointer itself, meaning that you can't have this pointer point to anything else. This use of const is implied in all references because they can never be reassigned.

> - A constant pointer cannot be reassigned.
> - A pointer to a constant object cannot change that object.
> - A constant pointer to a constant object cannot be reassigned, nor can it be used to modify the object.
> - A reference to a constant object cannot change the object.
> - A reference to a constant object is often called a constant reference, but it is the object that is constant. All references are themselves constant and need no such designation!

> This bears special attention because it is contradictory and confusing. A *constant pointer* means that the pointer itself is constant. A *constant reference* is programmer shorthand for a reference to a constant object.

You can tell what the keyword const refers to in a pointer declaration by drawing an imaginary dotted line down through the asterisk. If the const is to the right of the line, it is modifying the pointer; if it is to the left of the line, it is modifying the object itself.

The pointer we are passing in to GetAreaByRef is both a constant pointer and a pointer to a constant object. You can't reassign this pointer to point to a different object, and you can't use this pointer to modify the object. We call such a pointer a *constant pointer to a constant object*.

When we invoke GetAreaByRef by passing in the pointer, no copy constructor is called.

Why Isn't the Default Copy Constructor Sufficient?

To see why the default copy constructor is insufficient, we must modify the Rectangle class. Listing 7.3 shows the new code.

 Warning   As shown here, this code will crash.

Listing 7.3   Dangerous Code

```
1:    #include <iostream>
2:    using namespace std;
3:
4:    class Point     // holds x,y coordinates
5:    {
6:    public:
7:        Point (int x, int y);
8:        Point (const Point & rhs);
9:        ~Point()
10:       {
11:           cout << "In Point destructor(";
12:           cout << this << ")" << endl;
13:       }
14:       void SetX(int x) { itsX = x; }
15:       void SetY(int y) { itsY = y; }
```

continues

Listing 7.3   continued

```
16:          int GetX()const { return itsX;}
17:          int GetY()const { return itsY;}
18:     private:
19:          int itsX;
20:          int itsY;
21:     };    // end of Point class declaration
22:
23:     class  Rectangle
24:     {
25:     public:
26:
27:          Rectangle (int top, int left, int bottom, int right);
28:     //     Rectangle(const Rectangle& rhs);
29:          ~Rectangle()
30:          {
31:               cout << "In Rectangle destructor (";
32:               cout << this << ")" << endl;
33:               delete itsUpperLeft;
34:               delete itsLowerRight;
35:          }
36:
37:
38:          Point * GetUpperLeft() const { return itsUpperLeft; }
39:          Point * GetLowerRight() const { return itsLowerRight; }
40:          int GetDepth() const { return itsDepth;   }
41:
42:
43:          int GetWidth() const;
44:          int GetHeight() const;
45:          int GetArea() const;
46:
47:     private:
48:          Point * itsUpperLeft;
49:          Point *  itsLowerRight;
50:
51:          int itsDepth;
52:
53:     };
54:
55:     int GetArea(Rectangle r)
56:     {
57:          cout << "\nIn GetArea()..." << endl;
58:          return r.GetArea();
59:     }
60:
61:     int GetAreaByRef(const Rectangle& rectRef)
62:     {
63:          cout << "In GetAreaByRef(const Rectangle&)..." << endl;
64:          return rectRef.GetArea();
65:     }
```

```
66:
67:    int GetAreaByRef(const Rectangle * const pRect)
68:    {
69:        cout << "In GetAreaByRef(const Rectangle * const)...";
70:        cout << endl;
71:        return pRect->GetArea();
72:    }
73:
74:    Rectangle::Rectangle(int top, int left, int bottom, int right):
75:    itsUpperLeft(new Point (left,top)),
76:    itsLowerRight(new Point(right,bottom))
77:    {
78:        cout << "In rectangle constructor(";
79:        cout << this << ")\n" << endl;
80:    }
81:
82:    /*
83:    Rectangle::Rectangle(const Rectangle & rhs):
84:    itsLowerRight(new Point(*rhs.GetLowerRight())),
85:    itsUpperLeft(new Point(*rhs.GetUpperLeft())),
86:    itsDepth(rhs.GetDepth())
87:    {
88:        cout << "In Rectangle copy constructor(";
89:        cout << this << ")\n" << endl;
90:    }
91:    */
92:
93:    int Rectangle::GetWidth() const
94:    {
95:        int rightX = itsLowerRight->GetX();
96:        int leftX = itsUpperLeft->GetX();
97:        int width = rightX - leftX;
98:        cout << "GetWidth. rightX: " << rightX;
99:        cout << " leftX:   " << leftX << ".  Width:  ";
100:        cout << width << endl;
101:        return width;
102:    }
103:
104:    int Rectangle::GetHeight() const
105:    {
106:        int topY = itsUpperLeft->GetY();
107:        int bottomY = itsLowerRight->GetY();
108:        int height = topY - bottomY;
109:        cout << "GetHeight. topY: " << topY << " bottomY: ";
110:        cout << bottomY << ".  Height: " << height << endl;
111:        return height;
112:    }
113:
114:    // compute area of the rectangle by finding corners,
115:    // establish width and height and then multiply
```

continues

Listing 7.3   continued

```
116:    int Rectangle::GetArea() const
117:    {
118:           int Width = GetWidth();
119:           int Height = GetHeight();
120:           return (Width * Height);
121:    }
122:
123:    Point::Point (int x, int y):
124:    itsX(x),
125:    itsY(y)
126:    {
127:        cout << "In Point constructor(";
128:        cout << this << ")" << endl;
129:    }
130:
131:    Point::Point(const Point & rhs):
132:    itsX(rhs.GetX()),
133:    itsY(rhs.GetY())
134:    {
135:        cout << "In Point copy constructor(";
136:        cout << this << ")" << endl;
137:    }
138:
139:    int main()
140:    {
141:        cout << "Constructing the rectangle..." << endl;
142:        Rectangle r1 (100, 20, 50, 80 );
143:
144:        cout << "\nCalling GetArea()..." << endl;
145:        cout << "r1 area: " << GetArea(r1);
146:        cout << "\n" << endl;
147:
148:
149:        cout << "Calling GetAreaByRef(const Rectangle&)...";
150:        cout << endl;
151:        cout << "r1 area: " << GetAreaByRef(r1);
152:        cout << "\n" << endl;
153:
154:
155:        cout << "Calling GetAreaByRef(const Rectangle * const)...";
156:        cout << endl;
157:        cout << "r1 area: " << GetAreaByRef(&r1) << "\n" << endl;
158:
159:        return 0;
160:    }
```

Output

Constructing the rectangle...
In Point constructor(00481D10)

```
In Point constructor(00481B50)
In rectangle constructor(0012FF68)


Calling GetArea()...

In GetArea()...
GetWidth. rightX: 80 leftX:   20.  Width:  60
GetHeight. topY: 100 bottomY: 50.  Height: 50
In Rectangle destructor (0012FF0C)
In Point destructor(00481D10)
In Point destructor(00481B50)
r1 area: 3000

Calling GetAreaByRef(const Rectangle&)...
In GetAreaByRef(const Rectangle&)...
GetWidth. rightX: -572662307 leftX:    -572662307.  Width:  0
GetHeight. topY: -572662307 bottomY: -572662307.  Height: 0
r1 area: 0

Calling GetAreaByRef(const Rectangle * const)...
In GetAreaByRef(const Rectangle * const)...
GetWidth. rightX: -572662307 leftX:    -572662307.  Width:  0
GetHeight. topY: -572662307 bottomY: -572662307.  Height: 0
r1 area: 0

In Rectangle destructor (0012FF68)
In Point destructor(00481D10)
```

7

Analysis

The output reflects that garbage values have been introduced about halfway through this program. You will almost certainly find that this program, running as shown, crashes. Why?

Let's examine the changes that were made. `Rectangle` no longer holds two `Point` objects by value. Instead, it holds pointers to the `Point` objects (line 48). This is not at all an unusual construct. It enables you to create constructors that do not initialize the `Point` pointers, and it just creates a rectangle whose pointers are null.

The member methods must now interact with the `Point` objects using pointer syntax, but that is not burdensome. The `Rectangle` constructor, of course, must allocate memory for the `Point` members, as shown in the constructor (line 74). In the initialization routine, `Rectangle` initializes each member pointer by invoking `new` on `Point`, thus allocating memory on the heap. For example

```
75:     itsUpperLeft(new Point (left,top)),
```

This creates a new `Point` object, passing in `left` and `top` to the `Point` constructor, and then initializes `itsUpperLeft` to the address that is returned by `new`.

All this works just fine, but when we call `GetArea` and pass in `r1`, a copy of `r1` must be created, as was illustrated earlier. Because we've commented out the copy constructor, the default copy constructor—which is provided by the compiler—is called.

Remember that the default copy constructor does nothing more than a *bitwise* (or *shallow*) copy.

A *shallow copy* (also called a *bitwise* copy) makes a copy of each member variable, bit by bit.

This means that the new copy will have a pointer called `itsUpperLeft`, which is identical to the pointer in the original object. Both will contain the same address; therefore, both will point to the same object in memory, as shown in Figure 7.3.

Figure 7.3

Using the default copy constructor.

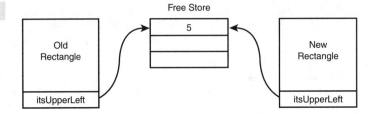

When we return from `GetArea()`, the `Rectangle`'s destructor is run to destroy the copy. Because `Rectangle` now allocates memory for the `Point` objects, its destructor must delete the `Point` objects to avoid a memory leak (line 33). This is normally fine, but the shallow copy means that the temporary `Rectangle` deletes the same `Point` objects that are pointed to by the original `Rectangle` (see Figure 7.4).

Figure 7.4

Creating a stray pointer.

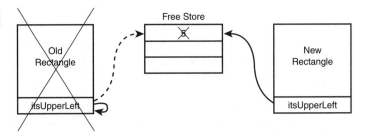

This is a disaster waiting to happen. The first time the original `Rectangle` object uses its `Pointer` to `itsUpperLeft`, the program will crash. Even if it doesn't crash, the pointer is now pointing to garbage in memory, and when we try to retrieve the values, we get back whatever happens to be in that memory.

Note You might get lucky and find that the values you expect are returned, which means that the compiler hasn't reused that memory. This is a Pyrrhic victory, however, because the compiler *can* reuse that memory at any time. In fact, this is no victory at all: It only means that your program will crash unpredictably, making it much harder to debug.

Writing Your Own Copy Constructor

This is why we write our own copy constructor. We want to ensure that we do a *deep copy*, allocating new memory for each object that is pointed to. Thus, when we return from GetArea(), the *copy* of the points are deleted, not the original points (as illustrated in Figure 7.5).

 deep copy—A copy that allocates memory and makes a duplicate rather than an alias.

Figure 7.5

Deep copy illustrated.

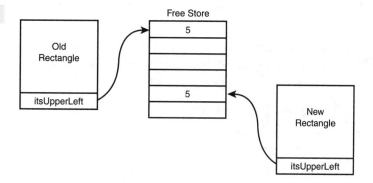

To see this, uncomment the copy constructor (line 28) and its implementation (line 83). In the implementation of the copy constructor, we now allocate a new Point object (line 84) and pass into that object the object that is returned by calling GetLowerRight (which returns a pointer) and dereferencing it.

Thus, what is passed to the constructor is a Point object, which invokes the Point's copy constructor explicitly. It is as if we had written

```
Point * pTemp = rhs.GetLowerRight(); // get the pointer
const Point & pRef = *pTemp; // derefernece
itsLowerRight = new Point (pRef); // create memory and initialize
```

when actually we've combined all these steps into a single initialization.

Recompile and run the program. This time it works as expected.

The Assignment Operator

Before we leave this topic, let's take a look at the fourth Miranda method, the assignment operator. You might want to assign one rectangle to another:

```
Rectangle a(5,10,15,20);
Rectangle b(20,30,10,50);
// ... use b for a while
b = a;  // assignment
```

The default assignment operator that is provided by the compiler makes a shallow copy, so the same concerns we had about the copy constructor apply here as well. If the two objects end up with pointers that point to the same memory, when one of the rectangles is destroyed, the other is made invalid. When the function ends, both destructors are called. Whichever is called last causes a memory protection failure because it will try to delete an area of already-deleted memory.

There is an additional area of concern. Rectangle b has memory allocated for its existing variables that must not be lost, so we might want to clean up that memory before we make the assignment. As you'll see in a moment, this brings its own dangers.

I've rewritten the Rectangle class to include an assignment operator, and I've simplified the driver program so that we can focus on what happens when you assign one Rectangle to another. Listing 7.4 illustrates this.

Listing 7.4   Assignment Operator Demonstrated

```
0:   #include <iostream>
1:   using namespace std;
2:
3:   class Point      // holds x,y coordinates
4:   {
5:   public:
6:       Point (int x, int y);
7:       Point (const Point & rhs);
8:       ~Point()
9:       {
10:          cout << "In Point destructor(";
11:          cout << this << ")" << endl;
12:       }
13:      void SetX(int x) { itsX = x; }
14:      void SetY(int y) { itsY = y; }
15:      int GetX()const { return itsX;}
16:      int GetY()const { return itsY;}
17:
18:      Point & operator=(const Point & rhs);
19:   private:
20:       int itsX;
```

```
21:        int itsY;
22:    };     // end of Point class declaration
23:
24:    class  Rectangle
25:    {
26:    public:
27:        Rectangle (int top, int left, int bottom, int right);
28:        Rectangle(const Rectangle& rhs);
29:        ~Rectangle()
30:        {
31:            cout << "In Rectangle destructor (";
32:            cout << this << ")" << endl;
33:            delete itsUpperLeft;
34:            delete itsLowerRight;
35:        }
36:
37:        Point * GetUpperLeft() const { return itsUpperLeft; }
38:        Point * GetLowerRight() const { return itsLowerRight; }
39:        int GetDepth() const { return itsDepth;  }
40:
41:        Rectangle & operator=(const Rectangle & rhs);
42:
43:        int GetWidth() const;
44:        int GetHeight() const;
45:        int GetArea() const;
46:
47:    private:
48:        Point * itsUpperLeft;
49:        Point * itsLowerRight;
50:        int itsDepth;
51:    };
52:
53:    Rectangle::Rectangle
54:    (
55:        int top,
56:        int left,
57:        int bottom,
58:        int right
59:    ):
60:    itsUpperLeft(new Point (left,top)),
61:    itsLowerRight(new Point(right,bottom))
62:    {
63:        cout << "In rectangle constructor(";
64:        cout << this << ")\n" << endl;
65:    }
66:
67:    Rectangle::Rectangle(const Rectangle & rhs):
68:    itsLowerRight(new Point(*rhs.GetLowerRight())),
69:    itsUpperLeft(new Point(*rhs.GetUpperLeft())),
```

continues

Listing 7.4   continued

```
70:    itsDepth(rhs.GetDepth())
71:    {
72:        cout << "In Rectangle copy constructor(";
73:        cout << this << ")\n" << endl;
74:    }
75:
76:    int Rectangle::GetWidth() const
77:    {
78:        int rightX = itsLowerRight->GetX();
79:        int leftX = itsUpperLeft->GetX();
80:        int width = rightX - leftX;
81:        return width;
82:    }
83:
84:    int Rectangle::GetHeight() const
85:    {
86:        int topY = itsUpperLeft->GetY();
87:        int bottomY = itsLowerRight->GetY();
88:        int height = topY - bottomY;
89:        return height;
90:    }
91:
92:    // compute area of the rectangle by finding corners,
93:    // establish width and height and then multiply
94:    int Rectangle::GetArea() const
95:    {
96:        int Width = GetWidth();
97:        int Height = GetHeight();
98:        return (Width * Height);
99:    }
100:
101:    Rectangle & Rectangle::operator =(const Rectangle& rhs)
102:    {
103:        cout << "In Rectangle assignment operator...\n";
104:
105:        if ( this != &rhs )
106:        {
107:            itsDepth = rhs.itsDepth;
108:            delete itsUpperLeft;
109:            itsUpperLeft = new Point(*rhs.itsUpperLeft);
110:            *itsLowerRight = *rhs.itsLowerRight;
111:        }
112:        return *this;
113:    }
114:
115:    Point::Point (int x, int y):
116:    itsX(x),
117:    itsY(y)
118:    {
119:        cout << "In Point constructor(";
```

```
120:        cout << this << ")" << endl;
121:    }
122:
123:    Point::Point(const Point & rhs):
124:    itsX(rhs.GetX()),
125:    itsY(rhs.GetY())
126:    {
127:        cout << "In Point copy constructor(";
128:        cout << this << ")" << endl;
129:    }
130:
131:    Point & Point::operator =(const Point & rhs)
132:    {
133:        cout << "In Point assignment operator...\n";
134:
135:        if ( this != &rhs )
136:        {
137:            itsX = rhs.itsX;
138:            itsY = rhs.itsY;
139:        }
140:        return *this;
141:    }
142:
143:    int main()
144:    {
145:        cout << "Constructing the rectangles. r1..." << endl;
146:        Rectangle r1 (100, 20, 50, 80 );
147:        cout << "r2..." << endl;
148:        Rectangle r2 (50, 10, 25, 40);
149:
150:        cout << "r1 area: " << r1.GetArea() << endl;
151:        cout << "r2 area: " << r2.GetArea() << endl;
152:
153:        cout << "\nAssigning r2 = r1...\n";
154:        cout << "\n" << endl;
155:
156:        r2 = r1;
157:
158:        cout << "\nr1 area: " << r1.GetArea() << endl;
159:        cout << "r2 area: " << r2.GetArea() << "\n" << endl;
160:
161:        cout << "Exiting and deleting the rectangles...\n";
162:
163:        return 0;
164:    }
```

Output

```
Constructing the rectangles. r1...
In Point constructor(00481D10)
In Point constructor(00481B50)
In rectangle constructor(0012FF68)
```

```
r2...
In Point constructor(00481B10)
In Point constructor(00481AD0)
In rectangle constructor(0012FF5C)

r1 area: 3000
r2 area: 750

Assigning r2 = r1...


In Rectangle assignment operator...
In Point assignment operator...
In Point destructor(00481B10)
In Point copy constructor(00481B10)

r1 area: 3000
r2 area: 3000

Exiting and deleting the rectangles...
In Rectangle destructor (0012FF5C)
In Point destructor(00481B10)
In Point destructor(00481AD0)
In Rectangle destructor (0012FF68)
In Point destructor(00481D10)
In Point destructor(00481B50)
```

Analysis

The significant changes occur at line 18, where the Point assignment operator is declared; at line 41, where the Rectangle assignment operator is declared; and at lines 101 and 131, where they are implemented.

To get an idea of how these work, let's walk through the driver program, beginning on line 143. We declare two local Rectangle objects, r1 and r2, and print their area on lines 150 and 151.

On line 156 we assign the Rectangle r1 to r2. This invokes the Rectangle assignment operator on line 101. The line

```
r2 = r1
```

is translated by the compiler into

```
r2.operator=(r1);
```

Now, at last, you can see the meaning of the parameter name rhs: It stands for *r*ight *h*and *s*ide because that parameter stands for the argument on the right hand side of the assignment operator. Using this name for the copy constructor makes a bit less sense, but it became a custom because these two methods are so similar.

Thus, in the implementation on line 101, the `Rectangle` whose method is active is r1, and the parameter, rhs, is actually r1, passed in as a constant reference.

Assigning to `itsDepth` is simple: We just get the value from rhs (that is, from r1). What can we do about the pointers? We actually have two choices. The first choice is shown on lines 108 and 109: I've deleted the current value and created a new `Point` object on the heap, initialized with the value from rhs. This calls the copy constructor on `Point`, as is reflected in the output.

This approach is required when you have a variable-length object such as a string. You can't assume that you have enough room in memory to just copy over rhs's data in that case. In this case, we know that the `Point` object is a fixed size object, so we can just copy over the object by value, calling `Point`'s assignment operator as we do on line 110 (and as is reflected in the output).

Actually, even for a variable-length object such as a string, if that object's assignment operator is clever enough, you don't have to worry about reallocating the memory: You can have the object do it for you. Thus, `Rectangle` should be safe just writing

```
itsMemberVariable = rhs.itsMemberVariable;
```

If `itsMemberVariable` is of variable length, it is up to `itsMemberVariable`'s class's assignment operator to manage the memory.

Now, why the test on line 105? Because we've decided to manage the memory on lines 108 and 109, we must be careful. What happens if we write

```
r1 = r1;
```

In this case, we'd be assigning back to the original object. If we were to delete `itsUpperLeft`, we'd have no value to assign back in when we allocate memory on 109. We'd have just deleted it on 108, which is a disaster waiting to happen!

Of course, you'd never write

```
r1 = r1;
```

on purpose, but it is easy for such a thing to happen by mistake in the presence of references. You might write

```
r1 = r2;
```

thinking you were safe, but r2 might be a reference to r1, leading you right back to

```
r1 = r1;
```

To protect against this problem, we check first. If the `this` pointer is different from the address of `rhs`, we know that we have two different objects, and we can update the memory. If they are the same, the update is skipped. In either case, we return the object by reference.

Notice that the return value is not a constant, but it is a reference. This allows your user-defined classes to act more like built-in types. Specifically, just as you can write

```
int x;
int y;
int z = 7;
x = y = z;
```

you can also write

```
Rectangle r1(100,20,40,80);
Rectangle r2(50,10,20,40);
Rectangle r3(25,5,10,20);
r3 = r2 = r1;
```

The compiler translates this into

```
r3.operator=(r2.operator=(r1));
```

and the values from `r1` are assigned to both `r2` and `r3`.

When It Looks Like Assignment But Isn't

Try this: Add the following line to `main()` in Listing 7.4 and set a break point on the new line:

```
Rectangle r3 = r2;
```

Before you step into the break point, where do you expect to go? If you said the copy constructor, pat yourself on the back: This looks like assignment, but it isn't. It is initialization. In initialization, `r3` does not yet exist: It will be initialized with the value in `r2`. This generates exactly the same code as if you had written

```
Rectangle r3(r2);
```

Back to Linked Lists

We now understand, finally, why the `GetSolution()` method in `Game` returns the `LinkedList` as a reference:

```
const LinkedList & GetSolution () const { return solution; }
```

It does so, specifically, to avoid the cost of passing the `LinkedList` object by value. We took a pretty long digression to come to that understanding, but you now understand what happens when you *don't* pass by value. Furthermore, you now have an idea about all the tricky aspects of managing the resulting calls to the copy constructor, and possibly to the assignment operator.

We are ready now to modify LinkedList to be a bit more object-oriented. We'll pick that up in Chapter 8, "Using Polymorphism."

Chapter 8

Using Polymorphism

The linked list class works, but it cries out for a bit of improvement. Each node in the list is forever checking to see whether there is a next node in the list before taking action:

```
void Node::Insert(char theChar)
{
    if ( ! nextNode )
        nextNode = new Node(theChar);
    else
        nextNode->Insert(theChar);
}
```

This creates code that is a bit more difficult to maintain. As an object-oriented designer, I notice that I'm asking each node to be capable of being the head node in the list, an internal node in the list, or the tail of the list. There is nothing special about these positions—they are just nodes.

Because any node can be internal or the tail, it can't know whether it has a next node, so it must test. If a node knew that it was an internal node, it would always know that there was a next node ("If I'm not the tail, there must be at least one after me"). If it knew that it was the tail, it would know there was no next node (such is the meaning of being the tail node; objects live a very existential existence, and they often major in epistemology).

Specialization

This leads me to a redesign. In it, I have three types of nodes: One is the head node, one is the tail, and the third is the internal node.

You've already seen that the LinkedList class you created can mark the head node position, and that this class has special responsibilities such as supporting an offset operator. Let's break out the InternalNode from the TailNode.

When we say that the LinkedList, InternalNode, and TailNode are all nodes, this tells us that we are thinking about a specialization/generalization relationship. The LinkedList, InternalNode, and TailNode are specializations of Node. The LinkedList has the special requirement that it act as an interface to the list, which leads me to the design shown in Figure 8.1

Figure 8.1

Node Specialization.

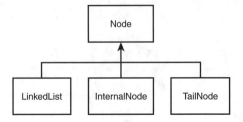

In this design, shown here in UML notation, we indicate that the LinkedList, InternalNode, and TailNode are all kinds of Node. This brings us back to the conversation about specialization/generalization in Chapter 1, "Introduction."

The specialization relationship establishes an *is-a* relationship: That is, a TailNode *is-a* Node. Furthermore, the specialization relationship indicates that TailNode adds to the definition of Node. It says that this is a special kind of Node—one that marks the end of a list.

Similarly, InternalNode specializes Node to mean a node that manages associated data and that, by implication, does not mark the tail of the list.

Finally, LinkedList is-a node, a very special node that marks the head of the list and that provides an interface to users of the list. We could have called this the *head node*, but we want to focus on the user's perception: To the user, the head node *is* the linked list. Thus, we bridge the gap between the architect's view (in which this is the head node in a linked list) and the user's view (in which this *is* the linked list) by having it inherit from Node but calling it LinkedList.

The specialization/generalization relationship is reciprocal. Because LinkedList, TailNode, and InternalNode specialize Node, Node in turn becomes a generalization of the commonality between all three of these classes. Programmers talk about *factoring out* common features from the derived classes up into the base

> classes. Thus, you can factor out all the common responsibilities of the three
> classes up into Node.

Benefits from Specialization

The first benefit you receive from this design is that Node can serve to hold the common characteristics of LinkedList, InternalNode, and TailNode. The things they have in common in this design are that any Node can exist in a list, that you can tell any Node to insert a new data object, and that you can tell a Node to display itself.

In addition, by specializing Node, this design of TailNode maintains the Node features but adds the special capability to mark the end of the list. This specialization is manifest in the differences in how TailNode responds to a request to Insert data, which it handles differently than, for example, an InternalNode does.

Polymorphism

The need to handle Insert() in a special way might be a good reason to create a new class, but you can imagine that it would make your code much more complicated. Each Node would have to know what it pointed to: If it pointed to an InternalNode, it would call InternalNodeInsert, and if it pointed to a TailNode, it would call TailNodeInsert. What a bother.

We want to say, "I have a Node, I don't know what kind. It might be an InternalNode or it might be a TailNode. When I call Insert(), I want my Node to act one way if it is an InternalNode, and in a different way if it is a TailNode."

This is called polymorphism: *poly* means *many* and *morph* means *form*. We want the Node to take on many forms. C++ supports polymorphism, which means that the client can call Insert on the Node and the compiler will take care of making the right thing happen. In this case, the right thing means that if the Node is really an InternalNode, InternalNode::Insert() will be called; if the Node is really a TailNode, TailNode::Insert() will be called instead.

Abstract Data Types

You want to create InternalNode objects to hold your data, and you want to create a single TailNode object and a single LinkedList object. You will never instantiate a Node object, though. The Node object exists only as an abstraction so that you can say "I will call the next node," and not worry about which kind of node it is. The Node class is called an *abstract data type (ADT)* because it exists only to provide an abstraction for the classes that inherit from it.

8

The classes that are derived from your ADT (in this case, `LinkedList`, `InternalNode`, and `TailNode`) can be *concrete*, and thus can have objects instantiated. Alternatively, you can derive ADTs from other ADTs. Ultimately, however, you must derive a concrete class so that you can create objects.

abstract data type—A class that provides a common interface to a number of classes that derive from it. You can never instantiate an abstract data type.

concrete class—A class that is not abstract and that can therefore be instantiated.

How This Is Implemented in C++

Until now, we've not discussed a word about how all this is implemented in C++. That is because we have rightly been focused on design, not implementation.

The *design* calls for all three of these classes to specialize `Node`. You *implement* that design concept of specialization by using inheritance. Thus, you will have `LinkedList`, `TailNode`, and `InternalNode` inherit from `Node`.

The Syntax of Inheritance

When you declare a class, you can indicate the class from which it derives by writing a colon after the class name, the type of derivation (public or otherwise), and the class from which it derives. For now, focus only on public inheritance because that is what implements the design concept of specialization/generalization.

Thus, to indicate that `InternalNode` is a specialization of `Node`, or that `InternalNode` *derives* from `Node`, you write

```
class InternalNode : public Node
```

When one class specializes another, we say that the specialized class is *derived* from the more general class, and that the more general class is the *base class*.

The class from which you derive must have been declared already, or you receive a compiler error.

Overriding Functions

A `LinkedList` object has access to all the member functions in class `Node`, as well as to any member functions the declaration of the `LinkedList` class might add. It can also *override* a base class function. Overriding a function means changing the implementation of a base class function in a derived class. When you instantiate an object of the derived class and call an overridden method, the right thing happens.

When a derived class creates a function with the same return type and signature as a member function in the base class, but with a new implementation, it is said to *override* that method.

This is very handy because it allows an `InternalNode` to specialize how it handles some methods (such as `Insert()`) and simply inherit the implementation of other methods.

When you override a function, its signature must be identical to the signature of the function in the base class. The signature is the function prototype, other than the return type: the name, the parameter list, and the keyword `const` (if it is used).

Virtual Methods

I have emphasized the fact that an `InternalNode` object is-a `Node` object. So far that has meant only that the `InternalNode` object has inherited the attributes (data) and capabilities (methods) of its base class. In C++, however, the is-a relationship runs deeper than that.

C++ extends its polymorphism, allowing pointers to base classes to be assigned to derived class objects. Thus, you can write

```
Node * pNode = new InternalNode;
```

This creates a new `InternalNode` object on the heap and returns a pointer to that object, which it assigns to a pointer to `Node`. This is fine because an `InternalNode` is-a `Node`.

In fact, this is the key to polymorphism. You can create all kinds of Windows—they can each have a `draw()` method that does something different (the list box draws a rectangle, the radio button draws a circle). You can create a pointer to a Window without regard to what type of Window you have, and when you call

```
pWindow->Draw();
```

the Window is drawn properly.

Similarly, you can have a pointer to any kind of `Node`, a `LinkedList`, an `InternalNode`, or a `TailNode`, and you can call `Insert()` on that node without regard to what kind of `Node` it is. The right thing will happen.

Here's how it works: You use the pointer to invoke a method on `Node`, for example `Insert()`. If the pointer is really pointing to a `TailNode`, and if `TailNode` has overridden `Insert()`, the overridden version of `Insert` is called. If `TailNode` does not override `Insert()`, it inherits this method from its base class, `Node`, and `Node::Insert()` is called.

This is accomplished through the magic of virtual functions.

Note C++ programmers use the terms *method* and *function* interchangeably. This confusion comes from the fact that C++ has two parents: the object-oriented languages such as SmallTalk, which use the term *method*, and C, which uses the term *function*.

How Virtual Functions Work

When a derived object, such as an `InternalNode` object, is created, first the constructor for the base class is called, and then the constructor for the derived class is called. Figure 8.2 shows how the `InternalNode` object looks after it is created. Note that the `Node` part of the object is contiguous in memory with the `InternalNode` part.

Figure 8.2

The `InternalNode` *object after it is created.*

When a virtual function is created in an object, the object must keep track of that function. Many compilers build a virtual function table, called a *v-table*. One of these tables is kept for each type, and each object of that type keeps a virtual table pointer (called a *vptr* or *v-pointer*) that points to that table. (Although implementations vary, all compilers must accomplish the same thing, so you won't be too wrong with this description.)

v-table—The virtual function table used to achieve polymorphism.

vptr or v-pointer—The Virtual Function Table Pointer, which is provided for every object from a class with at least one virtual method.

Each object's vptr points to the v-table that, in turn, has a pointer to each of the virtual functions. When the `Node` part of the `InternalNode` is created, the vptr is initialized to point to the correct part of the v-table, as shown in Figure 8.3.

When the `InternalNode` constructor is called and the `InternalNode` part of this object is added, the vptr is adjusted to point to the virtual function overrides (if any) in the `InternalNode` object (see Figure 8.4).

When a pointer to a `Node` is used, the vptr continues to point to the correct function, depending on the "real" type of the object. Thus, when `Insert()` is invoked, the correct (`InternalNode`) version of the function is invoked.

Figure 8.3

The v-table of a node.

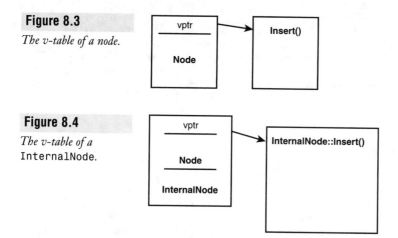

Figure 8.4

The v-table of a `InternalNode`.

Virtual Destructors

It is legal and common to pass a pointer to a derived object when a pointer to a base object is expected. What happens when that pointer to a derived subject is deleted? If the destructor is virtual, as it should be, the right thing happens: The derived class's destructor is called. Because the derived class's destructor automatically invokes the base class's destructor, the entire object is properly destroyed.

The rule of thumb is this: If any of the functions in your class are virtual, the destructor needs to be virtual as well.

EXCURSION

The ANSI/ISO standard dictates that you *can* vary the return type, but few compilers support this. If you change the signature—the name, number, or type of parameters or whether the method is **const**—you are not overriding the method, you are adding a new method.

It is important to note that if you add a new method with the same name as another method in the base class, you hide the base class method and the client can't get to it. Take a look at Listing 8.1, which illustrates this point.

Hiding the Base Class Method

```
0:  #include <iostream>
1:  using namespace std;
2:
3:  class Base
4:  {
5:  public:
6:      Base() { cout << "Base constructor\n"; }
```

continues

continued

```
7:      virtual ~Base() { cout << "Base destructor\n"; }
8:      virtual void MethodOne() { cout << "Base MethodOne\n"; }
9:      virtual void MethodTwo() { cout << "Base MethodTwo\n"; }
10:      virtual void MethodThree()
11:          { cout << "Base MethodThree\n"; }
12:  private:
13:  };
14:
15:  class Derived : public Base
16:  {
17:  public:
18:      Derived() { cout << "Derived constructor\n"; }
19:      virtual ~Derived() { cout << "Derived destructor\n"; }
20:      virtual void MethodOne() { cout << "Derived MethodOne\n"; }
21:      virtual void MethodTwo() { cout << "Derived MethodTwo\n"; }
22:      virtual void MethodThree(int myParam)
23:          { cout << "Derived MethodThree\n"; }
24:  private:
25:  };
26:
27:  int main()
28:  {
29:
30:      Base * pb = new Base;
31:      pb->MethodOne();
32:      pb->MethodTwo();
33:      pb->MethodThree();
34:  //    pb->MethodThree(5);
35:      delete pb;
36:      cout << endl;
37:
38:      Base * pbd = new Derived;
39:      pbd->MethodOne();
40:      pbd->MethodTwo();
41:      pbd->MethodThree();
42:  //    pbd->MethodThree(5);
43:      delete pbd;
44:      cout << endl;
45:
46:      Derived * pd = new Derived;
47:      pd->MethodOne();
48:      pd->MethodTwo();
49:  //    pd->MethodThree();
50:      pd->MethodThree(5);
51:      delete pd;
52:
53:      return 0;
54:  }
```

Output

```
Base constructor
Base MethodOne
Base MethodTwo
Base MethodThree
Base destructor

Base constructor
Derived constructor
Derived MethodOne
Derived MethodTwo
Base MethodThree
Derived destructor
Base destructor

Base constructor
Derived constructor
Derived MethodOne
Derived MethodTwo
Derived MethodThree
Derived destructor
Base destructor
```

Analysis

In this example, we create a **Base** class and a **Derived** class. The **Base** class declares three methods virtual on lines 8–10, which will be overridden in the **Derived** class.

The overridden **MethodThree** differs from the base class's version in that it takes an extra parameter. This overloads the method (rather than overrides it) and *hides* the base class method. What is the effect? Let's see.

On line 30 we declare a pointer to a **Base** object, and we use this pointer to invoke **MethodOne**, **MethodTwo**, and both versions of **MethodThree**. The second, shown on line 34, won't compile and so is commented out. It won't compile because **Base** objects know nothing about this overload version.

The output shows that a **Base** constructor is called, followed by the three **Base** methods, ending with a call to the **Base** destructor. Pretty much as we might expect.

On line 38 we declare a pointer to a **Base** and initialize it with a **Derived**. This is the polymorphic form: We assign a specialized object to a pointer to a more general object. We call **MethodOne**, **MethodTwo**, and **MethodThree**, and they compile fine until we try to compile the version that takes an **int**. Because this is a pointer to a **Base**, it can't find this method and won't compile.

8

Let's look at the output. We see the **Base** constructor, and then the **Derived** constructor. That is how derived objects are constructed: base first. We then see a call to the **Derived MethodOne**. Polymorphism works! Here we have a **Base** pointer, but because we assigned a **Derived** object to it, when we call a virtual method, the right method is called. This is followed by a call to **Derived MethodTwo**, and then to **Base MethodThree**! As far as the **Base** pointer is concerned, **Base MethodThree** has not been overridden, so **Derived** inherits the **Base** method. Finally, the object is destroyed in the reverse order in which it was created.

The final set of code begins on line 46, where we create a **Derived Pointer** and initialize it with a **Derived** object. This time we can't call the version of **MethodThree** that was declared in **Base** because our new **Derived** object hides it. This proves the rule: If you overload a base class in the derived class, you must explicitly implement every version of the method (in this case you'd have to implement the version with no parameters) in the derived class, or it is hidden from your derived objects.

The output reflects the fact that this **Derived** object calls (of course) only derived methods.

To avoid the hiding, we can move the version of the method that takes an integer up into **Base**, or at a minimum we can implement the version with no parameters in the derived class. If we choose the first option, we can use both methods polymorphically. If we choose the latter, at least we can access the base method using a derived object.

We can, actually, overcome many of these problems with a bit more magic. Let's take them in turn. To solve the first problem (shown on line 34), we have only to overload **MethodThree** in **Base**:

```
3:   class Base
4:   {
5:   public:
6:       Base() { cout << "Base constructor\n"; }
7:       virtual ~Base() { cout << "Base destructor\n"; }
8:       virtual void MethodOne() { cout << "Base MethodOne\n"; }
9:       virtual void MethodTwo() { cout << "Base MethodTwo\n"; }
10:      virtual void MethodThree()
11:          { cout << "Base MethodThree\n"; }
         virtual void MethodThree(int param)
                 { cout << "Base MethodThree(int)\n"; }
12:  private:
13:  };
```

To solve the problem on lines 42 and 49, we need only invoke the base class's method directly:

```
42:  //   pbd->Base::MethodThree(5);
```

Here we use the **Base** class name, followed by the scoping operator (`::`), to invoke the **Base** version of this method. Hey! Presto! Now we've "unhidden" it, and we can call it.

Implementing Polymorphism

All this is fine in theory, but it remains highly abstract until you see it implemented in code. Let's take a look at the implementation of the newly object-oriented LinkedList (see Listing 8.2).

Listing 8.1   LinkedList

```
0:  #ifndef LINKEDLIST_H
1:  #define LINKEDLIST_H
2:
3:  #include "def0514.h"
4:
5:  class Node   // abstract data type
6:  {
7:  public:
8:      Node(){}
9:      virtual ~Node() {}
10:     virtual void Display() const { }
11:     virtual int HowMany(char c) const = 0;
12:     virtual Node * Insert(char theCharacter) = 0;
13:     virtual char operator[](int offset) = 0;
14: private:
15: };
16:
17: class InternalNode: public Node
18: {
19: public:
20:     InternalNode(char theCharacter, Node * next);
21:     virtual ~InternalNode();
22:     virtual void Display() const;
23:     virtual int HowMany(char c) const;
24:     virtual Node * Insert(char theCharacter);
25:     virtual char operator[](int offset);
26:
27: private:
28:     char myChar;
29:     Node * nextNode;
30: };
31:
32: class TailNode : public Node
33: {
34: public:
35:     TailNode(){}
36:     virtual ~TailNode(){}
37:     virtual int HowMany(char c) const;
38:     virtual Node * Insert(char theCharacter);
39:     virtual char operator[](int offset);
40:
```

continues

Listing 8.1 continued

```
41:   private:
42:
43:   };
44:
45:   class LinkedList : public Node
46:   {
47:   public:
48:        LinkedList();
49:        virtual ~LinkedList();
50:        virtual void Display() const;
51:        virtual int HowMany(char c) const;
52:        virtual char operator[](int offset);
53:
54:        bool Add(char c);
55:        void SetDuplicates(bool dupes);
56:
57:   private:
58:        Node * Insert(char c);
59:        bool duplicates;
60:        Node * nextNode;
61:   };
62:
63:   #endif
```

Analysis

This analysis begins on line 5 with the declaration of the Node class. Note that all the methods, with the exception of the constructor, are virtual.

Constructors cannot be virtual; destructors need to be virtual if any method is virtual; and I've made the rest of the methods virtual because I expect that they can be overridden in at least some of the derived classes.

Note that the first three methods—the constructor, the destructor, and Display()— all have inline implementations that do nothing. HowMany() (line 11), however, does not have an inline implementation. If you check Listing 8.2, which has the implementation for the classes that are declared in Listing 8.1, you will not find an implementation for Node::HowMany().

That is because Node::HowMany() is declared to be a *pure* virtual function by virtue of the designation at the end of the declaration, = 0. This indicates to the compiler that this method *must* be overridden in the derived class. In fact, it is the presence of one or more pure virtual functions in your class declaration that creates an ADT. To recap: In C++, an abstract data type is created by declaring one or more pure virtual functions in the class.

pure virtual function—A member function that *must* be overridden in the derived class, and which makes the class in which it is declared an Abstract Data Type. You create a pure virtual function by adding = 0 to the function declaration.

The Node class is, therefore, an ADT from which you derive the concrete nodes you'll instantiate in the program. Every one of these concrete types must override the HowMany() and Insert() methods, as well as the offset operator. If a derived type fails to override even one of these methods, it too is abstract, and no objects can be instantiated from it.

On line 17, you see the declaration of the InternalNode class, which derives from Node. As you can see on lines 23–25, this class does override the three pure virtual functions of Node; thus, this is a concrete class from which you can instantiate objects.

Although we put the keyword virtual on lines 22–25, it is not necessary. When a method is virtual, it remains virtual all the way down the hierarchy of derived classes. So we could have left this designation out here, as we did on line 21.

InternalNode adds two private variables: myChar and nextNode. It is clear why myChar can't be in Node: Only InternalNode classes have a character for which they are responsible. Why not put nextNode up in the base class, then? After all, nodes exist in a linked list. You'd expect all nodes to have a nextNode.

This is true of all nodes *except* for TailNode. Because TailNode does not have a nextNode, it doesn't make sense for this attribute to be in the base class.

You can put this pointer in the base and then give TailNode a null nextNode pointer. That might work, but it doesn't map to the semantics of a Node. A Node is an object that lives in a linked list. It is not part of our definition that a Node must point to another Node, only that it must be in the list. TailNodes are in the list, but they don't point to a nextNode. Thus, this pointer is not an intrinsic aspect of a Node, so I've left it out of the base class.

The declaration for TailNode begins on line 32, and once again you can see that the pure virtual functions are overridden. The distinguishing characteristics of TailNode are shown in the implementation of these methods, which we'll consider in a moment.

Finally, on line 45 you see LinkedList declared. Again, the pure virtual methods are overridden, but this time, on lines 54 and 55, you see new public methods: Add and SetDuplicates. These methods support the functionality of this class, to provide an interface for the LinkedList to the client classes.

Note also that on line 58 we've moved Insert() to the private section of LinkedList. The only Node class that any non-Node interacts with is this one, and Insert is not part of the LinkedList class's public interface. When a client wants to add a character to the list, it calls LinkedList::Add(), which is shown on line 54.

Node's Insert() method is public, however—when nodes interact with one another (for example, when LinkedList is adding objects to an InternalNode), the InsertMethod is used.

Let's look at the implementation of LinkedList in Listing 8.3, adding Game in Listings 8.4 and 8.5, and the driver program Decryptix! in Listing 8.6. This enables us to step through a few methods using the new object-oriented linked list.

Listing 8.2   Linked List Implementation

```
0:   #include "LL 0802.cpp"
1:
2:   InternalNode::InternalNode(char theCharacter, Node * next):
3:   myChar(theCharacter),nextNode(next)
4:   {
5:   }
6:
7:   InternalNode::~InternalNode()
8:   {
9:       delete nextNode;
10:  }
11:
12:  void InternalNode::Display() const
13:  {
14:      cout << myChar; nextNode->Display();
15:  }
16:
17:  int InternalNode::HowMany(char theChar) const
18:  {
19:      int myCount = 0;
20:      if ( myChar == theChar )
21:          myCount++;
22:      return myCount + nextNode->HowMany(theChar);
23:  }
24:
25:  Node * InternalNode::Insert(char theCharacter)
26:  {
27:      nextNode = nextNode->Insert(theCharacter);
28:      return this;
29:  }
30:
31:  char InternalNode::operator[](int offSet)
32:  {
33:      if ( offSet == 0 )
34:          return myChar;
35:      else
36:          return (*nextNode)[—offSet];
37:  }
```

```
38:
39:
40:   int TailNode::HowMany(char theChar) const
41:   {
42:       return 0;
43:   }
44:
45:   Node * TailNode::Insert(char theChar)
46:   {
47:       return new InternalNode(theChar, this);
48:   }
49:
50:   char TailNode::operator[](int offset)
51:   {
52:       ASSERT(false);
53:       return ' ';
54:   }
55:
56:
57:
58:   LinkedList::LinkedList():
59:   duplicates(true)
60:   {
61:       nextNode = new TailNode;
62:   }
63:
64:   LinkedList::~LinkedList()
65:   {
66:       delete nextNode;
67:   }
68:
69:   void LinkedList::Display() const
70:   {
71:       nextNode->Display();
72:   }
73:
74:   int LinkedList::HowMany(char theChar) const
75:   {
76:       return nextNode->HowMany(theChar);
77:   }
78:
79:   Node * LinkedList::Insert(char theChar)
80:   {
81:           nextNode = nextNode->Insert(theChar);
82:           return nextNode;
83:   }
84:
85:   char LinkedList::operator[](int offSet)
86:   {
87:       return (*nextNode)[offSet];
88:   }
```

continues

Listing 8.2   continued

```
89:
90:
91:
92:   bool LinkedList::Add(char theChar)
93:   {
94:        if ( duplicates || HowMany(theChar) == 0 )
95:        {
96:             Insert(theChar);
97:             return true;
98:        }
99:        else
100:            return false;
101:  }
102:
103:
104:  void LinkedList::SetDuplicates(bool dupes)
105:  {
106:       duplicates = dupes;
107:  }
```

Listing 8.3   Game Header

```
0:   #ifndef GAME_H
1:   #define GAME_H
2:
3:   #include "defvals.h"
4:   #include "LL_0801.h"
5:
6:   class Game
7:   {
8:   public:
9:        Game();
10:       ~Game(){}
11:       void Display(const LinkedList * pList)const
12:       {
13:            pList->Display();
14:       }
15:
16:       void Play();
17:       const LinkedList &  GetSolution() const
18:       {
19:            return solution;
20:       }
21:
22:       void Score(
23:            const char * thisGuess,
24:            int & correct,
25:            int & position
26:            );
27:
```

```
28:    private:
29:              int HowMany(const char * theString, char theChar);
30:              LinkedList solution;
31:              int howManyLetters;
32:              int howManyPositions;
33:              int round;
34:              bool duplicates;
35:    };
36:
37:    #endif
```

Listing 8.4   Game Implementation

```
0:    #include <time.h>
1:    #include "game0803.h"
2:    #include "defvals.h"
3:
4:    Game::Game():
5:         round(1),
6:         howManyPositions(0),
7:         howManyLetters(0),
8:         duplicates(false)
9:    {
10:
11:         bool valid = false;
12:         while ( ! valid )
13:         {
14:              while ( howManyLetters < minLetters
15:                   || howManyLetters > maxLetters )
16:              {
17:                   cout << "How many letters? (" ;
18:                   cout << minLetters << "-" << maxLetters << "): ";
19:                   cin >> howManyLetters;
20:                   if ( howManyLetters < minLetters
21:                        || howManyLetters > maxLetters )
22:                   {
23:                        cout << "please enter a number between ";
24:                        cout << minLetters << " and " << maxLetters << endl;
25:                   }
26:              }
27:
28:              while ( howManyPositions < minPos ||
29:                   howManyPositions > maxPos )
30:              {
31:                   cout << "How many positions? (";
32:                   cout << minPos << "-" << maxPos << "): ";
33:                   cin >> howManyPositions;
34:                   if ( howManyPositions < minPos ||
35:                        howManyPositions > maxPos )
36:                   {
37:                        cout << "please enter a number between ";
```

8

continues

Listing 8.4   continued

```
38:                              cout << minPos <<" and " << maxPos << endl;
39:                         }
40:                    }
41:
42:               char choice = ' ';
43:               while ( choice != 'y' && choice != 'n' )
44:               {
45:                    cout << "Allow duplicates (y/n)? ";
46:                    cin >> choice;
47:               }
48:
49:               duplicates = choice == 'y' ? true : false;
50:               solution.SetDuplicates(duplicates);
51:
52:               if ( ! duplicates && howManyPositions > howManyLetters )
53:               {
54:          cout << "I can't put " << howManyLetters;
55:          cout << " letters in ";
56:          cout << howManyPositions ;
57:          cout << "positions without duplicates! Please try again.\n";
58:          howManyLetters = 0;
59:          howManyPositions = 0;
60:               }
61:          else
62:               valid = true;
63:     }
64:
65:
66:     srand( (unsigned)time( NULL ) );
67:
68:     for ( int i = 0; i < howManyPositions; )
69:     {
70:          int nextValue = rand() % (howManyLetters);
71:          char theChar = alpha[nextValue];
72:          if ( solution.Add(theChar) )
73:               i++;
74:     }
75:
76:     cout << "Exiting constructor. List: ";
77:     solution.Display();
78:
79: }
80:
81: inline int Game::HowMany(const char * theString, char theChar)
82: {
83:     int count = 0;
84:     for ( int i = 0; i < strlen(theString); i++)
85:          if ( theString[i] == theChar )
86:               count ++;
87:     return count;
```

```
88:    }
89:
90:    void Game::Play()
91:    {
92:         char guess[80];
93:         int correct = 0;
94:         int position = 0;
95:         bool quit = false;
96:
97:         while ( position < howManyPositions )
98:         {
99:
100:               cout << "\nRound " << round;
101:               cout << ". Enter " << howManyPositions;
102:               cout << " letters between ";
103:               cout << alpha[0] << " and ";
104:               cout << alpha[howManyLetters-1] << ": ";
105:
106:               cin >> guess;
107:
108:               if ( strlen(guess) != howManyPositions )
109:               {
110:                    cout << "\n ** Please enter exactly ";
111:                    cout << howManyPositions << " letters. **\n";
112:                    continue;
113:               }
114:
115:
116:               round++;
117:
118:               cout << "\nYour guess: " << guess << endl;
119:
120:               Score(guess,correct,position);
121:               cout << "\t\t" << correct << " correct, ";
122:               cout << position << " in position." << endl;
123:         }
124:
125:               cout << "\n\nCongratulations! It took you ";
126:
127:               if ( round <= 6 )
128:                    cout << "only ";
129:
130:               if ( round-1 == 1 )
131:                    cout << "one round!" << endl;
132:               else
133:                    cout << round-1 << " rounds." << endl;
134:
135:    }
136:
137:
138:    void Game::Score(
```

continues

Listing 8.4   continued

```
139:                        const char * thisGuess,
140:                        int & correct,
141:                        int & position
142:                        )
143:  {
144:      correct = 0;
145:      position = 0;
146:
147:
148:      for ( int i = 0; i < howManyLetters; i++)
149:      {
150:          int howManyInGuess = HowMany(thisGuess, alpha[i]);
151:          int howManyInAnswer = solution.HowMany(alpha[i]);
152:          correct += howManyInGuess < howManyInAnswer ?
153:              howManyInGuess : howManyInAnswer;
154:      }
155:
156:      for (  i = 0; i < howManyPositions; i++)
157:      {
158:          if ( thisGuess[i] == solution[i] )
159:              position++;
160:      }
161:
162:      ASSERT ( position <= correct );
163:
164:  }
```

Listing 8.5   Decryptix! Driver Program

```
0:   #include "def0514.h"
1:   #include "game0803.h"
2:
3:   int main()
4:   {
5:
6:       cout << "Decryptix. (c)Copyright 1999 Liberty Associates,";
7:       cout << " Inc. Version 0.3\n\n" << endl;
8:       bool playAgain = true;
9:
10:      while ( playAgain )
11:      {
12:          char choice = ' ';
13:          Game theGame;
14:          theGame.Play();
15:
16:          cout << "\nThe answer: ";
17:          theGame.GetSolution().Display();
```

```
18:              cout << "\n\n" << endl;
19:
20:              while ( choice != 'y' && choice != 'n' )
21:              {
22:                   cout << "\nPlay again (y/n): ";
23:                   cin >> choice;
24:              }
25:
26:              playAgain = choice == 'y' ? true : false;
27:         }
28:
29:     return 0;
30:  }
```

Analysis

 Note The Game class declaration is unchanged from the previous version, and is reproduced here only as a convenience.

Let's start the analysis with the construction of the solution member variable of Game. Put a break point on line 58 of Listing 8.2. When the break point is hit, the first thing you do is check the call stack to see when in the execution of the program this constructor was called:

```
LinkedList::LinkedList() line 62
Game::Game() line 10 + 58 bytes
main() line 14 + 8 bytes
```

As you can see, main() called the Game constructor, which in turn called the LinkedList constructor. Line 14 of main() looks like this:

```
        Game theGame;
```

It's just as you expected—the construction of a Game object. Line 10 of Game is the opening brace, shown in the code as line 9 of Listing 8.4. Because the LinkedList member variable (solution) was not initialized, the compiler calls its constructor just before entering the body of Game's constructor.

Returning to Listing 8.2, line 58, note that the LinkedList initializes its duplicates member variable to true (line 59); then, on line 61, it creates a new TailNode and sets its own nextNode to point to the Tail. This creates an empty linked list, as shown in Figure 8.5.

Figure 8.5

An empty linked list.

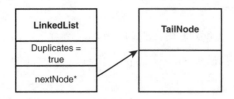

LinkedList is thus automatically initialized to a first Node (LinkedList) and a last Node (TailNode); neither of them contains any data, but together they create the structure of the list.

If you continue stepping through the code, you find yourself in the body of the Game constructor (line 11 of Listing 8.4). Set a break point on line 66 and run to that break point so that you skip examining the initial user interface code that has not changed from previous chapters.

When you are prompted, choose five letters in five positions. The break point is hit, and we generate a seed for the random number generator, based on the time (as discussed in previous chapters). On line 70, we generate a random number and use that as an offset into the alpha array to generate our first character. By line 72 we have that first character, which in my case is 'd'.

Stepping into the Add method causes us to jump to line 92 of Listing 8.2. On line 94, duplicates is tested and fails (we're not allowing dupes); therefore, the call to HowMany is made, passing in the parameter.

Stepping in here brings us to line 74. The LinkedList implementation of this is to return the value that is generated by calling HowMany on whatever the LinkedList points to. Step in, and you'll find yourself in the HowMany() method of TailNode. This makes sense; right now, LinkedList points to TailNode.

Because TailNode holds no data, it returns 0 regardless of what character it is given. This is returned to LinkedList::HowMany(), which in turn returns it to LinkedList::Add() on line 94. Because this satisfies the second condition in the OR statement, enter the body of the if statement on line 96.

Stepping into the Call to Insert jumps to line 80, the implementation of LinkedList::Insert(). LinkedList's strategy is to pass this request on to whatever it points to. Stepping in brings us to line 47, the implementation of TailNode::Insert().

TailNode always inserts a node when it is asked to. It knows that it is the tail, so it doesn't have to check—it can just make the insertion. This is the critical difference from the previous version. You'll remember that in Chapter 6, "Using Linked Lists,"

`Node` responded to `Insert` as follows:

```
void Node::Insert(char theChar)
{
    if ( ! nextNode )
        nextNode = new Node(theChar);
    else
        nextNode->Insert(theChar);
}
```

That is, it was necessary to see whether there were any more `Node`s in the list. If not (if the current `Node` was the `Tail`), a new `Node` could be inserted. On the other hand, if the current `Node` was not the `Tail`, and therefore was an `InternalNode`, the `Insert` request would be passed down the list.

The new design obviates the need for the test: The `TailNode` knows that it is the tail, and it can just make the insertion. This simple division of responsibility is, in a small way, the very heart of object-oriented software development.

Let's examine the implementation in some detail. Line 47 returns the address of the new `InternalNode` that is created by passing in the character that is received as a parameter and the `this` pointer of the `TailNode`.

This jumps to the constructor for `InternalNode`, shown on line 2. Here you see the creation of the `InternalNode`. The character is inserted into the `InternalNode`'s `myChar` member variable, and the `this` pointer from the `TailNode` is stored in the `nextNode` pointer of `InternalNode`.

The address of this `InternalNode` is then passed back to the caller of `TailNode::Insert()`, and in this case is assigned to the `nextNode` member variable of `LinkedList` (as shown on line 81). Finally, this address is returned by `LinkedList::Insert`, but the calling function—`LinkedList::Add()` on line 96— makes no use of it, and it is thrown on the floor. On line 97, we return `true` to the calling function on line 72 of Listing 8.4

We have now added a first letter to the linked list, and it worked great. It takes a lot longer to explain the process than to perform it. Next, let's track the second letter, now that you have an `InternalNode` in the linked list.

Adding a Second Letter

Return to line 92 of Listing 8.2. Once again, this steps you into `LinkedList::HowMany()` (line 74), this time passing in `'b'`.

This time, `LinkedList`'s `nextNode` points to an `InternalNode` (the one holding `'d'`), so we now jump to line 17. Here a local variable `myCount` is initialized to zero. The

InternalNode's member variable myCount ('d') is compared to the parameter theChar ('b'). Because they are not the same, myCount remains zero.

We now invoke HowMany() on the node that is pointed to by this InternalNode's nextNode pointer. Right now, the pointer points to TailNode, which we examined previously; it simply returns zero. That zero is added to myCount (also zero) for a total of zero, which is the value that is returned to LinkedList::Add().

This causes the second half of the OR statement on line 94 to return true (HowMany('b') equals zero), so the body of the if statement executes. This causes the call on Insert() to execute, with a jump to line 80, which is the implementation of LinkedList::Insert(). Again, LinkedList's strategy is to pass this request on to whatever it points to, which in this case is InternalNode's Insert() method (as shown on line 27). InternalNode's strategy is to call Insert() on the object to which its nextNode pointer points (in this case TailNode), and then to set its nextNode pointer to whatever value is returned.

Because the nextNode is the TailNode, InternalNode::Insert is now called. As you saw just a moment ago, it creates a new InternalNode for 'b' and tells that new node to point to the tail. It then returns the address of the new node, which is now assigned to the nextNode pointer of the node that holds 'd'. Thus, 'b' is appended to the list, as shown in Figure 8.6.

Figure 8.6

Appending 'b'.

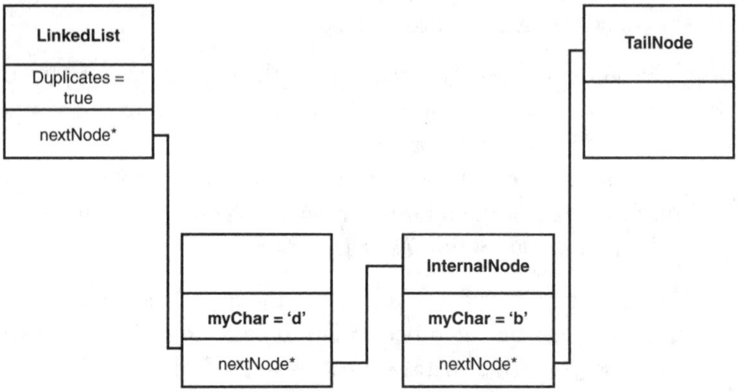

Examining operator[]

Let's take a look at Game::Score, beginning on line 138 of Listing 8.4. You've examined the fundamental logic in detail in previous chapters. (We're particularly interested in the letter by letter comparisons.) You've seen how LinkedList::HowMany() works; now take a look at the offset operator as it is used on line 158.

Stepping in to this code steps into `Linkedlist::Operator[]` on line 87 of Listing 8.2.

 Note

Along the way, I've added test code at line 77 to print out the answer so that I can examine the behavior of the system as I test it. You want to remove both lines 76 and 77 before releasing this code.

Not surprisingly, all `LinkedList` does here is invoke this same operator on the node to which it points. Stepping in from line 87 brings you to line 31, `InternalNode::operator[]`. Take a look at your auto member variables, and you'll find that `myChar` is `'d'`, just as you might expect. The offset that was passed in is now tested. If it is `0`, the call was for the first letter in the list. You will be at the first letter in the list, and you can return `myChar`, which is the case now. The letter `'d'` is returned to `LinkedList`; `LinkedList` returns it to the calling method, `score()`, which—on line 158 of Listing 8.4—is compared with the value of the first character in the guess.

This is repeated, but with `i` set to `1`. A call to `solution[1]` is invoked, bringing us back into `LinkedList::operator[]` on line 87 of Listing 8.2.

Stepping in from line 87 brings you back to `InternalNode::operator[]` on line 31. Take a look at your auto member variables, and you'll find that `myChar` is again `'d'`—you're back at the first `InternalNode` in the list. The offset that was passed in (1) is now tested. Because it is not zero, the `if` statement on line 33 fails and the body of the `else` statement on line 36 executes:

```
36:          return (*nextNode)[-offSet];
```

This invokes the offset operator on the next `Node` in the list, passing in the decremented `offSet` value. Stepping in appears to bring us back to the top of the same method, but check your variables—`myChar` is now b, and `offset` is now zero. Perfect: You'll return the second letter in the list, exactly as you wanted.

The linked list works as you want, and by using inheritance, you've delegated responsibility for monitoring the head and tail of the list to specialized nodes. This simplifies the code and makes it easier to maintain.

The problem with this linked list, however, is that it can only be used by nodes that hold single characters. What if you have other data that you want to insert into your linked list? Must you really rewrite the linked list each time you change the kind of object that is contained? The next chapter, "Implementing Templates," takes a look at modifying your linked list so that it can handle any kind of data.

Chapter 9

Implementing Templates

In the preceding chapter, "Using Polymorphism," you modified your linked list to make it a bit more object-oriented. You are now ready to add a much-desired feature to your program: the capability to keep a history of past guesses so that when you are contemplating a guess you can review the results you've received so far.

Creating the History

To accomplish this goal, you want to keep track of previous guesses and how they were scored. We'll create a class for this and call it Guess.

A guess consists of a string that is guessed and the score that is received. We'll start by creating a Score class, which for now will simply consist of two integers and accessor methods to retrieve and set these values. These will represent the number of correct guesses, and how many of the correct guesses were in the correct position. Our Guess object now combines a Score with a string of characters, as shown in Listing 9.1.

The Guess class will record each guess and will be aggregated in a collection we'll call history. Together, they will represent all the guesses offered so far in the game so that the player can review what he has already tried.

Listing 9.1 The Guess Class

```
0:  #ifndef GUESS_H
1:  #define GUESS_H
2:
3:  #include "def0514.h"
4:  #include "Scor0902.h"
```

continues

Listing 9.1   continued

```
5:
6:   class Guess
7:   {
8:   public:
9:       Guess();
10:      Guess(const char * guess, int howManyRight,
10a:          int howManyInPosition);
11:      Guess(const Guess& rhs);
12:      ~Guess();
13:      const Score&  GetScore() const { return theScore; }
14:      const char * GetString() const { return string; }
15:      friend ostream& operator<<
15a:         (ostream& ostr, const Guess& theGuess);
16:      bool operator==(const Guess& rhs) const;
17:      Guess & operator=(const Guess& rhs);
18:
19:  private:
20:      char * string;
21:      Score theScore;
22:  };
23:
24:  #endif
```

 Note   This listing uses definedValues.h, which was shown in Listing 6.4 and which is unchanged here.

Lines 20 and 21 contain the two member variables. The member variable string is a character array that contains the player's guess. The member variable theScore is of type Score, the declaration of which is shown in Listing 9.2.

Listing 9.2   The score Class

```
0:   #ifndef SCORE_H
1:   #define SCORE_H
2:
3:   class Score
4:   {
5:   public:
6:       Score(int right, int pos);
7:       Score();
8:       Score(const Score& rhs);
9:       virtual ~Score();
10:       int GetInPosition() const;
11:       int GetCorrect() const;
```

```
12:       bool operator==(const Score& rhs) const;
13:       Score & operator=(const Score& rhs);
14:
15: private:
16:       int howManyInPosition;
17:       int howManyRight;
18: };
19:
20: #endif
```

Both of these classes overload their copy constructor and assignment operator. In the case of Guess, this is particularly important because the member variable string is a pointer to a string in memory. When a Guess is copied—either explicitly or implicitly—this memory must be managed, as was explained in the discussion of deep copy in Chapter 7, "The Canonical Methods."

Overloaded Operators

The Guess class overloads the equality operator (==) in addition to the assignment operator (=). A Guess class must be capable of answering the question of whether it is equal to another Guess class because this is part of the semantics of being in a linked list. For example, InternalNode includes this bit of code:

```
if ( myData == theData )
    myCount++;
```

myData is the data that is held by the InternalNode. If you are going to put a Guess object into the list, you must be capable of calling this code when myData and theData are both objects of type Guess. By overloading this method, you can make this comparison. You'll see the implementation of this in just a moment.

 Note   Note that I've renamed myChar to myData to be a bit more general because we might have non-character objects held in the node.

9

Writing Class Data to cout

You also must be capable of passing the Guess to the << operator of cout, which is, after all, how InternalNode implements the Display() method:

```
cout << myData; nextNode->Display();
```

Again, because myData can be of type Guess, you must be capable of supporting this notation. When myData is a char variable, you have no problem: cout knows how to print a character. If, however, it is a Guess, you have a problem. Overloading operator << in Guess won't help. This code translates to

```
cout.operator<<(myData)
```

and you have no way of providing its implementation to cout. You don't own the code to cout and can't change it, so you are a bit stuck. Fortunately, C++ provides a solution. The idiom is to create a global function that returns an ostream object (cout is an ostream object), and which takes two parameters—an ostream object and a constant reference to a user-defined type:

```
ostream& operator<< (ostream& theStream,  const Guess& theGuess)
{
    theStream << theGuess.GetString() << "\t";
    theStream << theGuess.GetScore().GetCorrect();
    theStream << " correct, ";
    theStream << theGuess.GetScore().GetInPosition();
    theStream << " in position\n";
    return theStream;
}
```

Having done this, you need only to declare this method to be a friend of the Guess class, as shown on line 15 of Listing 9.1. The effect is that when you call

```
cout << myData;
```

and myData is of type Guess, the global method is called, passing cout for theStream and myData for theGuess.

EXCURSION

Friend Classes and Methods

If you want to expose private member data or functions to another class without making them public to the world, you must declare the class to which you want to grant access in order to be a friend. This extends the interface of your class to include the friend class. That is, the friend class can access all your private data and methods.

It is important to note that friendship cannot be transferred. Just because you are my friend and Joe is your friend doesn't mean that Joe is my friend. Friendship is not inherited, either. Again, just because you are my friend and I'm willing to share my secrets with you doesn't mean that I'm willing to share my secrets with your children.

Finally, friendship is not reciprocal. Assigning Class One to be a friend of Class Two does not make Class Two a friend of Class One. Just because you are willing to tell me your secrets doesn't mean I am willing to tell you mine.

Friend classes should be used with caution. If two classes are inextricably entwined and one must frequently access data in the other, there might be good reason to use this declaration. But use it sparingly: It is often just as easy to use the public accessor methods, and doing so enables you to change one class without having to recompile the other.

Note

You will often hear novice C++ programmers complain that friend declarations "undermine" the encapsulation that is so important to object-oriented programming. This is, frankly, errant nonsense. The friend declaration makes the declared friend part of the class interface, and is no more an undermining of encapsulation than is public derivation.

You accomplish the declaration by putting the word *friend* into the class that is granting the access rights. That is, I can declare you to be my friend, but you can't declare yourself to be my friend.

Friend Functions

At times you will want to grant this level of access not to an entire class, but only to one or two functions of that class. You can do this by declaring the member functions of the other class to be friends, rather than declaring the entire class to be a friend. In fact, you can declare any function to be a friend function, regardless of whether it is a member function of another class.

You're now ready to add `Guess` to `LinkedList`, but `LinkedList` is not ready to receive it. Examine the declarations for `Node`, `InternalNode`, and `LinkedList` from Listing 8.1, which is reproduced here as Listing 9.3.

Listing 9.3   Node Declarations

```
0:  #ifndef LINKEDLIST_H
1:  #define LINKEDLIST_H
2:
3:  #include "def0514.h"
4:
5:  class Node  // abstract data type
6:  {
7:  public:
8:      Node(){}
9:      virtual ~Node() {}
10:     virtual void Display() const { }
11:     virtual int HowMany(char c) const = 0;
12:     virtual Node * Insert(char theCharacter) = 0;
13:     virtual char operator[](int offset) = 0;
14: private:
15: };
16:
17: class InternalNode: public Node
```

continues

Listing 9.3   continued

```
18:    {
19:    public:
20:           InternalNode(char theCharacter, Node * next);
21:           ~InternalNode();
22:           virtual void Display() const;
23:           virtual int HowMany(char c) const;
24:           virtual Node * Insert(char theCharacter);
25:           virtual char operator[](int offset);
26:
27:    private:
28:           char myChar;
29:           Node * nextNode;
30:    };
31:
32:    class TailNode : public Node
33:    {
34:    public:
35:           TailNode(){}
36:           ~TailNode(){}
37:           virtual int HowMany(char c) const;
38:           virtual Node * Insert(char theCharacter);
39:           virtual char operator[](int offset);
40:
41:    private:
42:
43:    };
44:
45:    class LinkedList : public Node
46:    {
47:    public:
48:           LinkedList();
49:           ~LinkedList();
50:           virtual void Display() const;
51:           virtual int HowMany(char c) const;
52:           virtual char operator[](int offset);
53:
54:           bool Add(char c);
55:           void SetDuplicates(bool dupes);
56:
57:    private:
58:           Node * Insert(char c);
59:           bool duplicates;
60:           Node * nextNode;
61:    };
62:
63: #endif
```

Each of these methods is intimately tied to characters. How can we ask this list to store a Guess? One option is to re-create the linkedList, substituting Guess each time we now see char, as shown in Listing 9.4.

Listing 9.4   LinkedList for Guess Objects

```
0:  #ifndef LINKEDLIST_H
1:  #definef LINKEDLIST_H
2:
3:  #include "def0514.h"
4:
5:  class GuessNode  // abstract data type
6:  {
7:  public:
8:      GuessNode(){}
9:      virtual ~GuessNode() {}
10:     virtual void Display() const { }
11:     virtual int HowMany(const Guess& theData) const = 0;
12:     virtual GuessNode * Insert(const Guess& theData) = 0;
13:     virtual const Guess& operator[](int offset) = 0;
14: private:
15: };
16:
17: class GuessInternalNode: public GuessNode
18: {
19: public:
20:     GuessInternalNode(const Guess& theData, GuessNode * next);
21:     ~GuessInternalNode();
22:     virtual void Display() const;
23:     virtual int HowMany(const Guess& thedata) const;
24:     virtual GuessNode * Insert(const Guess& theData);
25:     virtual const Guess& operator[](int offset);
26:
27: private:
28:     Guess myData;
29:     GuessNode * nextNode;
30: };
31:
32: class GuessTailNode : public GuessNode
33: {
34: public:
35:     GuessTailNode(){}
36:     ~GuessTailNode(){}
37:     virtual int HowMany(const Guess& data) const;
38:     virtual GuessNode * Insert(const Guess& data);
39:     virtual const Guess& operator[](int offset);
40:
41: private:
42:
43: };
44: class GuessLinkedList : public GuessNode
45: {
```

continues

Listing 9.4   continued

```
46:  public:
47:      GuessLinkedList();
48:      ~GuessLinkedList();
49:      virtual void Display() const;
50:      virtual int HowMany(const Guess& data) const;
51:      virtual const Guess& operator[](int offset);
52:
53:      bool Add(const Guess& data);
54:      void SetDuplicates(bool dupes);
55:
56: private:
57:      GuessNode * Insert(const Guess&  data);
58:      bool duplicates;
59:      GuessNode * nextNode;
60:  };
```

This will work, but it is a nightmare. Each time you create a new object to put in a list, all the functionality of the linked list must be reproduced. Worse, if you change how the LinkedList works, you must replicate that change in every "version" of the list.

The answer, of course, is *templates*, which are a way to say to the compiler, "I'm going to tell you the actual type of the thing at runtime." We *parameterize* the class, making the type of the object that is stored a parameter—a value defined at runtime.

Thus, rather than having a Node that holds a char and another that holds a Guess, we simply tell the compiler that we have a Node that holds a T, where T will be defined when we actually run the program.

parameterized classes—Classes that operate on objects whose type is defined at runtime.

templates—The principal implementation mechanism for parameterized classes in C++.

Listing 9.5 shows the redeclaration of the LinkedList classes using templates.

Listing 9.5   LinkedList with Templates

```
0:  #ifndef LINKEDLIST_H
1:  #define LINKEDLIST_H
2:
3:  #include "def0514.h"
4:
5:  template <class T>
6:  class Node  // abstract data type
7:  {
```

```
8:   public:
9:        Node(){}
10:        virtual ~Node() {}
11:        virtual void Display() const { }
12:        virtual int HowMany(const T& theData) const = 0;
13:        virtual Node<T> * Insert(const T& theData) = 0;
14:        virtual const T& operator[](int offset) = 0;
15:   private:
16:   };
17:
18:   template <class T>
19:   class InternalNode: public Node<T>
20:   {
21:   public:
22:        InternalNode(const T& theData, Node<T> * next);
23:        ~InternalNode();
24:        virtual void Display() const;
25:        virtual int HowMany(const T& thedata) const;
26:        virtual Node<T> * Insert(const T& theData);
27:        virtual const T& operator[](int offset);
28:
29:   private:
30:        T myData;
31:        Node<T> * nextNode;
32:   };
33:
34:   template <class T>
35:   class TailNode : public Node<T>
36:   {
37:   public:
38:        TailNode(){}
39:        ~TailNode(){}
40:        virtual int HowMany(const T& data) const;
41:        virtual Node<T> * Insert(const T& data);
42:        virtual const T& operator[](int offset);
43:
44:   private:
45:
46:   };
47:
48:   template <class T>
49:   class LinkedList : public Node<T>
50:   {
51:   public:
52:        LinkedList();
53:        ~LinkedList();
54:        virtual void Display() const;
55:        virtual int HowMany(const T& data) const;
56:        virtual const T& operator[](int offset);
57:
58:        bool Add(const T& data);
```

9

Listing 9.5   continued

```
59:        void SetDuplicates(bool dupes);
60:
61:  private:
62:       Node<T> * Insert(const T&  data);
63:       bool duplicates;
64:       Node<T> * nextNode;
65:  };
```

You'll notice in this declaration that every place we originally had char, we've now substituted T. Note also that while I was making the change, I changed the parameters and return types from pass by value to pass by reference. It is one thing to throw characters around, making copies willy-nilly; it is quite another to throw larger objects around memory.

Let's take a quick look at the syntax for templates. Each parameterized declaration begins with the keyword template, followed by the declaration of the thing that is parameterized (in this case, this is the class). Here we use the letter *T* for the class variable, but you can use anything. That is, we might have written

```
template <class foo>
```

and then substituted foo everywhere thetype is to be used; for example, we've used T on line 12 as the type of the parameter that is passed to HowMany.

That's really all there is to it: Use the keyword template, declare a variable name for the class type. and then substitute the variable everywhere you use the class type.

> **Note**
>
> In more complex template definitions, you might need two classes (for example, one for the parameter and one for the return type). In that case, you just create a template with two variables:
>
> template <class T, class X>
>
> Then just substitute as needed.

Definition in the Header

When working with templates, you must put the implementation for the parameterized classes in the header file with the declaration. Thus, lines 69–193 of LinkedList.h contain the implementation, as shown in Listing 9.6.

Listing 9.6   Implementing the Templates

```
69:  template <class T>
70:  Node<T> * InternalNode<T>::Insert(const T& theData)
```

```
71:   {
72:        nextNode = nextNode->Insert(theData);
73:        return this;
74:   }
75:
76:   template <class T>
77:   const T& InternalNode<T>::operator[](int offSet)
78:   {
79:        if ( offSet == 0 )
80:             return myData;
81:        else
82:             return (*nextNode)[-offSet];
83:   }
84:
85:   template <class T>
86:   int TailNode<T>::HowMany(const T& theData) const
87:   {
88:        return 0;
89:   }
90:
91:   template <class T>
92:   Node<T> * TailNode<T>::Insert(const T& theData)
93:   {
94:        return new InternalNode<T>(theData, this);
95:   }
96:
97:   template <class T>
98:   const T& TailNode<T>::operator[](int offset)
99:   {
100:        ASSERT(false);
101:        T * pT = new T;;
102:        return *pT;   // memory leak but can't get here!
103:   }
104:
105:   template <class T>
106:   InternalNode<T>::InternalNode(const T& theData, Node<T> * next):
107:   myData(theData),nextNode(next)
108:   {
109:   }
110:
111:   template <class T>
112:   InternalNode<T>::~InternalNode()
113:   {
114:
115:        delete nextNode;
116:   }
117:
118:   template <class T>
119:   void InternalNode<T>::Display() const
120:   {
```

continues

Listing 9.6   continued

```
121:        cout << myData; nextNode->Display();
122:    }
123:
124:    template <class T>
125:    int InternalNode<T>::HowMany(const T& theData) const
126:    {
127:        int myCount = 0;
128:        if ( myData == theData )
129:            myCount++;
130:        return myCount + nextNode->HowMany(theData);
131:    }
132:
133:
134:    template <class T>
135:    LinkedList<T>::LinkedList():
136:    duplicates(false)
137:    {
138:        nextNode = new TailNode<T>;
139:    }
140:
141:    template <class T>
142:    LinkedList<T>::~LinkedList()
143:    {
144:        delete nextNode;
145:    }
146:
147:    template <class T>
148:    void LinkedList<T>::Display() const
149:    {
150:        nextNode->Display();
151:    }
152:
153:    template <class T>
154:    int LinkedList<T>::HowMany(const T& theData) const
155:    {
156:        return nextNode->HowMany(theData);
157:    }
158:
159:    template <class T>
160:    Node<T> * LinkedList<T>::Insert(const T& theData)
161:    {
162:            nextNode = nextNode->Insert(theData);
163:            return nextNode;
164:    }
165:
166:    template <class T>
167:    const T& LinkedList<T>::operator[](int offSet)
168:    {
169:        return (*nextNode)[offSet];
170:    }
```

```
171:
172:
173:
174:    template <class T>
175:    bool LinkedList<T>::Add(const T& theData)
176:    {
177:          if ( duplicates || HowMany(theData) == 0 )
178:          {
179:                Insert(theData);
180:                return true;
181:          }
182:          else
183:                return false;
184:    }
185:
186:
187:    template <class T>
188:    void LinkedList<T>::SetDuplicates(bool dupes)
189:    {
190:          duplicates = dupes;
191:    }
192:
193:    #endif
```

Analysis

The syntax here is much the same as for the declaration. On line 69 we see the keyword `template` used again. The only surprising part is the declaration of the return type on line 70. But yes, we return a `Node<T>` rather than a simple `Node` because it is important that we return a character `Node` or a `Guess Node` as appropriate. The essential point is that the type of the actual object that is returned is determined at runtime by how we define `T`.

how too pro̅ nouns' it	I pronounce <T> as "of T," so Node<T> is pronounced "Node of T."

9

Note also that the class whose method we're defining on line 70 is declared to be `InternalNode<T>` rather than just `InternalNode`. This enables us to be quite specific in what we intend; in fact, we can specialize some methods based on the specific type of parameterized type, if necessary. In other words, you can, for one or two methods, decide that you'll have a special `InsertMethod` for `InternalNode` of `Guess`, which will not behave like the more general method shown here.

We don't do this in this particular example, but that functionality gives us a great deal of flexibility in our use of templates.

Create the Non-Parameterized Type First

This, by the way, is how I always create parameterized types: I get them working first with a specific type (char, in this case), and then generalize to the use of templates. That way I know, for example, that the LinkedList *should* work when I add the correct parameters.

Instantiating the Template

When you declare an object to be a specific kind of LinkedList, for example when you write

```
LinkedList<Guess> history;
```

the compiler uses the template you've created to instantiate a LinkedList in which Guess is substituted everywhere you have written T. Similarly, if you write

```
LinkedList<char> solution;
```

the compiler again uses your template to create a LinkedList with char substituted for T (identical to the one you created in Chapter 8).

We see this in the declaration of Game, as shown in Listing 9.7.

Listing 9.7   Game Class Declaration

```
0:  #ifndef GAME_H
1:  #define GAME_H
2:
3:  #include "def0514.h"
4:  #include "gues0901.h"
5:  #include "LL_0906.h"
6:
7:  class Guess;
8:
9:  class Game
10: {
11: public:
12:     Game();
13:     ~Game(){}
14:     void Play();
15:     bool IsValid(char c)const;
16:     const LinkedList<char>& GetSolution() const;
17:     void DisplayAnswer();
18:     void Score(
19:         const char * thisGuess,
20:         int & correct,
21:         int & position
22:         );
23:     bool HandleFlag(char flag);
```

```
24:        void ShowHint();
25:        void ShowHistory();
26:        void ShowHelp();
27:
28:   private:
29:        int HowMany(
30:            const char * theString,
31:            char theChar
32:            );
33:
34:        LinkedList<char> solution;
35:        LinkedList<Guess> history;
36:
37:        int howManyLetters;
38:        int howManyPositions;
39:        int round;
40:        int hintCtr;
41:        bool duplicates;
42:   };
43:
44:   #endif
```

On line 34 we declare `solution` to be a `LinkedList` of characters, and on line 35 we declare `history` to be a `LinkedList` of `Guess` objects.

The fact that the compiler makes an instance for every declaration of the parameterized class is somewhat "expensive" in that it causes your code to become larger than you might expect. The `LinkedList` is, after all, copied and re-created once to hold characters, and again to hold guesses. On the other hand, it is much more reliable and maintainable than is re-creating the linked list by hand. Every instance of the `LinkedList` shares every change to the template, no matter what type of object it is holding.

Using the History Object

9

The purpose of the history object is to enable the user to review his previous guesses and the scores he has received. To do so, you must create a `Guess` object after each guess is scored and store it in the `Game`'s `history` member variable, which is actually a `LinkedList<Guess>`.

Let's see it at work in Listing 9.8, the implementation of `Game`.

Listing 9.8   Implementing `Game`

```
0:   #include "game0907.h"
1:   #include "def0514.h"
2:   #include <time.h>
```

continues

Listing 9.8 continued

```
 3:
 4:  Game::Game():
 5:  round(1),
 6:  howManyPositions(0),
 7:  howManyLetters(0),
 8:  hintCtr(0),
 9:  duplicates(false)
10:  {
11:
12:      bool valid = false;
13:      while ( ! valid )
14:      {
15:          while ( howManyLetters < minLetters ¦¦
16:              howManyLetters > maxLetters )
17:          {
18:              cout << "How many letters? (";
19:              cout << minLetters << "-" << maxLetters << "): ";
20:              cin >> howManyLetters;
21:              if ( howManyLetters < minLetters ¦¦
22:                  howManyLetters > maxLetters )
23:              {
24:                  cout << "please enter a number between " ;
25:                  cout << minLetters << " and ";
25a:                 cout << maxLetters << endl;
26:              }
27:          }
28:
29:          while ( howManyPositions < minPos ¦¦
30:              howManyPositions > maxPos )
31:          {
32:              cout << "How many positions? (";
33:              cout << minPos << "-" << maxPos << "): ";
34:              cin >> howManyPositions;
35:              if ( howManyPositions < minPos ¦¦
36:                  howManyPositions > maxPos )
37:              {
38:                  cout << "please enter a number between ";
39:                  cout << minPos <<" and " << maxPos << endl;
40:              }
41:          }
42:
43:          char choice = ' ';
44:          while ( choice != 'y' && choice != 'n' )
45:          {
46:              cout << "Allow duplicates (y/n)? ";
47:              cin >> choice;
48:          }
49:
50:          duplicates = choice == 'y' ? true : false;
51:          solution.SetDuplicates(duplicates);
```

```
52:
53:              if ( ! duplicates &&
54:                  howManyPositions > howManyLetters )
55:              {
56:                  cout << "I can't put " << howManyLetters;
57:                  cout << " letters in " << howManyPositions;
58:                  cout << " positions without duplicates! ";
58a:                 cout << "Please try again.\n";
59:                  howManyLetters = 0;
60:                  howManyPositions = 0;
61:              }
62:              else
63:                  valid = true;
64:          }
65:
66:
67:          srand( (unsigned)time( NULL ) );
68:
69:
70:          for ( int i = 0; i < howManyPositions; )
71:          {
72:              int nextValue = rand() % (howManyLetters);
73:              char theChar = alpha[nextValue];
74:              if ( solution.Add(theChar) )
75:                  i++;
76:          }
77:
78:          cout << "Exiting constructor. List: ";
79:          solution.Display();
80:
81:  }
82:
83:
84:  void Game::DisplayAnswer()
85:  {
86:      solution.Display();
87:  }
88:
89:  const LinkedList<char>& Game::GetSolution() const
90:  {
91:      return solution;
92:  }
93:
94:  inline int Game::HowMany(const char * theString, char theChar)
95:  {
96:      int count = 0;
97:      for ( int i = 0; i < strlen(theString); i++)
98:          if ( theString[i] == theChar )
99:              count ++;
100:      return count;
101:  }
```

continues

Listing 9.8   continued

```
102:
103:   bool Game::IsValid(char c) const
104:   {
105:       bool isValid = false;
106:
107:       for ( int i = 0; i < howManyLetters; i++ )
108:           if ( alpha[i] == c )
109:               isValid = true;
110:
111:       return isValid;
112:   }
113:
114:   void Game::Play()
115:   {
116:       char guess[80];
117:       int correct = 0;
118:       int position = 0;
119:       bool quit = false;
120:
121:       while ( position < howManyPositions )
122:       {
123:
124:           cout << "\nRound " << round << ". Enter -? or ";
125:           cout << howManyPositions << " letters between ";
126:           cout << alpha[0] << " and ";
127:           cout << alpha[howManyLetters-1] << ": ";
128:
129:           cin >> guess;
130:
131:           if ( guess[0] == '-' )// got a flag
132:           {
133:               quit = HandleFlag(guess[1]);
134:               if ( quit )
135:                   break;
136:               continue;
137:           }
138:
139:           if ( strlen(guess) < howManyPositions )
140:           {
141:               cout << "\n ** Please enter exactly ";
142:               cout << howManyPositions << " letters. **\n";
143:               continue;
144:           }
145:
146:           round++;
147:
148:           cout << "\nYour guess: " << guess << endl;
149:
150:           Score(guess,correct,position);
151:           cout << "\t\t" << correct << " correct, ";
```

```
152:              cout << position << " in position." << endl;
153:
154:              Guess thisRound(guess,correct,position);
155:              history.Add(thisRound);
156:          }
157:
158:      if ( ! quit )
159:      {
160:              cout << "\n\nongratulations! It took you ";
161:
162:              if ( round <= 6 )
163:                  cout << "only ";
164:
165:              if ( round-1 == 1 )
166:                  cout << "one round!" << endl;
167:              else
168:                  cout << round-1 << " rounds." << endl;
169:          }
170:
171:  }
172:
173:  void Game::Score(
174:                      const char * thisGuess,
175:                      int & correct,
176:                      int & position
177:                      )
178:  {
179:      correct = 0;
180:      position = 0;
181:
182:
183:      for ( int i = 0; i < howManyLetters; i++)
184:      {
185:          int howManyInGuess = HowMany(thisGuess, alpha[i]);
186:          int howManyInAnswer = solution.HowMany(alpha[i]);
187:          correct += howManyInGuess < howManyInAnswer ?
188:              howManyInGuess : howManyInAnswer;
189:      }
190:
191:      for (  i = 0; i < howManyPositions; i++)
192:      {
193:          if ( thisGuess[i] == solution[i] )
194:              position++;
195:      }
196:
197:      ASSERT ( position <= correct )
198:
199:  }
200:
201:
202:  void Game::ShowHistory()
```

continues

Listing 9.8   continued

```
203:    {
204:         history.Display();
205:
206:    }
207:
208:    void Game::ShowHint()
209:    {
210:         if ( hintCtr < howManyPositions )
211:         {
212:             cout << "\nHINT!! Position " << hintCtr+1;
213:             cout << ": " << solution[hintCtr] << endl;
214:             hintCtr++;
215:         }
216:    }
217:
218:    void Game::ShowHelp()
219:    {
220:         cout << "\t-h Hint\n\t-s Show history\n";
221:         cout << "\t-? Help\n\t-q quit\n" << endl;
222:    }
223:
224:    bool Game::HandleFlag(char flag)
225:    {
226:         bool quit = false;
227:         switch (flag)
228:         {
229:         case 'h':
230:             ShowHint();
231:             break;
232:         case 's':
233:             ShowHistory();
234:             break;
235:         case '?':
236:             ShowHelp();
237:             break;
238:         case 'q':
239:             quit = true;
240:             break;
241:         default:
242:             cout << "\nUnknown flag. Ignored.\n";
243:             break;
244:         }
245:         return quit;
246:    }
```

Let's take a look at Game::Play(), beginning on line 114. Assume that the user enters abcde. Because the first character is not -, the if statement on line 131 fails and we continue on line 139, where we test to make sure that the user has entered the correct number of characters. He has, so we skip the `if` statement, and on line 146 we increment the round number. We then show the guess to the user on line 148. On line 150 we pass the user's guess to `Score`, which fills the member variables `correct` and `position` with the number that he has correct and the number that he has in the right position.

You're all set, but you must record this guess, along with the score; do this by instantiating a `Guess` object on line 154. This branches us to the constructor of the `Guess` class, shown in Listing 9.9.

 Note   We check for a dash (-) because this is how the user signals that he wants to take a special action. This is discussed later in this chapter.

Listing 9.9 `Guess` Implementation

```
0:  #include "gues0901.h"
1:
2:  Guess::Guess(
3:                  const char * guess,
4:                  int howManyRight,
5:                  int howManyInPosition):
6:  theScore(howManyRight, howManyInPosition)
7:  {
8:       int len = strlen(guess);
9:       string = new char[len+1];
10:      strcpy(string, guess);
11:
12: }
13:
14: Guess::Guess(const Guess& rhs):
15: theScore(rhs.theScore)
16: {
17:      int len = strlen(rhs.string);
18:      string = new char[len+1];
19:      strcpy(string, rhs.string);
20:
21: }
22:
23: Guess::Guess():
24: string(0)
25: {}
26:
27: Guess::~Guess()
28: {
29:      if ( string )
```

continues

Listing 9.9   continued

```
30:              delete string;
31:  }
32:
33:
34:
35:  bool Guess::operator==(const Guess& rhs) const
36:  {
37:      return ( (strcmp(string,rhs.string) == 0 ) &&
38:          ( theScore == rhs.theScore ) );
39:  }
40:
41:  Guess & Guess::operator=(const Guess& rhs)
42:  {
43:      if ( this != & rhs )
44:      {
45:          theScore = rhs.theScore;
46:          int len = strlen(rhs.string);
47:          string = new char[len+1];
48:          strcpy(string, rhs.string);
49:      }
50:      return *this;
51:  }
```

We pick up our analysis in the constructor of Guess on line 2, where the member variables are initialized and a copy of the string is saved in the string member variable by way of a deep copy.

On line 46 we use the standard library function strlen to get the length of a null-terminated c-style string of characters, which we store in the local variable len. On line 48 we use the standard library strcpy to copy that string into the member variable string.

With that, we return to line 155 of Listing 9.8, where we call Add on the member variable history, passing in the Guess we just created.

This causes us to jump to line 175 of Listing 9.6. In this case, the type T is Guess and the parameter theData is the Guess that was just created. The member variable duplicates is false; we enter HowMany, passing in the Guess and jumping to line 154, where the LinkedList node immediately calls HowMany on the tail Node. This is the same logic we've seen before.

The first time through, you'll remember, we get back 0 (there are no entries in the list at all yet). The second time through we'll have an InternalNode, and we find ourselves at line 125.

When we saw this before (using a linked list that held just characters), we compared the character that was passed in as a parameter with the character held by the InternalNode. This time we'll be comparing the Guess that is passed in as a parameter with the Guess that is held as data. We see this on line 128.

Because Guess is a user-defined class, the compiler messages this line from

```
myData == theData
```

into

```
myData.operator==(theData)
```

and processing jumps to line 44 of Listing 9.9, where the strings and scores are compared. Note that this design eliminates duplicate guesses from the history.

The comparison returns true if the string in the new Guess is the same as the string in the old, and if the Score in the new Guess is the same as the Score in the old.

 Note

This example uses the old c-style strings and the strcmp method from the old standard library, which takes two parameters—both pointers to c-style null-terminated character strings—and returns 0 if they are identical. All this manipulation of c-style strings is replaced by the string class from the Standard Template Library, which is covered in Chapter 10, "Leveraging the Standard Template Library."

As you can see, adding a Guess to the history LinkedList is directly parallel to adding a character to the solution.

Using the History

All this work to store off the Guess enables us to display, on demand, a history of guesses to the user. Let's assume that we've entered three answers, and on the fourth line the user enters -s, requesting that the game display the history of guesses entered so far.

If the user types a string that begins with a dash, we detect that on line 131 of Listing 9.8. This calls HandleFlag(), passes the letter immediately after the dash (guess[1]), and causes processing to jump to line 224.

The flags we support are 'h' for Hint, 's' for Show History (which is the one we want), '?' to show the help, and 'q' to quit the game. The user has entered -s, so we branch to ShowHistory() on line 202.

9

Here we invoke `Display()` on the history member variable, which you probably remember is a `LinkedList<Guess>`. This in turn calls `Display` on each of the nodes in the list. The `InternalNode`'s `Display` method passes the member variable `myData` to `cout`, which causes the global operator `<<` method to be invoked.

Getting It Right

Of course, getting this right is very difficult, and making it efficient, flexible, reusable, and robust to boot requires many months of work. Fortunately, the STL solves this problem—and many others—for us.

There is a great deal of complexity in the STL, much of it beyond the scope of this book, but the essence of it is this: Someone who knows what he is doing has already created a suite of very flexible, very efficient, very robust container classes so that you don't have to. This is a wonderful thing; it is reuse at its best.

In fact, the STL is so well designed and the classes are so useful that the right question is not, "Do I use an STL container or write my own?" but rather, "Why *wouldn't* I use the STL?" In fact, for many of us, there is no question at all: We just use the STL and assume that whatever tiny benefit we might achieve in a customized solution for our particular needs is swamped by the overwhelming benefit of using a well tested and highly optimized STL class.

Chapter 10

Leveraging the Standard Template Library

The C++ Standard now includes the Standard Libraries, which in turn include the Standard Template Library (STL). Previous primers have treated this as a very advanced topic, but this is now an integral part of the language, and all C++ programs of any size will likely include STL classes from now on as C++ programmers become more proficient with the library.

Converting Decryptix! to STL

Our linked list class is useful, but it is limited in its functionality and it's not terribly efficient. We can spend a fair amount of development time fleshing it out, making it faster, more robust, and perhaps even reusable, but the authors of the STL have done this work for us.

The STL includes a number of useful classes, including the vector class. C++ inherits arrays from C, and with that comes a host of limitations, including inefficient use of memory. The major problem with arrays occurs because you must declare how large they are at compile time. If you don't know how many objects you want to store, this is difficult to get right. If you choose too small an array, you might run out of room and not be able to store all you need to. If you choose too large an array, you waste many bytes of memory.

Vectors overcome these limitations by providing array-like indexed access in a fast, efficient, robust class that provides its own memory management. Vectors will expand automatically as you add to them, so they can start out small and grow as needed.

In this chapter we'll convert our linked lists to vectors. While we're at it, we'll convert our Score class, which exists only to hold two integers, to an STL pair class. pair is a class that is created specifically to hold paired values, which is just what we need.

Collection Classes

Vectors are one type of collection. The STL supports a number of collections, and it supports other classes for modifying and extending the functionality of collections. A comprehensive treatment of the STL is beyond the scope of this book, but is offered in *STL From Scratch* by Pablo Halpern (ISBN: 0-7897-2128-7).

Working with Vectors

Although you can treat a vector much like an array (using offset notation), you walk through a vector with an *iterator*. An iterator is much like a pointer—in fact, you can use a simple pointer as an iterator over an array—but typically an iterator is implemented as a small class. The advantage is that an iterator can maintain its state: It can know where it is in the array. The idiom for using iterators is to create one that points to the beginning of a collection and another that points to the end. You can then start at the beginning and walk the collection from beginning to end.

iterator—An object that is used to point to a particular element in a collection. Iterators are used to incrementally examine or edit each member in turn.

When a programmer talks about walking a collection, he means starting at a given point in the collection and iterating over each member in turn.

Let's take a look at the code, and you'll see how this is done. Listing 10.1 shows the Game class.

Listing 10.1   Declaring the Game Object

```
0:  #ifndef GAME_H
1:  #define GAME_H
2:
3:  #include "defvals.h"
4:  #include "gues1002.h"
5:
6:  class Guess;
7:
8:  class Game
9:  {
10:  public:
11:      Game();
```

```
12:        ~Game(){}
13:        void Display(vector<char> charVec)const;
14:        bool HandleFlag(char flag);
15:        bool IsValid(char theChar)const;
16:        vector<char> GetSolution() const;
17:        void Play();
18:        void Score(
19:            vector<char> thisGuess,
20:            int & correct,
21:            int & position
22:            );
23:        void ShowHint();
24:        void ShowHistory();
25:        void ShowHelp();
26:
27:   private:
28:        vector<char> solution;
29:        vector<Guess> history;
30:        int hintCtr;
31:        int howManyLetters;
32:        int howManyPositions;
33:        bool duplicates;
34:        int round;
35:   };
36:
37:   #endif
```

 Note   This listing uses definedValues.h, which was shown in Listing 6.4 and which is unchanged here.

As you can see on lines 28 and 29, `solution` and `history` are now declared to be vectors rather than linked lists. The vector is implemented as a template, and the same syntax we used for `LinkedList` applies here. Thus, `solution` is a vector of `char`, and `history` is a vector of `Guess`.

On line 6 I forward declare the `Guess` class because `Game` has a vector of `Guess` objects. A forward declaration says, "This is an object, and I'll declare it for you before I use any instances of it." You can forward declare when using a class in a collection type as shown here, or when member variables are pointers or references to that type; if you use an instance, however, you must include the header file.

Why a Vector of `char` and Not a String?

The STL also offers a very robust `string` class for the manipulation of strings of characters. I've chosen to treat this as a vector of characters rather than as a string because I'm interested in the individual letters as objects—not in the semantics of strings of characters. Either choice might work, but this more closely reflects how I think about the solution: as a collection of individual letters. In fact, by doing so, I can later change this from a collection of letters to, for example, a collection of colors, without significantly changing my implementation.

Listing 10.2 provides the declaration for Guess.

Listing 10.2   Declaration of Guess

```
0:  #ifndef GUESS_H
1:  #define GUESS_H
2:
3:  #include <vector>
4:  using namespace std;
5:
6:  #include "defvals.h"
7:
8:  class Guess
9:  {
10:  public:
11:      Guess(
12:          vector<char>theGuess,
13:          int howManyRight,
14:          int howManyInPosition
15:          );
16:      ~Guess(){}
17:      pair<int, int> GetScore()const { return score; }
18:      vector<char> GetString() const { return myString; }
19:      void Display() const;
20:
21:  private:
22:      vector<char> myString;
23:      pair<int, int> score;
24:  };
25:
26:  #endif
```

On line 22 we change our LinkedList of characters to a vector of characters, and on line 23 we change our Score class to a pair. The only job for the Score class was to store two related integers, which is the very purpose of a pair. The pair type is parameterized: In this case, we're holding two integers, but we might as easily have held two different user-defined types.

GetScore() now returns the member variable score, so its return type is changed to reflect that it will return a pair of integers; also, GetString now returns a vector of characters.

Let's look at the implementation of Game in Listing 10.3, Guess in 10.4, and the driver program in Listing 10.5

Listing 10.3   Game **Class Implementation**

```
0:   #include "game1001.h"
1:   #include "defvals.h"
2:   #include <string>
3:   #include <ctime>
4:   #include <algorithm>
5:   using namespace std;
6:
7:   Game::Game():
8:        round(1),
9:        howManyPositions(0),
10:       howManyLetters(0),
11:       hintCtr(0),
12:       duplicates(false)
13:  {
14:
15:       bool valid = false;
16:       while ( ! valid )
17:       {
18:           while ( howManyLetters < minLetters
19:                   ¦¦ howManyLetters > maxLetters )
20:           {
21:               cout << "How many letters? (";
22:               cout << minLetters << "-";
23:               cout << maxLetters << "): ";
24:               cin >> howManyLetters;
25:               if ( howManyLetters < minLetters ¦¦
26:                    howManyLetters > maxLetters )
27:               {
28:                   cout << "please enter a number between ";
29:                   cout << minLetters << " and ";
30:                   cout << maxLetters << endl;
31:               }
32:           }
33:
34:           while ( howManyPositions < minPos
35:                   ¦¦ howManyPositions > maxPos )
36:           {
37:               cout << "How many positions? (";
38:               cout << minPos << "-" << maxPos << "): ";
39:               cin >> howManyPositions;
40:               if ( howManyPositions < minPos ¦¦
41:                    howManyPositions > maxPos )
42:               {
43:                   cout << "please enter a number between ";
44:                   cout << minPos <<" and " << maxPos << endl;
45:               }
46:           }
```

continues

Listing 10.3   continued

```
47:
48:            char choice = ' ';
49:            while ( choice != 'y' && choice != 'n' )
50:            {
51:                    cout << "Allow duplicates (y/n)? ";
52:                    cin >> choice;
53:            }
54:
55:            duplicates = choice == 'y' ? true : false;
56:
57:            if ( ! duplicates &&
58:                howManyPositions > howManyLetters )
59:            {
60:                    cout << "I can't put " << howManyLetters;
61:                    cout << " letters in " << howManyPositions;
62:                    cout << " positions without duplicates! ";
62a:                   cout << "Please try again.\n";
63:                    howManyLetters = 0;
64:                    howManyPositions = 0;
65:            }
66:            else
67:                    valid = true;
68:        }
69:
70:        srand( (unsigned)time( NULL ) );
71:
72:        for ( int i = 0; i < howManyPositions; )
73:        {
74:            int nextValue = rand() % (howManyLetters);
75:            char theChar  = alpha[nextValue];
76:            if ( ! duplicates && i > 0 )
77:            {
78:                    vector<char>::iterator where =
79:                        find(solution.begin(), solution.end(),theChar );
80:                    if ( where != solution.end() )
81:                        continue;
82:            }
83:            solution.push_back(theChar);
84:            i++;
85:
86:        }
87:    }
88:
89:    void Game::Display(vector<char> charVec)const
90:    {
91:        copy(
92:            charVec.begin(),
93:            charVec.end(),
94:            ostream_iterator<char>(cout," "));
95:    }
96:
```

```
97:   bool Game::IsValid(char c) const
98:   {
99:        bool isValid = false;
100:
101:       for ( int i = 0; i < howManyLetters; i++ )
102:            if ( alpha[i] == c )
103:                 isValid = true;
104:
105:       return isValid;
106:  }
107:
108:  void Game::Play()
109:  {
110:       vector<char> thisGuess;
111:       int correct = 0;
112:       int position = 0;
113:       bool quit = false;
114:
115:       while ( position < howManyPositions )
116:       {
117:            thisGuess.clear();
118:            string guess;
119:
120:            cout << "\nRound " << round;
121:            cout << ". Enter -? or ";
122:            cout << howManyPositions;
123:            cout << " letters between ";
124:            cout << alpha[0];
125:            cout << " and ";
126:            cout << alpha[howManyLetters-1] << ": ";
127:
128:            cin >> guess;
129:
130:            if ( guess[0] == '-' )// got a flag
131:            {
132:                 quit = HandleFlag(guess[1]);
133:                 if ( quit )
134:                      break;
135:                 continue;
136:            }
137:
138:            if ( guess.length() < howManyPositions )
139:            {
140:                 cout << "\n ** Please enter exactly ";
141:                 cout << howManyPositions << " letters. **\n";
142:                 continue;
143:            }
144:
145:            bool lineIsValid = true;
146:
147:                 for ( int i = 0; i < howManyPositions; i++)
148:                 {
149:                      lineIsValid = IsValid(guess[i]);
```

continues

10

Listing 10.3   continued

```
150:                          if ( ! lineIsValid )
151:                              break;
152:                     }
153:
154:
155:             if ( lineIsValid )
156:                 for ( int i = 0; i < howManyPositions; i++)
157:                     thisGuess.push_back(guess[i]);
158:             else
159:             {
160:
161:                     cout << "Please enter only letters between ";
162:                     cout << alpha[0] << " and ";
163:                     cout << alpha[howManyLetters-1] << "\n";
164:                     continue;
165:             }
166:
167:             round++;
168:
169:             cout << "\nYour guess: ";
170:             Display(thisGuess);
171:
172:             Score(thisGuess,correct,position);
173:             cout << "\t\t" << correct << " correct, ";
174:             cout << position << " in position." << endl;
175:             Guess thisRound(thisGuess,correct,position);
176:             history.push_back(thisRound);
177:         }
178:
179:         if ( ! quit )
180:         {
181:             cout << "\n\nCongratulations! It took you ";
182:
183:             if ( round <= 6 )
184:                 cout << "only ";
185:
186:             if ( round-1 == 1 )
187:                 cout << "one round!" << endl;
188:             else
189:                 cout << round-1 << " rounds." << endl;
190:         }
191:
192: }
193:
194: vector<char> Game::GetSolution() const
195: {
196:     return solution;
197: }
198:
199: bool Game::HandleFlag(char flag)
```

```
200:    {
201:        bool quit = false;
202:        switch (flag)
203:        {
204:        case 'h':
205:            ShowHint();
206:            break;
207:        case 's':
208:            ShowHistory();
209:            break;
210:        case '?':
211:            ShowHelp();
212:            break;
213:        case '!':
214:            Display(GetSolution());
215:            break;
216:        case 'q':
217:            quit = true;
218:            break;
219:        default:
220:            cout << "\nUnknown flag. Ignored.\n";
221:            break;
222:        }
223:        return quit;
224:    }
225:
226:    void Game::Score(
227:            vector<char> thisGuess,
228:            int & correct,
229:            int & position
230:            )
231:    {
232:        correct = 0;
233:        position = 0;
234:
235:        for (
236:            int i = 0;
237:            i < howManyLetters;
238:            i++
239:                )
240:        {
241:            int howManyInGuess =
242:                count (thisGuess.begin(),
243:                    thisGuess.end(), alpha[i]);
243a:           int howManyInAnswer =
244:                count (solution.begin(), solution.end(), alpha[i]);
245:            correct += _MIN(howManyInGuess, howManyInAnswer);
246:        }
247:
248:        for (  i = 0; i < howManyPositions; i++)
249:        {
```

continues

Listing 10.3   continued

```
250:                    if ( thisGuess[i] == solution[i] )
251:                        position++;
252:            }
253:    }
254:
255:    void Game::ShowHelp()
256:    {
257:        cout << "\t-h Hint\n\t-s Show history\n";
258:        cout << "\t-? Help\n\t-q quit\n";
258a:       cout << endl;
259:    }
260:
261:    void Game::ShowHistory()
262:    {
263:        for (
264:            vector<Guess>::const_iterator it = history.begin();
265:            it != history.end();
266:            it++
267:               )
268:        {
269:            it->Display();
270:        }
271:    }
272:
273:    void Game::ShowHint()
274:    {
275:        if ( hintCtr < howManyPositions )
276:        {
277:            cout << "\nHINT!! Position " << hintCtr+1;
278:            cout << ": " << solution[hintCtr] << endl;
279:            hintCtr++;
280:        }
281:    }
```

Listing 10.4   Guess Implementation

```
0:   #include "gues1002.h"
1:
2:   Guess::Guess(
3:           vector<char>guess,
4:           int howManyRight,
5:           int howManyInPosition
6:           ):
7:   myString(guess),
8:   score(howManyRight, howManyInPosition)
9:   {
10:  }
11:
12:   void Guess::Display() const
13:   {
14:       copy(
15:           myString.begin(),
```

```
16:              myString.end(),
17:              ostream_iterator<char>(cout," ")
18:              );
19:        cout << "\t";
20:        cout << score.first;
21:        cout << " correct, ";
22:        cout << score.second;
23:        cout << " in position\n";
24:  }
```

Listing 10.5   Driver Program

```
0:   #include <iostream>
1:   #include <vector>
2:   #include <iterator>
3:   #include <algorithm>
4:   #include <time.h>
5:   #include <utility>
6:   #include "defvals.h"
7:   #include "game1001.h"
8:   #include "gues1002.h"
9:
10:  using namespace std;
11:
12:  int main()
13:  {
14:        cout << "Decryptix. (c)Copyright 1999";
15:        cout << " Liberty Associates, Inc.";
16:        cout << "Version 10\n\n" << endl;
17:        bool playAgain = true;
18:
19:        while ( playAgain )
20:        {
21:             char choice = ' ';
22:             Game * g = new Game;
23:             g->Play();
24:
25:             cout << "\nThe answer: ";
26:             g->Display(g->GetSolution());
27:             cout << "\n\n" << endl;
28:             delete g;
29:
30:             while ( choice != 'y' && choice != 'n' )
31:             {
32:                  cout << "\nPlay again (y/n): ";
33:                  cin >> choice;
34:             }
35:
36:             playAgain = choice == 'y' ? true : false;
37:        }
38:        return 0;
```

continues

10

Listing 10.5	continued

```
39:  }
40:
41:
```

Output

```
0:  Decryptix. (c)Copyright 1999 Liberty Associates, Inc.Version 10
1:  How many letters? (2-26): 5
2:  How many positions? (2-10): 5
3:  Allow duplicates (y/n)? n
4:  Round 1. Enter -? or 5 letters between a and e: abcde
5:  Your guess: a b c d e        5 correct, 2 in position.
6:   Round 2. Enter -? or 5 letters between a and e: -h
7:   HINT!! Position 1: a
8:   Round 2. Enter -? or 5 letters between a and e: abdce
9:   Your guess: a b d c e       5 correct, 3 in position.
10:   Round 3. Enter -? or 5 letters between a and e: abdec
11:   Your guess: a b d e c       5 correct, 1 in position.
12:  Round 4. Enter -? or 5 letters between a and e: -?
13:        -h Hint
14:        -s Show history
15:        -? Help
16:        -q quit
17:  Round 4. Enter -? or 5 letters between a and e: -s
18:  a b c d e      5 correct, 2 in position
19:  a b d c e      5 correct, 3 in position
20:  a b d e c      5 correct, 1 in position
21:  Round 4. Enter -? or 5 letters between a and e: adbce
22:  Your guess: a d b c e        5 correct, 5 in position.
23:  Congratulations! It took you only 4 rounds.
24:  The answer: a d b c e
25:  Play again (y/n): n
```

Examining the Output

Let's start with the output: I've collapsed this output to squeeze out white space caused by skipped lines, and I've added line numbers to facilitate the analysis.

The game begins on line 0 with the copyright information, and then the user is prompted for how many letters and positions, and whether duplicates are allowed. We've chosen to play with five letters in five positions, no duplicates. Our first guess is abcde, which on line 5 is scored as five correct, of which two are in the correct position.

In round 2, rather than entering a guess, we enter -h, asking for a hint. We're told that the first position is *a*. We guess abdce on line 8, and this is scored on line 9 as five correct, of which three are in the correct position. Our next guess is abdec: Once again, five are correct, but only one is in the correct position.

At this point we want to review the previous scores, so we enter -? to find out how to do so; the help is displayed beginning on line 13. On line 17 we enter -s, which requests the history of guesses; beginning on line 18, the three previous rounds are reviewed. This is enough information to determine the answer. If *a* must be in the first position, bdce has two correct, and bdec has none correct (because the *a* must be right for both of these guesses); the answer must be adbce. That is our guess, and we're correct.

Initializing the Game

Let's track the implementation to see how the vectors are used. We'll start with a break point on line 71 of Listing 10.3, where we generate a random number and turn it into a letter within the range of letters we want (in this case, the letter *a*). On line 73 we check to see whether we're allowing duplicates. Because we are not, we test i, which is currently 0 (this being the first letter to add), so the if statement is skipped. We'll simply add the letter to the vector, which we accomplish on line 80 with a call to push_back(). This method, push_back(), is used with a number of STL containers, including vector. The purpose of push_back() is to add an item to the *end* of the vector. The effect of this call is to add the letter that is held in theChar to the vector solution.

On line 81 i is incremented, and we jump to the top of the for loop on line 69. A second value is generated (*d*), and on line 73 we pass both tests and enter the if statement. It is time to test whether *d* is already in the vector. We do this by creating an iterator that we'll name where. We initialize where with the results of a call to the find() STL function, which sets the iterator where to point to the first occurrence of theChar within solution.

On line 75 we want to check whether the iterator that is returned is pointing to the iterator that marks the end of the vector. If so, the character was not in the vector. We actually reverse this logic by saying that if the iterator that is returned (where) is not set to the end, the character *was* found. Thus we must go and generate a new character, so we call continue to repeat the loop without incrementing i.

If where is now equal to end() (one past the last item in the vector), the character is not in the solution, the if statement on line 77 fails, and we do not continue; instead, we proceed to line 80, where the character is added to solution. After we've added a character for each position, solution is set and the constructor for

10

`Game` ends. This returns us to line 23 in Listing 10.5, where we invoke `Play()`, which causes us to branch to line 104 in Listing 10.3.

The `Play()` Method

The method `Game::Play()` begins when we declare a local vector of characters named `thisGuess` and local variables to represent how many choices were correct and how many were in the correct position. Finally, on line 110 a local Boolean value, `quit`, is initialized `false`.

On line 112 we begin a `while` loop to solicit guesses from the player. We begin by clearing out all the entries from the local vector `thisGuess` with a call to the vector member method `clear()`. The result is an empty vector.

We declare a Standard Library `string` variable, `guess`, on line 115. We must use this to hold the user's guess because `cin` doesn't know how to write to a vector of characters; it does, however, know how to write to a string, which we do on line 125.

On line 127 we test whether the first character in the string is a hyphen, which indicates a flag. It is not (our guess is `abcde`), so processing continues on line 135. Here we check that the player has entered the correct number of letters. Because we have, the `if` statement fails and we continue on line 142, where the local Boolean value `lineIsValid` is initialized to `true`.

On line 144 we begin looping through the string, passing each letter in turn to the method `IsValid`, which is implemented on line 94. This does a brute force search through `alpha`, looking for a letter within the range of letters we are accepting. Thus, if we are using five letters, this searches through *a*, *b*, *c*, *d*, and *e* to find the letter that is offered. If the letter that was guessed is not in the valid range, `isValid` returns `false`; otherwise, it returns `true`. The return value is tested on line 147. If any of the letters are not valid, the `for` loop breaks, and the returned value (in this case `false`) is tested on line 152.

If, by line 152, `lineIsValid` is `true`, all the characters in the guess are valid; we can add them to the `thisGuess` vector of characters, which we do by adding each of them, one by one, calling `push_back`.

If `lineIsValid` is not `true`, it means that we received at least one invalid character, and we prompt the user to try again.

Displaying the Contents of a Vector

When we have a valid guess, we display it to the user by calling `Display` on line 167 and passing in our vector of characters. This branches to line 86, where we accomplish the display by calling the STL method `copy`. The purpose of `copy` is to copy a range of a vector into another collection.

You call `copy` by passing in three iterators:

- An iterator that points to the start of the source
- An iterator that points to the end of the source
- An iterator that points to the start of a new collection

The argument to `Game::Display` is the character vector we passed in, here called `charVec`. We get an iterator to the first character in the vector by calling the member method `begin()` on that vector; similarly, we get an iterator that points to the end of the vector by calling `end()`. These are the first two parameters to `copy`. The iterator we want to pass as the third argument is a special iterator: one designed to iterate over an `ostream` object such as `cout`. This enables us to copy the characters directly to the standard output.

We do this by instantiating an unnamed `ostream` iterator of `char`, passing to the constructor an instance of an `ostream` object (in this case `cout`) as the first parameter, and providing a delimiter with which to separate each member of the vector (in this case, a space). The net effect of all this is that we print each character in the vector, separated by a space, as shown in the output on line 5.

Scoring the Guess

On line 169, the vector of characters that now contains the guess is passed to `Score()`, causing processing to branch to line 223.

The `for` loop that begins on 232 iterates through `alpha` (our array of the letters of the alphabet) for each letter in use. Thus, if we are using five letters, this iterates once for each of the five letters *a* through *e*.

We count how often each letter appears in `thisGuess`, and how often it appears in the solution. Then we compute the number correct by taking the lesser of these two counts.

We begin on line 238 by initializing the local integer variable `howManyInGuess` with the result that is obtained by calling the STL function `count`, which takes as arguments an iterator that points to the beginning of a vector, an iterator that points to the end of a vector, and an instance of an object to look for (in this case, a letter). The method `begin()` returns an iterator to the beginning of the vector and, as you might guess, `end()` returns an iterator to the end of the vector. `__MIN` is a standard C-library method that takes two integers and returns the smaller value.

The net effect of this entire `for` loop is that we have a count of how many letters are correct in the guess, even if we are allowing duplicates in the solution. We must now determine how many are in the correct position, which we do on line 245 by iterating through the guess and solution and seeing if there is any match in exact position.

Creating the History

When `Score()` returns, processing resumes at line 170 of Listing 10.3, where the score is printed. We then create a `Guess` object named `thisRound` on line 172 to hold this guess and its score, and to be added to the `History` vector of guesses for review later. This invokes the `Guess` constructor, shown on line 2 of Listing 10.4. The vector of characters is passed in as an argument, as are the integers that represent how many letters the player guessed correctly and how many are in the right position.

On line 7 we initialize the member variable `myString` with the `Guess`. This invokes the copy constructor on the vector of `char`. On line 8, we initialize `score` with the two integer variables. Checking the declaration of the `Guess` class, line 20 of Listing 10.2 shows that `score` is a pair of integers. A pair is just an ordered collection of two items, named internally `first` and `second`. With this initialization, the constructor returns, bringing us back to line 172 of Listing 10.4, where we now add our newly created `Guess` object to our history vector by calling `push_back()` and passing in the `Guess` object. This completes one round of play.

When the user is prompted for an entry, he can enter `-s`, as we saw in the output. This is trapped in `Play()` on line 127 and handled by passing in the letter that immediately follows the dash to `HandleFlag()`, the implementation of which is shown on line 196. Passing in `s` causes the `case` statement on line 204 to execute, calling `ShowHistory()`, which is implemented on line 258.

When programmers talk of *trapping* a flag, they mean noting it before taking any further action, and then acting accordingly. Typically, when a flag is trapped you take an action and then start over as if the flag didn't exist.

ShowHistory

`ShowHistory()` works by iterating through the `history` vector, calling `Display()` on each item in the vector. We do this with a `for` loop. In the initialization of the `for` loop, we create an iterator over a vector of `Guess` objects named `it` (short for *iterator*, not *Cousin It!*). We declare this a *constant* iterator because we'll only use this iterator to call constant methods on our `Guess`. We initialize this iterator to the result of calling `begin()` on `history`. Thus, we initialize it to the beginning of the vector. That completes the initialization of the `for` loop (signaled by the first semicolon).

The test of the `for` loop follows:

```
it != history.end();
```

That is, the iterator is not pointing at the end of the vector. Note that `end` is declared as just past the last object in the vector. When this returns `false`—when `it == history.end()`—we are done looping. Finally, at the end of each loop we'll increment the iterator. Iterators overload the `++` operator to indicate that they are to point at the next object in the vector.

The iterator `it` points to an object of type `Guess` at any given moment. When we call `it->Display()`, it's exactly as if we had extracted that object from the vector and called `Display()` on it. Processing branches to the implementation of `Guess`' `Display()` method, shown on line 12 of Listing 10.4.

`Display` again copies each member of its vector of characters to `cout`. This is followed on line 19 by printing a tab character, followed by the first member of the pair `score` (which, you probably remember, held the number of correct letters). We then print the word *correct* on line 21, and then pass `cout` the member variable second from `score`. Because `first` and `second` are just integers, `cout` knows how to deal with them. Note that we're not passing the pair object itself, just the members `first` and `second`, which are themselves integers.

Examining the Hints

You will notice from the output that on one round, we ask the game for a hint by passing in the `-h` flag. As before, this branches to `HandleFlag()`; this time, though, instead of branching to `ShowHistory()`, we branch to `ShowHint()` on line 270. Here we look at the `hintCtr` member variable, which is initialized to `0` in the constructor (on line 8). We compare this with `howManyPositions` to see whether we've already provided a hint for every letter. In our case, `hintCtr` is zero (this is the first time we're supplying a hint), and `howManyPositions` is 5 (the number of letters to be guessed). Because zero is less than five, the `if` statement on line 273 returns true, and we'll enter the body of the `if` statement; then, on line 274 we'll print a message for the `Hint`. On line 275 we use the `hintCtr` member variable as an offset into the `solution` vector, returning a character that is passed to `cout` to be printed to the screen.

Finally, on line 276 we increment `hintCtr` so that the next time we request a hint, we'll see the next letter in the solution.

10

Chapter 11

The Computer Guesses

Now that you have things working with templates, it is time to extend the functionality of your program and redesign it accordingly.

Teaching the Computer to Guess

The very first feature you want to add to the computer is the capability to guess a code you create. To do so, you have to think about what it is you do when *you* guess a code the computer has created. Let's examine one game:

```
Your guess: a b c d e          5 correct, 1 in position.
Round 2. Enter -? or 5 letters between a and e: bacde
Your guess: b a c d e          5 correct, 1 in position.
Round 3. Enter -? or 5 letters between a and e: badce
Your guess: b a d c e          5 correct, 1 in position.
Round 4. Enter -? or 5 letters between a and e: dcbae
Your guess: d c b a e          5 correct, 5 in position.
The answer: d c b a e
```

I've told the computer that I'll be playing with five letters in five positions, with no duplicates, so I know that the letters are *a* through *e*. My first guess is abcde; the result is five correct, one in position. On my second guess, I'll reverse *a* and *b*. If I lose the one that is in position, I know that one of these was right, but whatever the score I'll learn something. It turns out that I still have one in position.

Next, I leave *b* and *a* in the same position but reverse *c* and *d*. This also leaves one in position, so *e* is in the fifth position (that being the only logical conclusion from the scores so far). Because *a* and *b* are not in the first two positions, they must be in the third and fourth, so I'll reverse the two sets and guess dcbae. That proves to be the correct answer (the only other possible answers were dcabe, cdabe, and cdbae).

I find the answer by looking at whether a guess is consistent with what I know so far; I want the computer to do the same.

Capturing the Rules

How might we teach the computer to look for consistency in this way? On close examination, we find that there are a number of different clues we can use to speed up the computer's guess.

First, we can check to see whether it is possible to force some letters. For example, if I guess ababa and I learn that two of my letters match, I know that *a* and *b* must appear in the answer. Thus, if the number of unique letters in my guess is less than or equal to the number of correct letters, the unique letters in my guess must be correct. Call this *Force Rule 1*.

The next observation is that if we learn that zero letters in the current guess match the solution, we can eliminate all the letters in the guess from every position. We'll call this *Eliminate Rule 1*.

If we find that the number correct in this guess is exactly equal to the number already known to be forced (under Force Rule 1), the non-forced letters can be eliminated. Thus, if we guess *abcde* and we know that *ab* are forced, and the number correct is two, *cde* can be eliminated from all positions. We'll call this *Eliminate Rule 2*.

Now we examine how many are in position. If we note that none are in position, we can keep track and reduce our guesses. Thus, if we guess *abcde* and the In Position score is zero, we know that *a* cannot be in position 1, *b* cannot be in position 2, and so forth. Call this *Eliminate Rule 3*.

We'll capture these rules in a class that is responsible for managing the string of letters that is under consideration, and we'll call it a SmartString. A SmartString consists of a vector of smart characters. Each character knows its current value (for example, *c*) and the range of possible values in that character's position. The smart character doesn't need to know its position; that responsibility belongs to the string. The character just needs to know "I could be *a*, *b*, *c*, *e*, or *g*, but right now I'm *c*."

Decrypter Classes

We want to create a class for the computer and another for the human. We can also factor out their common capabilities into an abstract base class—Decrypter. Listing 11.1 shows the declaration for the class Decrypter.

Listing 11.1 `Decrypter` Class

```
0:  #ifndef DECRYPTER_H
1:  #define DECRYPTER_H
2:
3:  #include "defvals.h"
4:  #include "guess.h"
5:
6:  class Decrypter
7:  {
8:  public:
9:      Decrypter (bool duplicates);
10:     virtual ~Decrypter();
11:     void Display(vector<char> charVec) const;
12:     virtual bool HandleFlag (char flag) = 0;
13:     virtual void Play() = 0;
14:     virtual void ShowHelp() = 0;
15:     void ShowHistory();
16:
17: protected:
18:     bool duplicates;
19:     vector<Guess> history;
20:     int round;
21: };
22:
23: #endif
```

> This listing uses definedValues.h, which was shown in Listing 6.4 and which is unchanged here.

Analysis

We know that this is an abstract data type because there is at least one pure virtual function (`HandleFlag` on line 12, as well as `Play` and `ShowHelp`).

Each *pure* virtual function indicates that the concrete derived classes must override the behavior; thus, every derived class is expected to override these three methods. For example, all derived classes will implement a `Play()` method. The two we know of, `Computer` and `Human`, each have their own `Play()` methods, and although the interface to this method is identical, the actual implementation will be totally different. The base class, `Decrypter`, provides the interface; the derived classes supply the implementation.

11

The best way to analyze the implementation of the computer playing is to walk through a game and examine how the smart characters and smart strings interact to optimize the computer player's performance.

We start in main(), which is shown in Listing 11.2.

Listing 11.2   Driver Program

```
0:  #include <iostream>
1:  // Driver program to create a game and demonstrate
2:  // Computer guessing the solution
3:
4:  #include "defvals.h"
5:  #include "game.h"
6:  #include "guess.h"
7:
8:  using namespace std;
9:
10:  int main()
11:  {
12:
13:      cout << "Decryptix. (c)Copyright 1999";
14:      cout << "Liberty Associates, Inc.";
15:      cout << "Version 4.0\n\n" << endl;
16:      cout << "There are two ways to play Decryptix:";
17:      cout << "either you can guess a pattern I create,\n";
18:      cout << "or I can guess your pattern.\n\n";
19:      cout << "If you are guessing, I will think of a ";
20:      cout << "pattern of letters (e.g., abcde).\n";
21:      cout << "On each turn, you guess the pattern and ";
22:      cout << "I will tell you how many letters you \n";
23:      cout << "got right, and how many of the correct ";
24:      cout << "letters were in the correct position.\n\n";
25:      cout << "The goal is to decode the puzzle as quickly ";
26:      cout << "as possible. You control how many\n";
27:      cout << "letters can be used and how many positions ";
28:      cout << "(e.g., 5 possible letters in 4\n";
29:      cout << "positions) as well as whether or not the ";
30:      cout << "pattern might contain duplicate \n";
31:      cout << "letters (e.g., aabcd).\n\n";
32:      cout << "If I'm guessing, you think of a pattern ";
33:      cout << "and score each of my answers.\n\n";
34:      bool playAgain = true;
35:
36:      while ( playAgain )
37:      {
38:          char choice = ' ';
39:          Game * g = new Game;
40:          g->Play();
41:
42:          delete g;
43:
```

```
44:        while ( choice != 'y' && choice != 'n' )
45:        {
46:            cout << "\nPlay again (y/n): ";
47:            cin >> choice;
48:        }
49:
50:        playAgain = choice == 'y' ? true : false; 51:        }
52:
53:    return 0;
54: }
```

Analysis

Let's take a moment to examine this program in some detail. The main() function begins in its usual way, on line 10, by printing out a useful set of instructions to the player:

```
Decryptix. (c)Copyright 1999Liberty Associates, Inc.Version 4.0

There are two ways to play Decryptix:either you can guess a pattern I create,
or I can guess your pattern.

If you are guessing, I will think of a pattern of letters (e.g., abcde).
On each turn, you guess the pattern and I will tell you how many letters you
got right, and how many of the correct letters were in the correct position.

The goal is to decode the puzzle as quickly as possible. You control how many
letters can be used and how many positions (e.g., 5 possible letters in 4
positions) as well as whether or not the pattern might contain duplicate
letters (e.g., aabcd).

If I'm guessing, you think of a pattern and score each of my answers.
```

Implementing Game

On line 39 we instantiate a new Game object, and on line 40 we call Play on that object. Listing 11.3 shows the declaration of the Game object.

Listing 11.3   The Game Class

```
0:  #ifndef GAME_H
1:  #define GAME_H
2:
3:  #include "defvals.h"
4:  #include "guess.h"
5:  #include "SmartStr.h"
6:
7:  class Guess;
8:  class Decrypter;
```

11

continues

Listing 11.3 continued

```
 9:
10:  class Game
11:  {
12:  public:
13:      Game();
14:      ~Game(){}
15:
16:      void Play();
17:
18:      static int howManyLetters;
19:      static int howManyPositions;
20:
21:  private:
22:      void DisplayTime(int secs);
23:      bool VerifyComputerChoices();
24:      bool duplicates;
25:
26:      Decrypter * pDecrypter;
27:
28:  };
29:
30:  #endif
```

Analysis

Many things have changed in this implementation of Game. First—and most importantly—we now have a pointer to a Decrypter. This will be assigned to point to either a computer or a human when we begin play. You might note a few other significant changes, but I'm going to hold off on explaining these until we come to their use as we work through the program. We've progressed to the construction of a Game object on the heap (line 39 of Listing 11.2). This brings us to the implementation of Game, which is shown in Listing 11.4.

Listing 11.4 Game Implemented

```
 0:  #include "game.h"
 1:  #include "defvals.h"
 2:  #include "SmartStr.h"
 3:  #include "Decrypter.h"
 4:  #include "Human.h"
 5:  #include "computer.h"
 6:
 7:  #include <time.h>
 8:
 9:  int Game::howManyLetters = 0;
10:  int Game::howManyPositions = 0;
11:
12:  Game::Game()
```

```
13:   {
14:       for ( ;; )
15:       {
16:           // get user's preference for how many possible letters
17:           while ( howManyLetters < minLetters ||
18:               howManyLetters > maxLetters )
19:           {
20:               cout << "How many letters? (";
21:               cout << minLetters << "-" << maxLetters << "): ";
22:               cin >> howManyLetters;
23:               if ( howManyLetters < minLetters ||
24:                   howManyLetters > maxLetters )
25:               {
26:                   cout << "please enter a number between ";
27:                   cout << minLetters << " and ";
28:                   cout << maxLetters << endl;
29:               }
30:           }
31:
32:           // get user's preference for how many slots (positions)
33:           while ( howManyPositions < minPos ||
34:               howManyPositions > maxPos )
35:           {
36:               cout << "How many positions? (";
37:               cout << minPos << "-" << maxPos << "): ";
38:               cin >> howManyPositions;
39:               if ( howManyPositions < minPos ||
40:                   howManyPositions > maxPos )
41:               {
42:                   cout << "please enter a number between ";
43:                   cout << minPos <<" and " << maxPos << endl;
44:               }
45:           }
46:
47:           char choice = ' ';
48:           while ( choice != 'y' && choice != 'n' )
49:           {
50:               cout << "Allow duplicates (y/n)? ";
51:               cin >> choice;
52:           }
53:
54:           duplicates = choice == 'y' ? true : false;
55:
56:           if ( ! duplicates &&
57:               howManyPositions > howManyLetters )
58:           {
59:               cout << "\nI can't put " << howManyLetters;
60:               cout << " letters in " << howManyPositions;
61:               cout << " positions without duplicates! ";
62:               cout << "Please try again.\n\n";
63:               howManyLetters = 0;
```

11

continues

Listing 11.4   continued

```
64:              howManyPositions = 0;
65:              continue;
66:          }
67:
68:          choice = ' ';
69:          while ( choice != 'h' && choice != 'c' )
70:          {
71:              cout << "Who guesses. (H)uman";
72:              cout << " or (C)omputer? (h/c)? ";
73:              cin >> choice;
74:          }
75:
76:          bool ok = choice == 'h' ?
77:              true : VerifyComputerChoices();
78:          if( ok )
79:          {
80:              if ( choice == 'h' )
81:                  pDecrypter = new Human(duplicates);
82:              else
83:                  pDecrypter = new Computer(duplicates);
84:
85:              break;
86:          }
87:      }
88:  }
89:
90:  void Game::DisplayTime(int totalSeconds)
91:  {
92:      int totalDays = totalSeconds / SecondsInDay;
93:      int totalHours = totalSeconds / SecondsInHour;
94:      int totalMinutes = totalSeconds / SecondsInMinute;
95:      if ( totalDays > 1 )
96:          cout << totalDays << " days! ";
97:
98:      else if ( totalHours > 1 )
99:          cout << totalHours << " hours! ";
100:
101:      else if ( totalMinutes > 1 )
102:          cout << totalMinutes << " minutes. ";
103:
104:      else
105:          cout << totalSeconds << " seconds. ";
106:  }
107:
108:  void Game::Play()
109:  {
110:
111:      int start = time( NULL );
112:
113:      pDecrypter->Play();
```

```
114:
115:     // report elapsed time
116:     int end = time( NULL );
117:     int totalSeconds = end - start;
118:
119:     cout << "\nTotal elapsed time, this game: ";
120:     DisplayTime(totalSeconds);
121:
122:     cout << "\n";
123:
124:     howManyLetters = 0;
125:     howManyPositions = 0;
126: }
127:
128:
129: bool Game::VerifyComputerChoices()
130: {
131:     int totalGuesses = 1;
132:
133:     if ( duplicates )
134:         for ( int i = 0; i < howManyPositions; i++ )
135:             totalGuesses *= howManyLetters;
136:     else
137:         for (
138:             int i = howManyLetters;
139:             i > howManyLetters - howManyPositions;
140:             i—
141:             )
142:             totalGuesses *= i;
143:
144:     int totalSeconds = totalGuesses / GUESSES_PER_SECOND;
145:
146:     if ( totalSeconds > 2 )
147:     {
148:         cout << "\n\nYou are asking me to guess ";
149:         cout << "from a possible ";
150:         cout << totalGuesses;
151:         cout <<   " combinations.";
152:
153:         cout << "\nI can get through about ";
154:         cout <<   GUESSES_PER_SECOND;
155:         cout << " guesses per second. ";
156:         cout << "If the puzzle is tough,";
157:         cout << "\na single guess could take me more than ";
158:
159:         DisplayTime(totalSeconds);
160:
161:         char confirm = ' ';
162:         while ( confirm != 'y' && confirm != 'n' )
163:         {
164:             cout << "\n\nAre you sure (y/n)? ";
```

continues

Listing 11.4   continued

```
165:                cin >> confirm;
166:         }
167:
168:         if ( confirm == 'n' )
169:         {
170:             howManyLetters = 0;
171:             howManyPositions = 0;
172:             return false;
173:         }
174:     }
175:     else
176:     {
177:         cout << "Choosing among " << totalGuesses;
178:         cout << " possible combinations...\n\n";
179:     }
180:
181:     return true;
182:
183: }
```

Analysis

The constructor begins on line 12. Here's the problem we want to solve: If the computer is guessing, and if we make the problem very difficult, each guess can take a long time. We want to provide a quick estimate of how long each round will take; if it is a long time, we want to offer the user a chance to choose a smaller number of letters or positions. To do this, we need to do two things:

1. Write a member function to do the computation. We'll call it VerifyComputerChoices().

2. Put the entire set up in a loop so that if the user says he does not want the current choices, he can try again.

Forever Loops

We can create such a loop in many different ways. One common way is to create a Boolean flag value called quit, and then initialize it to false. Next, create a loop that continues until quit is set true:

```
bool quit = false;
while ( ! quit )
{
    // code here
    if ( someCondition )
        quit = true;
}
```

Such a loop continues until `someCondition` is met in which case `quit` is set `true`, and the `while` loop ends. We've chosen an alternative approach. We create a forever loop on line 14. Note that there are only two semicolons: There is no setup, no test, no action in the `for` loop—it will continue forever.

Note

> Some programmers like to define
>
> ```
> #define EVER ;;
> allowing them to write
> for ( EVER )
> {
> //...
> }
> ```
>
> which conveys that this loop goes on forever.

The only thing that can stop this loop from repeating endlessly is a `break` statement, which we see on line 85. You'll note that this break is only called if `ok` is `true`, and we set `ok` to `true` on line 76 if the user chooses human or if `VerifyComputerChoices` returns `true` (which we'll examine shortly).

Let's back up and take this one step at a time. Lines 17–30 use the same logic we've seen before to find out how many letters the user wants to play. Lines 32–45 find out how many positions. Lines 47–54 establish whether we're using duplicates; if not, lines 56–66 check to ensure that we have a logically consistent set of decisions. All this we've seen before.

Human Guesses

Lines 68–77 are responsible for figuring out whether a human is to guess the code set by the computer, or if the computer is to guess the human player's code.

If the human is guessing, `choice` is set to `h`, `ok` is set to `true`, and the `if` statement on line 78 passes us into line 80, where we create a new `Human` player, passing in the `duplicates` flag and assigning the new `Human` to the `pDecrypter` member variable. As we've seen before, it is fine to assign the address of a `Human` to a pointer to `Decrypter` because a `Human` *is-a* `Decrypter`.

We'll follow this path for now and come back to what happens if the computer is guessing later in this chapter. Let's assume that we are choosing five letters in five positions, with no duplicates. We come to line 73 and we choose `h` for human guesses. On line 81 we set `pDecrypter` to the result of calling new `Human`, passing in

11

false for duplicates. This, of course, invokes the Human constructor. Listing 11.5 shows the declaration of the Human class, and Listing 11.6 shows the implementation.

Listing 11.5 Human **Class Declaration**

```
0:  #ifndef HUMAN_H
1:  #define HUMAN_H
2:
3:  #include "Decrypr.h"
4:
5:  class Human : public Decrypter
6:  {
7:  public:
8:  Human (bool duplicates);
9:  virtual  ~Human ();
10:
11:  vector<char> GetSolution () const;
12:  bool HandleFlag (char flag);
13:  bool IsValid  (char c) const;
14:  void Play ();
15:  void Score  (
16:          vector<char> thisGuess,
17:          int & correct,
18:          int & position
19:          );
20:
21:  private:
22:  void ShowHint ();
23:  void ShowHelp ();
24:
25:  int hintCtr;
26:  vector<char> solution;
27:
28:  };
29:
30:  #endif
```

Listing 11.6 Human **Class Implementation**

```
0:  #include "Human.h"
1:  #include "Game.h"
2:  #include <string>
3:
4:  Human::Human(bool dupes) :
5:  Decrypter(dupes),
6:  hintCtr(0)
7:  {
8:
9:  }
10:
11:  Human::~Human()
12:  {
```

```
13:
14:    }
15:
16:    vector<char> Human::GetSolution() const
17:    {
18:        return solution;
19:    }
20:
21:    // Handle any flag from user (-?,-q, etc.)
22:    bool Human::HandleFlag(char flag)
23:    {
24:        bool quit = false;
25:        switch (flag)
26:        {
27:        case 'h':
28:            ShowHint();
29:            break;
30:        case 's':
31:            ShowHistory();
32:            break;
33:        case '?':
34:            ShowHelp();
35:            break;
36:        case '!':
37:            Display(GetSolution());
38:            break;
39:        case 'q':
40:            quit = true;
41:            break;
42:        default:
43:            cout << "\nUnknown flag. Ignored.\n";
44:            break;
45:        }
46:        return quit;
47:    }
48:
49:    bool Human::IsValid(char theChar) const
50:    {
51:        bool isValid = false;
52:
53:        for ( int i = 0; i < Game::howManyLetters; i++ )
54:            if ( alpha[i] == theChar )
55:                isValid = true;
56:
57:        return isValid;
58:    }
59:
60:    void Human::Play()
61:    {
62:        vector<char> thisGuess;
63:        int correct = 0;
```

continues

Listing 11.6   continued

```
64:        int position = 0;
65:        bool quit = false;
66:        round++;
67:
68:        srand( (unsigned)time( NULL ) );
69:
70:        for ( int i = 0; i <
71:            Game::howManyPositions; )
72:        {
73:            int nextValue = rand() % (Game::howManyLetters);
74:            char theChar = alpha[nextValue];
75:            if ( ! duplicates && i > 0 )
76:            {
77:                vector<char>::iterator where =
78:                    find(solution.begin(), solution.end(),theChar);
79:                if ( where != solution.end() )
80:                    continue;
81:            }
82:            solution.push_back(theChar);
83:            i++;
84:        }
85:
86:        while ( position < Game::howManyPositions )
87:        {
88:            thisGuess.clear();
89:            string guess;
90:
91:            cout << "\nRound " << round;
92:            cout << ". Enter -? or ";
93:            cout << Game::howManyPositions;
94:            cout << " letters between ";
95:            cout << alpha[0] << " and ";
96:            cout << alpha[Game::howManyLetters-1] << ": ";
97:
98:            cin >> guess;
99:
100:           if ( guess[0] == '-' )// got a flag
101:           {
102:               quit = HandleFlag(guess[1]);
103:               if ( quit )
104:                   break;
105:               continue;
106:           }
107:
108:           if ( guess.length() < Game::howManyPositions )
109:           {
110:               cout << "\n ** Please enter exactly ";
111:               cout << Game::howManyPositions << " letters. **\n";
112:               continue;
113:           }
```

```
114:
115:            bool lineIsValid = true;
116:
117:            // ensure they've entered only possible letters
118:            for ( int i = 0; i < Game::howManyPositions; i++)
119:            {
120:                lineIsValid = IsValid(guess[i]);
121:                if ( ! lineIsValid )
122:                    break;
123:            }
124:
125:            // create the guess for display
126:            if ( lineIsValid )
127:                for (
128:                    int i = 0;
129:                    i < Game::howManyPositions;
130:                    i++
131:                    )
132:                    thisGuess.push_back(guess[i]);
133:            else
134:            {
135:
136:                cout << "Please enter only letters between ";
137:                cout << alpha[0] << " and ";
138:                cout << alpha[Game::howManyLetters-1] << "\n";
139:                continue;
140:            }
141:
142:            round++;
143:            cout << "\nYour guess: ";
144:            Display(thisGuess);
145:
146:            // compute and report how they did
147:            Score(thisGuess,correct,position);
148:            cout << "\t\t" << correct << " correct, ";
149:            cout << position << " in position." << endl;
150:
151:            // crate a record and record it in the history vector
152:            Guess thisRound(thisGuess,correct,position);
153:            history.push_back(thisRound);
154:        }
155:
156:    if ( ! quit )
157:    {
158:        cout << "\nThe answer: ";
159:        Display(GetSolution());
160:        cout << "\n\n" << endl;
161:
162:        cout << "\n\nCongratulations! It took you ";
163:
164:        if ( round <= 6 )
```

continues

Listing 11.6   continued

```
165:                    cout << "only ";
166:
167:             if ( round-1 == 1 )
168:                    cout << "one round!" << endl;
169:             else
170:                    cout << round-1 << " rounds." << endl;
171:         }
172:
173:
174:  }
175:
176:
177:  // human guessing, see how many letters & position match
178:  void Human::Score(
179:                        vector<char> thisGuess,
180:                        int & correct,
181:                        int & position
182:                        )
183:  {
184:      correct = 0;
185:      position = 0;
186:
187:      // for every possible letter,
188:      // how many are in each the answer and the guess
189:      for ( int i = 0; i < Game::howManyLetters; i++)
190:      {
191:          int howManyInGuess = count(
192:                              thisGuess.begin(),
193:                              thisGuess.end(),
194:                              alpha[i]
195:                              );
196:          int howManyInAnswer = count(
197:                                  solution.begin(),
198:                                  solution.end(),
199:                                  alpha[i]
200:                                  );
201:          correct += _MIN(howManyInGuess, howManyInAnswer);
202:      }
203:
204:      // for each position in the guess
205:      // how many match the solution
206:      for (  i = 0; i < Game::howManyPositions; i++)
207:      {
208:          if ( thisGuess[i] == solution[i] )
209:                position++;
210:      }
211:  }
212:
```

```
213:    // When human is guessing, reveal each letter one by one
214:    void Human::ShowHint()
215:    {
216:        if ( hintCtr < Game::howManyPositions )
217:        {
218:            cout << "\nHINT!! Position ";
219:            cout << hintCtr+1 << ": ";
220:            cout << solution[hintCtr] << endl;
221:            hintCtr++;
222:        }
223:    }
224:        // result of pressing -?
225:    void Human::ShowHelp()
226:    {
227:        cout << "\t-h Hint\n\t-s Show history\n\t";
228:        cout << "-? Help\n\t-q quit\n" << endl;
229:    }
```

Analysis

The constructor of Human is shown on line 3 of Listing 11.6. The first thing that happens in the initialization phase is that the parameter (dupes) is passed up to the base class Decrypter. This is common: Derived classes often explicitly initialize their base class.

The declaration for the base class Decrypter is shown in Listing 11.1 and reproduced here for your convenience as Listing 11.7. The implementation is shown in Listing 11.8.

Listing 11.7   Reproduction of Listing 11.1

```
0:  #ifndef DECRYPTER_H
1:  #define DECRYPTER_H
2:
3:  #include "defvals.h"
4:  #include "guess.h"
5:
6:  class Decrypter
7:  {
8:  public:
9:      Decrypter   (bool duplicates);
10:     virtual ~Decrypter   ();
11:     void Display (vector<char> charVec) const;
12:     virtual bool HandleFlag (char flag) = 0;
13:     virtual void Play () = 0;
14:     virtual void ShowHelp () = 0;
15:     void ShowHistory ();
```

11

continues

Listing 11.7   continued

```
16:
17:   protected:
18:       bool duplicates;
19:       vector<Guess> history;
20:       int round;
21:   };
22:
23:   #endif
```

Listing 11.8   Decrypter Implemented

```
0:    #include "Decryptr.h"
1:
2:    Decrypter::Decrypter(bool hasDuplicates):
3:    duplicates(hasDuplicates),
4:    round(0)
5:    {
6:
7:    }
8:
9:    Decrypter::~Decrypter()
10:   {
11:
12:   }
13:
14:
15:   void Decrypter::Display(vector<char> charVec) const
16:   {
17:       copy(
18:           charVec.begin(),
19:           charVec.end(),
20:           ostream_iterator<char>(cout," ")
21:           );
22:   }
23:
24:   // Iterate through history of guesses and display results
25:   void Decrypter::ShowHistory()
26:   {
27:       for (
28:           vector<Guess>::const_iterator it =
29:               history.begin();
30:           it != history.end();
31:           it++
32:           )
33:       {
34:           it->Display();
35:       }
36:   }
```

Analysis

The initialization in `Decrypter` in turn takes the `dupes` parameter and uses it to initialize the member variable, `duplicates`. In addition, the member variable `round` is initialized to `0`.

The `Human` constructor and the `Decrypter` constructor take no further action, so control is returned to line 81 in Listing 11.4, where the address of the newly created `Human` object is assigned to the pointer `pDecrypter` (see Figure 11.1).

Figure 11.1

Assigning
`pDecrypter`.

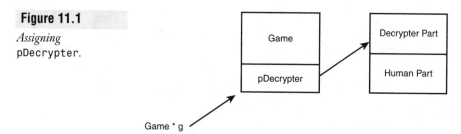

On line 85 we hit the `break` statement, ending the forever loop and thus ending the `Game` constructor. Note that the semantics of this constructor are that a `Game` object is not valid until it is pointing to a fully initialized `Decrypter` of some kind.

Control now resumes at line 40 of Listing 11.2, where we invoke `Play()` on the game pointer, thus branching to line 108 of Listing 11.4.

We begin by initializing a local variable, `start`, with the current time. Then, on line 113, we invoke the `Play()` method on the `Decrypter`. By looking ahead to lines 116–126, you'll notice that we do little else in `Game::Play`. We note the elapsed time of playing the game and set `howManyLetters` and `howManyPositions` back to zero for the next time we play, but all the action is now in the `Play()` method of the `Decrypter`. This is just as it should be: The game is delegating this responsibility to the object that knows how to do it—the `Decrypter`. It is as if the Game said, "Okay, I'll keep track of how long this takes. Now go ahead and play."

In our case, because `pDecrypter` points to a `Human` and because `Play` is a virtual function, this invokes the `Human` implementation of `Play()` as shown on line 59 of Listing 11.6.

This is a fundamental design rule: *Put the responsibility in the class that has the knowledge.* Because `Human` has the knowledge of how a human guesser plays, that is where the responsibility for `Play()` belongs.

11

How **Human** Plays

Staying with Listing 11.6, on line 62 we create a vector of characters to hold the first guess, and on lines 63–65 we initialize a few variables to their starting position. (So far, the human has guessed zero correct answers, of which zero are in position, and he does not yet want to quit.) We also increment round to 1 to get us started:

```
62:      vector<char> thisGuess;
63:      int correct = 0;
64:      int position = 0;
65:      bool quit = false;
66:      round++;
```

Next comes some logic we've seen before, in which we fill the solution vector with randomly generated letters. This is identical to the work formerly done in the Game object, moved here to Human because this is human guessing-specific activity. That is, when the computer is guessing, this won't be done.

On line 85 we begin the logic of prompting the human player for his guess; again, we've seen this before, and it was covered in some detail in Chapter 10, "Leveraging the Standard Template Library." All this logic, through scoring the guess and creating the Guess object to store in History, is just as we've seen it before, simply moved here to Human to encapsulate this responsibility in the class that must manage it. There are no surprises here.

Computer **Guesses**

The interesting new material begins when the computer is guessing. Let's play again; this time we'll choose 10 letters in five positions with no duplicates, but the computer will be guessing. We'll pick up the action on line 71 of Listing 11.4, where we prompt for Human guessing or Computer. When we enter c for computer, we come to line 76. Here the Boolean value ok is initialized with the value of the ternary operator. Let's pick this apart. The ternary operator is written as follows:

```
choice == 'h' ? true : VerifyComputerChoices();
```

This must resolve to true or false. It works like this: If choice equals 'h', the first value (true) is returned. If, on the other hand, choice does not equal 'h', the value that is returned from calling VerifyComputerChoices() is returned. We'd expect that method to return a Boolean, and that is just what it does.

The net effect is this: If we choose c for the computer to play, VerifyComputerChoices() is invoked, and if that does not return true, the loop repeats. If it does return `true`, the `if` statement on line 78 is satisfied, and `pDcrypter` is assigned to a new `Computer` object on line 83:

```
78:         if( ok )
79:         {
80:             if ( choice == 'h' )
81:                 pDecrypter = new Human(duplicates);
82:             else
83:                 pDecrypter = new Computer(duplicates);
```

Stepping into `VeryifyComputerChoices()`

The call to `VerifyComputerChoices()` causes us to jump to line 129. The goal of this method is to make an estimate of how long it might take the computer to guess the answer on each round. To do this, we need to know how many possible combinations of letters there are.

Let's think about how we might solve this problem before we analyze the code. If we allow duplicates, the number of letters we can use must be multiplied by itself for each position. Thus, the number of possible combinations is L^P, where L is the number of different letters and P is the number of different positions. With four letters in three positions, we have 4*4*4, or 64, possible combinations.

If we do *not* allow duplicates, however, we cannot have the combinations *aaaa*, *aaab*, *aabb*, and so on. In fact, if *a* is in the first position, it can not be in positions 2, 3, or 4. Thus, for each position, we must decrement the possible variants. Therefore, the total number is 4*3*2, or 24, possible combinations. More generally, the answer is L*L-1...*(L-P+1). Thus, for five letters in three positions, the final multiplication is times 5-3+1, or 3, so it is 5*4*3.

We can capture this in the algorithms shown on lines 131–142:

```
131:    int totalGuesses = 1;
132:
133:    if ( duplicates )
134:        for ( int i = 0; i < howManyPositions; i++ )
135:            totalGuesses *= howManyLetters;
136:    else
137:        for (
138:            int i = howManyLetters;
139:            i > howManyLetters - howManyPositions;
140:            i—
141:            )
142:            totalGuesses *= i;
```

Substitute real numbers and prove to yourself that this works. Let's try five letters in three positions. If we are not allowing duplicates, the `for` loop runs three times (i=0, i=1, i=2), so we'll multiply 1*5 = 5, 5*5 = 25, 25*5 = 225. That is correct because 5^3 is 225.

If we are *not* allowing duplicates, the `else` clause runs and is translated into the following:

```
for (
     i = 5;
     i > 5-3
     i—
   )
```

This runs thrice, resulting in 1 *= 5, which is 5, and then 5 *= 4, which is 20, and then 20 *= 3, which is 60. There are 60 combinations of five letters in three positions if you don't allow duplicates.

We then compute how many seconds the computer might have to guess by dividing the total number of guesses by a constant, GUESSES_PER_SECOND, which we defined in definedValues.h as 10,000. This number, 10,000, is based on my own experience with this program; you might want to use a more sophisticated number, based on actual machine speed.

 Note

If you get ambitious, you can have the system keep track of how long it takes to make a series of guesses and then adjust its average speed accordingly. That kind of heuristic learning is beyond the scope of this book and is left as an exercise for the masochistic reader. If you do undertake this project, remember the Heisenberg uncertainty analogy: The very act of measuring the duration might affect the duration.

On line 146 I check whether the total number of seconds I've computed is greater than two. (This means, in effect, that there are more than 20,000 combinations.) If so, I prompt the user and give him a sense of what he is up against. For example, if you ask for 20 letters in five positions, you get the following warning:

```
You are asking me to guess from a possible 1860480 combinations.
I can get through about 10000 guesses per second. If the puzzle is tough,
a single guess could take me more than 3 minutes.
```

Because 20 letters in five positions without duplicates creates 1,860,480 combinations, it can take a while for the computer to generate a guess—and that number grows to 3,200,000 if you allow duplicates!

To compute how long such a guess might take, we branch to `DisplayTime`, passing in the number of seconds. `DisplayTime` just does the division, and is shown on lines 90–106:

```
90:   void Game::DisplayTime(int totalSeconds)
91:   {
```

```
92:        int totalDays = totalSeconds / SecondsInDay;
93:        int totalHours = totalSeconds / SecondsInHour;
94:        int totalMinutes = totalSeconds / SecondsInMinute;
95:        if ( totalDays > 1 )
96:            cout << totalDays << " days! ";
97:
98:        else if ( totalHours > 1 )
99:            cout << totalHours << " hours! ";
100:
101:        else if ( totalMinutes > 1 )
102:             cout << totalMinutes << " minutes. ";
103:
104:        else
105:             cout << totalSeconds << " seconds. ";
106:    }
```

If the total time is less than two seconds or if the user decides to live with the delay, we return `true`; otherwise, we return `false`. You'll remember that we return this to the ternary operator on line 77:

```
76:        bool ok = choice == 'h' ?
77:                true : VerifyComputerChoices();
```

When we know that we have a computer guessing and we received `true` from `VerifyComputerChoices`, we are ready to create the new `Computer` object and assign it to `pDecrypter`, which we do on line 83:

```
83:            pDecrypter = new Computer(duplicates);
```

Creating the `Computer` Object

This brings us to the constructor for the new `Computer` object. Listing 11.9 shows the class declaration, and Listing 11.10 shows the implementation of the `Computer` class.

Listing 11.9 `Computer` Declaration

```
0:  #ifndef COMPUTER_H
1:  #define COMPUTER_H
2:
3:  #include "Decryptr.h"
4:
5:  class SmartString;
6:
7:  class Computer : public Decrypter
8:  {
9:  public:
10:      Computer(bool duplicates);
11:      virtual ~Computer();
12:      bool HandleFlag(char flag);
```

11

continues

Listing 11.9   continued

```
13:        void Play();
14:
15:  private:
16:        void GenerateAGuess();
17:        bool IsConsistent(vector<char> guess);
18:        Guess OfferGuess();
19:        void ShowHelp();
20:
21:        SmartString * mySmartString;
22:        int total;
23:  };
24:
25:  #endif
```

Listing 11.10   Computer Implementation

```
0:   #include "Computer.h"
1:   #include "smartstr.h"
2:   #include "Game.h"
3:
4:   Computer::Computer(bool dupes):
5:   Decrypter(dupes),
6:   total(0),
7:   mySmartString(0)
8:   {
9:
10:  }
11:
12:  Computer::~Computer()
13:  {
14:
15:  }
16:
17:  void Computer::GenerateAGuess()
18:  {
19:
20:      bool ok = true;
21:      int counter = 0;
22:      int start = time( NULL );
23:      do
24:      {
25:          counter++;
26:          total++;
27:          if ( counter % 10000 == 0 )
28:              cout << ".";
29:
30:          ok = mySmartString->GetNext();
31:
32:          if ( !ok )
33:          {
```

```
34:                    cout << "Something went wrong!";
35:                    cout << " Please start over\n";
36:                    round = 0;
37:                    delete mySmartString;
38:                    mySmartString = new SmartString(duplicates);
39:                    ShowHistory();
40:                    cout << "\n\n";
41:                    history.clear();
42:                    continue;
43:               }
44:
45:        } while ( !IsConsistent(mySmartString->GetString()) );
46:
47:        int end = time( NULL );
48:        int seconds = end - start;
49:        cout << "(" << counter ;
50:        cout << " strings eliminated this round; ";
51:        cout << total << " total.)";
52:        if ( seconds > 1 )
53:            cout << " [" << seconds << " seconds]";
54:        cout << "\n";
55: }
56:
57: // Handle any flag from user (-?,-q, etc.)
58: bool Computer::HandleFlag(char flag)
59: {
60:        bool quit = false;
61:        switch (flag)
62:        {
63:        case 's':
64:            ShowHistory();
65:            break;
66:        case '?':
67:            ShowHelp();
68:            break;
69:        case 'q':
70:            quit = true;
71:            break;
72:        default:
73:            cout << "\nUnknown flag. Ignored.\n";
74:            break;
75:        }
76:        return quit;
77: }
78:
79: bool Computer::IsConsistent(vector<char> theGuess)
80: {
81:
82:
83:        if ( ! duplicates)
84:        {
```

continues

Listing 11.10   continued

```
85:              for (
86:                  vector<char>::const_iterator it =
87:                      theGuess.begin();
88:                  it != theGuess.end();
89:                  it++
90:                  )
91:              {
92:                  int HowMany =
93:                      count(theGuess.begin(), theGuess.end(),*it); 94:
if ( HowMany > 1 )
95:                      return false;
96:              }
97:          }
98:
99:      bool isValid = true;
100:
101:     int correct;
102:     int position;
103:
104:     for (
105:         vector<Guess>::const_iterator it =
106:             history.begin();
107:         it != history.end();
108:         it++
109:         )
110:     {
111:
112:         vector <char> temp = it->GetString();
113:
114:         correct = 0;
115:         position = 0;
116:         for ( int i = 0; i < Game::howManyLetters; i++)
117:         {
118:             int howManyInGuess =
119:                 count (
120:                     theGuess.begin(),
121:                     theGuess.end(),
122:                     alpha[i]
123:                     );
124:             int howManyInAnswer =
125:                 count (temp.begin(), temp.end(), alpha[i]);
126:             correct += _MIN(howManyInGuess, howManyInAnswer);
127:         }
128:
129:         for (  i = 0; i < Game::howManyPositions; i++)
130:         {
131:             if ( theGuess[i] == temp[i] )
132:                 position++;
133:         }
134:
```

```
135:            if ( correct != it->GetScore().first ||
136:                    position != it->GetScore().second )
137:            {
138:                isValid = false;
139:                break;
140:            }
141:        }
142:
143:        return isValid;
144: }
145:
146: Guess Computer::OfferGuess()
147: {
148:        vector<char> theGuess =
149:            mySmartString->GetString();
150:        round++;
151:        int numCorrect, numInPosition;
152:        cout << "\n";
153:        Display(theGuess);
154:        cout << "Round " << round << ". ";
155:        cout << "Please record score. \t";
156:        cout << "How many correct?: ";
157:        cin >> numCorrect;
158:        cout << "\t\t\tHow many in position?: ";
159:        cin >> numInPosition;
160:        Guess thisGuess(theGuess,numCorrect,numInPosition);
162:        return thisGuess;
163:
164: }
165:
166: void Computer::Play()
167: {
168:
169:        if ( ! mySmartString )
170:            mySmartString = new SmartString(duplicates);
171:
172:        vector<char> theGuess;
173:        history.clear();
174:
175:        bool deletedCharacters = false;
176:
177:        for ( ;; )
178:        {
179:            Guess theGuess = OfferGuess();
180:            history.push_back(theGuess);
181:
182:            if ( theGuess.GetScore().second ==
183:                Game::howManyPositions )
184:                break;
185:
186:            if (
```

continues

11

Listing 11.10   continued

```
187:                    ! mySmartString->CanEliminateCharacters(theGuess) ||
188:                    ! IsConsistent(mySmartString->GetString())
189:                    )
190:                         GenerateAGuess();
191:        };
192:    }
193:
194:    // result of pressing -?
195:    void Computer::ShowHelp()
196:    {
197:        cout << "\t-s Show history\n\t-? Help\n";
198:        cout << "\t-q quit\n" << endl;
199:    }
```

Analysis

Before we begin the analysis of the constructor, we must examine the Computer class declaration closely.

On line 22 of Listing 11.9, we find a member variable total, which is declared to be an int. We'll use this integer to keep track of how many potential answers we've eliminated at any stage of the game. The goal of the computer guesser is to eliminate as many potential answers as possible to narrow down the field of guesses.

On the preceding line, however, we find a member variable that is a pointer to a smart string:

```
21:    SmartString * mySmartString;
```

This is key to our strategy of how to eliminate wrong answers. A smart string is a class that is responsible for knowing the potential answers and for eliminating answers that are known not to be possible. We'll see how this works in Chapter 12, "Delegating Responsibility."

In this chapter

- *Assigning Responsibility*
- *Watching it Work*
- *The Computer Plays*
- *Excursion: Static Member Variables*
- *Resuming the Analysis*
- *Eliminating Characters in Position*

Chapter 12

Delegating Responsibility

In the Chapter 11, "The Computer Guesses," we began to add the capability for the computer to guess the code that was established by the human player. Because the computer has no intuition, it must do this by working its way through every combination in a brute-force approach. We can significantly reduce the number of guesses the computer must make if we can eliminate some guesses because they are inconsistent, and if we can narrow the range of possible choices by either forcing some letters to be true or by eliminating some letters altogether.

Assigning Responsibility

It is a heuristic of good design that responsibilities be assigned to the class with the necessary knowledge, and also that any given class own one coherent set of responsibilities.

The Computer class has enough to do without worrying about which letters are valid. We'll create a smart string class to capture all we learn about the string as we proceed, and we'll create a smart character class to be responsible for capturing what we know about each position within the string.

Let's examine the smartString class in some detail. Listing 12.1 contains the declaration of the SmartString class, and Listing 12.2 contains the implementation.

Listing 12.1 SmartString Declaration

```
0:  #ifndef SMARTSTRING_H
1:  #define SMARTSTRING_H
2:
```

continues

Listing 12.1   continued

```
3:   #include "defvals.h"
4:   #include "SmartChr.h"
5:
6:   class Guess;
7:
8:   class SmartString
9:   {
10:  public:
11:      SmartString(bool dupes);
12:      virtual  ~SmartString();
13:
14:      bool CanEliminateCharacters(const Guess& theGuess);
15:      bool GetNext();
16:      vector<char> GetString();
17:      bool RemoveCurrentCharacters();
18:      bool RemoveCurrentCharactersInEveryPosition();
19:
20:  private:
21:      void ForceCharacters(const Guess & theGuess);
22:      int CountForcedInGuess(const Guess & theGuess);
23:      int CountUniqueLettersInGuess(const Guess & theGuess);
24:      bool In(vector <char> vec, char target) const;
25:
26:      vector<char> deadCharacters;
27:      bool duplicates;
28:      vector<char> forcedCharacters;
29:      vector<SmartChar> myString;
30:
31:  };
32:  #endif
```

Listing 12.2   SmartString Implementation

```
0:   #include "SmartStr.h"
1:   #include "Game.h"
2:   #include "Guess.h"
3:
4:   SmartString::SmartString(bool dupes):
5:   duplicates(dupes)
6:   {
7:       for ( int i = 0; i < Game::howManyPositions; i++ )
8:       {
9:           int j;
10:          if ( duplicates )
11:              j = 0;
12:          else
13:              j = i;
14:          SmartChar theChar(j);
15:          myString.push_back(theChar);
```

```
16:        }
17:    }
18:
19:    SmartString::~SmartString()
20:    {
21:
22:    }
23:
24:    vector<char> SmartString::GetString()
25:    {
26:        vector<char> outString;
27:
28:        for (
29:            vector<SmartChar>::iterator it = myString.begin();
30:            it != myString.end();
31:            it++
32:            )
33:        {
34:            char theChar = it->GetChar();
35:            outString.push_back(theChar);
36:        }
37:        return outString;
38:    }
39:
40:
41:    bool SmartString::GetNext()
42:    {
43:        vector<char> outString;
44:        vector<SmartChar>::reverse_iterator rit;
45:        rit = myString.rbegin();
46:
47:        bool rollover = rit->Increment();
48:        while ( rollover )
49:        {
50:            rit++;
51:            if ( rit == myString.rend() )
52:                return false;
53:            else
54:            {
55:                rollover = rit->Increment();
56:            }
57:        }
58:        return true;
59:    }
60:
61:
62:    // removes character that is currently shown
63:    // in a particular position
64:    bool SmartString::RemoveCurrentCharacters()
65:    {
```

12

continues

Listing 12.2   continued

```
66:       char theChar;
67:       bool anyDeleted = false;
68:
69:       for (
70:           vector<SmartChar>::iterator it = myString.begin();
71:           it != myString.end();
72:           it++
73:           )
74:       {
75:           theChar = it->GetChar();
76:
77:           if ( ! In(forcedCharacters,theChar) )
78:           {
79:               theChar = it->RemoveCurrent();
80:               // dead characters stop you from
81:               // reporting removal of characters already dead
82:               if (! In(deadCharacters,theChar) )
83:               {
84:                   deadCharacters.push_back(theChar);
85:                   cout << "Eliminating " << theChar;
86:                   cout << " from current position" << endl;
87:                   anyDeleted = true;
88:               }
89:           }
90:       }
91:       return anyDeleted;
92:   }
93:
94:
95:   // removes character that is currently shown
96:   // in a particular position from every position
97:   bool SmartString::RemoveCurrentCharactersInEveryPosition()
98:   {
99:       char theChar;
100:      bool anyDeleted = false;
101:      vector <char> currentGuess;
102:
103:      for (
104:          vector<SmartChar>::iterator it = myString.begin();
105:          it != myString.end();
106:          it++
107:          )
108:      {
109:          currentGuess.push_back(it->GetChar());
110:      }
111:
112:      for (
113:          vector<char>::iterator itc = currentGuess.begin();
114:          itc != currentGuess.end();
115:          itc++
```

```
116:                )
117:         {
118:             theChar = *itc;
119:             if ( ! In(forcedCharacters,theChar) )
120:             {
121:
122:                 for (
123:                     vector<SmartChar>::iterator it2 = myString.begin();
124:                     it2 != myString.end();
125:                     it2++
126:                     )
127:                 {
128:                     it2->Remove(theChar);
129:                     if (! In(deadCharacters,theChar) )
130:                     {
131:                         deadCharacters.push_back(theChar);
132:                         cout << "Eliminating " << theChar << endl;
133:                         anyDeleted = true;
134:                     }
135:                 }
136:             }
137:         }
138:     return anyDeleted;
139: }
140:
141: bool SmartString::CanEliminateCharacters(
142:                     const Guess & theGuess)
143: {
144:
145:     bool anyDeleted = false;
146:     ForceCharacters(theGuess);
147:     int forcedInAnswer = CountForcedInGuess(theGuess);
148:
149:     int overall = theGuess.GetScore().first;
150:     int inPos = theGuess.GetScore().second;
151:
152:
153:     if ( overall == 0 || overall == forcedInAnswer )
154:     {
155:         anyDeleted = RemoveCurrentCharactersInEveryPosition();
156:         return anyDeleted; // we did eliminate characters
157:     }
158:
159:     if ( inPos == 0 )
160:     {
161:         anyDeleted = RemoveCurrentCharacters();
162:         return anyDeleted; // we did eliminate characters
163:     }
164:
165:     return false;
```

12

continues

Listing 12.2   continued

```
166:    }
167:
168:    void SmartString::ForceCharacters(const Guess &theGuess)
169:    {
170:        int numDifferentLetters =
171:            CountUniqueLettersInGuess(theGuess);
172:        int score = theGuess.GetScore().first;
173:
174:        if ( score >= numDifferentLetters )
175:        {
176:            vector<char> theString =
177:                theGuess.GetString();
178:
179:            for (
180:                vector<char>::const_iterator it = theString.begin();
181:                it != theString.end();
182:                it++
183:                )
184:            {
185:                if ( ! In(forcedCharacters, *it) )
186:                    forcedCharacters.push_back(*it);
187:            }
188:        }
189:    }
190:
191:    int SmartString::CountUniqueLettersInGuess(
192:                        const Guess &theGuess)
193:    {
194:        vector<char> temp;
195:        vector<char> theString =
196:            theGuess.GetString();
197:
198:        for (
199:            vector<char>::const_iterator it = theString.begin();
200:            it != theString.end();
201:            it++
202:            )
203:        {
204:            if (! In(temp,*it) )
205:                temp.push_back(*it);
206:        }
207:
208:        // temp now has all the unique letters
209:
210:        return temp.size();
211:    }
212:
213:    int SmartString::CountForcedInGuess(
214:                        const Guess &theGuess)
215:    {
```

```
216:        int howManyForcedInGuess = 0;
217:        vector<char> theString = theGuess.GetString();
218:
219:        for (
220:            vector<char>::const_iterator it = theString.begin();
221:            it != theString.end();
222:            it++
223:            )
224:        {
225:            if ( In( forcedCharacters, *it ) )
226:                howManyForcedInGuess++;
227:        }
228:
229:        return howManyForcedInGuess;
230:
231:    }
232:
233:    bool SmartString::In(vector<char> vec, char target) const
234:    {
235:        vector<char>::iterator where =
236:            find(vec.begin(), vec.end(),target);
237:        return where != vec.end();
238:    }
```

Analysis

Let's begin by examining the header. The public interface includes methods such as `CanElminateCharacters`, `RemoveCurrentCharacters`, and `RemoveCurrentCharactersInEveryPosition`. We'll examine these in great detail when we work through the implementation of this class. The private section of the header includes a few member variables. First, on line 26 we have a vector of characters called `deadCharacters`, which keeps track of the characters that are no longer possible in any position. Next, we keep track of whether duplicates are allowed. On line 28 is a vector of characters, `forcedCharacters`, which keeps track of any characters we know are in the answer. Both `deadCharacters` and `forcedCharacters` are used only to store the information that this particular character is dead (or forced) *somewhere* in the string—they don't specify where, in which position:

```
26:    vector<char> deadCharacters;
27:    bool duplicates;
28:    vector<char> forcedCharacters;
29:    vector<SmartChar> myString;
```

When we have that information, we delegate it to the smart characters that compose the next member variable, `myString`, which is declared to be a vector of `SmartChar`. Listing 12.3 shows the declaration of `smartChar`, and Listing 12.4 has the implementation.

12

Listing 12.3 SmartChar **Declared**

```
 0:  #ifndef SMARTCHAR_H
 1:  #define SMARTCHAR_H
 2:
 3:  #include "defvals.h"
 4:
 5:  class SmartChar
 6:  {
 7:  public:
 8:      SmartChar(int letter = 0);
 9:      virtual ~SmartChar();
10:
11:      char GetChar() const;
12:      bool Increment();
13:      char RemoveCurrent();
14:      bool Remove(char c);
15:
16:  private:
17:      int myChar;
18:      vector<char> myCharacters;
19:
20:  };
21:
22:  #endif
```

Listing 12.4 SmartChar **Implemented**

```
 0:  #include "SmartChr.h"
 1:  #include "Game.h"
 2:
 3:  SmartChar::SmartChar(int letter):
 4:  myChar(letter)
 5:  {
 6:      for ( int i = 0; i < Game::howManyLetters; i++ )
 7:          myCharacters.push_back(alpha[i]);
 8:
 9:  }
10:
11:  SmartChar::~SmartChar()
12:  {
13:
14:  }
15:
16:  char SmartChar::GetChar() const
17:  {
18:      return myCharacters[myChar];
19:  }
20:
21:  bool SmartChar::Increment()
22:  {
```

```
23:        if ( ++myChar >= myCharacters.size() )
24:        {
25:            myChar = 0;
26:            return true;
27:        }
28:        return false;
29:    }
30:
31:    char SmartChar::RemoveCurrent()
32:    {
33:        char theChar = ' ';
34:
35:        if ( myCharacters.size() > 1 )
36:        {
37:            theChar = GetChar();
38:            myCharacters.erase( myCharacters.begin()+myChar );
39:            while ( myChar >= myCharacters.size() )
40:                myChar—;
41:        }
42:        return theChar;
43:    }
44:
45:    bool SmartChar::Remove(char theChar)
46:    {
47:        if ( myCharacters.size() > 1 )
48:        {
49:            vector<char>::iterator where =
50:                find(myCharacters.begin(), myCharacters.end(),theChar);
51:            if ( where != myCharacters.end() )
52:                myCharacters.erase(where);
53:            return true;
54:        }
55:        return false;
56:    }
```

Analysis

Understanding the Default Parameter

The smartChar class begins on line 8 of Listing 12.3 with the declaration of the constructor:

```
8:        SmartChar(int letter = 0);
```

The constructor takes a single parameter, an integer. We provide a *default* value for that integer (0) that will be assigned if none is provided by the calling function.

Thus, you can create a smartChar on the stack in one of two ways. You can write

```
SmartChar someChar(5);
```

12

which creates a SmartChar object named someChar and passes in the value 5; or you can write

```
SmartChar someChar;
```

which creates a SmartChar object named someChar and acts as if you had sent in the value 0. This has exactly the same impact as if you had written

```
SmartChar someChar(0);
```

Of course, you can also declare these on the heap. The equivalent statements are

```
SmartChar * pSomeChar = new SmartChar(5);
SmartChar * pSomeChar = new SmartChar;  // use the default
SmartChar * pSomeChar = new SmartChar(0);
```

If you peek ahead to line 4 of Listing 12.4 you'll find that the value of the parameter is assigned to the member variable myChar. Thus, if you write

```
SmartChar someChar(5);
```

when the constructor runs, the member variable myChar is initialized with the value 5; if you write

```
SmartChar someChar;
```

the member variable myChar is initialized with the value 0.

SmartChar in Detail

On lines 17 and 18 of Listing 12.3 we declare the two member variables:

```
17:      int myChar;
18:      vector<char> myCharacters;
```

The first, myChar, is an integer that we've seen already. The only other member variable, myCharacters, is a vector of characters.

Each SmartChar is in a specific position. myCharacters keeps track of every legal character for the current position. myChar keeps track of the offset of the current value for the position. Thus, if we are playing with five letters in five positions and the current guess is abcde, the smart character for position three will have a, b, c, d, e in its vector and 2 in myChar. (2 because a=0, b=1, and c=2, and this character is currently c.)

As we learn that a given position cannot have certain characters, we can eliminate those characters from the myCharacters vector. This will track our per-position knowledge.

Watching it Work

All this is rather complex in the abstract, but much easier to understand as we work our way through a problem. Let's return to the construction of the Computer object on line 5 of Listing 11.11:

```
4:  Computer::Computer(bool dupes):
5:  Decrypter(dupes),
6:  total(0),
7:  mySmartString(0)
8:  {
9:
10:  }
```

The Computer constructor takes a single parameter, dupes, which is provided by Game when it creates the Computer object. The very first thing that is done in the initialization of Computer is to chain up to the base class, Decrypter, passing along the Boolean argument.

As you'll remember, and as shown on line 2 of Listing 11.9, the Decrypter constructor does nothing except stash this value away and initialize its member variable round to 0:

```
2:  Decrypter::Decrypter(bool hasDuplicates):
3:  duplicates(hasDuplicates),
4:  round(0)
5:  {
6:
7:  }
```

The computer constructor then initializes its own member variable, total, and its pointer, mySmartString, to zero.

Note It is always legal—and a good idea—to initialize pointers to zero. This is a safe value for a pointer in C++, and it avoids the problem of random values being in the pointer when the pointer is used. With the value 0, if the pointer is used, you'll get an immediate error. Furthermore, although it is illegal to delete a pointer twice, it is fine to do so if its value is zero. Thus, if your code loses track of the fact that it has already deleted a pointer and deletes it again, it is safe if that pointer has been set to zero.

12

The Computer Plays

After the Computer is created, processing resumes in Game's constructor, which quickly finishes and restores control to main():

```
Game * g = new Game;
g->Play();
```

As you can see, the very next thing to happen is that Play() is called on the Game object:

```
void Game::Play()
{

    int start = time( NULL );

    pDecrypter->Play();
```

Game sets a clock to the current time to keep track of how long the game lasts, and then immediately calls Play() on whatever object pDecrypter points to, in this case our Computer object. This causes us to jump to line 166 in Listing 11.11:

```
166:   void Computer::Play()
167:   {
168:
169:       if ( ! mySmartString )
170:           mySmartString = new SmartString(duplicates);
```

The very first thing the Computer does is check its mySmartString member variable: If it is set to zero, the if statement will succeed. Remember, the value 0 is equal to the value false, so testing if mySmartString) is the same as testing if (mySmartString == 0). The latter is better form, but I put it here this way to remind you that you can test it either way, and it amounts to the same thing.

Creating a Smart String

Because this test succeeds, the code on line 170 runs and a new SmartString object is created. This jumps us to line 4 of Listing 12.2, where the member variable dupli-cates is initialized:

```
4:   SmartString::SmartString(bool dupes):
5:   duplicates(dupes)
6:   {
7:       for ( int i = 0; i < Game::howManyPositions; i++ )
8:       {
9:           int j;
10:          if ( duplicates )
11:              j = 0;
12:          else
13:              j = i;
```

```
14:         SmartChar theChar(j);
15:         myString.push_back(theChar);
16:     }
17: }
```

We now create a `for` loop to iterate through each position, creating a `smartChar` and adding it to the `SmartString`'s member variable, `myString`.

Note that if duplicates are allowed, we set the value of the `SmartChar` to 0; if they are not allowed, we set it to the current value of `i`, the counter variable. Thus, if we are using six letters in five positions and duplicates are allowed, our first string is aaaaa; if duplicates are not allowed, our first string is abcde.

We can see this at work by examining the constructor of `SmartChar`, which is called on line 14 and implemented on line 4 of Listing 12.4:

```
3:  SmartChar::SmartChar(int letter):
4:  myChar(letter)
5:  {
6:      for ( int i = 0; i < Game::howManyLetters; i++ )
7:          myCharacters.push_back(alpha[i]);
8:
9:  }
```

The member variable `myChar` is initialized to the value that is passed in (0 if duplicates are allowed, `i` if not). We then add all the letters that are legal in the `for` loop that is shown on line 6. Remember, this constructor is creating a single `SmartChar` that will hold a vector of legal letters for its position. Again, if we were playing six letters in five positions, we'd create five `SmartChar` members in the `SmartString` `myString` vector. Each of these `SmartChars` holds a vector of characters with the letters *a*, *b*, *c*, *d*, *e*, and *f*—the legal letters. All this is illustrated in Figure 12.1.

In this diagram, `Computer` has a member variable, `mySmartString`, that points to a `SmartString` object on the heap. That object in turn has four variables, one of which is `myString`, which is a vector of `SmartChar` objects. Each of these `SmartChar` objects has two variables: `myChar` (which holds the current offset into `myCharacters`) and `myCharacters` (a vector of char, which holds all the legal values).

If, after a while, we've proven that the first character cannot be *a*, *b*, or *c*; the second cannot be *b*, *c*, or *d*; the third can't be *b* or *d*; the fourth can't be *c*; the fifth can't be *a*; and the current guess is daceb, we would illustrate it as shown in Figure 12.2.

Here you see that each `SmartChar`'s vector has been reduced to hold only the legal values for that position, and that `myChar` has the value of the offset of the current choice. Thus, the third `smartChar`—which cannot be *a*, *b*, or *d* and whose current value is c—has a vector with only *a*, *c*, and *e*, and the offset is 1.

12

Figure 12.1

Computer, SmartString, *and* SmartChar.

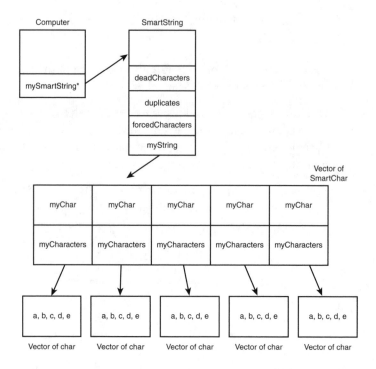

Computer::Play()

We resume our analysis on line 172 of Listing 11.11. We create a local vector of characters, theGuess, and we clear the history vector.

We create a local variable called deletedCharacters on line 175 and initialize its value to false. We're all set and ready to go, so we begin a forever loop on line 177:

```
177:    for ( ;; )
178:    {
179:        Guess theGuess = OfferGuess();
180:        history.push_back(theGuess);
181:
182:        if ( theGuess.GetScore().second ==
183:            Game::howManyPositions )
184:            break;
185:
186:        if (
187:            ! mySmartString->CanEliminateCharacters(theGuess) ||
188:            ! IsConsistent(mySmartString->GetString())
```

```
189:                    )
190:                        GenerateAGuess();
191:      };
```

Figure 12.2

Constraining the possible letters.

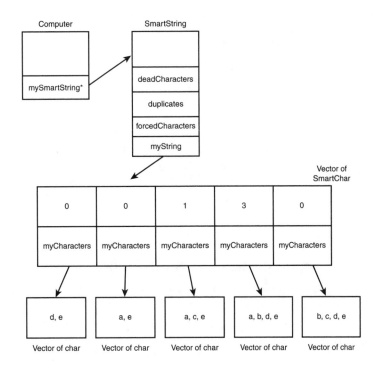

The logic of this loop is as follows: We offer a Guess to the user, and we return the results in a Guess object. The Guess object contains the guess itself as a vector of characters, and it contains an STL pair to represent the score, as we've seen before. Listing 12.5 contains the declaration of the Guess object, shown here for your convenience but unchanged from the preceding chapter.

Listing 12.5   Guess Declared

```
0:   #ifndef GUESS_H
1:   #define GUESS_H
2:
```

continues

12

Listing 12.5   continued

```
3:    #include "defvals.h"
4:
5:    class Guess
6:    {
7:    public:
8:        Guess(
9:        vector<char>guess,
10:        int howManyRight,
11:        int howManyInPosition);
12:        ~Guess() {}
13:
14:        void  Display() const;
15:        pair<int, int> GetScore() const;
16:        vector<char> GetString() const;
17:    private:
18:        pair<int, int> score;
19:        vector<char> myString;
20:    };
21:
22:    #endif
```

Generating Guesses: An Overview

Resuming on line 180 of Listing 11.11, we add the Guess we just got back from OfferGuess to the history:

```
177:      for ( ;; )
178:      {
179:          Guess theGuess = OfferGuess();
180:          history.push_back(theGuess);
181:
182:          if ( theGuess.GetScore().second ==
183:              Game::howManyPositions )
184:              break;
185:
186:          if (
187:              ! mySmartString->CanEliminateCharacters(theGuess) ||
188:              ! IsConsistent(mySmartString->GetString())
189:              )
190:                  GenerateAGuess();
191:      };
```

We then compare the score of how many were in position with the number of positions we have altogether. If they are the same, the computer has guessed the answer, and we're done. Otherwise, we want to generate another guess and try again, so we'll call GenerateAGuess() and then loop back to offer that guess.

That is all there is to it, but we want to reduce the number of guesses the computer makes. We'll engage a number of strategies to do so.

Our first effort consists of eliminating characters based on our results from the current guess. We'll do this before we generate another guess. If we can eliminate one of the current characters, when we get back from the call to `CanEliminateCharacters` the current guess is changed. We don't want to generate a new guess; we just want to offer this changed guess.

Thus, the logic on line 186 is as follows: If you have not eliminated any of the current characters, go ahead and generate a guess.

However, there is some chance that the string that results from eliminating characters will not need to be shown to the user. This would be true if the resulting string were not consistent with the other guesses we've tried so far. To handle this situation, we add the second half of the `if` statement on line 188. You can read this part of the `if` statement as follows: "If you *were* able to eliminate characters, you don't need to generate a guess *unless* the string that resulted is not consistent with our previous results."

Is the Guess Consistent?

The concept of being consistent is interesting. The idea is this: We have a history of guesses and their scores. We pretend that our current guess is the actual answer, and compare the previous guesses and their scores. Would we have scored them as we did if the current guess were the answer?

For example, consider the following history (for five letters in five positions):

> abcde—Five letters, one position
>
> baced—Five letters, one position

We are now looking at a potential guess: abdce. Could this have been the correct answer all along? No, because if this *were* the correct answer, the first guess would not be scored 5/1, but rather 5/3 (*a*, *b*, and *e* are in the right position). Because we know that the first guess was scored 5/1, abdce cannot be the right answer. It's not consistent with our previous guesses, so it can be eliminated.

Let's try another: Might edcba be the right answer?

Let's score the two guesses we have against edcba to see if the results are consistent with what we have so far. abcde would score five correct and one in position (the letter *c*), so that is consistent with the first guess's score. The second guess, baced, would be scored five correct and one in position (again, the letter *c*), so again this is consistent with the scores so far. Thus, we learn that although edcba might not be the right answer, it is at least consistent with what we know so far.

12

Again, our logic on line 188 says, "Okay, you have eliminated characters, so your string has changed, but is the new string consistent? If not, generate a guess."

GenerateAGuess calls IsConsistent with each potential guess so that what we get back from GenerateAGuess is a consistent (and potentially correct) answer.

We want to walk through this code in detail because it gets complicated quite quickly.

Generating a Guess, Details

Let's step through playing the Game, with the computer guessing, beginning on line 179:

```
177:     for ( ;; )
178:     {
179:         Guess theGuess = OfferGuess();
180:         history.push_back(theGuess);
181:
182:         if ( theGuess.GetScore().second ==
183:             Game::howManyPositions )
184:             break;
185:
186:         if (
187:             ! mySmartString->CanEliminateCharacters(theGuess) ||
188:             ! IsConsistent(mySmartString->GetString())
189:             )
190:                 GenerateAGuess();
191:     };
```

Assume that we've chosen seven letters in five positions, with no duplicates, and with the computer guessing. Let's further pretend that the actual answer is acgbf.

The computer begins by initializing its SmartString to abcde (because no duplicates are allowed). We jump to line 148, where we fill the local vector of characters theGuess with the string held in the SmartString (abcde). We increment the round and declare two local variables—numCorrect and numInPosition. We show the user the guess by calling Display(), and then we print out a request for the user to enter the score. The user sees abcde and must score it three correct (*abc*) and one in position (*a*). With this, we create a Guess object, passing in the string and the user's input.

On line 180, we add this Guess object to the history, which is a vector of Guess objects. We then test the score to see whether we have as many in position as there are positions. We do not (we have one in position out of five).

This brings us to line 187, where we call CanEliminateCharacters, passing in this guess. This causes us to jump to line 141 of Listing 12.2.

> **Note** The `Guess` object is passed in as a constant reference. This signals that we want the efficiency of pass-by-reference, but we don't want to allow this method to change the `Guess` object.

The Logic of `CanEliminateCharacters`

This method—trying to eliminate characters—is quite complex and actually applies a number of rules. The very first thing it does, in fact, is to pass the `Guess` to another method, `ForceCharacters`, which tries to see whether it can identify any characters that *must* be in the answer. Regardless of the success of this effort, we next check to see whether there are any forced characters in the current guess, and we keep track of them in `forcedInAnswer`.

If we have zero correct letters or if the number of correct letters is equal to the number of forced letters in the answer, we know that all the non-forced letters in the answer can be eliminated. In fact, they can be eliminated in every position!

Thus, if we have abcde and we know that there are two forced letters and two correct letters in this string, none of the non-forced letters can be in the answer at all. If so, we call `RemoveCurrentCharactersInEveryPosition`. This takes the letters *a*, *b*, *c*, *d*, and *e* out of every position *unless* those letters are in the `forcedCharacters` vector. Thus, if *a* and *c* are forced, only *b*, *d*, and *e* are eliminated, which is just what we want.

If we can delete characters this way, we're done, and we return the number we deleted. If not, we check to see whether we have zero letters in position. If so, we know that the current letters must all be wrong, and each smart character can eliminate its current choice as a possibility. Thus, if we have abcde and none are in the correct position, we know that the first character cannot be *a*, the second cannot be *b*, and so forth.

If we can't do any of this, `CanEliminateCharacters` returns `false`.

With that overview, let's step through it in detail.

`CanEliminateCharacters` in Detail

We therefore come into `CanEliminateCharacters` on line 141, with `theGuess` holding the string abcde and the score 3/1 (three correct letters, one in position):

```
141:   bool SmartString::CanEliminateCharacters(
142:                     const Guess & theGuess)
143:   {
```

12

```
144:
145:        bool anyDeleted = false;
146:        ForceCharacters(theGuess);
```

We initialize anyDeleted to false, and then on line 146 we pass theGuess in to ForcedCharacters, which brings us to line 168 of Listing 12.2:

```
168:   void SmartString::ForceCharacters(const Guess &theGuess)
169:   {
170:        int numDifferentLetters =
171:            CountUniqueLettersInGuess(theGuess);
```

The first thing that is done in this method is to call CountUniqueLettersInGuess, passing in the Guess. This brings us to line 191:

```
191:   int SmartString::CountUniqueLettersInGuess(
192:                          const Guess &theGuess)
193:   {
194:        vector<char> temp;
195:        vector<char> theString =
196:            theGuess.GetString();
197:
198:        for (
199:            vector<char>::const_iterator it = theString.begin();
200:            it != theString.end();
201:            it++
202:            )
203:        {
204:            if (! In(temp,*it) )
205:                temp.push_back(*it);
206:        }
207:
208:        // temp now has all the unique letters
209:
210:        return temp.size();
211:   }
```

We create a local vector of characters called temp, and another that holds a copy of the string from the Guess. We iterate through temp, and for each character in the guess, we test whether it is in the vector temp. If not, we add it. When we're done, temp has one entry for each unique letter in the guess. We return the size of that vector, which is how many unique letters are in the guess. In our case, this value is 5.

This brings us back to line 171:

```
168:   void SmartString::ForceCharacters(const Guess &theGuess)
169:   {
170:        int numDifferentLetters =
171:            CountUniqueLettersInGuess(theGuess);
172:        int score = theGuess.GetScore().first;
```

```
173:
174:      if ( score >= numDifferentLetters )
175:      {
176:          vector<char> theString =
177:              theGuess.GetString();
178:
179:          for (
180:              vector<char>::const_iterator it = theString.begin();
181:              it != theString.end();
182:              it++
183:              )
184:          {
185:              if ( ! In(forcedCharacters, *it) )
186:                  forcedCharacters.push_back(*it);
187:          }
188:      }
189: }
```

The local variable score is set to the number of correct letters, which in our case is three. We now compare these values, and if the score (3) is greater than or equal to the number of different letters, we know they must all be correct, in which case we push them into the vector forcedCharacters. Unfortunately, we can't do that this time, so we return empty-handed, resuming on line 147:

```
146:      ForceCharacters(theGuess);
147:      int forcedInAnswer = CountForcedInGuess(theGuess);
```

We now call CountForcedInGuess, which compares the total number of forced characters in the guess. This is shown on line 213:

```
214:                  const Guess &theGuess)
215: {
216:      int howManyForcedInGuess = 0;
217:      vector<char> theString = theGuess.GetString();
218:
219:      for (
220:          vector<char>::const_iterator it = theString.begin();
221:          it != theString.end();
222:          it++
223:          )
224:      {
225:          if ( In( forcedCharacters, *it ) )
226:              howManyForcedInGuess++;
227:      }
228:
229:      return howManyForcedInGuess;
230:
231: }
```

12

We simply iterate through the guess, checking to see whether any of the letters in the guess are in the vector `forcedCharacters`. In this case, we'll return 0 and resume on line 148:

```
141:   bool SmartString::CanEliminateCharacters(
142:                          const Guess & theGuess)
143:   {
144:
145:       bool anyDeleted = false;
146:       ForceCharacters(theGuess);
147:       int forcedInAnswer = CountForcedInGuess(theGuess);
148:
149:       int overall = theGuess.GetScore().first;
150:       int inPos = theGuess.GetScore().second;
151:
152:
153:       if ( overall == 0 || overall == forcedInAnswer )
154:       {
155:           anyDeleted = RemoveCurrentCharactersInEveryPosition();
156:           return anyDeleted; // we did eliminate characters
157:       }
158:
159:       if ( inPos == 0 )
160:       {
161:           anyDeleted = RemoveCurrentCharacters();
162:           return anyDeleted; // we did eliminate characters
163:       }
164:
165:       return false;
166:   }
```

On line 149 we set the local variable `overall` to the number of correct letters (3), and we set `inPos` to the number in the correct position (1).

On line 153 we test `overall` to see if it is 0 or equal to the number of forced letters in the answer. In this case we fail both tests:

```
153:       if ( overall == 0 || overall == forcedInAnswer )
154:       {
155:           anyDeleted = RemoveCurrentCharactersInEveryPosition();
156:           return anyDeleted; // we did eliminate characters
157:       }
```

On line 159 we test to see if none of the guessed letters are in the correct position. Again, because one is, we fail this test and we return `false`, indicating that we eliminated no letters at all. This brings us back to line 188 of Listing 11.11:

```
159:       if ( inPos == 0 )
160:       {
161:           anyDeleted = RemoveCurrentCharacters();
162:           return anyDeleted; // we did eliminate characters
163:       }
```

The return value is `false`, but we test the `NOT` value, so this side of the `OR` statement passes. Because it does, we do not even try the second half of the statement—we go right to `GenerateAGuess`. This makes sense; having been unable to eliminate characters we do not need to test whether the current guess is consistent, it is unchanged, and we do need to generate a new guess.

GenerateAGuess

We step into this method on line 17 of Listing 11.11. Again, we initialize some variables, including a local time keeper that will track how long it takes us to come up with a consistent guess:

```
20:      bool ok = true;
21:      int counter = 0;
22:      int start = time( NULL );
```

The local variable `counter` tracks how many strings we eliminate in this try, and `total` tracks how many have been eliminated in this game:

```
27:          if ( counter % 10000 == 0 )
28:              cout << ".";
```

On line 27 we check to see whether we've passed a multiple of 10,000 strings tried. If so, we'll print a dot to the screen to tell the user we're still working. If our estimates are right, this will print one dot approximately every second.

On line 30, we ask `mySmartString` to `GetNext()`:

```
30:          ok = mySmartString->GetNext();
```

This branches to line 41 of Listing 12.2. The goal of this method is to get the next string. A string, you remember, is composed of `SmartCharacters`.

You'll also remember that the string is initialized to aaaaa if we are allowing duplicates or abcde if we are not. Let's assume that we're allowing duplicates and that we are playing with three letters (*a, b, c*) in five positions. We begin with aaa. The next string is aab, the one that follows is aac. Now what? The next string is aba. This is just like your car odometer: After 001 comes 002, and then 003, all the way up to 009, which is followed by 010. The tens place rolls over.

We must do the same here. After we hit the highest legal letter (*c*), we must roll over to *a* but bump up the next one to the left.

In this case we're using seven letters (*a–g*) in five positions with no duplicates, so the first guess is abcde, followed by abcdf, and then abcdg; but the one after that will be abcea. Make sure you understand why.

Resuming with the code in `GetNext`, we must iterate backward through `myString`. To do that, we use a special *reverse* iterator, one that goes backward. We declare this on

12

line 44, declaring rit to be a reverse iterator. We then assign rit to myString.rbe-gin, which is the beginning position of a reverse iterator (for example, the end of the vector). Each increment bumps the iterator *back* one position.

On line 47 we call Increment(), which invokes SmartChar::Increment (shown on line 21 of Listing 12.4). This code is very simple: It just checks to see if it is time to rollover. If so, it sets itself to its first character and returns true; otherwise, it returns false.

We resume on line 48 of 12.2, and if rollover is true, we enter the while loop. On line 50 we increment the reverse iterator, causing it to move back a SmartChar. Thus, if we were pointing to the last character, we're now pointing to the penultimate one. We then increment this one, and if it rolls over, we continue working our way back. So, if the string is abcgg, the increment rolls the last *g* to *a*, but incrementing the earlier *g* causes it to roll as well, incrementing the *c*. The result is abdaa, which is just what we want.

If we run out of letters and cannot resolve the roll over, we return false; otherwise, we return true, resuming on line 32 of Listing 11.11. If we do return false, ok is set to false, and we have run out of letters without hitting the solution. This can only mean that the user has given us false information. We tell him that something went wrong, show him all the previous guesses and their scores, and then restart the game, setting round to zero, clearing out the history, and offering a new starting string.

Assuming that this does not happen, we continue on line 45, noting that we are in a do...while loop. Having generated a guess, we must now go see whether that guess is consistent with our previous scores.

IsConsistent in Detail

The computer generates strings in order, so the next string it generates will be abcdf. This is the string that is passed to IsConssitent(). The question is this: Would you get the same score you got last time (3/1) if the answer *had* been abcdf (remembering that the answer actually is acgbf)?

Let's see, if the guess was abcde and the answer had been abcdf, we'd expect to see four right, with all four in position. What we got was three right with one in position, so this string is eliminated as inconsistent:

```
83:     if ( ! duplicates)
84:     {
85:        for (
86:           vector<char>::const_iterator it =
87:              theGuess.begin();
88:           it != theGuess.end();
89:           it++
```

```
90:                )
91:            {
92:                int HowMany =
93:                    count(theGuess.begin(), theGuess.end(),*it);
94:                if ( HowMany > 1 )
95:                    return false;
96:            }
97:        }
```

We enter IsConsistent on line 83. We are not allowing duplicates, so the if statement succeeds. We create an iterator against the Guess and iterate over every letter in the Guess, counting how many times that letter appears in the guess. The net effect is that if there are any duplicates, we can immediately return false. In abcdf there are no duplicates, so we proceed to line 99:

```
99:     bool isValid = true;
100:
101:     int correct;
102:     int position;
103:
104:     for (
105:         vector<Guess>::const_iterator it =
106:             history.begin();
107:         it != history.end();
108:         it++
109:         )
110:     {
111:
112:         vector <char> temp = it->GetString();
113:
114:         correct = 0;
115:         position = 0;
116:         for ( int i = 0; i < Game::howManyLetters; i++)
117:         {
118:             int howManyInGuess =
119:                 count (
120:                     theGuess.begin(),
121:                     theGuess.end(),
122:                     alpha[i]
123:                     );
124:             int howManyInAnswer =
125:                 count (temp.begin(), temp.end(), alpha[i]);
126:             correct += _MIN(howManyInGuess, howManyInAnswer);
127:         }
128:
129:         for (  i = 0; i < Game::howManyPositions; i++)
130:         {
131:             if ( theGuess[i] == temp[i] )
132:                 position++;
133:         }
134:
135:         if ( correct != it->GetScore().first ||
```

12

```
136:                    position != it->GetScore().second )
137:            {
138:                isValid = false;
139:                break;
140:            }
141:        }
142:
143:        return isValid;
144:    }
```

We now iterate through `theHistory`, pulling each string out of the history and scoring it against this guess. This code is nearly identical to the code in `Human` in which we score the human's guess. In a future version of this program, it might make sense to consolidate this code in `Decrypter` so that we can avoid having them get out of synch with one another.

Take a look at line 116:

```
116:            for ( int i = 0; i < Game::howManyLetters; i++)
```

We want to count through this `for` loop once for each letter, so we need to know how many letters we're playing with. This information is stored in `Game`. How do we gain access?

EXCURSION

Static Member Variables

The normal way to handle this is to ask **Game** for this value:

```
theGame.GetHowManyLetters();
```

This calls a member method of **Game**, which returns an integer. Unfortunately, we do not have an object of type **Game** to ask. We can turn ourselves inside out getting one, but that entails passing the **Game** object in to the **Computer** just so we can get this information. This solution is too ugly.

Alternatively, **Game** can tell **Computer** how many letters in how many positions when it creates the **Computer**, and the **Computer** object can stash this information away in a member variable. This solution is better, but terribly inefficient. Why should **Computer** keep this duplicate information? It doesn't really need it, and **Game** already knows. We'd rather keep this under the control of **Game**.

A third alternative is to make the value a global variable, which is a variable that is declared outside the scope of any class or method and which is available to any object anywhere in your code. Yech! This is a total violation of encapsulation, and is terribly error prone. Bugs that are created by global variables are very hard to find.

The final alternative—the one I've used—is to make the variable a static member of **Game**. A *static member* is similar to a global variable in that it is accessible from anywhere in your code, but it is *scoped* to the **Game** and can only be reached by using the scoping operator (as shown on line 116).

Static member variables are not allocated memory when you create objects of the class. You must do so explicitly, as shown on lines 9 and 10 of Listing 11.5. Note that these variables are initialized outside of any member methods.

One important fact about static member methods is that they exist on a class—not an object—level. This means that there is only one value for **howManyLetters**, no matter how many **Game** objects we create. This can be very useful if you have a class with many objects but you need to keep a count that is shared among every object.

Methods can be static as well. The advantage of a static method is that you can call it without having an instance of the class. Thus, if **Game** has a static method **myMethod** that is declared as follows

```
class Game
{
public:
//...
    static int MyMethod();
//...
};
```

you can call that method from **main** without a **Game** object:

```
int main()
{
//...


    int x = Game::MyMethod();
//...
    return 0;
}
```

Alternatively, you can call the same method with an object:

```
int main()
{
//...
    Game theGame;
    int x = theGame.MyMethod();
//...
    return 0;
}
```

The only limitation of static member methods is that they cannot be constant. You'll remember from Chapter 5, "Playing the Game," that constant member methods have a constant **this** pointer, but static member methods have no **this** pointer at all!

12

The Effect of Static

Static methods and members are a way to provide the advantages of global methods and variables, but they are scoped to a specific class and are therefore less error prone. We use a static member method here to provide global access to the member variables howManyLetters and howManyPositions.

We can make this code cleaner (and more encapsulated) by making these static member variables private and by using static member methods GetHowManyLetters() and GetHowManyPositions().

Resuming the Analysis

By line 133 of Listing 11.11, we've completed scoring the first item in theHistory against this current guess. If the score we get is not the same as the score we received, we know this string cannot be correct. In fact, correct is four and position is four, but the score that was received by this entry was three and one, so isValid is set false and we return it to the do...while loop in GenerateAGuess. This causes GenerateAGuess to generate the next string, abcdg, and to test it.

We will, in fact, eliminate 310 strings this way before generating the next potentially valid guess: acbfg. After this is displayed and scored, we'll enter CanEliminateCharacters again, where, you'll remember, we immediately call ForceCharacters:

```
174:      if ( score >= numDifferentLetters )
```

Because we have scored five letters and there are five positions, the test on line 174 of Listing 12.2 succeeds and each of the characters (*a, c, b, f,* and *g*) is added to the forcedCharacters vector on line 186:

```
185:              if ( ! In(forcedCharacters, *it) )
186:                  forcedCharacters.push_back(*it);
```

This returns us to CanEliminateCharacters line 147:

```
147:      int forcedInAnswer = CountForcedInGuess(theGuess);
```

The local variable forcedInAnswer is initialized with 5, overall with 5, and inPos with 2:

```
153:      if ( overall == 0 || overall == forcedInAnswer )
154:      {
155:          anyDeleted = RemoveCurrentCharactersInEveryPosition();
156:          return anyDeleted; // we did eliminate characters
157:      }
```

On line 153 we detect that overall (5) is equal to forcedInAnswer (5), so we enter the body of the if statement on line 155 and call RemoveCurrentCharactersInEveryPosition. This code, beginning on line 97, is not going to do much this time because it removes every one of the current characters unless that character is in forcedCharacters. This time, however, every one of the characters is in forcedCharacters, so nothing is accomplished. The local Boolean anyDeleted remains false, and that is what is returned. On line 156 that same value of false is returned to Play, so once again GenerateAGuess is called.

This time, an additional 198 strings are eliminated as inconsistent (for a total of 508), and the user is shown acfgb. Let's examine this. Had the answer actually been acfgb, the first guess abcde would have scored three letters correct (*abc*) and one in the correct position (*a*). The second guess, acbfg, would have scored five letters correct, and two in the correct position (*ac*). That is what they scored, so this answer is consistent with what we know so far.

We score this one 5/2 again. The same logic applies: We cannot eliminate any characters because the computer has already found all five. The computer eliminates the next 18 strings and then guesses acgbf, which is the correct answer. A total of 526 strings were eliminated as inconsistent, and the computer got the answer in just four rounds of guessing: abcde, acbfg, acfgb, and then acgbf. Not bad.

Let's examine one more game, in which we play with 10 letters (*a* through *j*) in five positions, with no duplicates, and in which the answer is ghijf.

The computer first generates abcde.

We score this 0/0, which causes CanEliminateCharacters to note that overall is now 0 and to call RemoveCurrentCharactersInEveryPosition. This branches to line 97 in Listing 12.2, where we iterate through the string and extract each character in the guess (abcde). We then check to see whether each character is in forcedCharacters on line 119. If it is not, we iterate through the string on line 123, and for each SmartChar in the string we call Remove, passing in the character. We then add each character to the vector deadCharacters if it is not already there.

The net effect of all this is that abcde is eliminated. This returns us to line 187 of Listing 11.11, where CanEliminateCharacters has returned true, so the NOT statement is false. The second half of the OR statement must be entered, calling IsConsistent() on the string that results from eliminating these characters.

What string is that? It is fghij. Why? You'll remember that the first guess was abcde, which means that the myChar variables were set to 0, 1, 2, 3, and 4, and the

12

possible characters were *a*, *b*, *c*, *d*, *e*, *f*, *g*, *h*, *i*, and *j*. We eliminated *a*, *b*, *c*, *d*, and *e* from each, so the characters that are left are *f*, *g*, *h*, *i*, and *j*. Because the myChar value has not changed, these offsets now correspond to *f*, *g*, *h*, *i*, and *j*. That is the very first string to check, and we now check to see if it is consistent with the answers that are already in history.

The only thing in history is abcde. If the answer had been fghij we would have scored 0/0, which is what we did score, so this is consistent. Given that it is consistent, there is no reason to generate a guess, so that step is skipped (the if statement fails) and we resume on line 179, offering the player the guess fghij.

This we'll score 5/0. We have all the letters, but none is in the right position. We thus force these five letters, eliminate the next 528 strings as inconsistent, and generate the guess gfijh. This scores 5/3. We eliminate the next 248 strings and generate ghijf. Thus, we find the right answer in four guesses.

Eliminating Characters in Position

Let's look at one more example. This time, let's assume that we are playing with seven letters in five positions, with no duplicates, and with the computer guessing. Our answer is gadbe.

For the first guess, the computer guesses abcde. We score this 4/1. The four correct letters are abde and the one correct position is *e*.

The next guess is acbef, after eliminating 302 alternatives as inconsistent. We'll score this 3/0.

There are no forced characters as a result of this or the previous guess, and we pick up the analysis on line 159 of Listing 12.2:

```
159:        if ( inPos == 0 )
160:        {
161:            anyDeleted = RemoveCurrentCharacters();
162:            return anyDeleted; // we did eliminate characters
163:        }
```

Because the number in position *is* zero, we enter the body of the if statement and we call RemoveCurrentCharacters. This instructs the SmartString that, because none of these letters is in the correct position, we can safely remove the current characters from the list of possible characters. That is not to say, for example, that there are no *a*s in the answer, only that the very first letter must not be *a*, the second letter must not be *c*, the third must not be *b*, the fourth must not be *e*, and the fifth must not be *f*.

This branches to line 64, where we iterate over myString and get each character in turn:

```
69:     for (
70:         vector<SmartChar>::iterator it = myString.begin();
71:         it != myString.end();
72:         it++
73:         )
74:     {
75:         theChar = it->GetChar();
```

We check each character on line 77 to make sure that it is not in forcedCharacters, our array of letters that cannot be deleted:

```
77:         if ( ! In(forcedCharacters,theChar) )
78:         {
79:             theChar = it->RemoveCurrent();
```

If it is not in forcedCharacters, we remove it by calling RemoveCurrent() on the smartChar. This branches to line 31 of Listing 12.4, where we extract the character (so we can report its removal), and then we erase that character from our array of possible characters:

```
37:         theChar = GetChar();
38:         myCharacters.erase( myCharacters.begin()+myChar );
39:         while ( myChar >= myCharacters.size() )
40:             myChar—;
```

Note that myChar (the offset into the array that points to the current character) is unchanged as long as we're not pointing past the end of the array. Thus, just by removing a character, we now point to a new character. If the character we remove is the last in array (in this case *g*), myChar must be decremented to ensure that it points to a valid letter.

To review, before we removed the characters, our string looked like Figure 12.3.

Immediately after we removed the characters, our Smart string looked like Figure 12.4.

The value of the offsets hasn't changed, but the string that results *has* changed because letters were removed. For example, in the first character offset 0 pointed to *a*, but now it points to *b*. The same is true for all the others. The same five offsets that pointed to acbef now point to bdcfg. We check this value for consistency before offering it as a potential answer.

 Note   This code is not quite ready to run yet, but we will finish it up in chapter 13 and run it there.

12

Figure 12.3

Before we remove characters.

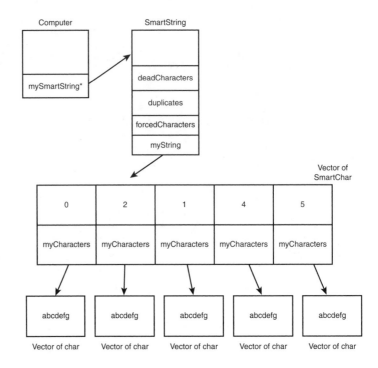

Figure 12.3

Before we remove characters.

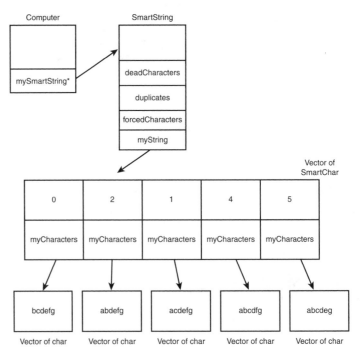

Figure 12.4

After removing characters.

Chapter 13

Persistence

Now that our game is working, the single most important feature we need to implement is the capability to save the game and restore it later. I found a need for this even as I was writing this chapter. My elder daughter, Robin, was bored on our flight from Boston to San Francisco, where we were going to visit my in-laws. I took out Decryptix!, and we began to play. About halfway through a particularly good game, we had to close the computer. We didn't want to lose the game, but we had no choice; we had to *shut the machine off* because we were landing. Time to add persistence.

Object Persistence

Objects are created in memory, either on the stack or on the heap. They live in memory until they are destroyed, and turning off the computer is guaranteed to destroy them irrevocably. *Object persistence* is the idea of writing these objects out of memory and storing them in some form of permanent storage, typically a disk file or a database.

Flavors of Persistence

Although it is possible to save objects in many different ways, the four most common choices are

- Save to a file
- Save to an object database
- Save to a relational database
- Save to a structured file such as the Windows Registry

Each has its advantages. For a simple game such as Decryptix!, we need no special database technology. We won't want to search for our objects or sort them in any way. We simply want to store the current state of the game to disk, and then restore it later. We'll do this by writing the objects to disk and saving them in a file. Then, when it is time to restore them, we'll read them from disk and write them back into memory. To make things very convenient, we'll allow the user to name the file so that we can store more than one game if we choose.

Designing Persistence

Many strategies handle persistence, depending on what you want to accomplish. For Decryptix!, I wanted to isolate and encapsulate as much of the responsibility for persistence as possible, shielding the classes from these issues when possible and minimizing replication of code.

A very hot trend in C++ is the creation and dissemination of design patterns, which are well-documented solutions to common problems encountered by C++ programmers. The approach I've taken follows the Serializer Design Pattern as described in *Design Patterns: Elements of Reusable Object-Oriented Software* (Addison-Wesley Professional Computing, ISBN: 0-201-63361-2) by Erich Gamma, Richard Helm, Ralph Johnson, and John Vlissides. This approach fully encapsulates the job of working with files inside three related classes: Storable, Reader, and Writer.

We start by creating an *abstract data type* (*ADT*) called Storable. This will serve as the base class for every class we want to store. The Writer and Reader classes will encapsulate knowledge of the file system and will behave in a way that is analogous to cin and cout.

Let's start by looking at the ADT Storable as shown in Listing 13.1.

Listing 13.1   The Storable Abstract Data Type

```
0:  #if !defined STORABLE_H
1:  #define STORABLE_H
2:
3:  #include <iostream>
4:  #include <fstream>
5:  #include <vector>
6:  using namespace std;
7:
8:  class Reader;
9:  class Writer;
10:
11:  class Storable
12:  {
13:  public:
```

```
14:      Storable(){}
15:      Storable(Reader&) {}
16:      virtual ~Storable(){}
17:      virtual void Write(Writer&) const = 0;
18:  };
```

Analysis

We begin by noting that this listing shows only part of the file storable.h. The rest of the file includes the declarations for the `Reader` and `Writer` classes, which we'll consider in a moment.

We begin on line 3 by including `iostream`, and then on line 4 we include `fstream`. `iostream` is responsible for managing input and output from the keyboard and monitor, respectively, and `fstream` is responsible for the same activities to and from the file system.

On lines 8 and 9, we forward declare the `Reader` and `Writer` class so that we can use references (or pointers) to objects of these classes in the `Storable` declaration.

The class itself is rather simple. We indicate that there is a default constructor on line 14 and that there is a constructor that takes a reference to a `Reader` object. This is a critical requirement of a `Storable` type: It can be created by passing in a `Reader` object, which we'll examine in just a moment.

`Storable` has only two other methods: the destructor and, most importantly, the `Write` method. `Write()` is pure virtual (indicated by `=0`), and every derived class must implement it.

The Reader and the Writer

The secret to making all this work is that the `Writer` is responsible for helping the object write itself to disk, and the `Reader` is responsible for helping the object read itself back into memory.

The only part of an object we need to write is the member data. The methods do not get stored to disk. The data we store can only be one of two possible types: built-in primitive types (for example, `long`, `char`, `int`) or a user-defined type (for example, `employee`, `cat`, `window`).

Every object that derives from `Storable` has a `Write()` method. In that method, the object delegates to the `Writer` object the responsibility for writing its own primitive data members. For members that are not of a primitive type, the object just tells the member to write itself. That object in turn comprises either primitive types or built-in types. We continue delegating until all the data members are written.

The Reader is the mirror image. It helps a storable object construct itself. The Reader knows how to read in primitive types, and if an object has user-defined types as member data, it just calls their constructor, passing in the same reader.

The Reader and Writer object declarations are shown in Listing 13.2, which shows the complete Storable.h file (which we began in the previous listing).

Listing 13.2   Storable.h

```
0:   #if !defined STORABLE_H
1:   #define STORABLE_H
2:
3:   #include <iostream>
4:   #include <fstream>
5:   #include <vector>
6:   using namespace std;
7:
8:   class Reader;
9:   class Writer;
10:
11:  class Storable
12:  {
13:  public:
14:      Storable(){}
15:      Storable(Reader&) {}
16:      virtual ~Storable(){}
17:      virtual void Write(Writer&) const = 0;
18:  };
19:
20:  class Reader
21:  {
22:  public:
23:      Reader(char * filename):fin(filename,ios::binary){}
24:      virtual ~Reader(){fin.close();}
25:      virtual Reader& operator >> (int&);
26:      virtual Reader& operator >> (const int&);
27:      virtual Reader& operator >> (char&);
28:      virtual Reader& operator >> (char*&);
29:      virtual Reader& operator >> (bool&);
30:      virtual Reader& operator >> (vector<char>&);
31:
32:  private:
33:      ifstream fin;
34:  };
35:
36:  class Writer
37:  {
38:  public:
39:      Writer(char * filename):fout(filename, ios::binary){};
```

13

```
40:      virtual ~Writer() {fout.close(); }
41:      virtual Writer& operator << (int &);
42:      virtual Writer& operator << (const int &);
43:      virtual Writer& operator << (char&);
44:      virtual Writer& operator << (char*&);
45:      virtual Writer& operator << (const char*&);
46:      virtual Writer& operator << (bool&);
47:      virtual Writer& operator << (const bool&);
48:      virtual Writer& operator << (const vector<char>&);
49:
50: private:
51:      ofstream fout;
52: };
53:
54: #endif
```

Let's examine the declaration in just a bit of detail before we see how these are implemented and used. On line 20 we declare the Reader class.

The constructor is shown on line 23, and it is very straightforward. When we construct a Reader object, we pass in a filename, and we use that string to construct the ifstream member variable fin. In the ifstream constructor, we pass in that filename and the flag binary.

> **Note** binary is a static member of the ios object, as described in the preceding chapter. Here we see that we can access this member without having an instance of an ios object by using the scoping operator (::)

The destructor, shown on line 24, closes the ifstream object. Thus, the lifetime of this object is controlled implicitly: It is created when the Reader is created and destroyed when the Reader is destroyed. We say that the Reader is *composed of* the ifstream object.

> **Note** When object A is composed of object B, B is created in A's constructor and destroyed in A's destructor.

The next lines are critical. We overload the >> operator for every primitive type we might want to read from disk. Thus, we can read both integers and constant integers, characters, pointers to characters, Booleans, and so forth. On line 30 we also overload operator >> for a vector of characters. We are going to let Reader and Writer manage the reading and writing of a vector of characters, relieving our other objects of this responsibility.

Writer shows exactly the same capabilities, but in reverse. We'll see how these work together when we examine the writing and subsequent reading of objects to and from disk.

User Interface Issues

We must make one other modification to the code: First and foremost, we must provide the player with a mechanism to indicate that he wants to save the current game. When the player is guessing, we already have the capability to put in a flag value when it is time to guess (for example, -s for show history). We'll add a new flag: -f for write to file.

We need to add this capability for the player to save the game even when the computer is guessing. Because this is not an event-driven program, we'll have to edge it in where we can. In an event-driven program—for example, in a typical Windows program such as Word—the program presents a menu and some widgets (buttons, list boxes, and so on). The user is then free to interact in any way he wants: Click a button, drop a list, and so forth. In our program, however, the user must interact in a prescribed order, so we must make sure we can handle the flag where it is presented.

We'll allow the user to enter a flag when it is time to score the computer's guess. This requires only a small change to the Computer::OfferGuess() method, which we'll discuss shortly.

All this is much clearer when we walk through the code, which we'll do right now. Decrypter, Computer, Human, Game, Guess, SmartString, and SmartChar must all now derive from Storable because each will be responsible for storing its state.

In addition, main() must change because we now ask the player whether he wants to resume an existing (saved) game or begin a new game. Listing 13.3 shows main().

Listing 13.3   The Driver Program

```
0:   #include <iostream>
1:   #include <iterator>
2:   #include <vector>
3:
4:   #include "defvals.h"
5:   #include "game.h"
6:   #include "guess.h"
7:
8:   using namespace std;
9:
10:  int main()
```

```
11:    {
12:
13:        cout << "Decryptix. (c)Copyright 1999 ";
14:        cout << "Liberty Associates, Inc.";
15:        cout << "Version 5\n\n" << endl;
16:        cout << "There are two ways to play Decryptix:";
17:        cout << "either you can guess a pattern I create,\n";
18:        cout << "or I can guess your pattern.\n\n";
19:        cout << "If you are guessing, I will think of a ";
20:        cout << "pattern of letters (e.g., abcde).\n";
21:        cout << "On each turn, you guess the pattern and ";
22:        cout << "I will tell you how many letters you \n";
23:        cout << "got right, and how many of the correct ";
24:        cout << "letters were in the correct position.\n\n";
25:        cout << "The goal is to decode the puzzle as quickly ";
26:        cout << "as possible. You control how many\n";
27:        cout << "letters can be used and how many positions ";
28:        cout << "(e.g., 5 possible letters in 4\n";
29:        cout << "positions) as well as whether or not the ";
30:        cout << "pattern might contain duplicate \n";
31:        cout << "letters (e.g., aabcd).\n\n";
32:        cout << "If I'm guessing, you think of a pattern ";
33:        cout << "and score each of my answers.\n\n";
34:        bool playAgain = true;
35:
36:        while ( playAgain )
37:        {
38:            Game * g;
39:
40:            char resume = ' ';
41:            while (
42:                resume != 'r' && resume != 'n' &&
43:                resume != 'R' && resume != 'N'
44:                )
45:            {
46:                cout << "R)esume existing game or start N)ew? ";
47:                cin >> resume;
48:            }
49:
50:            if ( resume == 'r' || resume == 'R')
51:            {
52:                char fileName[80];
53:                cout << "Resume from file named: ";
54:                cin >> fileName;
55:                cin.ignore(1,'\n');
56:
57:                Reader * reader = new Reader(fileName);
58:                g = new Game(*reader);
59:                delete reader;
60:            }
61:            else
```

continues

Listing 13.3   continued

```
62:                g = new Game;
63:
64:          g->Play();
65:
66:          delete g;
67:
68:          char choice = ' ';
69:          while ( choice != 'y' && choice != 'n' )
70:          {
71:              cout << "\nPlay again (y/n): ";
72:              cin >> choice;
73:          }
74:
75:          playAgain = choice == 'y' ? true : false;
76:      }
77:
78:      return 0;
79:  }
80:
```

 Note   This listing uses definedValues.h, which was shown in Listing 6.4 and which is unchanged here.

There is not much that is new in any of this until we reach line 38. This time we don't initialize the Game pointer; rather, we first determine whether we are restoring a saved game or starting a new game. If we are starting a new game, we'll instantiate the game on the heap, calling the default constructor as shown on line 62:

```
62:                g = new Game;
```

Let's follow this path to playing the game, saving it part of the way through and then restoring the game, which will bring us right back to this section of code.

On line 46 we prompt the user who will, in this case, enter n to indicate a new game. The if statement on line 50 fails, so we follow the else statement on line 61 and instantiate a new Game object on the heap. This calls the Game constructor, which prompts us to enter seven letters, five positions, and no duplicates. On line 64 we call Play(), which brings us into the body of the Game object. Listing 13.4 is the modified Game header, and 13.5 is the modified Game source code.

13

Listing 13.4 Game **Declared**

```
0:  #ifndef GAME_H
1:  #define GAME_H
2:
3:  #include "defvals.h"
4:  #include "guess.h"
5:  #include "SmartStr.h"
6:  #include "Storable.h"
7:
8:  class Guess;
9:  class Decrypter;
10:  class Reader;
11:  class Writer;
12:
13:  class Game : public Storable
14:  {
15:  public:
16:      Game();
17:      Game(Reader& rdr);
18:      ~Game(){}
19:
20:      void Play();
21:
22:      static int howManyLetters;
23:      static int howManyPositions;
24:
25:      void Write (Writer & wrtr) const; 26:
27:  private:
28:      void DisplayTime(int secs);
29:      bool VerifyComputerChoices();
30:      bool duplicates;
31:      void Store();
32:
33:      Decrypter * pDecrypter;
34:
35:  };
36:
37:  #endif
```

Analysis

On line 13 we note that Game now inherits publicly from Storable, which indicates that Game *is-a* Storable object. Game is thus required to implement a constructor that takes a reference to a Reader so that it can override the virtual Write function that takes a reference to a Writer object. To support these declarations, we *forward declare* the Reader and Writer objects.

> **Note**
>
> It is our goal not to clutter the header file with other included headers. To do so runs the risk of header A including B while B includes A, which the compiler will reject as a circular reference.
>
> Here is the issue: You cannot name a type that the compiler doesn't know about without first defining that type for the compiler. If we have a member variable of type `Writer`, we must include its header so that the compiler knows how large it is. If, however, we have only a *reference* or a *pointer* to a `Writer` object, we need only tell the compiler the name of that type, using a forward reference as shown on lines 10 and 11. Thus, we do not need to include the header file for these objects.
>
> We *do*, however, need to include the header file for the base class, `Storable` (you must always include the header for base classes). In our case, `Reader` and `Writer` are defined in storable.h, but we can easily move each to its own header files at a later time.

Finally, on line 25 we see the declaration of the `Write` method, which is consistent with the signature from `Storable`.

Listing 13.5   Game Implemented

```
0:   #include "game.h"
1:   #include "defvals.h"
2:   #include "SmartStr.h"
3:   #include "Decryptr.h"
4:   #include "Human.h"
5:   #include "computer.h"
6:
7:   #include <time.h>
8:
9:   int Game::howManyLetters = 0;
10:   int Game::howManyPositions = 0;
11:
12:
13:   Game::Game(Reader & rdr)
14:   {
15:       bool isHuman;
16:
17:       rdr >> isHuman;
18:
19:       if ( isHuman )
20:           pDecrypter = new Human(rdr);
21:       else
22:           pDecrypter = new Computer(rdr);
23:
24:       rdr >> duplicates;
25:       rdr >> howManyLetters;
```

```
26:        rdr >> howManyPositions;
27:        cout << "Game restored.\n";
28:
29:    }
30:
31:
32:    Game::Game()
33:    {
34:        for ( ;; )
35:        {
36:            // get user's preference for how many possible letters
37:            while ( howManyLetters < minLetters ||
38:                howManyLetters > maxLetters )
39:            {
40:                cout << "How many letters? (";
41:                cout << minLetters << "-" << maxLetters << "): ";
42:                cin >> howManyLetters;
43:                if ( howManyLetters < minLetters ||
44:                    howManyLetters > maxLetters )
45:                {
46:                    cout << "please enter a number between ";
47:                    cout << minLetters << " and ";
48:                    cout << maxLetters << endl;
49:                }
50:            }
51:
52:            // get user's preference for how many slots (positions)
53:            while ( howManyPositions < minPos ||
54:                howManyPositions > maxPos )
55:            {
56:                cout << "How many positions? (";
57:                cout << minPos << "-" << maxPos << "): ";
58:                cin >> howManyPositions;
59:                if ( howManyPositions < minPos ||
60:                    howManyPositions > maxPos )
61:                {
62:                    cout << "please enter a number between ";
63:                    cout << minPos <<" and " << maxPos << endl;
64:                }
65:            }
66:
67:            char choice = ' ';
68:            while ( choice != 'y' && choice != 'n' )
69:            {
70:                cout << "Allow duplicates (y/n)? ";
71:                cin >> choice;
72:            }
73:
74:            duplicates = choice == 'y' ? true : false;
75:
```

continues

Listing 13.5 continued

```
76:          if ( ! duplicates &&
77:              howManyPositions > howManyLetters )
78:          {
79:              cout << "\nI can't put " << howManyLetters;
80:              cout << " letters in " << howManyPositions;
81:              cout << " positions without duplicates! ";
82:              cout << "Please try again.\n\n";
83:              howManyLetters = 0;
84:              howManyPositions = 0;
85:              continue;
86:          }
87:
88:          choice = ' ';
89:          while ( choice != 'h' && choice != 'c' )
90:          {
91:              cout << "Who guesses. (H)uman";
92:              cout << " or (C)omputer? (h/c)? ";
93:              cin >> choice;
94:          }
95:
96:          bool ok = choice == 'h' ?
97:              true : VerifyComputerChoices();
98:          if( ok )
99:          {
100:             if ( choice == 'h' )
101:                 pDecrypter = new Human(duplicates);
102:             else
103:                 pDecrypter = new Computer(duplicates);
104:
105:             break;
106:         }
107:     }
108: }
109:
110: void Game::DisplayTime(int totalSeconds)
111: {
112:     int totalDays = totalSeconds / SecondsInDay;
113:     int totalHours = totalSeconds / SecondsInHour;
114:     int totalMinutes = totalSeconds / SecondsInMinute;
115:     if ( totalDays > 1 )
116:         cout << totalDays << " days! ";
117:
118:     else if ( totalHours > 1 )
119:         cout << totalHours << " hours! ";
120:
121:     else if ( totalMinutes > 1 )
122:         cout << totalMinutes << " minutes. ";
123:
124:     else
125:         cout << totalSeconds << " seconds. ";
```

13

```
126:    }
127:
128:    void Game::Play()
129:    {
130:
131:        int start = time( NULL );
132:
133:        bool StoreGame = pDecrypter->Play();
134:        if ( StoreGame )
135:            Store();
136:
137:
138:        // report elapsed time
139:        int end = time( NULL );
140:        int totalSeconds = end - start;
141:
142:        cout << "\nTotal elapsed time, this game: ";
143:        DisplayTime(totalSeconds);
144:
145:        cout << "\n";
146:
147:        howManyLetters = 0;
148:        howManyPositions = 0;
149:    }
150:
151:
152:    bool Game::VerifyComputerChoices()
153:    {
154:        int totalGuesses = 1;
155:
156:        if ( duplicates )
157:            for ( int i = 0; i < howManyPositions; i++ )
158:                totalGuesses *= howManyLetters;
159:        else
160:            for (
161:                int i = howManyLetters;
162:                i > howManyLetters - howManyPositions;
163:                i—
164:                )
165:                totalGuesses *= i;
166:
167:
168:        int totalSeconds = totalGuesses / GUESSES_PER_SECOND;
169:
170:        if ( totalSeconds > 2 )
171:        {
172:            cout << "\n\nYou are asking me to guess ";
173:            cout << "from a possible ";
174:            cout << totalGuesses;
175:            cout <<  " combinations.";
176:
```

continues

Listing 13.5 continued

```
177:            cout << "\nI can get through about ";
178:            cout <<  GUESSES_PER_SECOND;
179:            cout << " guesses per second. ";
180:            cout << "If the puzzle is tough,";
181:            cout << "\na single guess could take me more than ";
182:
183:            DisplayTime(totalSeconds);
184:
185:            char confirm = ' ';
186:            while ( confirm != 'y' && confirm != 'n' )
187:            {
188:                cout << "\n\nAre you sure (y/n)? ";
189:                cin >> confirm;
190:            }
191:
192:            if ( confirm == 'n' )
193:            {
194:                howManyLetters = 0;
195:                howManyPositions = 0;
196:                return false;
197:            }
198:        }
199:        else
200:        {
201:            cout << "Choosing among " << totalGuesses;
202:            cout << " possible combinations...\n\n";
203:        }
204:
205:        return true;
206:
207:    }
208:
209:
210:    void Game::Write(Writer & wrtr) const
211:    {
212:        pDecrypter->Write(wrtr);
213:        wrtr << duplicates;
214:        wrtr << howManyLetters;
215:        wrtr << howManyPositions;
216:    }
217:
218:
219:    void Game::Store()
220:    {
221:        char fileName[80];
222:        cout << "Store to file named: ";
223:        cin >> fileName;
224:        Writer * writer = new Writer(fileName);
```

```
225:      Write(*writer);
226:      delete writer;
227:  }
```

Analysis

We pick up the analysis with the invocation of Play, the implementation of which is shown beginning on line 128. We immediately invoke Play() on the pDecrypter, which in this scenario points to a Computer object. The result of this call is saved in the local Boolean variable StoreGame. If StoreGame is true, we store this play of the game, as we'll see shortly.

 Note

Many C++ programmers, especially those who come to C++ from C, might write the code shown on lines 133–135 as follows:

```
133:      if ( pDecrypter->Play() )
134:          Store();
```

This collapses the two steps into one, using the implicit and unnamed temporary Boolean that is returned from Play as the value to check in the if statement. Although this is perfectly valid in C++, it is somewhat more difficult to debug because you cannot easily examine the value (true or false) of the returned Boolean.

We continue our analysis in the body of Computer's Play() method, shown in Listings 13.6 and 13.7

Listing 13.6 Computer **Declared**

```
0:  #ifndef COMPUTER_H
1:  #define COMPUTER_H
2:
3:  #include "Decryptr.h"
4:
5:  class SmartString;
6:  class Reader;
7:  class Writer;
8:
9:  class Computer  : public Decrypter
10: {
11: public:
12:     Computer (bool duplicates);
13:     Computer (Reader & rdr);
```

continues

Listing 13.6   continued

```
14:        virtual ~Computer();
15:        bool HandleFlag(char flag, bool & isStoring);
16:        bool Play();
17:        virtual void Write(Writer& wrtr) const;
18:
19:   private:
20:        void GenerateAGuess ();
21:        bool IsConsistent (vector<char> guess);
22:        Guess OfferGuess(bool & quit, bool & isStoring);
23:
24:        void ShowHelp();
25:        SmartString * mySmartString;
26:        int    total;
27:   };
28:
29:   #endif
```

Listing 13.7   Computer Implemented

```
0:   #include "Computer.h"
1:   #include "smartstr.h"
2:   #include "Game.h"
3:   #include <string>
4:   #include <stdlib.h>
5:
6:
7:   Computer::Computer(bool dupes):
8:   Decrypter(dupes),
9:   total(0),
10:  mySmartString(0)
11:  {
12:  }
13:
14:  Computer::Computer(Reader & rdr):
15:  Decrypter(rdr)
16:  {
17:        mySmartString = new SmartString(rdr);
18:        rdr>>total;
19:        cout << "Computer restored.\n";
20:
21:  }
22:
23:  Computer::~Computer()
24:  {
25:
26:  }
27:
28:  void Computer::GenerateAGuess()
29:  {
30:
```

```
31:    bool ok = true;
32:    int counter = 0;
33:    int start = time( NULL );
34:    do
35:    {
36:        counter++;
37:        total++;
38:        if ( counter % 10000 == 0 )
39:            cout << ".";
40:
41:        ok = mySmartString->GetNext();
42:
43:        if ( !ok )
44:        {
45:            cout << "Something went wrong!";
46:            cout << " Please start over\n";
47:            round = 1;
48:            delete mySmartString;
49:            mySmartString = new SmartString(duplicates);
50:            ShowHistory();
51:            cout << "\n\n";
52:            history.clear();
53:            continue;
54:        }
55:
56:    } while ( !IsConsistent(mySmartString->GetString()) );
57:
58:    int end = time( NULL );
59:    int seconds = end - start;
60:    cout << "(" << counter ;
61:    cout << " strings eliminated this round; ";
62:    cout << total << " total.)";
63:    if ( seconds > 1 )
64:        cout << " [" << seconds << " seconds]";
65:    cout << "\n";
66: }
67:
68: // Handle any flag from user (-?,-q, etc.)
69: bool Computer::HandleFlag(char flag, bool & isStoring)
70: {
71:    bool quit = false;
72:    isStoring = false;
73:    switch (flag)
74:    {
75:    case 's':
76:        ShowHistory();
77:        break;
78:    case '?':
79:        ShowHelp();
80:        break;
81:    case 'f':
```

continues

Listing 13.7 continued

```
82:            isStoring = true;
83:            quit = true;
84:            break;
85:        case 'q':
86:            quit = true;
87:            break;
88:        default:
89:            cout << "\nUnknown flag. Ignored.\n";
90:            break;
91:        }
92:        return quit;
93:    }
94:
95:    bool Computer::IsConsistent(vector<char> theGuess)
96:    {
97:
98:
99:        if ( ! duplicates)
100:        {
101:            for (
102:                vector<char>::const_iterator it =
103:                    theGuess.begin();
104:                it != theGuess.end();
105:                it++
106:                )
107:            {
108:                int HowMany =
109:                    count(theGuess.begin(), theGuess.end(),*it);
110:                if ( HowMany > 1 )
111:                    return false;
112:            }
113:        }
114:
115:        bool isValid = true;
116:
117:        int correct;
118:        int position;
119:
120:        for (
121:            vector<Guess>::const_iterator it =
122:                history.begin();
123:            it != history.end();
124:            it++
125:            )
126:        {
127:
128:            vector <char> temp = it->GetString();
129:
130:            correct = 0;
131:            position = 0;
```

13

```
132:            for ( int i = 0; i < Game::howManyLetters; i++)
133:            {
134:                int howManyInGuess =
135:                    count (
136:                        theGuess.begin(),
137:                        theGuess.end(),
138:                        alpha[i]
139:                        );
140:                int howManyInAnswer =
141:                    count (temp.begin(), temp.end(), alpha[i]);
142:                correct += _MIN(howManyInGuess, howManyInAnswer);
143:            }
144:
145:            for (  i = 0; i < Game::howManyPositions; i++)
146:            {
147:                if ( theGuess[i] == temp[i] )
148:                    position++;
149:            }
150:
151:            if ( correct != it->GetScore().first ||
152:                    position != it->GetScore().second )
153:            {
154:                isValid = false;
155:                break;
156:            }
157:        }
158:
159:     return isValid;
160: }
161:
162: Guess Computer::OfferGuess(bool & quit, bool & isStoring)
163: {
164:     quit = false;
165:     isStoring = false;
166:     vector<char> theGuess =
167:         mySmartString->GetString();
168:     char temp[80];
169:     int numCorrect, numInPosition;
170:     for ( ;; )
171:     {
172:         cout << "\n";
173:         Display(theGuess);
174:         cout << "Round " << round << ". ";
175:         cout << "Please record score. \t";
176:         cout << "How many correct?: ";
177:         cin >> temp;
178:
179:         if ( temp[0] == '-' )// got a flag
180:         {
181:             quit = HandleFlag(temp[1], isStoring);
```

continues

Listing 13.7 continued

```
182:                if ( quit )
183:                {
184:                    numCorrect = 0;
185:                    numInPosition = 0;
186:                }
187:                else
188:                    continue;
189:            }
190:            else
191:            {
192:                numCorrect = atoi(temp);
193:                cout << "\t\t\tHow many in position?: ";
194:                cin >> numInPosition;
195:                round++;
196:            }
197:            break;
198:        }
199:    Guess thisGuess(theGuess,numCorrect,numInPosition);
200:    return thisGuess;
201:
202: }
203: bool Computer::Play()
204: {
205:
206:     bool quit;
207:     bool isStoring = false;
208:
209:     if ( ! mySmartString )
210:         mySmartString = new SmartString(duplicates);
211:
212:     vector<char> theGuess;
213:
214:     bool deletedCharacters = false;
215:
216:     for ( ;; )
217:     {
218:         Guess theGuess = OfferGuess(quit, isStoring);
219:         if ( quit )
220:             break;
221:
222:         history.push_back(theGuess);
223:
224:         if ( theGuess.GetScore().second ==
225:             Game::howManyPositions )
226:             break;
227:
228:         if (
229:             ! mySmartString->CanEliminateCharacters(theGuess) ||
230:             ! IsConsistent(mySmartString->GetString())
```

```
231:                )
232:                    GenerateAGuess();
233:        };
234:        return isStoring;
235: }
236:
237: // result of pressing -?
238: void Computer::ShowHelp()
239: {
240:        cout << "\t-s Show history\n\t-f store to File\n";
241:        cout << "\t-? Help\n\t-q quit\n" << endl;
242: }
243:
244: void Computer::Write(Writer & wrtr) const
245: {
246:        wrtr << false;  // no I'm not a human
247:        Decrypter::Write(wrtr);
248:        mySmartString->Write(wrtr);
249:        wrtr << total;
250:
251: }
```

Analysis

We resume our analysis on line 203 of Listing 13.7, with the implementation of Computer::Play(). There are no changes from the previous version until we enter OfferGuess() (shown on line 162). We want to obtain two results from OfferGuess back in Play. We want to return the Guess itself (as usual), but we also need to know whether the user has asked us to store the game. We create a local Boolean variable, isStoring, and pass it in to OfferGuess by reference, as shown on line 162. This allows OfferGuess to update this variable as a result of a request by the user to store the game.

Within OfferGuess, on line 173 we display the guess and ask the user to score the guess as to how many are correct. If, at this point, the user enters -f, we pass that flag to HandleFlag, shown on line 69. We are interested in the 'f' (for file) handler, which is shown on line 81. This simply sets the isStoring variable (again passed in by reference), as well as the quit Boolean, to true. quit is returned as the return value, and isStoring is returned by virtue of having been passed in by reference. OfferGuess returns with no score because quit was set true; the isStoring variable in Computer::Play is now marked true. This in turn returns to Game::Play, returning the value in isStoring (in this case true) and signaling the Game to store itself.

Assume for the moment that we played four rounds before entering the -f flag. We're playing seven letters in five positions with no duplicates. Our code is cbeda.

The four rounds proceed as they did in the preceding chapter, leading to the following guesses and scores:

```
abcde  3/0
bcdfg  4/2
bcegf  3/1
bdfag  4/0
```

At round 5, however, we signal that we want to store the current game. We pick up our story on line 179 of Listing 13.7, where the computer has offered a guess and the player has entered -f:

```
179:              if ( temp[0] == '-' )// got a flag
180:              {
181:                  quit = HandleFlag(temp[1], isStoring);
```

This branches to line 69, where the flag invokes the case 'f' clause of the Switch statement:

```
81:      case 'f':
82:              isStoring = true;
83:              quit = true;
```

This sets both the parameter isStoring and the local Boolean value quit to true. The latter, quit, is returned as the return value of the method and assigned to the value quit in OfferGuess(). This breaks us out of offering guesses and returns isStoring to Computer::Play() (see Listing 13.7, line 219). We break out of the forever loop and return isStoring to Game::Play() on line 133 of Listing 13.5. The return of isStoring == true causes the if statement on line 134 to evaluate true and the Game method Store() to be invoked, bringing us to line 219. Here is where the fun begins.

The game elicits a name from the end user by declaring a character buffer of 80 characters named fileName, and then prompting the user for input and capturing the input on line 223.

On line 224, we create a new Writer object on the heap, passing in the fileName we just created. This invokes Writer's constructor, which is shown on line 39 of Listing 13.2:

```
39:      Writer(char * filename):fout(filename, ios::binary){};
```

This inline implementation simply initializes the ofstream member variable fout with the file name we just passed in. An ofstream object is an output filestream object, used for writing out to files. The constructor of such an object takes two parameters: the name of the file and a flag indicating what kind of data you'll store in that file. We'll be storing binary (rather than text) data because we don't want the operating system to treat the data as text that can be read in an editor—we want the

13

data to be treated as a stream of bytes. We'll use the (static member) flag `binary` of the `ios` (`iostream`) object, which is the base object for `ofstream`.

The complexity of the myriad ways you can open and manipulate files is beyond the scope of this book. However, the simple method that is shown here opens a file for writing, and the file will be created as a stream of bytes.

After the file is open, we resume our analysis on line 224 of Listing 13.5, where `Game` now calls its own `Write()` method, passing in the newly created `Writer` object. Notice on the next line that when the call to `Write` returns, we'll delete the `Writer` to avoid a memory leak. This is good programming practice: The method that allocates the memory (on line 224) is the same method that deletes it (two lines later).

In the meantime, we have a lot of work to do. The call to `Write()` on line 225 kicks off a series of methods that will store the entire state of the game, including the history of guesses offered so far and the current state of the smart string and smart characters. Let's trace our way hrough it.

Writing out the Game

We'll examine the systematic details in just a moment, but before we begin, let's take a moment to think through what we want to accomplish.

The `Game` tells its `Decrypter` (in this case a `Computer`) to write itself. The `Computer` tells its base class, `Decrypter`, to write itself, which must write out its `history` member variable. This is a vector of `Guesses`, so each `Guess` must write itself out, including its pair of scores and its vector of characters. After `Decrypter` is done, `Computer` must write out its `SmartString` object, which in turn must tell each of its `SmartChar` objects to write themselves out to disk.

In short, by telling the `Game` to write itself, each of the objects in memory is written in a precise order. Later, when it is time to restore the `Game`, we'll read these objects up into memory in *exactly* the order in which they were written. Let's see how it is done, step by step.

Writing the Game, Step by Step

Remember that we start with the call to `Game::Store()`, where we create the `Writer` object, and then on line 225 we call the `Game` member method `Write()`:

```
219:   void Game::Store()
220:   {
221:       char fileName[80];
222:       cout << "Store to file named: ";
223:       cin >> fileName;
```

```
224:        Writer * writer = new Writer(fileName);
225:        Write(*writer);
226:        delete writer;
227:    }
```

The call to `Write()` invokes `Game::Write` on line 210. The very first thing the `Game` does is tell its member variable `pDecrypter`—which is a pointer to the current `Decrypter`, in this case the `Computer`—to write itself, passing in the same `Writer` object.

After this function call returns, the `Game` writes out the remaining member variables: duplicates, `howManyLetters`, and `howManyPositions`. For now, we need to see the result of calling `pDecrypter->Write(wrtr)`.

If you think that this will call the `Write` method on `pDecrypter`, you've forgotten about polymorphism! Because `pDecrypter` points to a computer object, this actually invokes `Computer::Write()`, shown on line 244 of Listing 13.7.

Writing Polymorphic Objects

We need to stop and think about what is going to happen when we read this object back up from disk. The `Game` will want to create a pointer to a `Decrypter`, but it won't know whether to create a computer or a human object. We need to signal to it that the object that is stored is a computer. The right object to store that signal is the computer itself. Thus, the first thing the computer does is write a Boolean to the disk. In this case, it writes `false`. When we store a human, we'll have it store `true`.

Line 246 illustrates how we store the value `false`:

```
246:        wrtr << false;
```

The compiler translates this into an overloaded operator call on the writer object:

```
wrtr.operator<<(false);
```

This is the essence of operator overloading, and it is this powerful technique that enables you to create classes, such as `writer`, that appear to work exactly like `cin` and `cout`.

This call brings us into the implementation of `writer`, which is shown in Listing 13.8 along with the implementation of `Reader`.

Listing 13.8 `Reader` and `Writer` **Implemented**

```
0:  #include "Storable.h"
1:  #include "defvals.h"
2:
```

```
3:  Writer & Writer::operator <<(int & data)
4:  {
5:      fout.write( (char*) &data, szInt);
6:      return *this;
7:  }
8:
9:  Writer & Writer::operator <<(const int & data)
10: {
11:     fout.write( (char*) &data, szInt);
12:     return *this;
13: }
14:
15: Writer & Writer::operator <<(char & data)
16: {
17:     fout.write( (char*) &data, szChar);
18:     return *this;
19: }
20:
21: Writer & Writer::operator <<(char *& data)
22: {
23:     int len = strlen(data);
24:     fout.write((char*)&len,szInt);
25:     fout.write(data,len);
26:     return *this;
27: }
28:
29: Writer & Writer::operator <<(const char *& data)
30: {
31:     int len = strlen(data);
32:     fout.write((char*)&len,szInt);
33:     fout.write(data,len);
34:     return *this;
35: }
36:
37: Writer & Writer::operator <<(bool & data)
38: {
39:     fout.write( (char*) &data, szBool);
40:     return *this;
41: }
42:
43: Writer & Writer::operator <<(const bool & data)
44: {
45:     fout.write( (char*) &data, szBool);
46:     return *this;
47: }
48:
49: Writer & Writer::operator <<(const vector<char>& vec)
50: {
51:     int len = vec.size();
52:     fout.write( (char*) &len, szInt );
53:     for (
```

continues

Listing 13.8   continued

```
54:            vector<char>::const_iterator it =
55:                vec.begin();
56:            it != vec.end();
57:            it++
58:            )
59:        {
60:            char theChar = it[0];
61:            fout.write( (char*) &theChar, szChar);
62:        }
63:        return *this;
64:    }
65:
66:    //******************** Reader ***************************
67:
68:    Reader & Reader::operator >>(int & data)
69:    {
70:        fin.read( (char*) &data, szInt);
71:        return *this;
72:    }
73:
74:    Reader & Reader::operator >>(const int & data)
75:    {
76:        fin.read( (char*) &data, szInt);
77:        return *this;
78:    }
79:
80:    Reader & Reader::operator >>(char & data)
81:    {
82:        fin.read( (char*) &data, szChar);
83:        return *this;
84:    }
85:
86:    Reader & Reader::operator >>(char *& data
87:    {
88:        int len;
89:        fin.read((char *) &len, szInt);
90:        data = new char[len+1];
91:        fin.read(data,len);
92:        data[len]='\0';
93:        return *this;
94:    }
95:
96:    Reader & Reader::operator >>(bool & data)
97:    {
98:        fin.read( (char*) &data, szBool);
99:        return *this;
100:   }
101:
102:   Reader & Reader::operator >>(vector<char>& vec)
103:   {
```

```
104:        char c;
105:        int len;
106:        fin.read( (char*) &len, szInt);
107:        for ( int i = 0; i < len; i++)
108:        {
109:            fin.read( (char*) &c, szChar);
110:            vec.push_back(c);
111:        }
112:        return *this;
113:    }
```

The overloaded operator that is invoked is shown on line 37. The Boolean value `false` is passed in by reference, and on line 39 we invoke the `write()` method on the `fout` member variable. This `write()` method takes two parameters: a pointer to the data to be written and the number of bytes to write.

We get a pointer to the data that is to be written by taking its address (using the address of symbol, &). This must be *cast* to a pointer to character (`char *`). We store the size of a Boolean in the constant `szBool`, which we declared in the header definedValues.h:

```
const int szBool = sizeof(bool);
```

`sizeof()` is a standard library method that returns the size of a type. Because `bool` objects are one byte, this returns the value 1, which is assigned to the constant integer `szBool`.

Thus, on line 39 we write out the value `false`, and then on line 40 we return the `Writer` object itself.

The very next thing that `Computer` does is to chain up to the `Write()` method in its base class, `Decrypter` (shown on line 247 of Listing 13.7).

This call invokes the `Write()` method on `pDecrypter`, shown on line 52 of Listing 13.9.

Listing 13.9 `Decrypter` **Implemented**

```
0:  #include "Decryptr.h"
1:  #include "Game.h"
2:
3:  Decrypter::Decrypter(bool hasDuplicates):
4:  duplicates(hasDuplicates),
5:  round(1)
6:  {
7:
8:  }
9:
```

continues

Listing 13.9 continued

```
10:   Decrypter::Decrypter(Reader & rdr):
11:   Storable(rdr)
12:   {
13:       rdr >> round;
14:       rdr >> duplicates;
15:       int size;
16:       rdr >> size;
17:       for ( int i = 0; i < size; i++)
18:       {
19:           Guess theGuess(rdr);
20:           history.push_back(theGuess);
21:       }
22:   }
23:
24:   Decrypter::~Decrypter()
25:   {
26:
27:   }
28:
29:   void Decrypter::Display(vector<char> charVec) const
30:   {
31:       copy(
32:           charVec.begin(),
33:           charVec.end(),
34:           ostream_iterator<char>(cout," ")
35:           );
36:   }
37:
38:   // Iterate through history of guesses and display results
39:   void Decrypter::ShowHistory()
40:   {
41:       for (
42:           vector<Guess>::const_iterator it =
43:               history.begin();
44:           it != history.end();
45:           it++
46:           )
47:       {
48:           it->Display();
49:       }
50:   }
51:
52:   void Decrypter::Write(Writer & wrtr) const
53:   {
54:       wrtr << round;
55:       wrtr << duplicates;
56:       int len = history.size();
57:       wrtr << len;
```

```
58:     for (
59:         vector<Guess>::const_iterator it =
60:             history.begin();
61:         it != history.end();
62:         it++
63:         )
64:     {
65:         it->Write(wrtr);
66:     }
67:  }
```

Decryptix! is ready to write itself out. First, we write the member variable round on line 54. This, again, invokes writer.operator<<(const int & data), passing in the value of round by reference. Processing jumps to line 9 of Listing 13.8, where the integer is written to disk. Once again we pass two arguments to fout: the value and the size of the integer (4 bytes).

We continue on line 55 of Listing 13.9, where we write out the member variable duplicates. After this, Decrypter wants to write out its member variable history. Remember that history is a vector of Guesses, so each member of that vector must be written to the disk.

Vectors are not storable; they know nothing about writers or readers. Therefore, someone must take responsibility for writing them to the disk. We have a few choices. We can teach the writer how to write vectors of Guesses to disk just as we have taught it to write integers. This is appealing because it encapsulates this responsibility in the Writer and is parallel to writing integers. I rejected this idea, however, because the design of the Writer class dictates that it needs to be a generic and reusable class that knows only about built-in types.

I could, of course, have created a derived type of Writer that knows about vectors of Guesses. Instead, I simply told the Decrypter to do this work because, after all, the Decrypter owns the vector of Guesses.

Frankly, any of these designs are reasonable; I chose this path because it seems consistent with how things work with other data. The Decrypter is responsible for knowing that it must write its member data to disk; here it also must know that it must write this vector.

The Decrypter accomplishes this task by iterating over the history vector—writing each element to disk, one by one, by calling Write() on that element and passing in the Writer object (as shown on line 65). Before doing so, however, it must write out how many elements are in the array so that when the array is restored Decrypter knows how many elements to read off the disk. Thus, on line 56 we call `size()` on the vector, which returns the number of elements; this is written out on line 57.

The call on line 65

```
65:        it->Write(wrtr);
```

invokes `Write()` on the element to which the iterator is pointing: a `Guess` object. To look at this code, we must examine the `Guess` declaration in Listing 13.10, and then the implementation in Listing 13.11.

Listing 13.10 Guess **Declared**

```
0:   #ifndef GUESS_H
1:   #define GUESS_H
2:
3:   #include "defvals.h"
4:   #include "storable.h"
5:
6:   class Reader;
7:   class Writer;
8:
9:   class Guess : public Storable
10:  {
11:  public:
12:    Guess(vector<char>guess, int howManyRight, int howManyInPosition);
13:      Guess(Reader & rdr);
14:      virtual ~Guess(){}
15:      void Display() const;
16:      pair<int, int> GetScore() const;
17:      vector<char>GetString() const;
18:      virtual void Write(Writer&) const;
19:
20:  private:
21:      pair<int, int> score;
22:      vector<char> string;
23:  };
24:
25:  #endif
```

Listing 13.11 Guess **Implemented**

```
0:   #include "guess.h"
1:
2:
3:   Guess::Guess(
3a:      vector<char>guess,
3b:      int howManyRight,
3c:      int howManyInPosition ):
4:   string(guess),
5:   score(howManyRight, howManyInPosition)
```

13

```
6:  {
7:  }
8:
9:  Guess::Guess(Reader & rdr)
10: {
11:     rdr >> score.first;
12:     rdr >> score.second;
13:     int len;
14:     rdr >> len;
15:     char theChar;
16:     for ( int i = 0; i < len; i++ )
17:     {
18:         rdr >> theChar;
19:         string.push_back(theChar);
20:     }
21:
22:
23: }
24:
25: void Guess::Display() const
26: {
27:     copy(
28:         string.begin(),
29:         string.end(),
30:         ostream_iterator<char>(cout," ")
31:         );
32:     cout << "\t" << score.first;
33:     cout << " correct, " << score.second;
34:     cout << " in position\n";
35: }
36:
37: pair<int, int> Guess::GetScore() const
38: {
39:     return score;
40: }
41:
42: vector<char> Guess::GetString() const
43: {
44:     return string;
45: }
46:
47: void Guess::Write(Writer & wrtr) const
48: {
49:     wrtr << score.first;
50:     wrtr << score.second;
51:     wrtr << string;
52: }
```

The implementation of Guess::Write is shown beginning on line 47 of
Listing 13.11. We start by writing the score, which is a pair of integers. We'll write

each integer separately. The two elements of a pair are called `first` and `second`: We pass `first` to the `Writer` object on line 50, and we pass `second` on line 52.

On line 51 we pass the member variable `string` to the `Writer` object. What's going on here? Isn't this a vector as well? I decided to implement the capability for a `Writer` to write out a vector of characters because they are so common throughout this program and others. Is this a good design decision? It is certainly a *defensible* design decision, but, frankly, I did it this way to demonstrate the possibility.

Because `Writer` knows how to write a `vector<char>`, `Guess` need not write out the length nor iterate over the contents of the vector. It can simply pass the vector to `Writer` as if it were a built-in type. Control passes to the overloaded operator in `Writer`, shown on line 49 of Listing 13.8.

Here we've taught the `Writer` the steps for writing out a vector of characters. We first write out the length as an integer on line 52, and then on lines 53–62 we iterate through the character vector, writing out each character in turn.

When the `Guess` is finished writing itself to disk, we return to `Decrypter::Write()`, where we write the next `Guess` in the history, and all subsequent `Guess` objects, until all four rounds of `Guesses` have been recorded to disk.

Upon completion of that work, `Decrypter::Write()` returns to `Computer::Write` (at line 244 of Listing 13.7). Having instructed its base class to write itself to disk, the `Computer` class now instructs its `SmartString` to write itself to disk, passing in, as usual, the `Writer` object.

This passes control to the `SmartString::Write` method. `SmartString`'s declaration is shown in Listing 13.12, and its implementation in Listing 13.13.

Listing 13.12 `SmartString` **Declared**

```
0:  #ifndef SMARTSTRING_H
1:  #define SMARTSTRING_H
2:
3:  #include "defvals.h"
4:  #include "SmartChr.h"
5:
6:  class Guess;
7:
8:  class SmartString
9:  {
10: public:
11:     SmartString(bool dupes);
12:     SmartString(Reader& rdr);
13:     virtual    ~SmartString();
14:
```

```
15:        bool CanEliminateCharacters (const Guess& theGuess);
16:        bool GetNext();
17:        vector<char> GetString();
18:        bool RemoveCurrentCharacters();
19:        bool RemoveCurrentCharactersInEveryPosition();
20:        void Write(Writer& wrtr) const;
21:
22:
23:    private:
24:
25:        void ForceCharacters(const Guess & theGuess);
26:        int CountForcedInGuess(const Guess & theGuess);
27:        int CountUniqueLettersInGuess(const Guess & theGuess);
28:        bool In(vector <char> vec, char target) const;
29:
30:        vector<char> deadCharacters;
31:        bool duplicates;
32:        vector<char> forcedCharacters;
33:        vector<SmartChar> myString;
34:    };
35:    #endif
```

Listing 13.13   `SmartString` Implemented

```
0:   #include "SmartStr.h"
1:   #include "Game.h"
2:   #include "Guess.h"
3:
4:   SmartString::SmartString(bool dupes):
5:   duplicates(dupes)
6:   {
7:       for ( int i = 0; i < Game::howManyPositions; i++ )
8:       {
9:           int j;
10:          if ( duplicates )
11:              j = 0;
12:          else
13:              j = i;
14:          SmartChar theChar(j);
15:          myString.push_back(theChar);
16:      }
17:  }
18:
19:  SmartString::SmartString(Reader & rdr)
20:  {
21:      rdr >> deadCharacters;
22:      rdr >> duplicates;
23:      rdr >> forcedCharacters;
24:      int size;
25:      rdr >> size;
```

continues

Listing 13.13   continued

```
26:     for ( int i = 0; i < size; i++)
27:     {
28:         SmartChar theSmartChar(rdr);
29:         myString.push_back(theSmartChar);
30:     }
31: }
32:
33: SmartString::~SmartString()
34: {
35:
36: }
37:
38: vector<char> SmartString::GetString()
39: {
40:     vector<char> outString;
41:
42:     for (
43:         vector<SmartChar>::iterator it = myString.begin();
44:         it != myString.end();
45:         it++
46:         )
47:     {
48:         char theChar = it->GetChar();
49:         outString.push_back(theChar);
50:     }
51:     return outString;
52: }
53:
54:
55: bool SmartString::GetNext()
56: {
57:     vector<char> outString;
58:     vector<SmartChar>::reverse_iterator it;
59:     it = myString.rbegin();
60:
61:     bool rollover = it->Increment();
62:     while ( rollover )
63:     {
64:         it++;
65:         if ( it == myString.rend() )
66:             return false;
67:         else
68:         {
69:             rollover = it->Increment();
70:         }
71:     }
72:     return true;
73: }
74:
75:
```

13

```
76:    // removes character that is currently shown
77:    // in a particular position
78:    bool SmartString::RemoveCurrentCharacters()
79:    {
80:        char theChar;
81:        bool anyDeleted = false;
82:
83:        for (
84:            vector<SmartChar>::iterator it = myString.begin();
85:            it != myString.end();
86:            it++
87:            )
88:        {
89:            theChar = it->GetChar();
90:
91:            if ( ! In(forcedCharacters,theChar) )
92:            {
93:                theChar = it->RemoveCurrent();
94:                // dead characters stop you from
95:                // reporting removal of characters already dead
96:                if (! In(deadCharacters,theChar) )
97:                {
98:                    deadCharacters.push_back(theChar);
99:                    cout << "Eliminating " << theChar;
100:                    cout << " from current position" << endl;
101:                    anyDeleted = true;
102:                }
103:            }
104:        }
105:        return anyDeleted;
106: }
107:
108:
109: // removes character that is currently shown
110: // in a particular position from every position
111: bool SmartString::RemoveCurrentCharactersInEveryPosition()
112: {
113:     char theChar;
114:     bool anyDeleted = false;
115:     vector <char> currentGuess;
116:
117:     for (
118:         vector<SmartChar>::iterator it = myString.begin();
119:         it != myString.end();
120:         it++
121:         )
122:     {
123:         currentGuess.push_back(it->GetChar());
124:     }
125:
```

continues

Listing 13.13   continued

```
126:     for (
127:         vector<char>::iterator itc = currentGuess.begin();
128:         itc != currentGuess.end();
129:         itc++
130:         )
131:     {
132:         theChar = *itc;
133:         if ( ! In(forcedCharacters,theChar) )
134:         {
135:
136:             for (
137:                 vector<SmartChar>::iterator it2 = myString.begin();
138:                 it2 != myString.end();
139:                 it2++
140:                 )
141:             {
142:                 it2->Remove(theChar);
143:                 if (! In(deadCharacters,theChar) )
144:                 {
145:                     deadCharacters.push_back(theChar);
146:                     cout << "Eliminating " << theChar << endl;
147:                     anyDeleted = true;
148:                 }
149:             }
150:         }
151:     }
152:     return anyDeleted;
153: }
154:
155: bool SmartString::CanEliminateCharacters
156:     (const Guess & theGuess)
157: {
158:
159:     bool anyDeleted = false;
160:     ForceCharacters(theGuess);
161:     int forcedInAnswer = CountForcedInGuess(theGuess);
162:
163:     int overall = theGuess.GetScore().first;
164:     int inPos = theGuess.GetScore().second;
165:
166:
167:     if ( overall == 0 ¦¦ overall == forcedInAnswer )
168:     {
169:         anyDeleted = RemoveCurrentCharactersInEveryPosition();
170:         return anyDeleted; // we did eliminate characters
171:     }
172:
173:     if ( inPos == 0 )
174:     {
175:         anyDeleted = RemoveCurrentCharacters();
```

```
176:              return anyDeleted; // we did eliminate characters
177:        }
178:
179:      return false;
180: }
181:
182: void SmartString::ForceCharacters(const Guess &theGuess)
183: {
184:      int numDifferentLetters =
185:          CountUniqueLettersInGuess(theGuess);
186:      int score = theGuess.GetScore().first;
187:
188:      if ( score >= numDifferentLetters )
189:      {
190:          vector<char> theString =
191:              theGuess.GetString();
192:
193:          for (
194:              vector<char>::const_iterator it = theString.begin();
195:              it != theString.end();
196:              it++
197:              )
198:          {
199:              if ( ! In(forcedCharacters, *it) )
200:                  forcedCharacters.push_back(*it);
201:          }
202:      }
203: }
204:
205: int SmartString::CountUniqueLettersInGuess
206:      (const Guess &theGuess)
207: {
208:      vector<char> temp;
209:      vector<char> theString =
210:          theGuess.GetString();
211:
212:      for (
213:          vector<char>::const_iterator it = theString.begin();
214:          it != theString.end();
215:          it++
216:          )
217:      {
218:          if (! In(temp,*it) )
219:              temp.push_back(*it);
220:      }
221:
222:      // temp now has all the unique letters
223:
224:      return temp.size();
225: }
226:
```

continues

Listing 13.13   continued

```
227:  int SmartString::CountForcedInGuess
228:      (const Guess &theGuess)
229:  {
230:      int howManyForcedInGuess = 0;
231:      vector<char> theString = theGuess.GetString();
232:
233:      for (
234:          vector<char>::const_iterator it = theString.begin();
235:          it != theString.end();
236:          it++
237:          )
238:      {
239:          if ( In( forcedCharacters, *it ) )
240:              howManyForcedInGuess++;
241:      }
242:
243:      return howManyForcedInGuess;
244:
245:  }
246:
247:  bool SmartString::In(vector<char> vec, char target) const
248:  {
249:      vector<char>::iterator where =
250:          find(vec.begin(), vec.end(),target);
251:      return where != vec.end();
252:  }
253:
254:  void SmartString::Write(Writer & wrtr) const
255:  {
256:      wrtr << deadCharacters;
257:      wrtr << duplicates;
258:      wrtr << forcedCharacters;
259:      int len = myString.size();
260:      wrtr << len;
261:      for (
262:          vector<SmartChar>::const_iterator it =
263:              myString.begin();
264:          it != myString.end();
265:          it++
266:          )
267:      {
268:          it->Write(wrtr);
269:      }
270:
271:  }
```

Analysis

We resume our analysis on line 254 of Listing 13.13. SmartString writes out its deadCharacters member variable, which we see declared as a vector of characters on line 30 of Listing 13.12. This will be written out exactly as we saw in the previous example.

Next, SmartString writes out the Boolean value duplicates, followed by the vector of characters forcedCharacters. Finally, SmartString must write out its member variable myString, which is a vector of SmartCharacter objects. The SmartString iterates through its vector, asking each SmartCharacter to write itself out in turn, as shown on line 268. SmartChar's declaration is shown in Listing 13.14, and its implementation is shown in Listing 13.15.

Listing 13.14   SmartChar **Declared**

```
0:  #ifndef SMARTCHAR_H
1:  #define SMARTCHAR_H
2:
3:  #include "defvals.h"
4:  #include "Storable.h"
5:
6:  class SmartChar : public Storable
7:  {
8:  public:
9:      SmartChar(int letter = 0);
10:     SmartChar(Reader& rdr);
11:     virtual ~SmartChar        ();
12:
13:     char GetChar () const;
14:     bool Increment ();
15:     char RemoveCurrent ();
16:     bool Remove (char c);
17:     void Write(Writer& wrtr) const;
18:
19:  private:
20:     int myChar;
21:     vector<char> myCharacters;
22:
23:  };
24:
25:  #endif
```

Listing 13.15   SmartChar **Implemented**

```
0:  #include "SmartChr.h"
1:  #include "Game.h"
2:
```

continues

Listing 13.15   continued

```
3:   SmartChar::SmartChar(int letter):
4:   myChar(letter)
5:   {
6:       for ( int i = 0; i < Game::howManyLetters; i++ )
7:           myCharacters.push_back(alpha[i]);
8:
9:   }
10:
11:  SmartChar::SmartChar(Reader & rdr)
12:  {
13:      rdr >> myChar;
14:      rdr >> myCharacters;
15:  }
16:
17:
18:  SmartChar::~SmartChar()
19:  {
20:
21:  }
22:
23:  char SmartChar::GetChar() const
24:  {
25:      return myCharacters[myChar];
26:  }
27:
28:  bool SmartChar::Increment()
29:  {
30:      if ( ++myChar >= myCharacters.size() )
31:      {
32:          myChar = 0;
33:          return true;
34:      }
35:      return false;
36:  }
37:
38:  char SmartChar::RemoveCurrent()
39:  {
40:      char theChar = ' ';
41:
42:      if ( myCharacters.size() > 1 )
43:      {
44:          theChar = GetChar();
45:          myCharacters.erase( myCharacters.begin()+myChar );
46:          while ( myChar >= myCharacters.size() )
47:              myChar—;
48:      }
49:      return theChar;
50:  }
51:
52:
```

```
53:  bool SmartChar::Remove(char theChar)
54:  {
55:      if ( myCharacters.size() > 1 )
56:      {
57:          vector<char>::iterator where =
58:              find(myCharacters.begin(), myCharacters.end(),theChar);
59:          if ( where != myCharacters.end() )
60:              myCharacters.erase(where);
61:          return true;
62:      }
63:      return false;
64:  }
65:
66:  void SmartChar::Write(Writer & wrtr) const
67:  {
68:      wrtr << myChar;
69:      wrtr << myCharacters;
70:  }
```

Again we resume in the Write method, this time of SmartChar, shown on line 66 of Listing 13.15. We see that SmartChar writes out its myChar integer, which represents the offset into its vector of characters. Then it passes that vector to the Writer object to be stored to disk.

When this completes, SmartChar returns to SmartString, which continues writing out its characters until it is done. Control then returns to Computer::Write on line 249 of Listing 13.7, where total is written to the disk. The member variable total represents the total number of strings eliminated to date, and this enables us to resume not only the game but also the statistics when we restore.

With this Computer::Write() concludes, and control returns to Game::Write() on line 213 of Listing 13.5. Game finishes by writing out its member variables duplicates, howManyLetters, and howManyPositions.

This returns us to the last line of Store() on line 226, where we delete the Writer object. We then return to Game::Play() on line 139, where we print out the elapsed time. We then exit back to Decryptix! on line 66 of Listing 13.3, where we delete the game itself and ask the player if he wants to play again. If the player says no, we return, exiting the program.

Chapter 14

Introducing Exceptions

In the preceding chapter, I demonstrated how to store the game to disk. In this chapter, I review how to *restore* the game *from* disk, reversing the storage procedure.

In addition, you'll take a look at handling exceptions.

When Something Exceptional Happens

Let's start by looking at exceptions. An exception signals that something has happened that prevents your program from continuing. For example, when customers interact with your program, it is possible for them to run out of memory or disk space. As a programmer, you can predict that this might happen, but there isn't much you can do to prevent it. What you *can* do is recover from the problem without crashing.

C++ handles these events by throwing *exceptions*. An exception is an object that signals a predictable but undesirable event that must be corrected before the program can proceed. Think of it as firing a flare gun up through the layers of your program.

exception—An object that signals a predictable but undesirable event.

The semantics of using exceptions is as follows: We *try* to accomplish a task, anticipating that the task might *raise* or *throw* an exception. If an exception is thrown, we *catch* the exception and then correct the situation or exit the program gracefully.

raise an exception—The same as throwing an exception. This signals that you have encountered a problem.

catch an exception—To handle the problem found elsewhere in the code.

In addition to exceptions that arise from running out of memory or disk space, you can define your own conditions that throw an exception. Let's look at an example. Assume that the computer is guessing a code generated by the human player. It is possible for the player to make a mistake in scoring that leaves the computer with no guesses that are consistent with all the previous possible guesses.

For example, let's assume we're playing with seven letters in five positions, with no duplicates, and with the computer guessing. The code is *baedc*, and the computer guesses *abcde*. We score this 5/1 (five correct, one in the right position). The computer then guesses *acbed*. The correct score for this is 5/0, but we make a mistake and score this 5/1 as well. The computer next guesses *adebc*, and we correctly score this 5/2. The computer is now stuck. Our mistake has left it with no guess that can possibly be consistent with these three scores.

You'll remember from Chapter 12, "Delegating Responsibility," that the computer will spin through each potential guess, not offering the guess to the player until the computer proves that it is consistent with all the answers that have come before. Because we scored the second guess incorrectly, every potential answer will be inconsistent: No answer matches all these previous scores!

Let's look at this in detail. When the time comes for the computer to offer a guess, we start in the *Computer* object's *GenerateAGuess()* method. The very first line of this method calls *GetNext()* on the smart string:

```
ok = mySmartString->GetNext();
```

This invokes *SmartString::GetNext()*, which is shown in Chapter 13, "Persistence," in Listing 13.13. I won't reproduce the code in its entirety—except to support exceptions as shown previously—because it is unchanged from Chapter 13. Listing 14.1 provides the relevant excerpt, using the line numbering from 13.13.

Listing 14.1   Excerpts from Listing 13.13 Revisited

```
55:  bool SmartString::GetNext()
56:  {
57:      vector<char> outString;
58:      vector<SmartChar>::reverse_iterator it;
59:      it = myString.rbegin();
60:
61:      bool rollover = it->Increment();
62:      while ( rollover )
63:      {
64:          it++;
65:          if ( it == myString.rend() )
66:              return false;
67:          else
```

```
68:                {
69:                    rollover = it->Increment();
70:                }
71:        }
72:        return true;
73:    }
```

14

The goal here is to get the next legal string. Thus, if we have *abcde*, we want to get *abcdf*.

On line 58 we create a *reverse* iterator to walk through the vector of smart characters, which we set on line 59 to point to the end of the vector. Because this is a *reverse* iterator, *rbegin* (reverse *begin*) points to the end of the iterator and *rend* (reverse *end*) points to the beginning. (Isn't programming fun?)

We then call *Increment()* on the *SmartChar* to which the iterator points. Listing 14.2 shows the excerpt from Listing 13.15 with the implementation of *SmartChar::Increment()*.

Listing 14.2   Excerpt from Listing 13.15

```
28:    bool SmartChar::Increment()
29:    {
30:        if ( ++myChar >= myCharacters.size() )
31:        {
32:            myChar = 0;
33:            return true;
34:        }
35:        return false;
36:    }
```

As you can see, we increment *myChar* on line 30, and if that puts it past the end of its vector of valid characters, we set it to *0* and return *true* (thus saying, "Yes, we did roll over"). If that does not cause a rollover, we set it to *false*. You can think of the *SmartChar*'s vector of *myCharacters* as a car odometer: If we roll over the highest number, we set the number back to zero and return *true* to say that we did so.

Now let's go back to Listing 14.1. As long as *SmartChar* signals that it did roll over, the iterator increments on the string, pointing to the next character, counting back from the end. We now tell the next—that is, the next one back from the end!—*smartChar* to increment. Why? Again, picture your car odometer. If the tens place rolls over, you must signal the hundreds place to increment.

Now, let's relate this back to the string. Assume for a moment that we have three positions, we're using five letters (*a* through *e*), and our string starts out *abc*. The next string is *abd*, and then *abe*. When we increment *abe*, the last letter (*e*) rolls over to *a*, and we need to bump the next to last letter (*b*) up to *c*, leaving us with *aca*. Got that? If you only have five letters in three positions, the next string after *abe* is *aca*.

The next time we generate a string, we'll get *acb*, *acc*, *acd*, *ace*, and then we roll again to *ada*. You can see how this can lead you to *aee*. When *aee* rolls, we go to *baa*, *bab*, and so forth. At some point, we get to *eee*. When we increment the last *e*, we get *eea*, but we must increment the middle *e*, which gives us *eaa*. Finally we must increment the first *e*, which gives us *aaa*, but we have no letters left to increment. Uh oh. This is the situation that is caught by line 65. We've reached the end of the vector, and we still have work to do.

In the old design we'd return *false* and allow the calling routine to handle the error. This might be a good place to throw an exception. Listing 14.3 shows the modified *SmartString* declaration, which uses exceptions to handle this problem.

Listing 14.3 SmartString **Modified**

```
 0:  #ifndef SMARTSTRING_H
 1:  #define SMARTSTRING_H
 2:
 3:  #include "defvals.h"
 4:  #include "SmartChr.h"
 5:
 6:  class Guess;
 7:
 8:  class SmartString
 9:  {
10:  public:
11:      SmartString(bool dupes);
12:      SmartString(Reader& rdr);
13:      virtual    ~SmartString();
14:
15:      bool CanEliminateCharacters    (const Guess& theGuess);
16:      void GetNext();
17:      vector<char> GetString();
18:      bool RemoveCurrentCharacters();
19:      bool RemoveCurrentCharactersInEveryPosition();
20:      void Write(Writer& wrtr) const;
21:
22:      class BadString
23:      {
24:      public:
25:          BadString(string err):
26:             errorString(err) {}
27:          ~BadString(){}
28:          const string & GetError() { return errorString; }
29:      private:
30:          string errorString;
31:      };
```

```
32:
33:  private:
34:      void ForceCharacters(const Guess & theGuess);
35:      int   CountForcedInGuess(const Guess & theGuess);
36:      int   CountUniqueLettersInGuess(const Guess & theGuess);
37:      bool In(vector <char> vec, char target) const;
38:
39:      vector<char> deadCharacters;
40:      bool duplicates;
41:      vector<char> forcedCharacters;
42:      vector<SmartChar> myString;
43:  };
44:  #endif
```

Analysis

You want to pay attention to a couple of things here. First, on line 16, `GetNext` now returns *void*. There is no need to return a bool value because we'll handle the problem with an exception.

Second, starting on line 22 we create a new class—*BadString*. What's going on here? We're still within the declaration of the *SmartString* class, so how can we declare a new class? This is called a *nested* class, and it is legal in C++—and quite useful.

nested class—A class that is declared within the scope of an outer class.

The only purpose of *BadString* is to act as an exception class for *SmartString*. We declare *BadString* within the class declaration for *SmartString*, thus *scoping* it to the *SmartString* class. This implements the design decision that *BadString* is to only be visible within the scope of *SmartString*.

If we want to create objects of type *BadString*, we can do so directly from within methods of *SmartString*, as shown in Listing 14.4.

Listing 14.4　Throwing a `BadString` Object

```
0:  void SmartString::GetNext()
1:  {
2:      vector<char> outString;
3:      vector<SmartChar>::reverse_iterator it;
4:      it = myString.rbegin();
5:
6:      bool rollover = it->Increment();
7:      while ( rollover )
8:      {
9:          it++;
```

continues

Listing 14.4   continued

```
10:              if ( it == myString.rend() )
11:                  throw new BadString("Unable to find valid string!\n");
12:              else
13:              {
14:                  rollover = it->Increment();
15:              }
16:          }
17:          return true;
18:      }
```

Analysis

This method from *SmartString* shows the revised implementation of *GetNext()*. On line 11, where we formerly returned *false*, we now throw the exception *BadString* by creating an instance on the heap. Because we are in a method of *SmartString*, we can access this constructor directly.

The object is caught in *Computer::GenerateAGuess()*. Because it is scoped to *SmartString*, we must identify it using the scoping operator, as shown in Listing 14.5.

Listing 14.5   Accessing the Contained Object

```
0:   void Computer::GenerateAGuess()
1:   {
2:
3:       bool ok = true;
4:       int counter = 0;
5:       int start = time( NULL );
6:       do
7:       {
8:           counter++;
9:           total++;
10:          if ( counter % 10000 == 0 )
11:              cout << ".";
12:
13:          try
14:          {
15:              mySmartString->GetNext();
16:          }
17:
18:          catch ( SmartString::BadString * pException )
19:          {
20:              cout << "\n\n" << pException->GetError();
21:              cout << " Please start over\n";
22:              round = 1;
23:              delete mySmartString;
```

```
24:              mySmartString = new SmartString(duplicates);
25:              ShowHistory();
26:              cout << "\n\n";
27:              history.clear();
28:              delete pException;
29:              continue;
30:          }
31:
32:      } while ( !IsConsistent(mySmartString->GetString()) );
33:
34:      int end = time( NULL );
35:      int seconds = end - start;
36:      cout << "(" << counter ;
37:      cout << " strings eliminated this round; ";
38:      cout << total << " total.)";
39:      if ( seconds > 1 )
40:          cout << " [" << seconds << " seconds]";
41:      cout << "\n";
42:  }
```

On line 13 we set up a *try* block, which says to the compiler, "I'm going to try something that might throw an exception." We then call *GetNext()*. If this method call (or any method it calls) throws an exception, that exception is presented to the *catch* blocks that immediately follow the *try* block.

catch blocks come in two flavors: those that specify what they catch (like the one shown on line 18), and those that do not. We'll consider the latter in just a moment.

The *catch* block on line 18 shows that it can catch a pointer to a *BadString* object. The *BadString* class is scoped within *SmartString*, so we use the scoping operator to resolve the name as shown.

Because the exception is a class, it can have both member methods and member variables. In this case, we use the method *GetError()* to print the error message. In a real-world application, we can make these objects as complex as necessary.

When we are done with the exception object, we delete the pointer, shown here on line 28. As an alternative, we can throw this same exception again at this point by just writing

```
throw;
```

or we can even create a new exception and throw the new exception from here. In either case, throwing a new or existing exception halts processing here and passes the exception back up the call stack to whichever calling method has the appropriate *catch* block.

Unwinding the Stack

This is a critical point. When you throw an exception, no further processing occurs in the current function. On line 11 of Listing 14.4, when we throw the *BadString* exception, we stop processing in the *GetNext()* method. The calling stack is unwound and local variables are destroyed. The calling method is checked for a *catch* block, and if none is found, that method too is unwound, working backward through the calling functions until a *catch* block is found.

If no *catch* block is found all the way back to *main*, the predefined term *terminate* method is called, whose default action is to call *default*. This global method, *default*, simply exits the program. You can write your own *terminate* method if you want to exit a bit more gracefully.

When the stack is unwound, local variables are destroyed just as they are if you return from the method. Pointers, however, are not deleted, and this can cause serious and significant memory leaks and other problems.

For example, let's examine the *Store()* method of *Game*, as shown in Listing 14.6.

Listing 14.6   Unwinding Past the Pointer

```
0: void Game::Store()
1: {
2:     char fileName[80];
3:     cout << "Store to file named: ";
4:     cin >> fileName;
5:     Writer * pWriter = new Writer(fileName);
6:     Write(*pWriter);
7:     delete pWriter;
8: }
```

Here we instantiate a *Writer* object on the heap, use it by calling *Game::Write* and passing in the dereferenced *Writer*, and then delete the *Writer* object. If *Write* (or one of the methods it calls) throws an exception, we'll exit this method wherever the exception is thrown, and we'll never have the opportunity to call *delete*. Thus, the *Writer* object will not be deleted, and we'll have a leak.

One way to solve this is to wrap the *Write* method in a *try* block and then delete *Writer* in the *catch* block. We can see this approach in Listing 14.5, where we catch the exception and delete the pointer.

This isn't always practical, but we can't tolerate letting pointers go undeleted. The answer is to wrap the pointer in an object that sits on the stack. We allocate the memory for the pointer in the object's constructor and deallocate it in the destructor. Thus, when the stack is unwound, the object is destroyed and the destructor frees the pointed to memory.

Such an object is called an *auto_ptr* (automatic pointer), and the standard library provides one for you. Listing 14.7 shows *Game::Store*, rewritten to use an *auto_ptr* to hold the pointer to the *Writer*.

Listing 14.7   Using an auto_ptr

```
0:   void Game::Store()
1:   {
2:       char fileName[80];
3:       cout << "Store to file named: ";
4:       cin >> fileName;
5:       auto_ptr<Writer> apWriter(new Writer(fileName));
6:       Write(*apWriter);
7:   }
```

On line 5 we create the *auto_ptr* object. As you can see, this is a parameterized object, so we must pass in the type (in this case, *Writer*). We then name the *auto_ptr* (*apWriter*) and initialize it by calling new *Writer*, passing the *fileName* in to the *Writer* constructor.

If you compare this with the construct of the pointer from Listing 14.6, you can get a better feel for what is going on:

```
Writer * pWriter = new Writer(fileName);
auto_ptr<Writer> apWriter(new Writer(fileName));
```

In the first example, *pWriter* is the name of the pointer variable that is of type pointer to *Writer*. In the second example, *apWriter* is of type *auto_ptr<Writer>*.

In the first example, we are creating a *Writer* object on the heap, passing in the *fileName* as a parameter to the constructor. In the second, we also create a *Writer* object on the heap, but we pass the address that is returned by *new* into the *auto_ptr*'s constructor. We might just as easily have written this second example as follows:

```
Writer * pWriter = new Writer(fileName);
auto_ptr<Writer> apWriter(pWriter);
```

Here I've created a temporary pointer to hold the address returned by *new*, and it is that temporary that I pass into the constructor of *auto_ptr*. The earlier example, combining these two steps, is the more common method, but either works.

> **Note**
>
> In no case do you need to delete this memory explicitly. The *auto_ptr* object *apWriter* now *owns* the pointer returned by *new*, and this pointer is deleted when *apWriter* goes out of scope.

Reading the Object from Disk

Now that we have exceptions working, we can look at how they help us handle unexpected problems when writing our objects to disk or reading them back into memory. The kinds of exceptions we might want to handle will include insufficient memory to create a new object and insufficient disk space to save an object.

Let's assume that we've been able to store the game as shown in Chapter 13. How do we get it back when it's time to resume play?

Let's fire up Decryptix! as shown in Listing 14.8.

Listing 14.8   Decryptix! Driver Program

```
0:  #include <iostream>
1:  #include <iterator>
2:  #include <vector>
3:
4:  #include "defvals.h"
5:  #include "game.h"
6:  #include "guess.h"
7:
8:  using namespace std;
9:
10: int main()
11: {
12:
13:     cout << "Decryptix. (c)Copyright 1999";
14:     cout << "Liberty Associates, Inc.";
15:     cout << "Version 4.0\n\n" << endl;
16:     cout << "There are two ways to play Decryptix:";
17:     cout << "either you can guess a pattern I create,\n";
18:     cout << "or I can guess your pattern.\n\n";
19:     cout << "If you are guessing, I will think of a ";
20:     cout << "pattern of letters (e.g., abcde).\n";
21:     cout << "On each turn, you guess the pattern and ";
22:     cout << "I will tell you how many letters you \n";
23:     cout << "got right, and how many of the correct ";
24:     cout << "letters were in the correct position.\n\n";
25:     cout << "The goal is to decode the puzzle as quickly ";
26:     cout << "as possible. You control how many\n";
27:     cout << "letters can be used and how many positions ";
28:     cout << "(e.g., 5 possible letters in 4\n";
29:     cout << "positions) as well as whether or not the ";
```

14

```
30:        cout << "pattern might contain duplicate \n";
31:        cout << "letters (e.g., aabcd).\n\n";
32:        cout << "If I'm guessing, you think of a pattern ";
33:        cout << "and score each of my answers.\n\n";
34:        bool playAgain = true;
35:
36:        while ( playAgain )
37:        {
38:            Game * g;
39:
40:            char resume = ' ';
41:            while ( resume != 'R' && resume != 'N' )
42:            {
43:                cout << "Resume existing game or start new?. (R)esume";
44:                cout << " or (N)ew? ";
45:                cin >> resume;
46:            }
47:
48:            if ( resume == 'R' )
49:            {
50:                char fileName[80];
51:                cout << "Resume from file named: ";
52:                cin >> fileName;
53:                cin.ignore(1,'\n');
54:
55:                Reader * reader = new Reader(fileName);
56:                g = new Game(*reader);
57:                delete reader;
58:            }
59:            else
60:                g = new Game;
61:
62:            try
63:            {
64:
65:                g->Play();
66:            }
67:
68:            catch (...)
69:            {
70:                cout << "Exception caught trying to play Game\n";
71:            }
72:
73:            delete g;
74:
75:            char choice = ' ';
76:            while ( choice != 'y' && choice != 'n' )
77:            {
78:                cout << "\nPlay again (y/n): ";
79:                cin >> choice;
```

continues

Listing 14.8 continued

```
80:           }
81:
82:           playAgain = choice == 'y' ? true : false;
83:       }
84:
85:       return 0;
86:  }
```

Output

Decryptix. (c)Copyright 1999Liberty Associates, Inc.Version 5.0

There are two ways to play Decryptix:either you can guess a pattern I
create, or I can guess your pattern.

If you are guessing, I will think of a pattern of letters (e.g., abcde).
On each turn, you guess the pattern and I will tell you how many letters
you got right, and how many of the correct letters were in the correct
position.

The goal is to decode the puzzle as quickly as possible. You control
how many letters can be used and how many positions (e.g., 5 possible
letters in 4 positions) as well as whether or not the pattern might
contain duplicate letters (e.g., aabcd).

If I'm guessing, you think of a pattern and score each of my answers.

Resume existing game or start new?. (R)esume or (N)ew? R

Analysis

We offer the user the choice to start a new game or resume an existing game. This
time, let's follow what happens if he asks to resume an existing game.

We begin in Decryptix.cpp, where the user has entered R to *resume a previous game*.
We prompt the user for a filename, and then we create a new *Reader* object, passing
in the filename as a parameter:

```
Reader * reader = new Reader(fileName);
```

This invokes the *Reader* constructor,

```
Reader(char * filename):fin(filename,ios::binary){}
```

which opens the file for reading. In this version of the program, we do no error
checking. If the user provides a filename for a file that does not exist or that was not

saved by Decryptix!, the results are unpredictable. In a future version of this program, we'll want to handle such an error.

After we have a *Reader* object, we can create a *Game* object, passing the reader to the overloaded *Game* constructor:

```
g = new Game(*reader);
```

This invokes the constructor that is shown in Listing 14.9.

Listing 14.9 Construction Using a Reader Object

```
0:  Game::Game(Reader & rdr)
1:  {
2:      bool isHuman;
3:
4:      rdr >> isHuman;
5:
6:      if ( isHuman )
7:          pDecrypter = new Human(rdr);
8:      else
9:          pDecrypter = new Computer(rdr);
10:
11:      rdr >> duplicates;
12:      rdr >> howManyLetters;
13:      rdr >> howManyPositions;
14:      cout << "Game restored.\n";
15:
16:  }
```

Analysis

The constructor declares a local Boolean variable, *isHuman*, and reads the first byte from the disk into that variable. It does this with the code that is shown on line 4, which the compiler translates into

```
rdr.operator>>(isHuman);
```

This causes processing to switch to the overloaded operator >>, which takes a Boolean

```
Reader & Reader::operator >>(bool & data)
{
    fin.read( (char*) &data, szBool);
    return *this;
}
```

where the data is read. The *read()* method of the *ifstream* object *fin* works much like the *write()* method of the *ofstream* object we saw previously. It accepts a pointer to character—to which we cast the Boolean variable data—and the size of the object. A Boolean is 1 byte, so we'll read one byte into this variable and then return the *Reader* object.

We return to line 6 of Listing 14.9, where we examine this newly restored variable. If it is *true*, we'll instantiate a *Human*. In this case it is *false*, so we'll instantiate a *Computer* object on the heap, passing the *Reader* object to the *Computer's* constructor (as shown in Listing 14.10).

Listing 14.10   *Computer's* **Constructor**

```
0:  Computer::Computer(Reader & rdr):
1:  Decrypter(rdr)
2:  {
3:      mySmartString = new SmartString(rdr);
4:      rdr>>total;
5:      cout << "Computer restored.\n";
6:
7:  }
```

Analysis

We begin execution of this constructor by initializing the base class (*Decrypter*), again passing in the *Reader* object. This immediately invokes the *Decrypter* overloaded constructor, as shown in Listing 14.11.

Listing 14.11   *Decrypter's* **Constructor**

```
0:  Decrypter::Decrypter(Reader & rdr):
1:  Storable(rdr)
2:  {
3:      rdr >> round;
4:      rdr >> duplicates;
5:      int size;
6:      rdr >> size;
7:      for ( int i = 0; i < size; i++)
8:      {
9:          Guess theGuess(rdr);
10:          history.push_back(theGuess);
11:      }
12:  }
```

Analysis

As you can see, *Decrypter* in turn initializes *its* base class, *Storable*, again passing in the *Reader* object and causing processing to jump to that constructor, which does nothing:

```
Storable(Reader&) {}
```

We resume in *Decrypter*'s constructor on line 3, where we read an integer value in from the disk and store it in the member variable *round*. We then read in the Boolean value *duplicates*.

Next we want to read in the member vector history, but we need to know how many bytes to read. We start by declaring a local integer variable size on line 5, and read in the next four bytes to fill that variable. With that value, we can enter the *for* loop on line 7, reading in *Guess* objects from the disk and pushing them into the vector.

Each time we create a *Guess* object on line 9, we invoke the *Guess* constructor, passing in the *Reader* object so that the *Guess* can be read in from the disk. The *Guess* constructor is shown in Listing 14.12

Listing 14.12 *Guess*'s **Constructor**

```
0:   Guess::Guess(Reader & rdr)
1:   {
2:       rdr >> score.first;
3:       rdr >> score.second;
4:       rdr >> string;
5:   }
```

Analysis

The *Guess* constructor reads four bytes from the disk and puts the contents into the *first* member of the pair *score*, which itself is a member variable of the *Guess* object. It then reads in the *second* member of that pair.

In exactly the same way that *Writer* supported writing character vectors, the *Reader* object supports reading them back. We take advantage of this on line 6 and direct the *Reader* object to fill the member variable *string*.

Completing this work, we return to Listing 14.11. On line 10, the *Guess* object is added to the end of the *history* vector.

When the *Decrypter* is finished adding the *Guesses* to its *history* member variable, it returns processing to the body of the *Computer* constructor, shown on line 3 of Listing 14.10. The first thing *Computer* does is create a new *SmartString* object, using the same *Reader* for the constructor:

```
3:       mySmartString = new SmartString(rdr);
```

This in turn calls the *SmartString* constructor, shown in Listing 14.13.

Listing 14.13 SmartString's Constructor

```
0:  SmartString::SmartString(Reader & rdr)
1:  {
2:      rdr >> deadCharacters;
3:      rdr >> duplicates;
4:      rdr >> forcedCharacters;
5:      int size;
6:      rdr >> size;
7:      for ( int i = 0; i < size; i++)
8:      {
9:          SmartChar theSmartChar(rdr);
10:          myString.push_back(theSmartChar);
11:      }
12: }
```

Analysis

This constructor restores the *deadCharacters* character vector, the Boolean value *duplicates*, and the character vector *forcedCharacters*. Finally, beginning on line 5, it restores its vector of *SmartChar* objects, as shown in Listing 14.14.

Listing 14.14 SmartChar's Constructor

```
0: SmartChar::SmartChar(Reader & rdr)
1: {
2:     rdr >> myChar;
3:     rdr >> myCharacters;
4: }
```

Analysis

This in turn calls the constructor for *SmartChar*, which does nothing but restore the integer variable *myChar* and the character vector *myCharacters*. *SmartString* then adds this to its vector of *SmartChar* objects, as shown on line 10 of Listing 14.13. This is done once for each position, so if the game we are restoring played seven letters in five positions, this is done once for each of the five positions.

After this is complete, we return to the *Computer* constructor, where on line 4 of Listing 14.10 we restore the next four bytes into the member variable *total*. We then print a message indicating that the *Computer* has been restored. We exit the *Computer*'s constructor, returning to the *Game*'s constructor on line 11 of Listing 14.9, reproduced here for your convenience:

```
0:  Game::Game(Reader & rdr)
1:  {
2:      bool isHuman;
```

```
3:
4:       rdr >> isHuman;
5:
6:       if ( isHuman )
7:            pDecrypter = new Human(rdr);
8:       else
9:            pDecrypter = new Computer(rdr);
10:
11:      rdr >> duplicates;
12:      rdr >> howManyLetters;
13:      rdr >> howManyPositions;
14:      cout << "Game restored.\n";
15:
16:  }
```

We finish restoring the game by reading the Boolean value *duplicates* and the two integers *howManyLetters* and *howManyPositions*. Note that there is no special processing for these static member variables; they are read from the disk like any other variables. Finally, on line 14 we print a message that the *Game* has been restored, and we exit the *Game* constructor, returning to line 57 of Listing 14.8:

```
55:            Reader * reader = new Reader(fileName);
56:            g = new Game(*reader);
57:            delete reader;
```

The entire process of restoring all these objects was invoked by the seemingly innocent code on line 56. Now that we've restored the game, we no longer need the *Reader* object, and it is destroyed on line 57. Finally, we will try to play the game. When we are finished, the *Game* object, so painfully restored, is destroyed:

```
62:            try
63:            {
64:
65:                g->Play();
66:            }
67:
68:            catch (...)
69:            {
70:                cout << "Exception caught trying to play Game\n";
71:            }
72:
73:            delete g;
```

The *catch* statement on line 68 is worth a moment's attention. This is the *catch* block for the *try* block that was created on line 62, and it says that it will catch *any* exception (...). Here we don't do anything terribly useful in the *catch* block, but you can imagine that we'd use this block to clean up the game, or even better, to give the player a chance to recover from whatever error condition caused the exception.

Restoring a Human

Restoration of a *Human* object, as opposed to a *Computer* object, is not terribly complex. In this case, the *Decrypter* that will be restored is the *Human* rather than the *Computer*. Like the *Computer*, however, the *Human* first restores the base class, *Decrypter*.

After this is done, the *Human* object constructor has little to do, as shown in Listing 14.15

Listing 14.15   Human Constructor

```
0: Human::Human(Reader & rdr):
1: Decrypter(rdr)
2: {
3:     rdr >> hintCtr;
4:     rdr >> solution;
5:     cout << "Solution and history restored.\n";
6: }
```

Analysis

The integer variable *hintCtr* is restored, and then the vector of characters, *solution*. After this is done, a message is printed and the *Human* constructor returns. Piece of cake.

Chapter 15

Next Steps

Congratulations! We started out with the simplest imaginable program, and we've built it up into a complex, useful, and fun game that illustrates all the fundamentals of C++.

You are now a competent C++ programmer, but you are by no means finished. You have much more to learn and many more books to read as you move from novice C++ programmer to expert.

Read Another Primer?

Now that you've worked your way through this learn-as-you-go approach, if you haven't done so already you might want to consider picking up a more traditional primer to review the concepts that are covered here in a bit more depth.

As for which primer to read, let me first admit that there are *many* good choices out there. Take a few minutes in your local bookstore and thumb through a few. Here are some general guidelines to keep in mind:

- Do you like the tone and approach?
- Does the book have enough examples? Are they explained in detail?
- Do you want exercises at the end of the chapter? If so, does this book have them? If so, does it supply the answers?
- What knowledge does the author assume you already have?
- Does the book cover C++ as an object-oriented language?

Obviously, I'm not objective—I have three other books designed for self study. *Sams Teach Yourself C++ In 21 Days, Third Edition* (ISBN: 0-672-31515-7) is a comprehensive text that is loaded with examples, quizzes, and exercises (and answers), and that covers every aspect of the language.

Sams Teach Yourself C++ In 24 Hours, Second Edition (ISBN: 0-672-31516-5) breaks things down into smaller chunks, leaves out the exercises, and skips some of the most esoteric aspects of C++.

Sams Teach Yourself C++ In 10 Minutes (ISBN: 0-672-31603-X) is a quick reference and gentle introduction to the language. This can serve as a fast and useful review when you don't need all the details.

There are also several other good books by other authors. Take your time and read a chapter or two before you buy.

Advanced Topics in C++

The very first advanced C++ book I'd recommend that you buy and read is Scott Meyers's *Effective C++, Second Edition* (Addison-Wesley, ISBN: 0-201-92488-9). This wonderful book provides 50 tips for using the language well, and needs to be on every C++ programmer's bookshelf. I have said many times that Scott Meyers has done more to improve the overall quality of C++ programming with this little gem than perhaps anyone else in the industry. In fact, I said it so many times that the publisher printed it on the back of his book!

Another advanced book that you might want to consider is my book *C++ Unleashed* (ISBN: 0-672-31239-5). This book presents a series of technical white papers on the core features of C++. *Unleashed* explores object-oriented analysis and design, as well as implementation issues that are associated with memory management, STL container classes, iterators, and algorithms. It will teach you how to manipulate data using dynamic data structures and recursion, efficient sorting algorithms, and advanced hashing and parsing techniques.

To gain insight into how C++ was created and how it has evolved, along with an understanding of why certain choices were made in the design of the language, consider *The Design and Evolution of C++* by Bjarne Stroustrup (Addison-Wesley, ISBN: 0-201-54330-3). Also, while you're peeking under the covers of C++, take a look at *Inside the C++ Object Model* by Stanley B. Lippman (Addison-Wesley, ISBN: 0-201-83454-5). Lippman is a former editor of *C++ Magazine*, and he is a guru of all things C++. This book looks at the underlying mechanisms of C++ and provides terrific insight into how the language works.

John Lakos's *Large-Scale C++ Software Design* (Addison-Wesley, ISBN: 0-201-63362-0) offers insight into building large, real-world, commercial softwar applications. This book is fairly advanced: I recommend that you read it only after reading several other books on this list.

Object-oriented Analysis, Design, and Patterns

This field is suddenly awash in good books, although many are a bit academic for my taste. Certainly, the flagship books must be *The Unified Software Development Process*, *The Unified Modeling Language User Guide*, and *The Unified Modeling Language Reference Manual*, all by the Three Amigos: Grady Booch, Ivar Jacobson, and James Rumbaugh.

As you might know, Booch, Jacobson, and Rumbaugh were individually considered great innovators in object-oriented analysis and design, and all three are now all with Rational Software, Inc. Together, they have promulgated both the Unified Modeling Language and the Rational Unified Process.

I have two books in this category: *Beginning Object-oriented Analysis and Design* (Wrox Press 1998, ISBN: 1-861-00133-9) and *Clouds To Code* (Wrox Press 1997, ISBN: 1-861-00095-2). *Beginning OOA&D* is a tutorial that covers the UML as well as analysis, design, and architectural mechanisms, including persistence, concurrency, and distributed objects. *Clouds to Code* is a detailed case study of the development of a real-world application, written as it happened. Both books are targeted to the working C++ programmer.

After you've read a book or two on object-oriented programming, be sure to pick up *Object-oriented Design Heuristics* by Arthur J. Riel (Addison Wesley, ISBN 0-201-63385-X). This wonderful book can help you understand the difference between great designs and mediocre ones. It is filled with world-class advice and guidance, and I recommend it highly.

Round out your knowledge of object-oriented analysis and design by subscribing to the Object Technology User Group (OTUG) mailing list: Write to `majordomo@rational.com`.

Design Patterns

Perhaps the hottest and most interesting trend in software development in the past decade is the advent of design patterns. These are an attempt to capture, name, and describe design solutions that can be reused in a variety of situations. The seminal work is *Design Patterns: Elements of Reusable Object-oriented Software* by Gama, et al. (Addison-Wesley, ISBN: 0-201-63361-2). Also take a look at the PLOP books (*Pattern Languages of Programming*), which are published by Addison-Wesley.

After you've read through several design patterns, you might want to pick up *Anti-Patterns: Refactoring Software, Architectures, and Projects in Crisis* by Brown et al. (Wiley Books, ISBN 0-471-19713-0).

Martin Fowler, author of the enormously popular *UML Distilled*, has extended the concept of design patterns to include *Analysis Patterns* (Addison-Wesley, ISBN: 0-201-89542-0). This book does for analysis what the other books do for design.

Magazines

You can do one more thing to strengthen your skills: Subscribe to a good magazine on C++ programming. The absolute best magazine of this kind, in my opinion, is *C++ Report* from SIGS Publications. Every issue is packed with useful articles. Save them. What you don't care about today might become critically important tomorrow. In the interest of full disclosure, I must confess that I write the *Object-oriented C++ From Scratch* column for *C++ Report*, but I started recommending it well before I began the column.

You can reach *C++ Report* at SIGS Publications, P.O. Box 2031, Langhorne, Pennsylvania 19047-9700.

Support Newsgroups

I provide a newsgroup for readers of my book at `www.delphi.com/LibertyBooks`, where you are encouraged to ask questions and discuss issues. I also frequent `comp.lang.c++` and `comp.lang.c++.moderated`. (If you want me to find the message there, be sure to include my full name in the message so that I can search for it on `www.deja.com`.) Many newsgroups can offer further information and support as you continue to study and learn.

Staying in Touch

If you have comments, suggestions, or ideas about this book or other books, I'd love to hear them. Please write to me at `jliberty@libertyassociates.com`, or check out my Web site at `www.libertyassociates.com`, where I provide an errata, source code, and FAQ for many of my books. I look forward to hearing from you.

Binary and Hexadecimal

You learned the fundamentals of arithmetic so long ago, it is hard to imagine what it would be like without that knowledge. When you look at the number 145 you instantly see "one hundred and forty-five" without much reflection.

Understanding binary and hexadecimal requires that you re-examine the number 145 and see it not as a number, but as a code for a number.

Start small: Examine the relationship between the number three and "3." The numeral 3 is a squiggle on a piece of paper; the number three is an idea. The numeral is used to represent the number.

The distinction can be made clear by realizing that three, 3, I I I, III, and *** all can be used to represent the same idea of three.

In base 10 (decimal) math you use the numerals 0, 1, 2, 3, 4, 5, 6, 7, 8, 9 to represent all numbers. How is the number ten represented?

One can imagine that we would have evolved a strategy of using the letter A to represent ten; or we might have used IIIIIIIII to represent that idea. The Romans used X. The Arabic system, which we use, makes use of position in conjunction with numerals to represent values. The first (right-most) column is used for "ones," and the next column is used for tens. Thus, the number fifteen is represented as 15 (read "one, five"); that is, 1 ten and 5 ones.

Certain rules emerge, from which some generalizations can be made:

1. Base 10 uses the digits 0–9.
2. The columns are powers of ten: 1s, 10s, 100s, and so on.

3. If the third column is 100, the largest number you can make with two columns is 99. More generally, with n columns you can represent 0 to (10^n-1). Thus, with 3 columns you can represent 0 to (10^3-1) or 0–999.

Other Bases

It is not a coincidence that we use base 10; we have 10 fingers. One can imagine a different base, however. Using the rules found in base 10, you can describe base 8:

1. The digits used in base 8 are 0–7.

2. The columns are powers of 8: 1s, 8s, 64, and so on.

3. With n columns you can represent 0 to 8^n-1.

To distinguish numbers written in each base, write the base as a subscript next to the number. The number fifteen in base 10 would be written as 15_{10} and read as "one, five, base ten."

Thus, to represent the number 15_{10} in base 8 you would write 17_8. This is read "one, seven, base eight." Note that it can also be read "fifteen" as that is the number it continues to represent.

Why 17? The 1 means 1 eight, and the 7 means 7 ones. One eight plus seven ones equals fifteen. Consider fifteen asterisks:

```
*****      *****
*****
```

The natural tendency is to make two groups, a group of ten asterisks and another of five. This would be represented in decimal as 15 (1 ten and 5 ones). You can also group the asterisks as

```
****          *******
****
```

That is, eight asterisks and seven. That would be represented in base eight as 17_8. That is, one eight and seven ones.

Around the Bases

You can represent the number fifteen in base ten as 15, in base nine as 16_9, in base 8 as 17_8, in base 7 as 21_7. Why 21_7? In base 7 there is no numeral 8. In order to represent fifteen, you will need two sevens and one 1.

How do you generalize the process? To convert a base ten number to base 7, think about the columns: in base 7 they are ones, sevens, forty-nines, three-hundred forty-threes, and so on. Why these columns? They represent 7^0, 7^1, 7^2, 7^4 and so forth. Create a table for yourself:

4	3	2	1
7^3	7^2	7^1	7^0
343	49	7	1

The first row represents the column number. The second row represents the power of 7. The third row represents the decimal value of each number in that row.

To convert from a decimal value to base 7, here is the procedure: Examine the number and decide which column to use first. If the number is 200, for example, you know that column 4 (343) is 0, and you don't have to worry about it.

To find out how many 49s there are, divide 200 by 49. The answer is 4, so put 4 in column 3 and examine the remainder: 4. There are no 7s in 4, so put a zero in the sevens column. There are 4 ones in 4, so put a 4 in the 1s column. The answer is 404_7.

To convert the number 968 to base 6:

5	4	3	2	1
6^4	6^3	6^2	6^1	6^0
1296	216	36	6	1

There are no 1296s in 968, so column 5 has 0. Dividing 968 by 216 yields 4 with a remainder of 104. Column 4 is 4. Dividing 104 by 36 yields 2 with a remainder of 32. Column 3 is 2. Dividing 32 by 6 yields 5 with a remainder of 2. The answer therefore is 4252_6.

5	4	3	2	1
6^4	6^3	6^2	6^1	6^0
1296	216	36	6	1
0	4	2	5	2

There is a shortcut when converting from one base to another base (such as 6) to base 10. You can multiply:

4 * 216	=	864
2 * 36	=	72
5 * 6	=	30
2 * 1	=	2
968		

Binary

Base 2 is the ultimate extension of this idea. There are only two digits: 0 and 1. The columns are:

Col:	8	7	6	5	4	3	2	1
Power:	2^7	2^6	2^5	2^4	2^3	2^2	2^1	2^0
Value:	128	64	32	16	8	4	2	1

To convert the number 88 to base 2, you follow the same procedure: There are no 128s, so column 8 is 0.

There is one 64 in 88, so column 7 is 1 and 24 is the remainder. There are no 32s in 24 so column 6 is 0.

There is one 16 in 24 so column 5 is 1. The remainder is 8. There is one 8 in 8, and so column 4 is 1. There is no remainder, so the rest of the columns are 0.

    0   1   0   1   1   0   0   0

To test this answer, convert it back:

1 * 64 = 64

0 * 32 = 0

1 * 16 = 16

1 * 8 = 8

0 * 4 = 0

0 * 2 = 0

0 * 1 = 0

              88

Why Base 2?

The power of base 2 is that it corresponds so cleanly to what a computer needs to represent. Computers do not really know anything at all about letters, numerals, instructions, or programs. At their core they are just circuitry, and at a given juncture there either is a lot of power or there is very little.

To keep the logic clean, engineers do not treat this as a relative scale (a little power, some power, more power, lots of power, tons of power), but rather as a binary scale ("enough power" or "not enough power"). Rather than saying "enough" or "not enough," they simplify it to "yes" or "no." Yes or no, or true or false, can be represented as 1 or 0. By convention, 1 means true or Yes, but that is just a convention; it could just as easily have meant false or no.

Once you make this great leap of intuition, the power of binary becomes clear: With 1s and 0s you can represent the fundamental truth of every circuit (there is power or there isn't). All a computer ever knows is, "Is you is, or is you ain't?" Is you is = 1; is you ain't = 0.

Bits, Bytes, and Nybbles

Once the decision is made to represent truth and falsehood with 1s and 0s, binary digits (or bits) become very important. Since early computers could send 8 bits at a time, it was natural to start writing code using 8-bit numbers — called *bytes*.

 Note   Half a byte (4 bits) is called a nybble!

With 8 binary digits you can represent up to 256 different values. Why? Examine the columns: If all 8 bits are set (1), the value is 255. If none is set (all the bits are clear or zero) the value is 0. 0–255 is 256 possible states.

What's a KB?

It turns out that 2^{10} (1,024) is roughly equal to 10^3 (1,000). This coincidence was too good to miss, so computer scientists started referring to 2^{10} bytes as 1KB or 1 kilobyte, based on the scientific prefix of kilo for thousand.

Similarly, 1024 * 1024 (1,048,576) is close enough to one million to receive the designation 1MB or 1 megabyte, and 1,024 megabytes is called 1 gigabyte (giga implies thousand-million or billion).

Binary Numbers

Computers use patterns of 1s and 0s to encode everything they do. Machine instructions are encoded as a series of 1s and 0s and interpreted by the fundamental circuitry. Arbitrary sets of 1s and 0s can be translated back into numbers by computer scientists, but it would be a mistake to think that these numbers have intrinsic meaning.

For example, the Intel 80×6 chip set interprets the bit pattern 1001 0101 as an instruction. You certainly can translate this into decimal (149), but that number per se has no meaning.

Sometimes the numbers are instructions, sometimes they are values, and sometimes they are codes. One important standardized code set is ASCII. In ASCII every letter and punctuation is given a 7-digit binary representation. For example, the lowercase letter "a" is represented by 0110 0001. This is not a number, although you can translate it to the number 97 (64 + 32 + 1). It is in this sense that people say that the letter "a" is represented by 97 in ASCII; but the truth is that the binary representation of 97, 01100001, is the encoding of the letter "a," and the decimal value 97 is a human convenience.

Hexadecimal

Because binary numbers are difficult to read, a simpler way to represent the same values is sought. Translating from binary to base 10 involves a fair bit of manipulation of numbers; but it turns out that translating from base 2 to base 16 is very simple, because there is a very good shortcut.

To understand this, you must first understand base 16, which is known as hexadecimal. In base 16 there are sixteen numerals: 0, 1, 2, 3, 4, 5, 6, 7, 8, 9, A, B, C, D, E, and F. The last six are arbitrary; the letters A–F were chosen because they are easy to represent on a keyboard. The columns in hexadecimal are

4	3	2	1
16^3	16^2	16^1	16^0
4096	256	16	1

To translate from hexadecimal to decimal, you can multiply. Thus, the number F8C represents:

F * 256 = 15 * 256 = 3840

8 * 16 =   128

C * 1 = 12 * 1 =   12

3980

Translating the number FC to binary is best done by translating first to base 10, and then to binary:

F * 16 = 15 * 16 = 240

C * 1 = 12 * 1 =   12

252

Converting 252_{10} to binary requires the chart:

Col:	9	8	7	6	5	4	3	2	1
Power:	2^8	2^7	2^6	2^5	2^4	2^3	2^2	2^1	2^0
Value:	256	128	64	32	16	8	4	2	1

There are no 256s.
1 128 leaves 124
1 64 leaves 60
1 32 leaves 28
1 16 leaves 12
1 8 leaves 4
1 4 leaves 0
0
0
1 1 1 1 1 1 0 0

Thus, the answer in binary is 1111 1100.

Now, it turns out that if you treat this binary number as two sets of 4 digits, you can do a magical transformation.

The right set is 1100. In decimal that is 12, or in hexadecimal it is C.

The left set is 1111, which in base 10 is 15, or in hex is F.

Thus, you have:

1111 1100

F   C

Putting the two hex numbers together is FC, which is the real value of 1111 1100. This shortcut always works. You can take any binary number of any length, and reduce it to sets of 4, translate each set of four to hex, and put the hex numbers together to get the result in hex. Here's a much larger number:

`1011 0001 1101 0111`

The columns are 1, 2, 4, 8, 16, 32, 64, 128, 256, 512, 1024, 2048, 4096, 8192, 16384, and 32768.

1 x 1 =	1
1 x 2=	2
1 x 4 =	4
0 x 8 =	0

1 x 16 =	16
0 x 32 =	0
1 x 64 =	64
1 x 128 =	128
1 x 256 =	256
0 x 512 =	0
0 x 1024 =	0
0 x 2048 =	0
1 x 4096 =	4,096
1 x 8192 =	8,192
0 x 16384 =	0
1 x 32768 =	32,768
Total:	45,527

Converting this to hexadecimal requires a chart with the hexadecimal values.

65535   4096   256   16   1

There are no 65,536s in 45,527 so the first column is 4096. There are 11 4096s (45,056), with a remainder of 471. There is one 256 in 471 with a remainder of 215. There are 13 16s (208) in 215 with a remainder of 7. Thus, the hexadecimal number is B1D7.

Checking the math:

B (11) * 4096 =	45,056
1 * 256 =	256
D (13) * 16 =	208
7 * 1 =	7
Total	45,527

The shortcut version would be to take the original binary number, 1011000111010111, and break it into groups of 4: 1011 0001 1101 0111. Each of the four then is evaluated as a hexadecimal number:

1011 =

1 x 1 =   1

1 x 2 =   2

0 x 4 =   0

1 x 8 =   8

Total   11

Hex: B

0001 =

1 x 1 =   1

0 x 2 =   0

0 x 4 =   0

0 * 8 =   0

Total   1

Hex: 1

1101 =

1 x 1 =   1

0 x 2 =   0

1 x 4 =   4

1 x 8 =   8

Total   13

Hex =   D

0111 =

1 x 1 =   1

1 x 2 =   2

1 x 4 =   4

0 x 8 =   0

Total   7

Hex: 7

Total Hex: B1D7

Appendix B

Operator Precedence

It is important to understand that operators have a precedence, but it is not essential to memorize the precedence.

Precedence—the order in which a program performs the operations in a formula. If one operator has precedence over another operator, it is evaluated first.

Higher precedence operators "bind tighter" than lower precedence operators; thus, higher precedence operators are evaluated first. The lower the rank in the following chart, the higher the precedence.

Table A.1. Operator precedence

Rank	Name	Operator
1	scope resolution	: :
2	member selection, subscripting, function calls, postfix increment and decrement	. -> ( ) ++ --
3	sizeof, prefix increment and decrement, complement, and, not, unary minus and plus, address of and dereference, new, new[], delete, delete[], casting, sizeof(),	++ -- ^ ! - + & * ( )
4	member selection for pointer	.* ->*
5	multiply, divide, modulo	* / %
6	add, subtract	+ -
7	shift	<< >>

continues

Table A.1 continued

Rank	Name	Operator
8	inequality relational	`<  <=  >  >=`
9	equality, inequality	`==  !=`
10	bitwise AND	`&`
11	bitwise exclusive OR	`^`
12	bitwise OR	`¦`
13	logical AND	`&&`
14	logical OR	`¦¦`
15	conditional	`?:`
16	assignment operators	`=  *=  /=  %=`
		`+=  -=  <<=  >>=`
		`&=  ¦=  ^=`
17	throw operator	`throw`
18	comma	`,`

Index

Other Related Titles

Using C++
Rob McGregor
ISBN: 0-7897-1667-4
$29.99 US/
$44.95 CAN

Bloodshed Dev-C++ is distributed under the GNU General Public License. Be sure to read it before using Dev-C++.

GNU GENERAL PUBLIC LICENSE

Version 2, June 1991 Copyright (C) 1989, 1991 FFree Software Foundation, Inc 675 Mass Ave, Cambridge, MA 02139, USA Everyone is permitted to copy and distribute verbatim copies of this license document, but changing it is not allowed.

Preamble

The licenses for most software are designed to take away your freedom to share and change it. By contrast, the GNU General Public License is intended to guarantee your freedom to share and change free software—to make sure the software is free for all its users. This General Public License applies to most of the Free Software Foundation's software and to any other program whose authors commit to using it. (Some other Free Software Foundation software is covered by the GNU Library General Public License instead.) You can apply it to your programs, too.

When we speak of free software, we are referring to freedom, not price. Our General Public Licenses are designed to make sure that you have the freedom to distribute copies of free software (and charge for this service if you wish), that you receive source code or can get it if you want it, that you can change the software or use pieces of it in new free programs; and that you know you can do these things.

To protect your rights, we need to make restrictions that forbid anyone to deny you these rights or to ask you to surrender the rights. These restrictions translate to certain responsibilities for you if you distribute copies of the software, or if you modify it.

For example, if you distribute copies of such a program, whether gratis or for a fee, you must give the recipients all the rights that you have. You must make sure that they, too, receive or can get the source code. And you must show them these terms so they know their rights.

We protect your rights with two steps: (1) copyright the software, and (2) offer you this license which gives you legal permission to copy, distribute and/or modify the software.

Also, for each author's protection and ours, we want to make certain that everyone understands that there is no warranty for this free software. If the software is modified by someone else and passed on, we want its recipients to know that what they have is not the original, so that any problems introduced by others will not reflect on the original authors' reputations.

Finally, any free program is threatened constantly by software patents. We wish to avoid the danger that redistributors of a free program will individually obtain patent licenses, in effect making the program proprietary. To prevent this, we have made it clear that any patent must be licensed for everyone's free use or not licensed at all.

The precise terms and conditions for copying, distribution and modification follow.

GNU GENERAL PUBLIC LICENSE

TERMS AND CONDITIONS FOR COPYING, DISTRIBUTION AND MODIFICATION

0. This License applies to any program or other work which contains a notice placed by the copyright holder saying it may be distributed under the terms of this General Public License. The "Program", below, refers to any such program or work, and a "work based on the Program" means either the Program or any derivative work under copyright law: that is to say, a work containing the Program or a portion of it, either verbatim or with modifications and/or translated into another language. (Hereinafter, translation is included without limitation in the term "modification".) Each licensee is addressed as "you".

Activities other than copying, distribution and modification are not covered by this License; they are outside its scope. The act of running the Program is not restricted, and the output from the Program is covered only if its contents constitute a work based on the Program (independent of having been made by running the Program). Whether that is true depends on what the Program does.

1. You may copy and distribute verbatim copies of the Program's source code as you receive it, in any medium, provided that you conspicuously and appropriately publish on each copy an appropriate copyright notice and disclaimer of warranty; keep intact all the notices that refer to this License and to the absence of any warranty; and give any other recipients of the Program a copy of this License along with the Program.

You may charge a fee for the physical act of transferring a copy, and you may at your option offer warranty protection in exchange for a fee.

2. You may modify your copy or copies of the Program or any portion of it, thus forming a work based on the Program, and copy and distribute such modifications or work under the terms of Section 1 above, provided that you also meet all of these conditions:

  a) You must cause the modified files to carry prominent notices stating that you changed the files and the date of any change.

  b) You must cause any work that you distribute or publish, that in whole or in part contains or is derived from the Program or any part thereof, to be licensed as a whole at no charge to all third parties under the terms of this License.

  c) If the modified program normally reads commands interactively when run, you must cause it, when started running for such interactive use in the most ordinary way, to print or display an announcement including an appropriate copyright notice and a notice that there is no warranty (or else, saying that you provide a warranty) and that users may redistribute the program under these conditions, and telling the user how to view a copy of this License. (Exception: if the Program itself is interactive but does not normally print such an announcement, your work based on the Program is not required to print an announcement.)

These requirements apply to the modified work as a whole. If identifiable sections of that work are not derived from the Program, and can be reasonably considered independent and separate works in themselves, then this License, and its terms, do not apply to those sections when you distribute them as separate works. But when you distribute the same sections as part of a whole which is a work based on the Program, the distribution of the whole must be on the terms of this License, whose permissions for other licensees extend to the entire whole, and thus to each and every part regardless of who wrote it.

Thus, it is not the intent of this section to claim rights or contest your rights to work written entirely by you; rather, the intent is to exercise the right to control the distribution of derivative or collective works based on the Program. In addition, mere aggregation of another work not based on the Program with the Program (or with a work based on the Program) on a volume of a storage or distribution medium does not bring the other work under the scope of this License.

3. You may copy and distribute the Program (or a work based on it, under Section 2) in object code or executable form under the terms of Sections 1 and 2 above provided that you also do one of the following:

  a) Accompany it with the complete corresponding machine-readable source code, which must be distributed under the terms of Sections 1 and 2 above on a medium customarily used for software interchange; or,

b) Accompany it with a written offer, valid for at least three years, to give any third party, for a charge no more than your cost of physically performing source distribution, a complete machine-readable copy of the corresponding source code, to be distributed under the terms of Sections 1 and 2 above on a medium customarily used for software interchange; or,

c) Accompany it with the information you received as to the offer to distribute corresponding source code. (This alternative is allowed only for noncommercial distribution and only if you received the program in object code or executable form with such an offer, in accord with Subsection b above.)

The source code for a work means the preferred form of the work for making modifications to it. For an executable work, complete source code means all the source code for all modules it contains, plus any associated interface definition files, plus the scripts used to control compilation and installation of the executable. However, as a special exception, the source code distributed need not include anything that is normally distributed (in either source or binary form) with the major components (compiler, kernel, and so on) of the operating system on which the executable runs, unless that component itself accompanies the executable.

If distribution of executable or object code is made by offering access to copy from a designated place, then offering equivalent access to copy the source code from the same place counts as distribution of the source code, even though third parties are not compelled to copy the source along with the object code.

4. You may not copy, modify, sublicense, or distribute the Program except as expressly provided under this License. Any attempt otherwise to copy, modify, sublicense or distribute the Program is void, and will automatically terminate your rights under this License. However, parties who have received copies, or rights, from you under this License will not have their licenses terminated so long as such parties remain in full compliance.

5. You are not required to accept this License, since you have not signed it. However, nothing else grants you permission to modify or distribute the Program or its derivative works. These actions are prohibited by law if you do not accept this License. Therefore, by modifying or distributing the Program (or any work based on the Program), you indicate your acceptance of this License to do so, and all its terms and conditions for copying, distributing or modifying the Program or works based on it.

6. Each time you redistribute the Program (or any work based on the Program), the recipient automatically receives a license from the original licensor to copy, distribute or modify the Program subject to these terms and conditions. You may not impose

any further restrictions on the recipients' exercise of the rights granted herein. You are not responsible for enforcing compliance by third parties to this License.

7. If, as a consequence of a court judgment or allegation of patent infringement or for any other reason (not limited to patent issues), conditions are imposed on you (whether by court order, agreement or otherwise) that contradict the conditions of this License, they do not excuse you from the conditions of this License. If you cannot distribute so as to satisfy simultaneously your obligations under this License and any other pertinent obligations, then as a consequence you may not distribute the Program at all. For example, if a patent license would not permit royalty-free redistribution of the Program by all those who receive copies directly or indirectly through you, then the only way you could satisfy both it and this License would be to refrain entirely from distribution of the Program.

If any portion of this section is held invalid or unenforceable under any particular circumstance, the balance of the section is intended to apply and the section as a whole is intended to apply in other circumstances.

It is not the purpose of this section to induce you to infringe any patents or other property right claims or to contest validity of any such claims; this section has the sole purpose of protecting the integrity of the free software distribution system, which is implemented by public license practices. Many people have made generous contributions to the wide range of software distributed through that system in reliance on consistent application of that system; it is up to the author/donor to decide if he or she is willing to distribute software through any other system and a licensee cannot impose that choice.

This section is intended to make thoroughly clear what is believed to be a consequence of the rest of this License.

8. If the distribution and/or use of the Program is restricted in certain countries either by patents or by copyrighted interfaces, the original copyright holder who places the Program under this License may add an explicit geographical distribution limitation excluding those countries, so that distribution is permitted only in or among countries not thus excluded. In such case, this License incorporates the limitation as if written in the body of this License.

9. The Free Software Foundation may publish revised and/or new versions of the General Public License from time to time. Such new versions will be similar in spirit to the present version, but may differ in detail to address new problems or concerns.

Each version is given a distinguishing version number. If the Program specifies a version number of this License which applies to it and "any later version", you have the option of following the terms and conditions either of that version or of any later version published by the Free Software Foundation. If the Program does not specify a version number of this License, you may choose any version ever published by the Free Software Foundation.

10. If you wish to incorporate parts of the Program into other free programs whose distribution conditions are different, write to the author to ask for permission. For software which is copyrighted by the Free Software Foundation, write to the Free Software Foundation; we sometimes make exceptions for this. Our decision will be guided by the two goals of preserving the free status of all derivatives of our free software and of promoting the sharing and reuse of software generally.

NO WARRANTY

11. BECAUSE THE PROGRAM IS LICENSED FREE OF CHARGE, THERE IS NO WARRANTY FOR THE PROGRAM, TO THE EXTENT PERMITTED BY APPLICABLE LAW. EXCEPT WHEN OTHERWISE STATED IN WRITING THE COPYRIGHT HOLDERS AND/OR OTHER PARTIES PROVIDE THE PROGRAM "AS IS" WITHOUT WARRANTY OF ANY KIND, EITHER EXPRESSED OR IMPLIED, INCLUDING, BUT NOT LIMITED TO, THE IMPLIED WARRANTIES OF MERCHANTABILITY AND FITNESS FOR A PARTICULAR PURPOSE. THE ENTIRE RISK AS TO THE QUALITY AND PERFORMANCE OF THE PROGRAM IS WITH YOU. SHOULD THE PROGRAM PROVE DEFECTIVE, YOU ASSUME THE COST OF ALL NECESSARY SERVICING, REPAIR OR CORRECTION.

12. IN NO EVENT UNLESS REQUIRED BY APPLICABLE LAW OR AGREED TO IN WRITING WILL ANY COPYRIGHT HOLDER, OR ANY OTHER PARTY WHO MAY MODIFY AND/OR REDISTRIBUTE THE PROGRAM AS PERMITTED ABOVE, BE LIABLE TO YOU FOR DAMAGES, INCLUDING ANY GENERAL, SPECIAL, INCIDENTAL OR CONSEQUENTIAL DAMAGES ARISINGOUT OF THE USE OR INABILITY TO USE THE PROGRAM (INCLUDING BUT NOT LIMITED TO LOSS OF DATA OR DATA BEING RENDERED INACCURATE OR LOSSES SUSTAINED BY YOU OR THIRD PARTIES OR A FAILURE OF THE PROGRAM TO OPERATE WITH ANY OTHER PROGRAMS), EVEN IF SUCH HOLDER OR OTHER PARTY HAS BEEN ADVISED OF THE POSSIBILITY OF SUCH DAMAGES.

END OF TERMS AND CONDITIONS

Appendix: How to Apply These Terms to Your New Programs

If you develop a new program, and you want it to be of the greatest possible use to the public, the best way to achieve this is to make free software which everyone can redistribute and change under these terms.

To do so, attach the following notices to the program. It is safest to attach them to the start of each source file to most effectively convey the exclusion of warranty; and each file should have at least the "copyright" line and a pointer to where the full notice is found

one line to give the program's name and a brief idea of what it does.

> *Copyright (C) 19yy <name of author>*

This program is free software; you can redistribute it and/or modify it under the terms of the GNU General Public License as published by the Free Software Foundation; either version 2 of the License, or (at your option) any later version.

This program is distributed in the hope that it will be useful, but WITHOUT ANY WARRANTY; without even the implied warranty of MERCHANTABILITY or FITNESS FOR A PARTICULAR PURPOSE. See the GNU General Public License for more details.

You should have received a copy of the GNU General Public License along with this program; if not, write to the Free Software Foundation, Inc., 675 Mass Ave, Cambridge, MA 02139, USA.

Also add information on how to contact you by electronic and paper mail. If the program is interactive, make it output a short notice like this when it starts in an interactive mode:

Gnomovision version 69, Copyright (C) 19yy name of author Gnomovision comes with ABSOLUTELY NO WARRANTY; for details type 'show w'. This is free software, and you are welcome to redistribute it under certain conditions; type 'show c' for details.

The hypothetical commands 'show w' and 'show c' should show the appropriate parts of the General Public License. Of course, the commands you use may be called something other than 'show w' and 'show c'; they could even be mouse-clicks or menu items—whatever suits your program.

You should also get your employer (if you work as a programmer) or your school, if any, to sign a "copyright disclaimer" for the program, if necessary. Here is a sample; alter the names:

Yoyodyne, Inc., hereby disclaims all copyright interest in the program 'Gnomovision' (which makes passes at compilers) written by James Hacker.

<signature of Ty Coon>,
1 April 1989
Ty Coon,
President of Vice

This General Public License does not permit incorporating your program into proprietary programs. If your program is a subroutine library, you may consider it more useful to permit linking proprietary applications with the library. If this is what you want to do, use the GNU Library General Public License instead of this License.

CD-ROM Installation

Windows 95 Installation Instructions

1. Insert the CD-ROM disc into your CD-ROM drive.
2. From the Windows 95 desktop, double-click on the My Computer icon.
3. Double-click on the icon representing your CD-ROM drive.
4. Double-click on the icon titled START.EXE to run the CD-ROM interface.

 Note If Windows 95 is installed on your computer and you have the AutoPlay feature enabled, the START.EXE program starts automatically whenever you insert the disc into your CD-ROM drive.

Windows NT Installation Instructions

1. Insert the CD-ROM disc into your CD-ROM drive.
2. From File Manager or Program Manager, choose Run from the File menu.
3. Type *<drive>*\START.EXE and press Enter, where *<drive>* corresponds to the drive letter of your CD-ROM. For example, if your CD-ROM is drive D:, type D:\START.EXE and press Enter. This will run the CD-ROM interface.